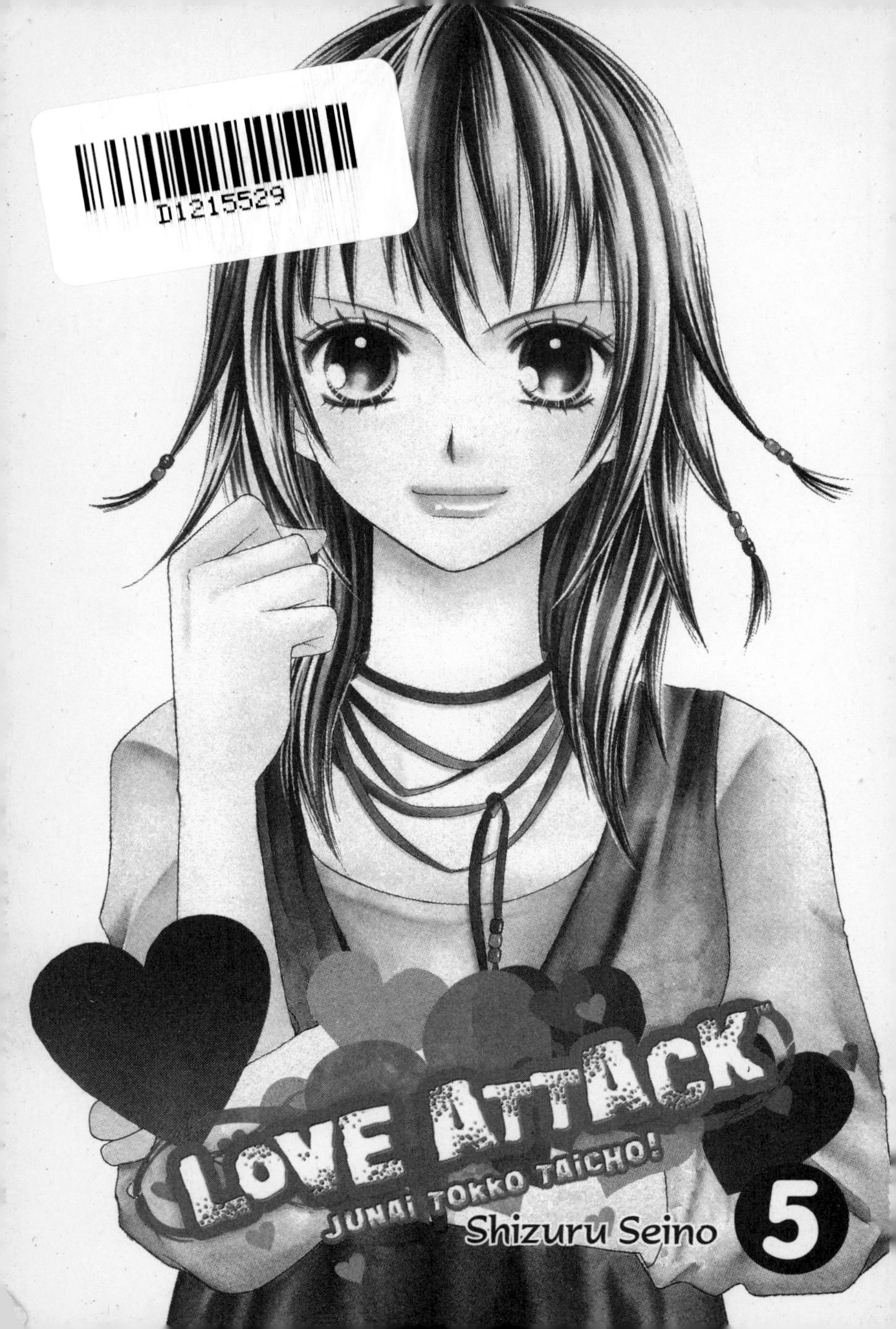
LOVE ATTACK™
JUNAI TOKKO TAICHO!
Shizuru Seino
5

Love Attack Volume 5
Created by Shizuru Seino

Translation - Adrienne Beck
English Adaptation - Magdalena Llexim
Retouch and Lettering - Star Print Brokers
Production Artist - Vicente Rivera, Jr.
Graphic Designer - James Lee

Editor - Hyun Joo Kim
Pre-Production Supervisor - Vicente Rivera, Jr.
Pre-Production Specialist - Lucas Rivera
Managing Editor - Vy Nguyen
Senior Designer - Louis Csontos
Senior Designer - James Lee
Senior Editor - Bryce P. Coleman
Senior Editor - Jenna Winterberg
Associate Publisher - Marco F. Pavia
President and C.O.O. - John Parker
C.E.O. and Chief Creative Officer - Stu Levy

A  Manga

TOKYOPOP and ⊙ are trademarks or registered trademarks of TOKYOPOP Inc.

TOKYOPOP Inc.
5900 Wilshire Blvd. Suite 2000
Los Angeles, CA 90036

E-mail: info@TOKYOPOP.com
Come visit us online at www.TOKYOPOP.com

ISBN: 978-1-4278-0910-0

First TOKYOPOP printing: January 2009
10 9 8 7 6 5 4 3 2 1
Printed in the USA

LOVE ATTACK™

JUNAI TOKKO TAICHO!

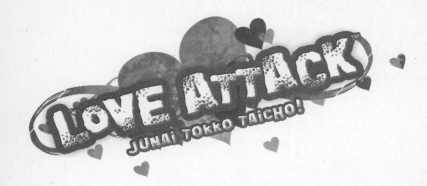

Vol. 5

by
Shizuru Seino

TOKYOPOP®

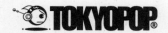

HAMBURG // LONDON // LOS ANGELES // TOKYO

LOVE ATTACK™

JUNAI TOKKO TAICHO!

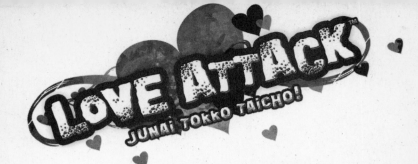

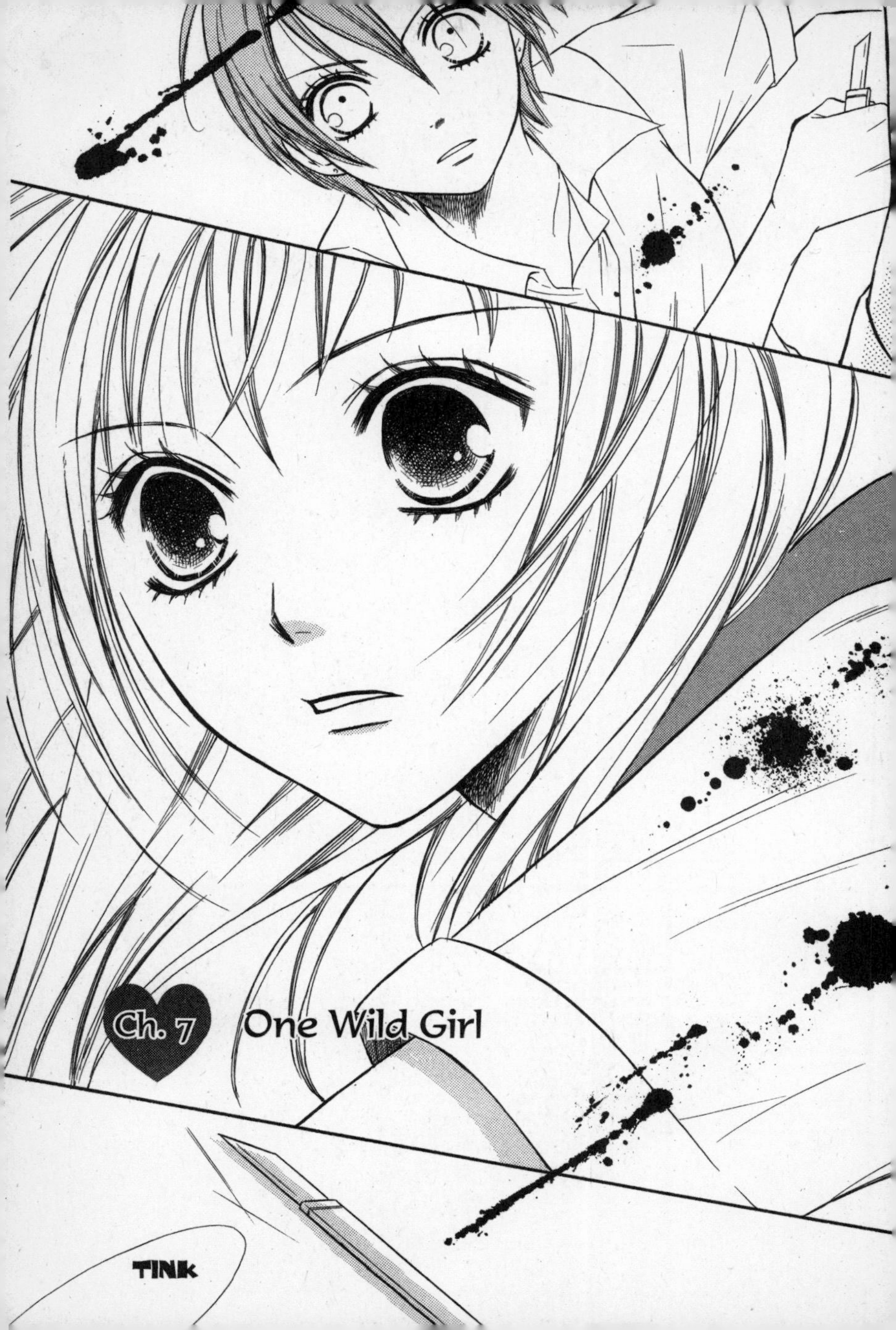
Ch. 7 One Wild Girl
TINK

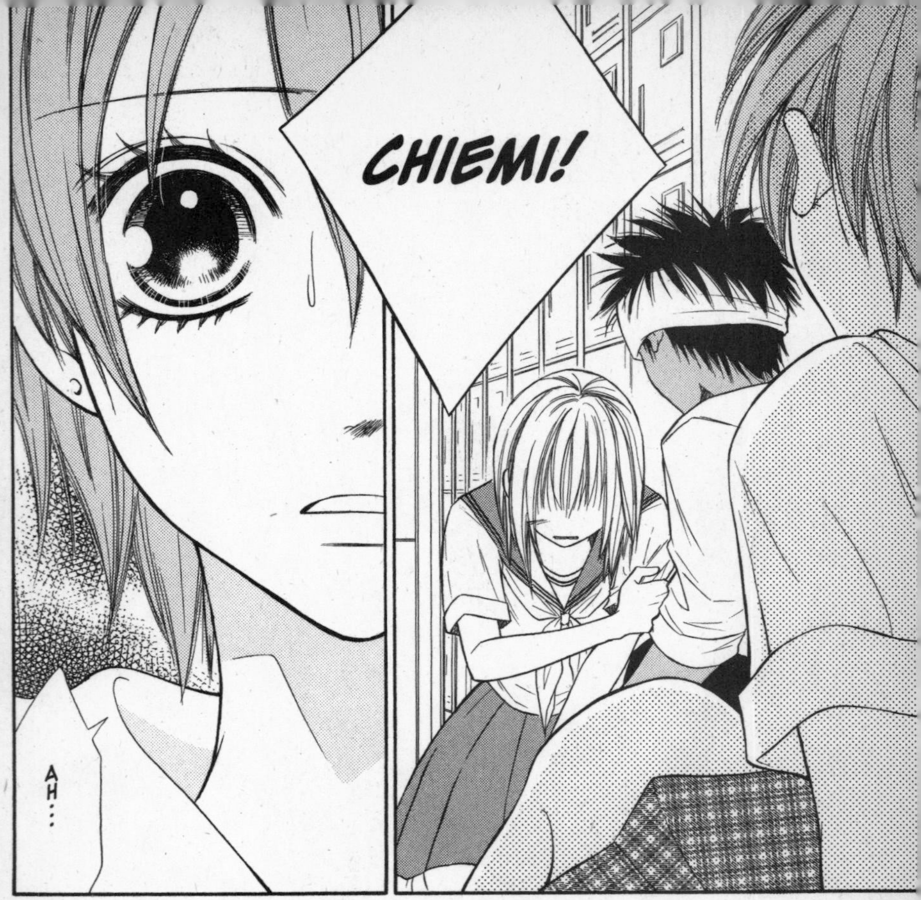
CHIEMI!
AH...

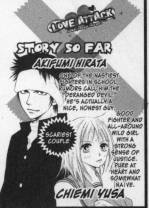

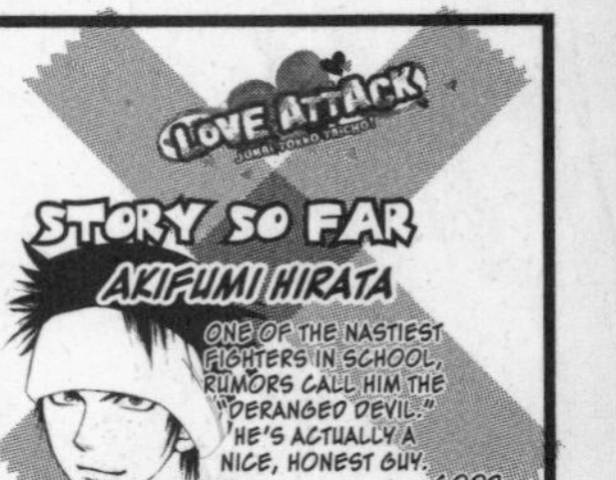
LOVE ATTACK
STORY SO FAR
AKIFUMI HIRATA
ONE OF THE NASTIEST FIGHTERS IN SCHOOL, RUMORS CALL HIM THE "DERANGED DEVIL." HE'S ACTUALLY A NICE, HONEST GUY.
SCARIEST COUPLE
GOOD FIGHTER AND ALL-AROUND WILD GIRL WITH A STRONG SENSE OF JUSTICE. PURE AT HEART AND SOMEWHAT NAIVE.
CHIEMI YUSA

★ STUCK BETWEEN A ROCK AND A HARD PLACE DUE TO A LONG RECORD OF FIGHTING IN SCHOOL, CHIEMI IS GIVEN A CHOICE: REFORM PROBLEM-CHILD AKIFUMI HIRATA OR BE EXPELLED! BUT WHEN CHIEMI DISCOVERS THAT HIRATA IS REALLY JUST A NICE GUY WITH A BAD REP, THE TWO END UP DATING.

★ JUST AS THINGS ARE SETTLING DOWN, HIRATA'S CHILDHOOD FRIEND AKIO KURAMORI APPEARS. IN LOVE WITH HIRATA HERSELF, AKIO STARTS HARASSING CHIEMI WITH WORSE AND WORSE PRANKS. HIRATA AND CHIEMI ALMOST BREAK UP OVER THE ORDEAL, BUT THEY EVENTUALLY COME TO AN UNDERSTANDING.

★ SEEING HIRATA AND CHIEMI RECOVER AS A COUPLE, AKIO SNAPS. SHE TRIES TO SLIT HER OWN WRIST WITH A BOX CUTTER RIGHT IN FRONT OF THEM, BUT CHIEMI JUMPS IN TO STOP HER. BUT A FLAILING AKIO MANAGES TO HIT CHIEMI WITH THE BLADE...

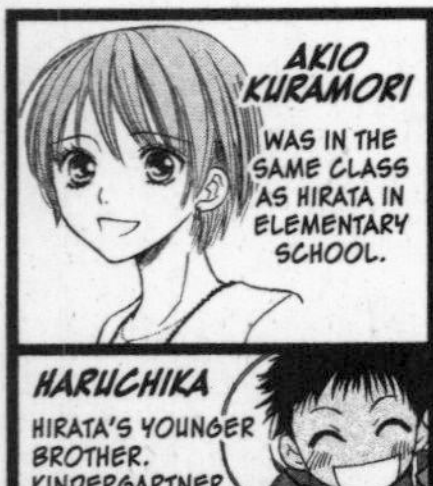
AKIO KURAMORI
WAS IN THE SAME CLASS AS HIRATA IN ELEMENTARY SCHOOL.
HARUCHIKA
HIRATA'S YOUNGER BROTHER. KINDERGARTNER.
YUKARI
SHARP-TONGUED BUT RESPONSIBLE.
HIRODA
POMPADOUR HAIRSTYLE IS HIS TRADEMARK. GRANDIOSE.

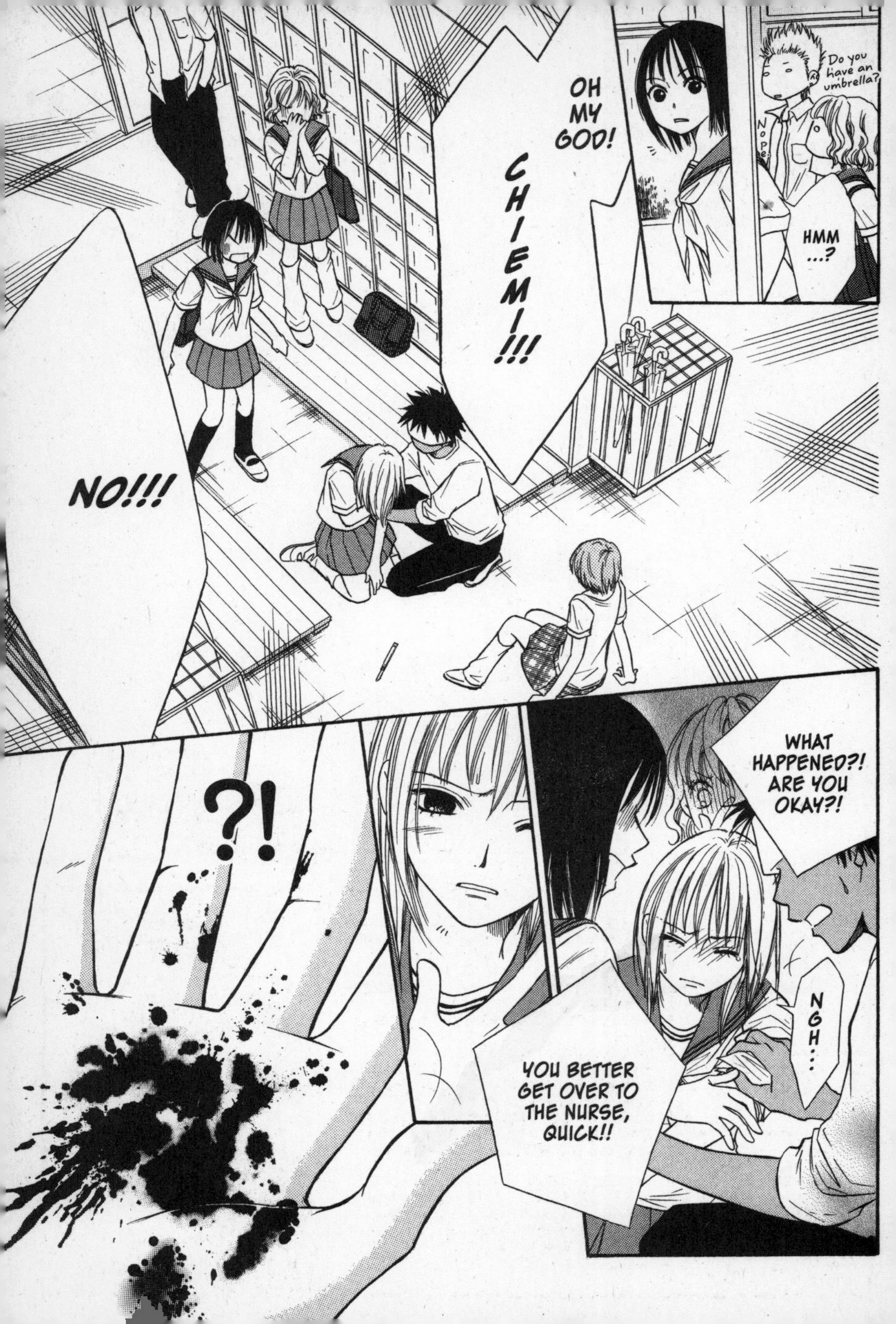
Do you have an umbrella?
Nope.
HMM ...?
OH MY GOD!
CHIEMI!!!
NO!!!
WHAT HAPPENED?! ARE YOU OKAY?!
NGH...
YOU BETTER GET OVER TO THE NURSE, QUICK!!
?!

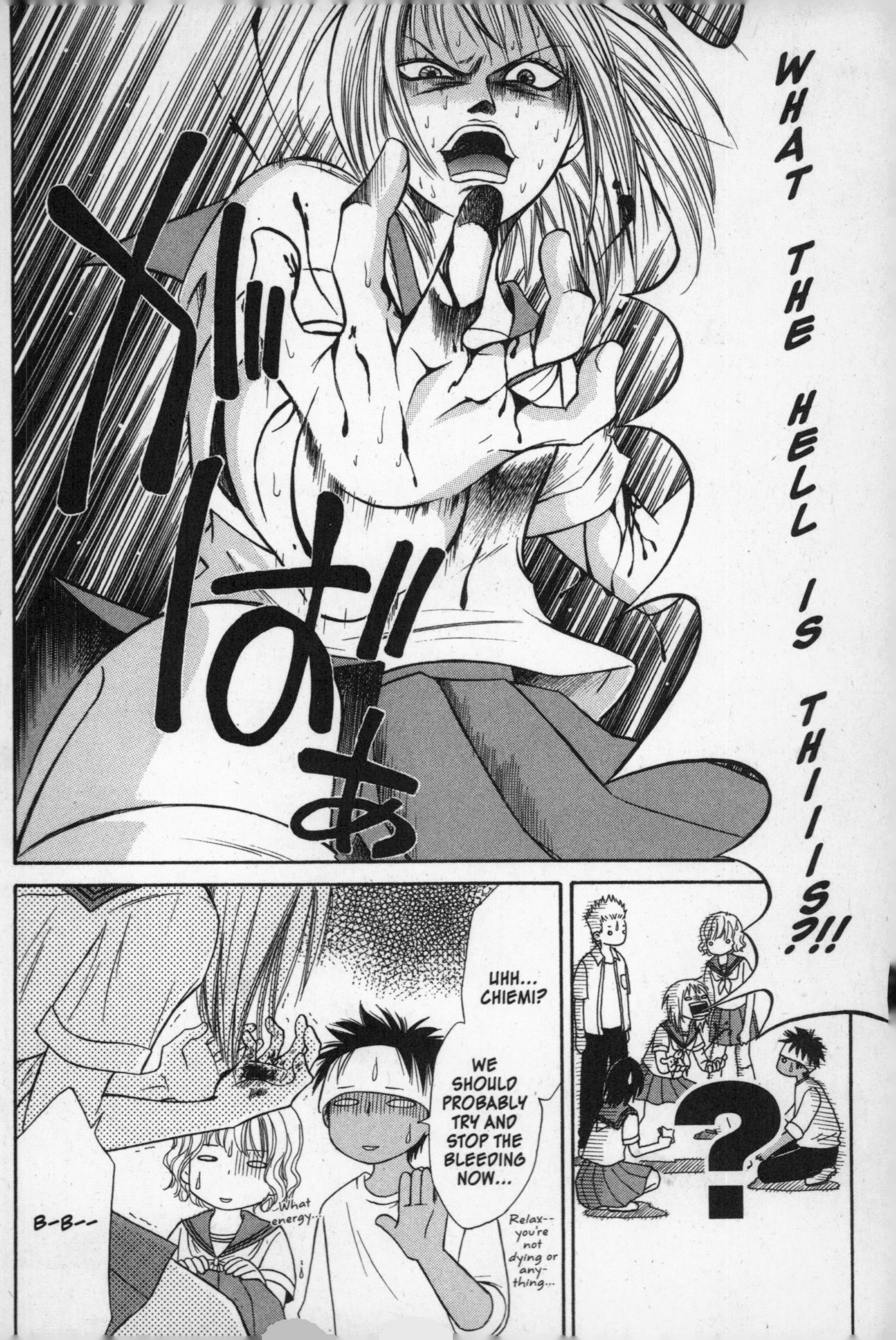
WHAT THE HELL IS THIIIIS?!!
?
UHH... CHIEMI?
WE SHOULD PROBABLY TRY AND STOP THE BLEEDING NOW...
Relax-- you're not dying or anything...
What energy...
B--B--

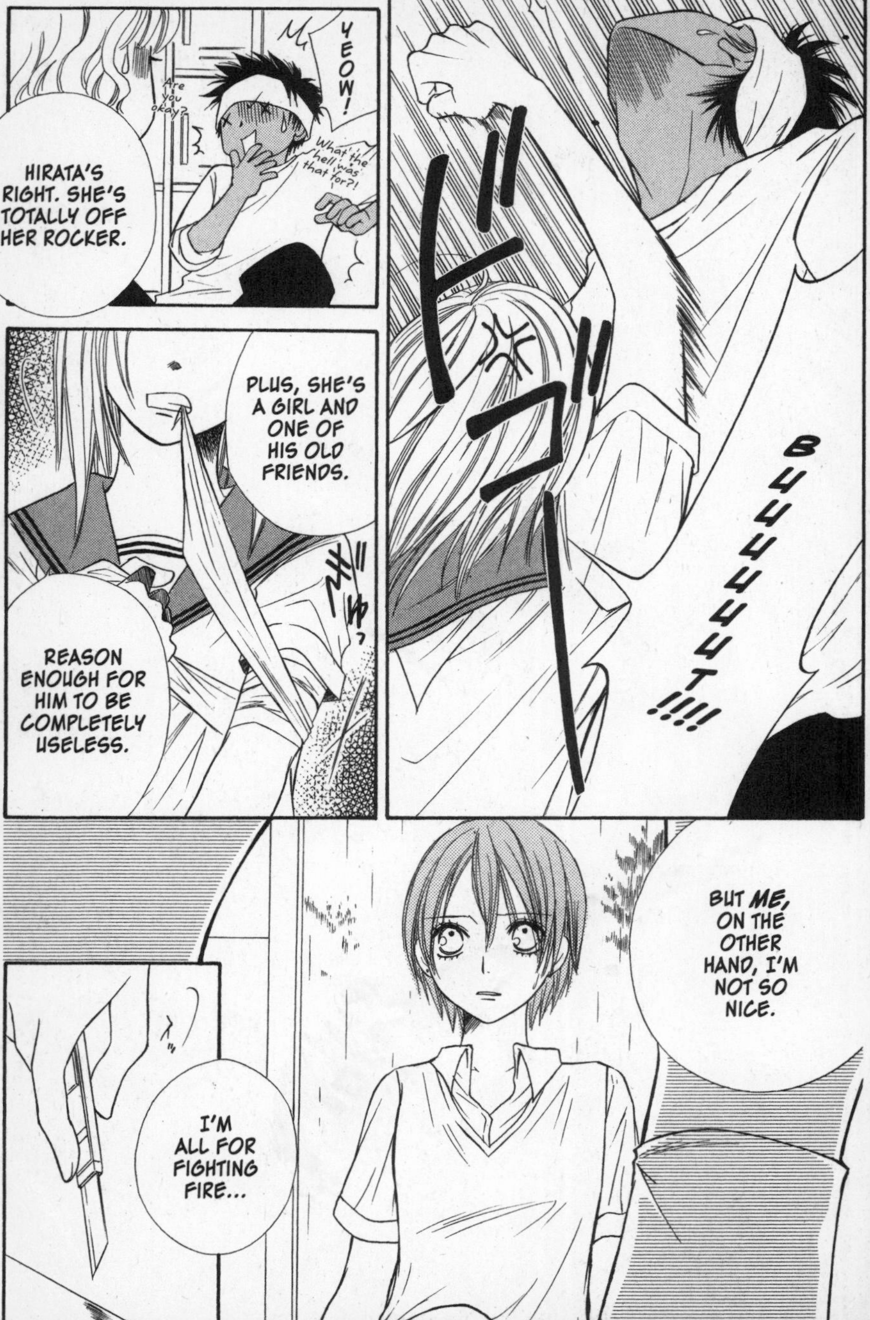
ドゴー
BUUUUUUUT!!!!
YEOW!
Are you okay?
What the hell was that for?!
HIRATA'S RIGHT. SHE'S TOTALLY OFF HER ROCKER.
PLUS, SHE'S A GIRL AND ONE OF HIS OLD FRIENDS.
REASON ENOUGH FOR HIM TO BE COMPLETELY USELESS.
BUT ME, ON THE OTHER HAND, I'M NOT SO NICE.
I'M ALL FOR FIGHTING FIRE...

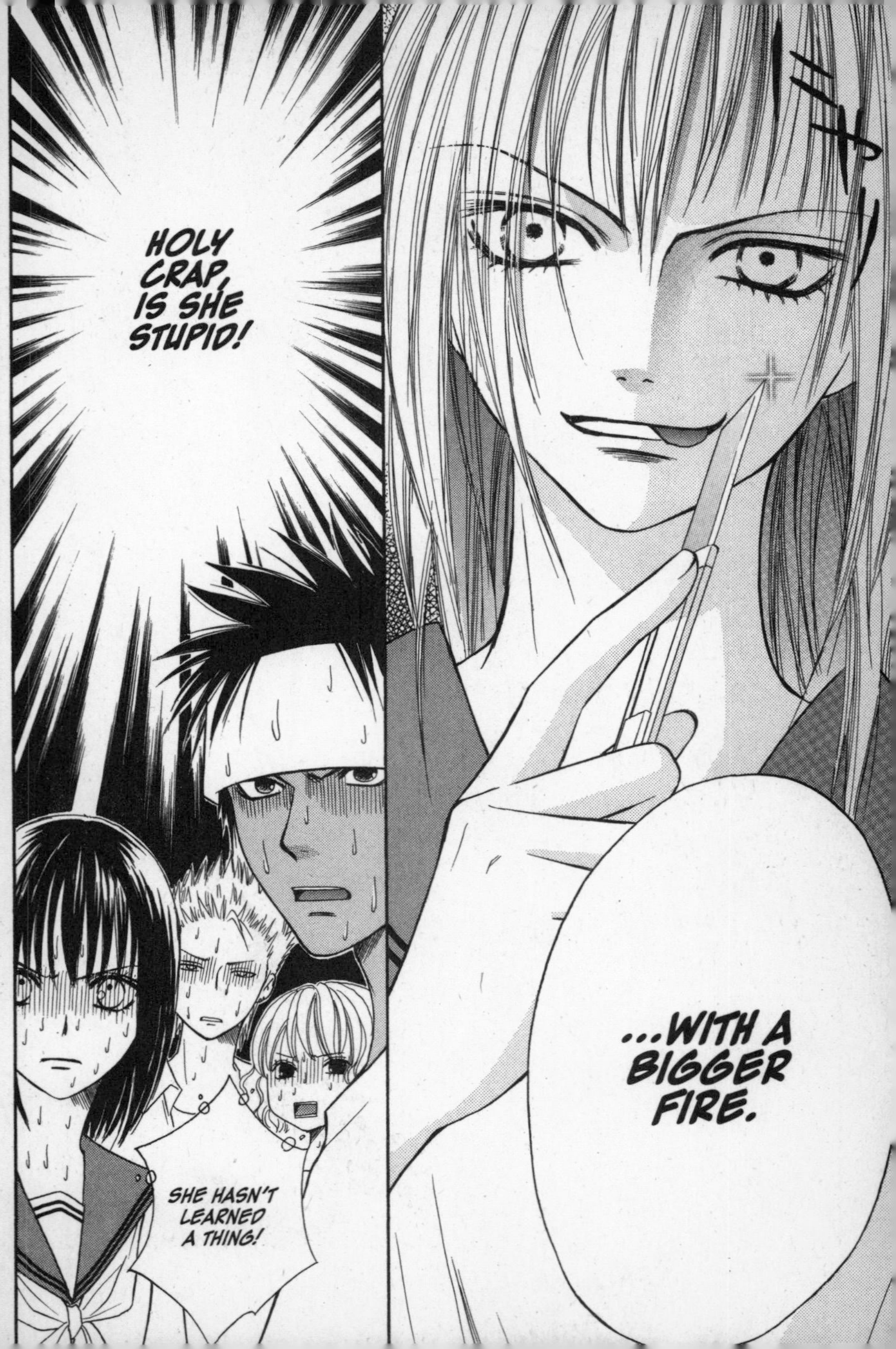
...WITH A BIGGER FIRE.
HOLY CRAP, IS SHE STUPID!
SHE HASN'T LEARNED A THING!

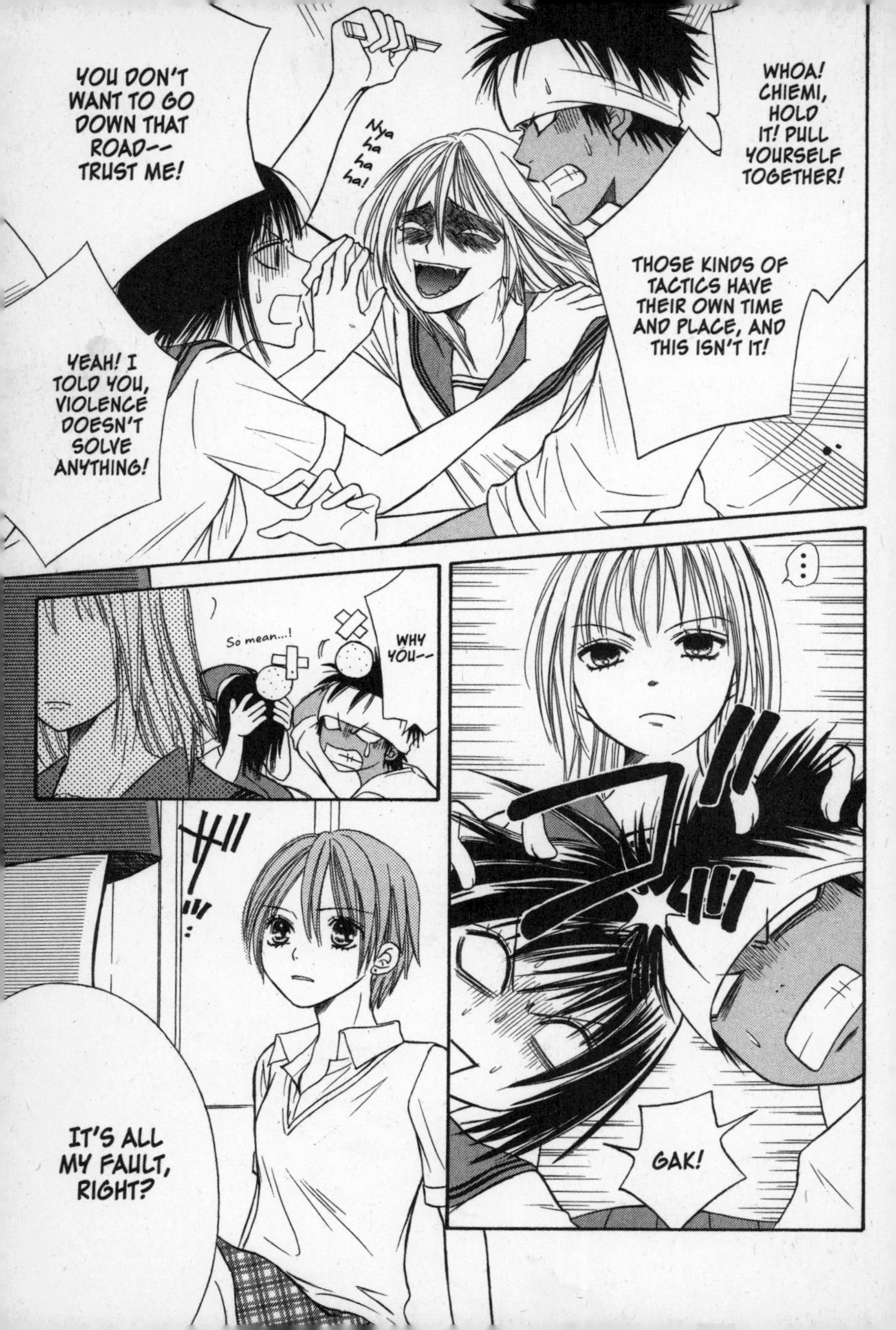

WHOA! CHIEMI, HOLD IT! PULL YOURSELF TOGETHER!
Nya ha ha ha!
YOU DON'T WANT TO GO DOWN THAT ROAD--TRUST ME!
THOSE KINDS OF TACTICS HAVE THEIR OWN TIME AND PLACE, AND THIS ISN'T IT!
YEAH! I TOLD YOU, VIOLENCE DOESN'T SOLVE ANYTHING!
...
GAK!
WHY YOU--
So mean...!
IT'S ALL MY FAULT, RIGHT?

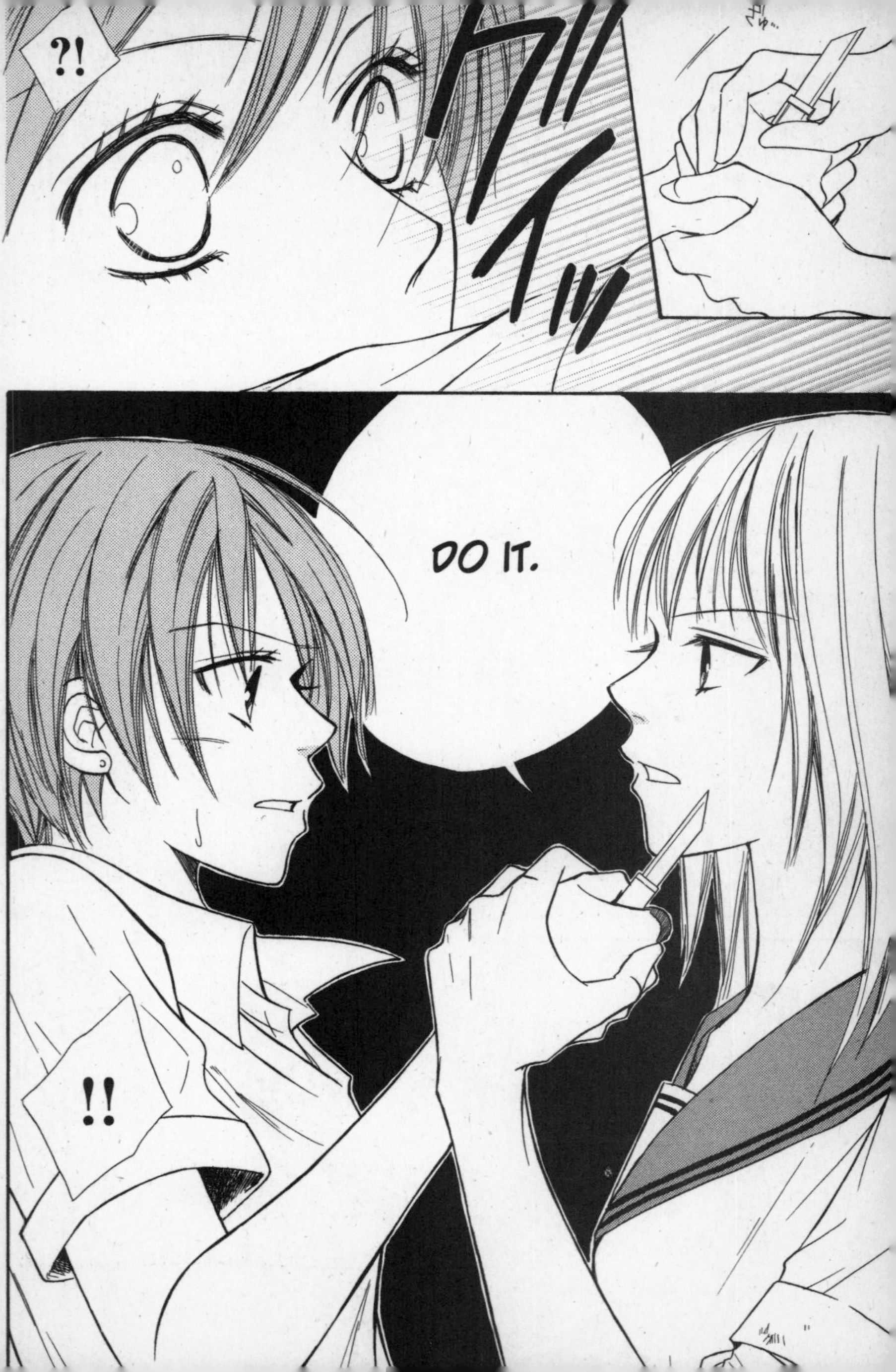
グイッ
?!
DO IT.
!!

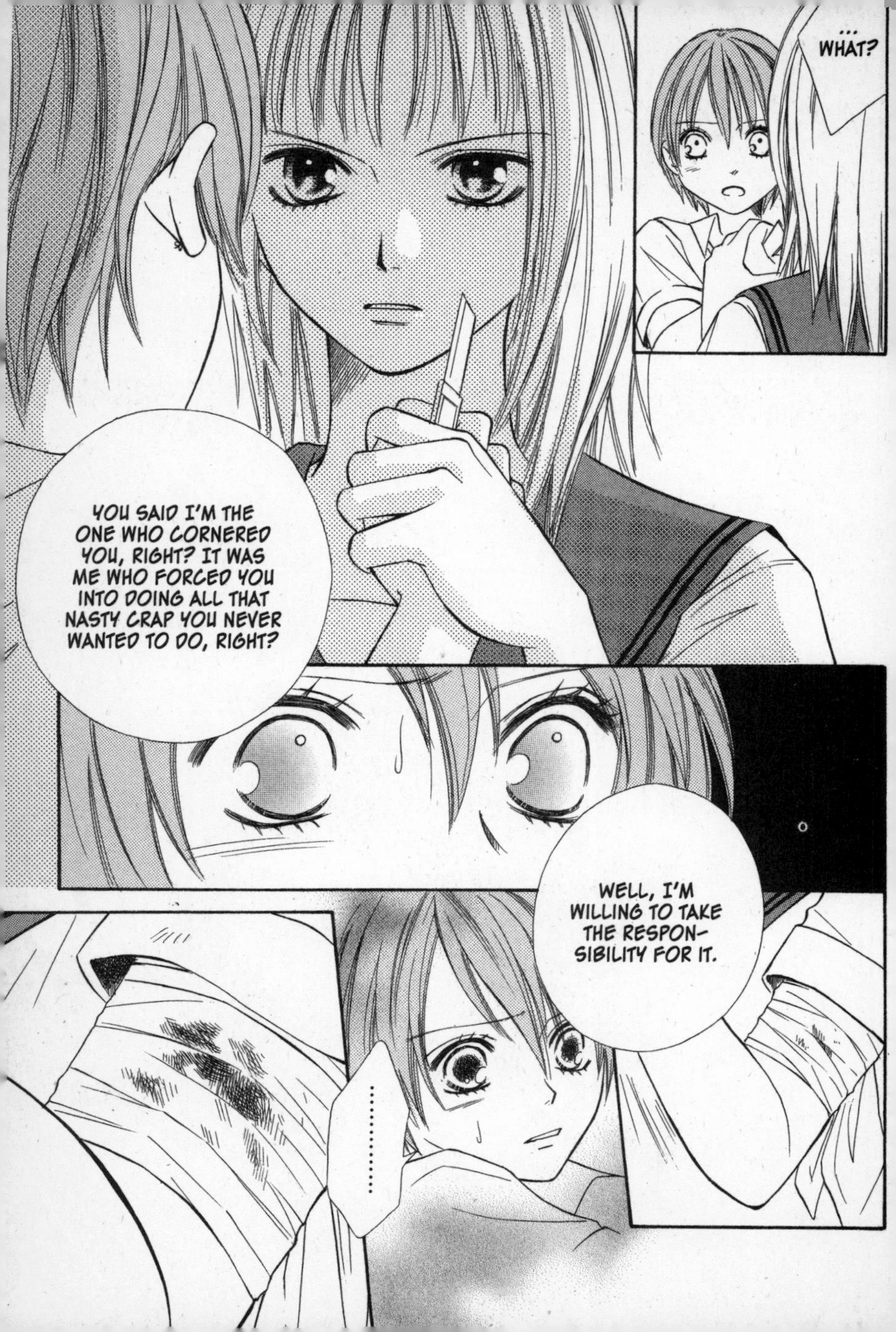
...WHAT?
YOU SAID I'M THE ONE WHO CORNERED YOU, RIGHT? IT WAS ME WHO FORCED YOU INTO DOING ALL THAT NASTY CRAP YOU NEVER WANTED TO DO, RIGHT?
WELL, I'M WILLING TO TAKE THE RESPON-SIBILITY FOR IT.
......

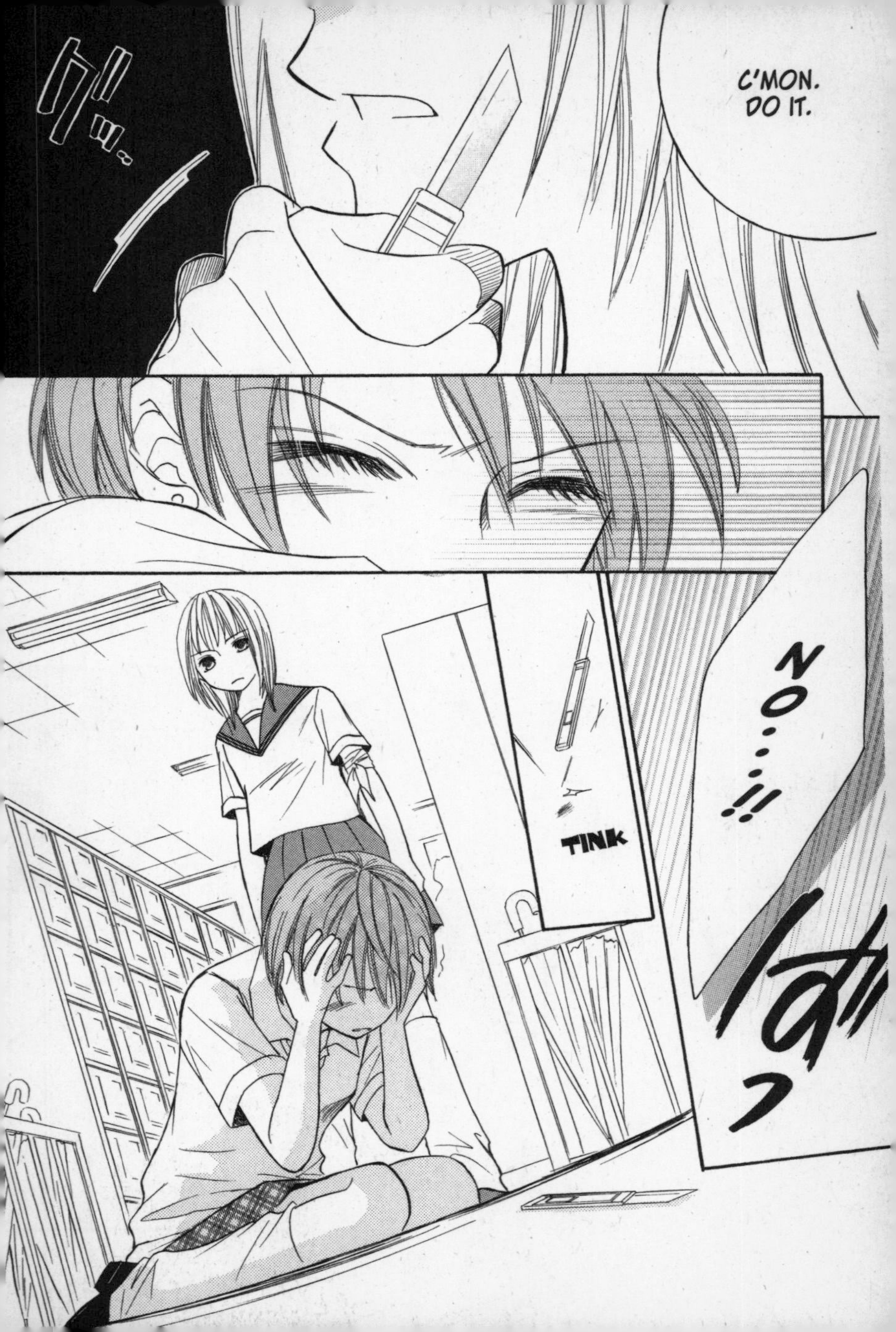
C'MON.
DO IT.
NO...!!
TINK
はっ

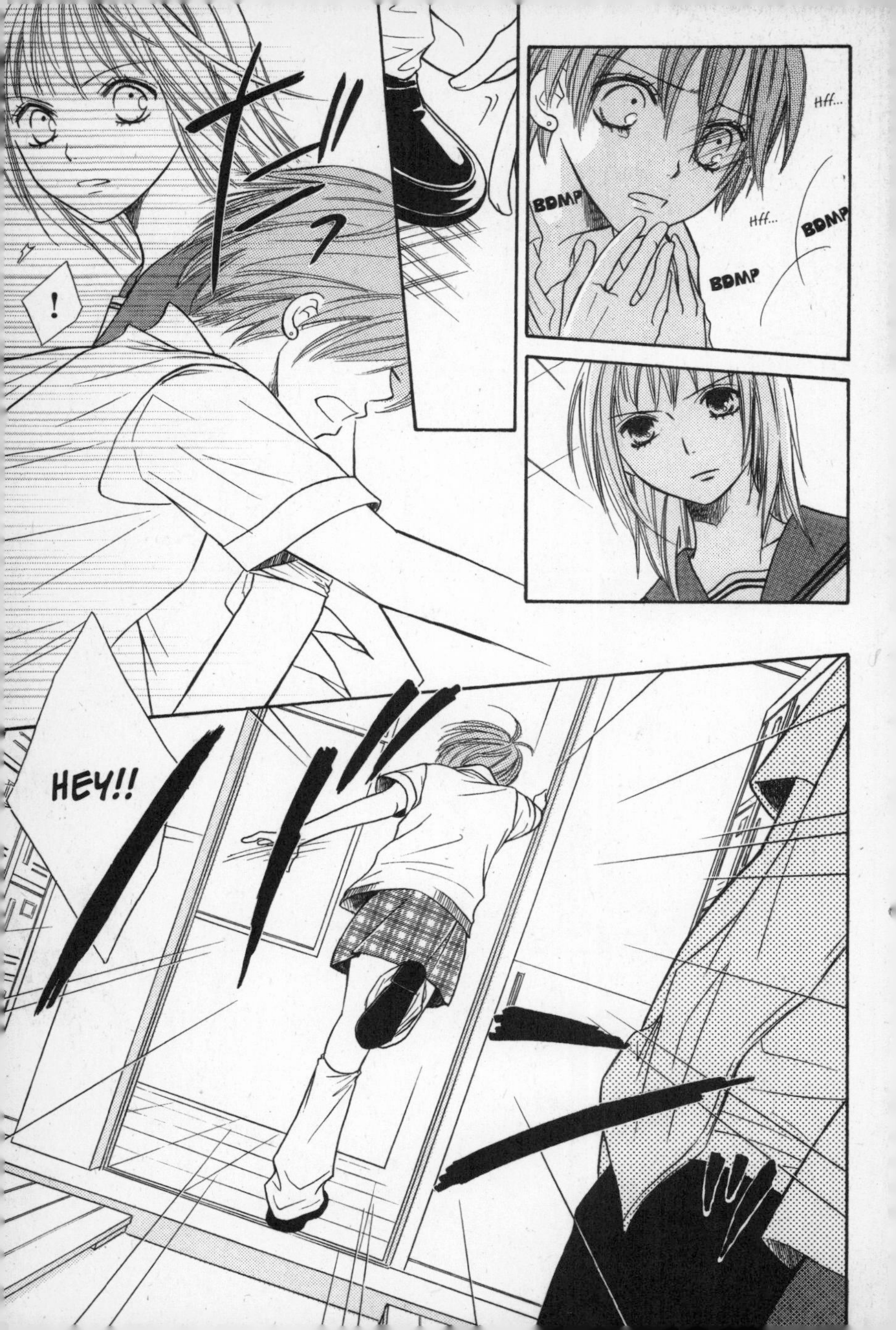
Hff...
BDMP
Hff...
BDMP
BDMP
!
HEY!!

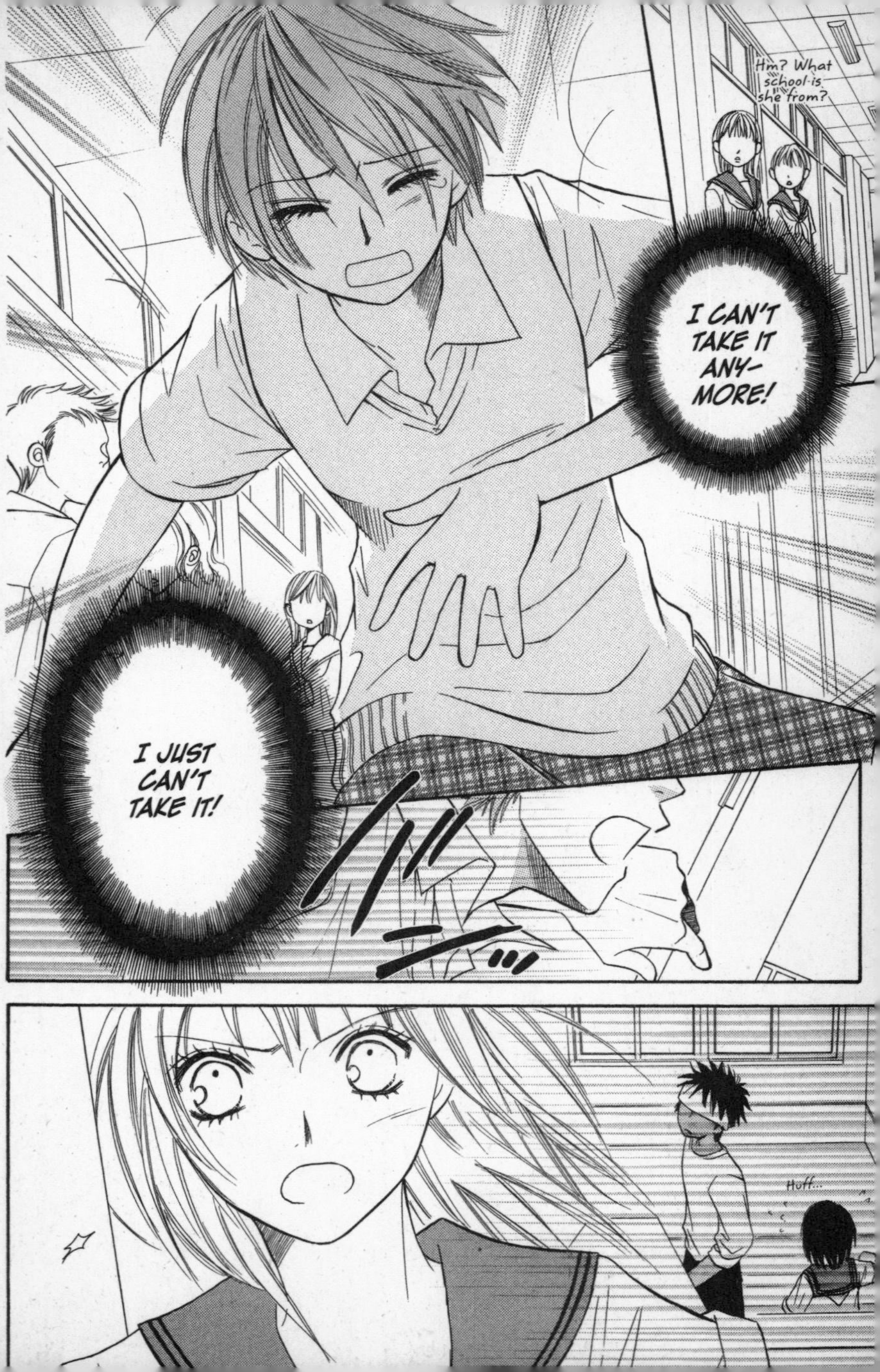
Hm? What school is she from?
I CAN'T TAKE IT ANY-MORE!
I JUST CAN'T TAKE IT!
Huff...

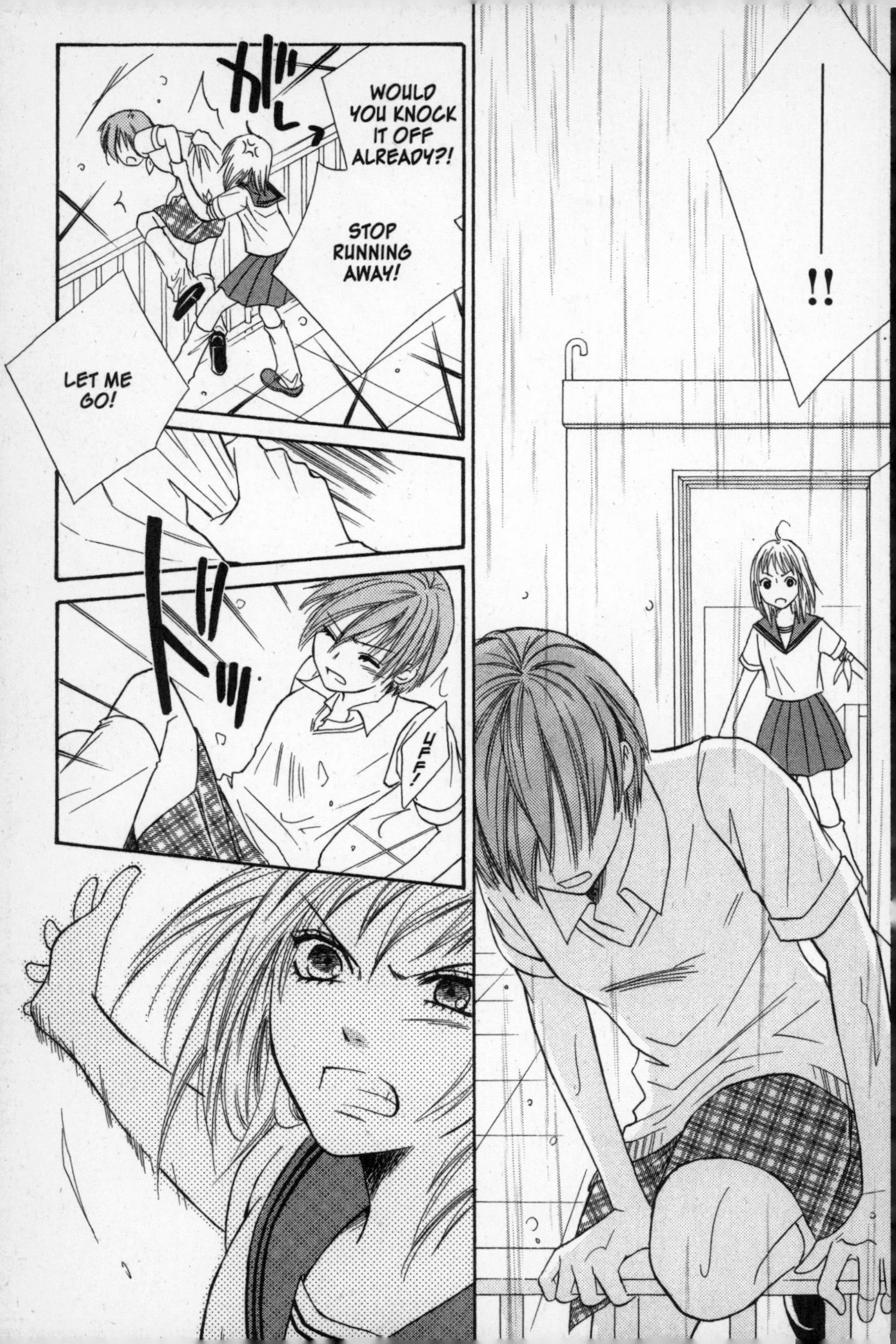
!!
WOULD YOU KNOCK IT OFF ALREADY?!
STOP RUNNING AWAY!
LET ME GO!
UFF!

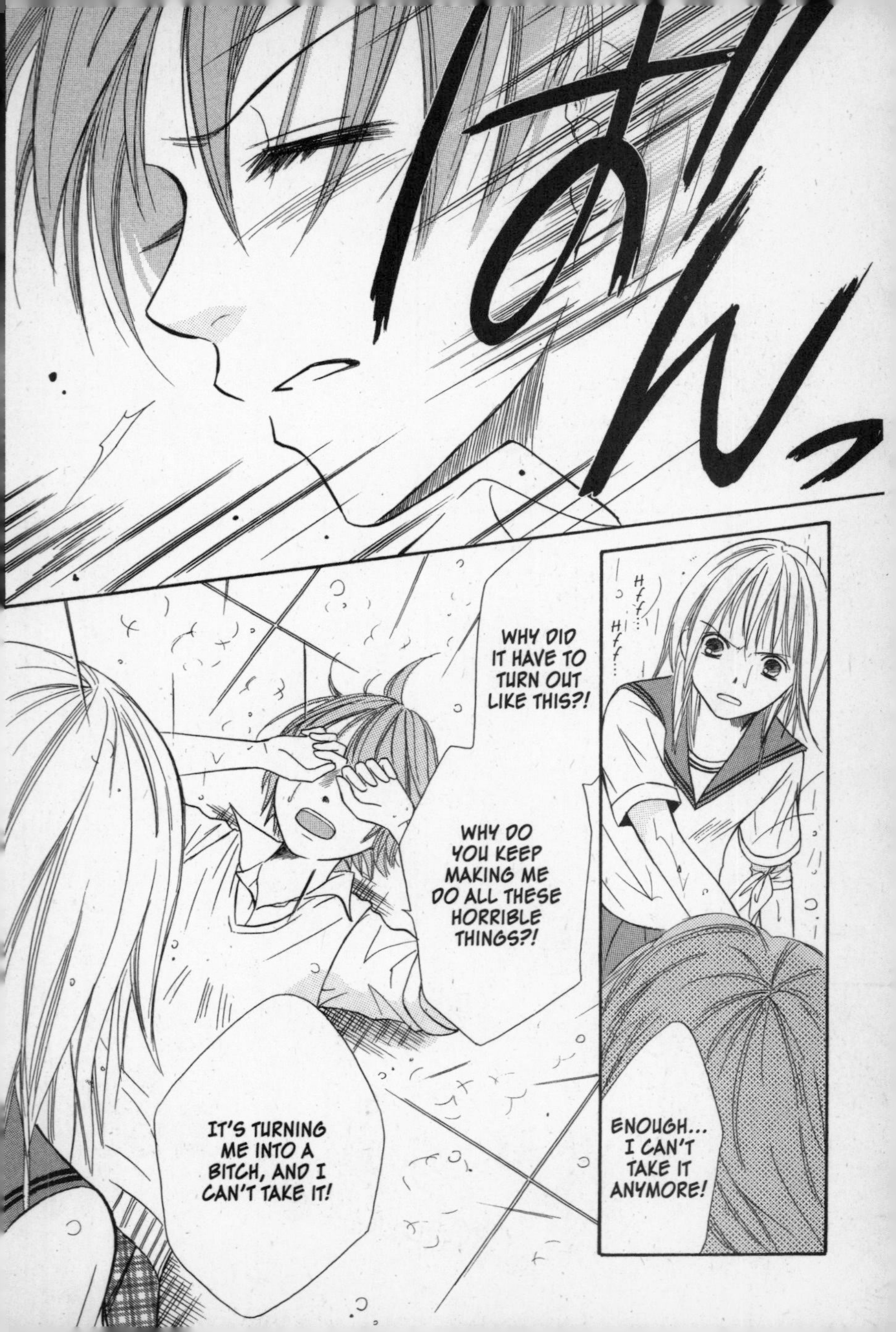
はんっ
Hff... Hff...
ENOUGH... I CAN'T TAKE IT ANYMORE!
WHY DID IT HAVE TO TURN OUT LIKE THIS?!
WHY DO YOU KEEP MAKING ME DO ALL THESE HORRIBLE THINGS?!
IT'S TURNING ME INTO A BITCH, AND I CAN'T TAKE IT!

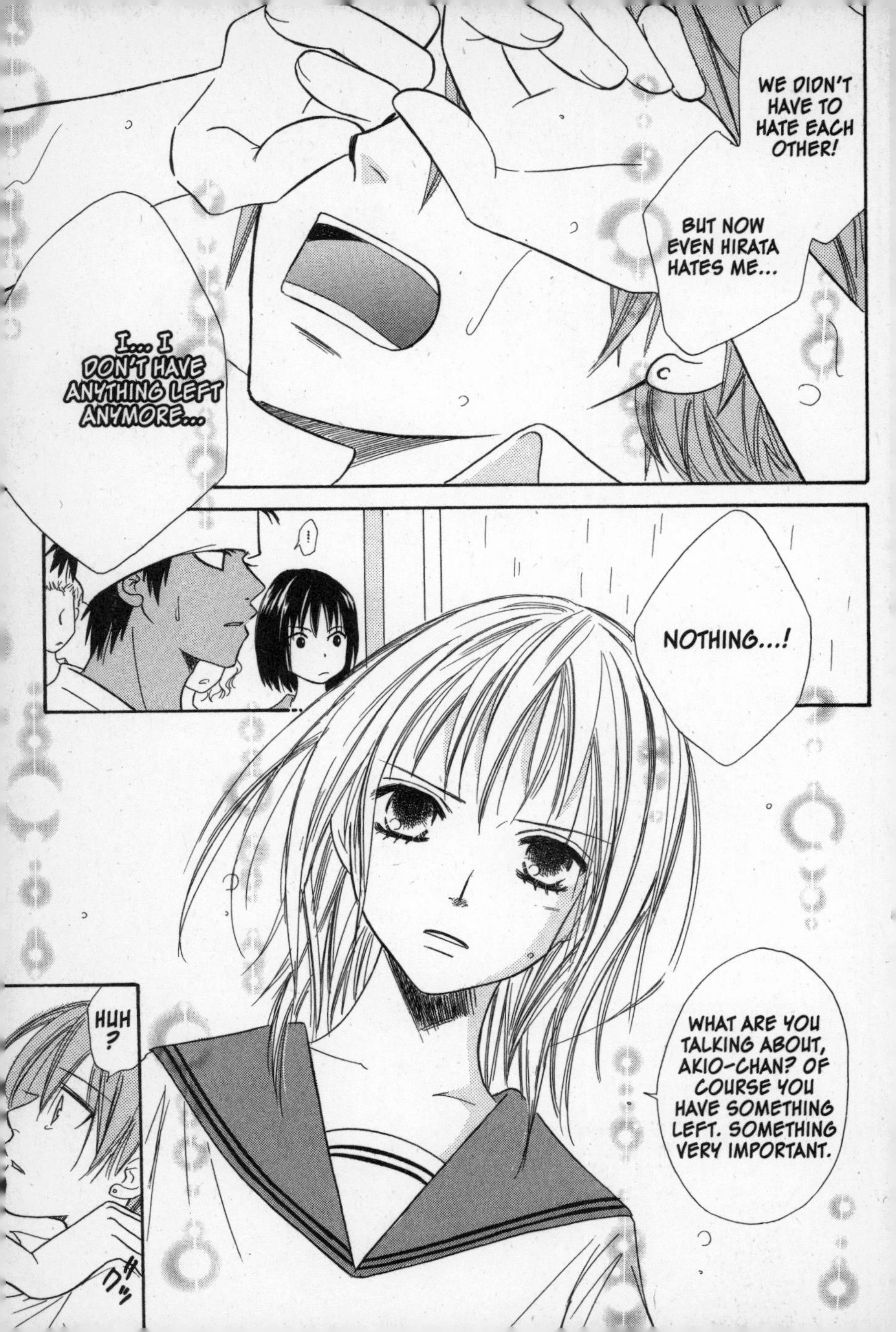
WE DIDN'T HAVE TO HATE EACH OTHER!
BUT NOW EVEN HIRATA HATES ME...
I... I DON'T HAVE ANYTHING LEFT ANYMORE...
NOTHING...!
!...
WHAT ARE YOU TALKING ABOUT, AKIO-CHAN? OF COURSE YOU HAVE SOMETHING LEFT. SOMETHING VERY IMPORTANT.
HUH?

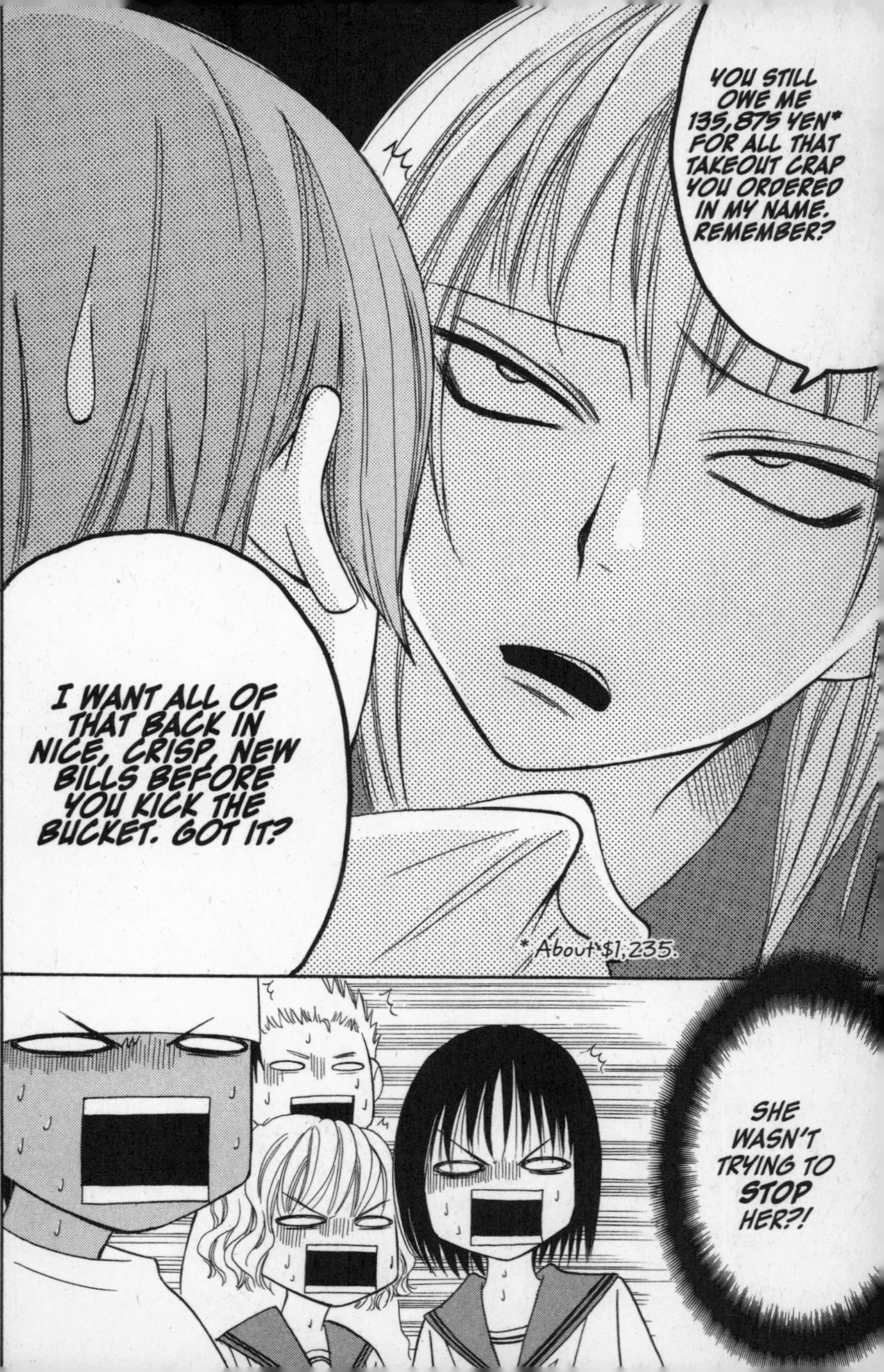
YOU STILL OWE ME 135,875 YEN* FOR ALL THAT TAKEOUT CRAP YOU ORDERED IN MY NAME. REMEMBER?
I WANT ALL OF THAT BACK IN NICE, CRISP, NEW BILLS BEFORE YOU KICK THE BUCKET. GOT IT?
* About $1,235.
SHE WASN'T TRYING TO STOP HER?!

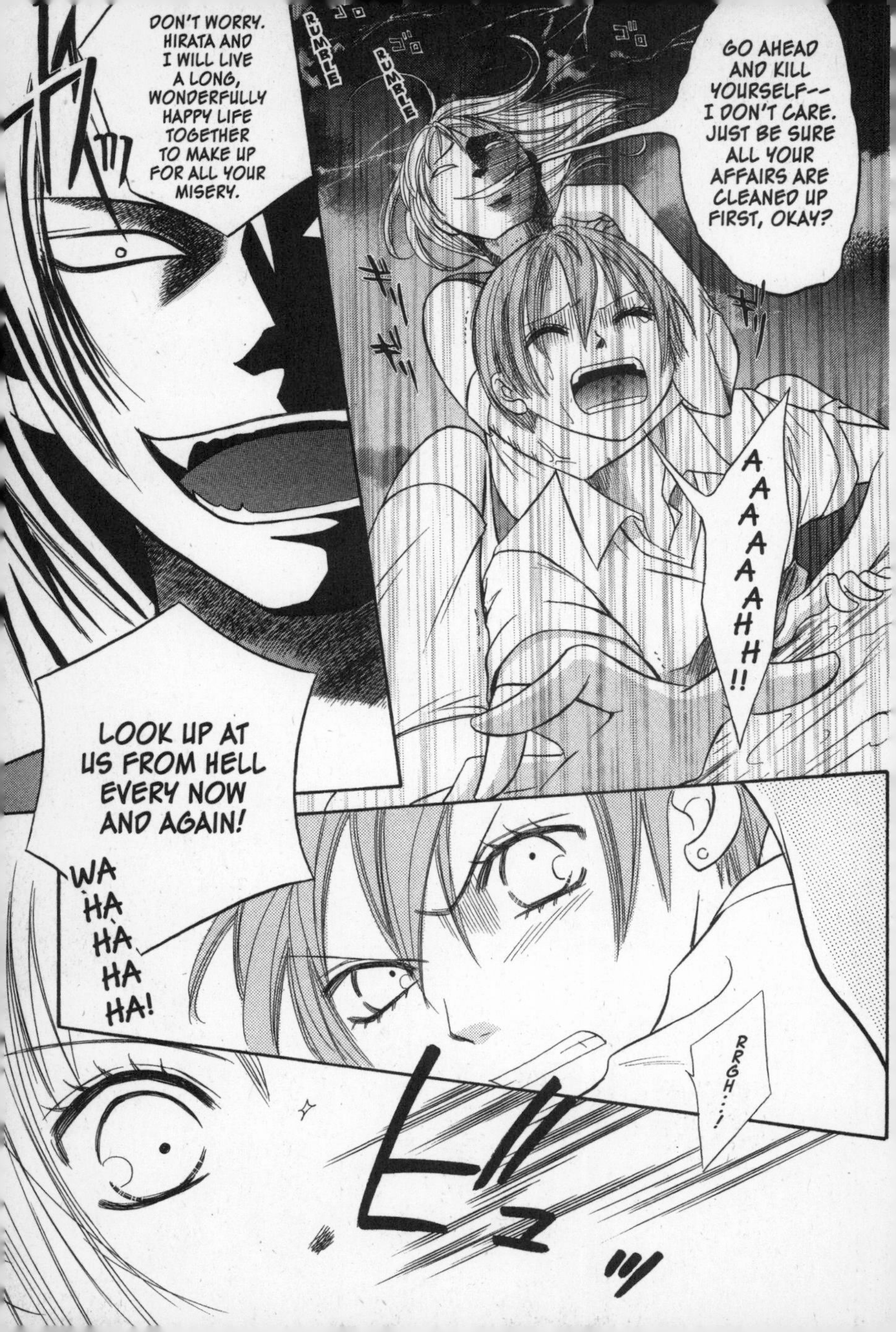
RUMBLE
RUMBLE
GO AHEAD AND KILL YOURSELF-- I DON'T CARE. JUST BE SURE ALL YOUR AFFAIRS ARE CLEANED UP FIRST, OKAY?
AAAAAAHH!!
DON'T WORRY. HIRATA AND I WILL LIVE A LONG, WONDERFULLY HAPPY LIFE TOGETHER TO MAKE UP FOR ALL YOUR MISERY.
LOOK UP AT US FROM HELL EVERY NOW AND AGAIN!
WA HA HA HA HA HA!
RRGH...!

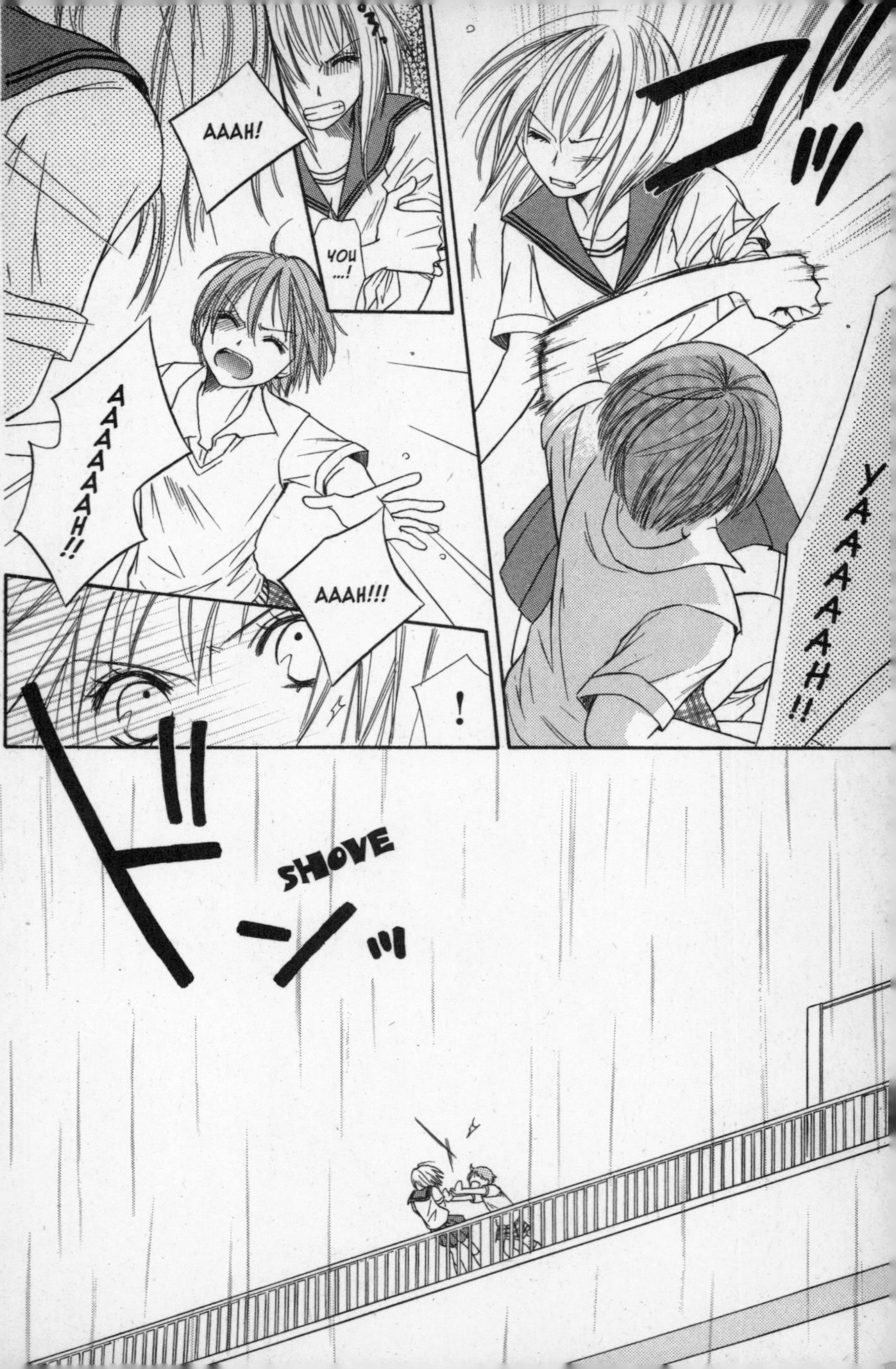
YAAAAAAH!!
YOU ...!
AAAH!
AAAAAAAH!!
AAAH!!!
!
SHOVE

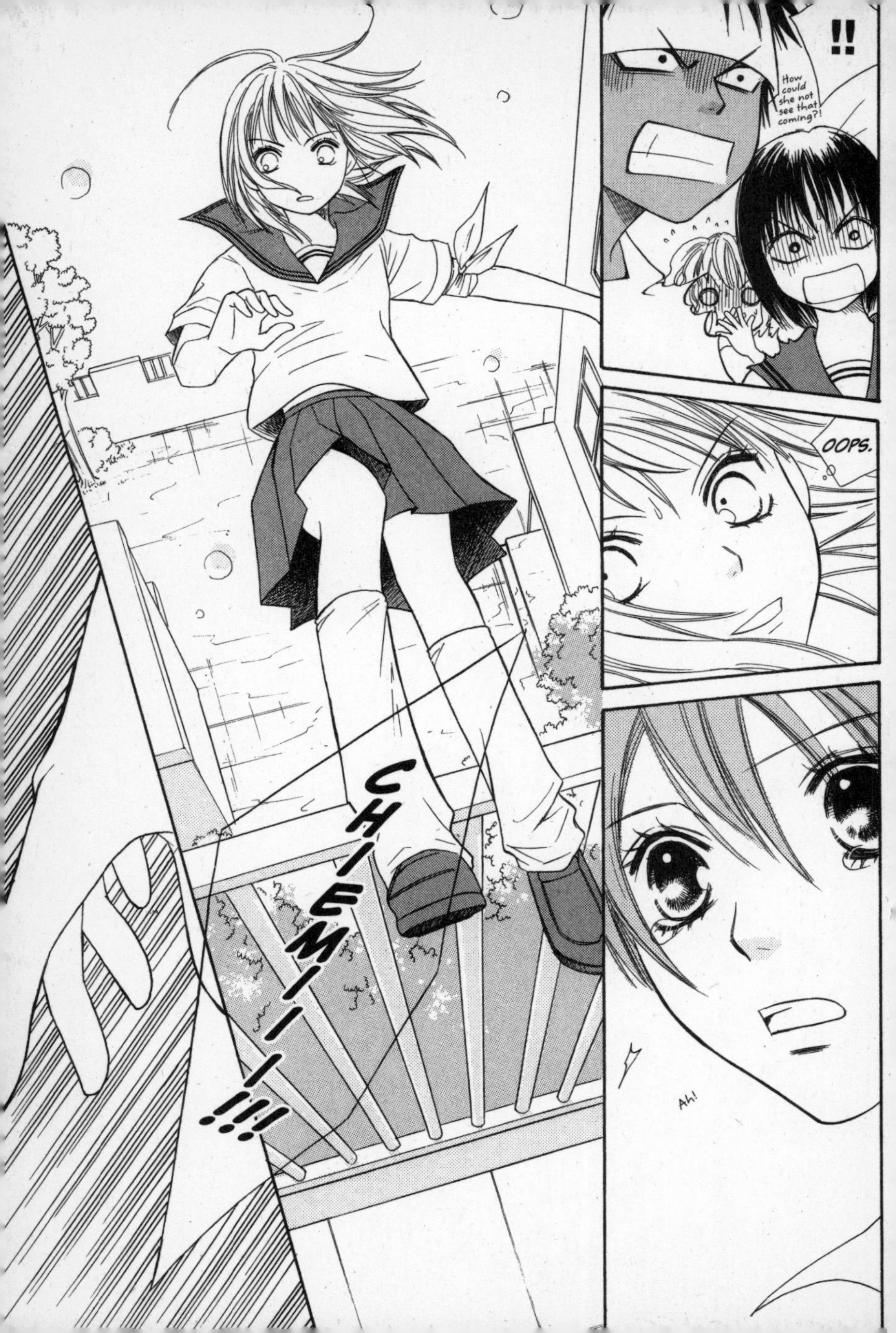
!!
How could she not see that coming?!
OOPS.
Ah!
CHIEMI-I-I-I!!!!

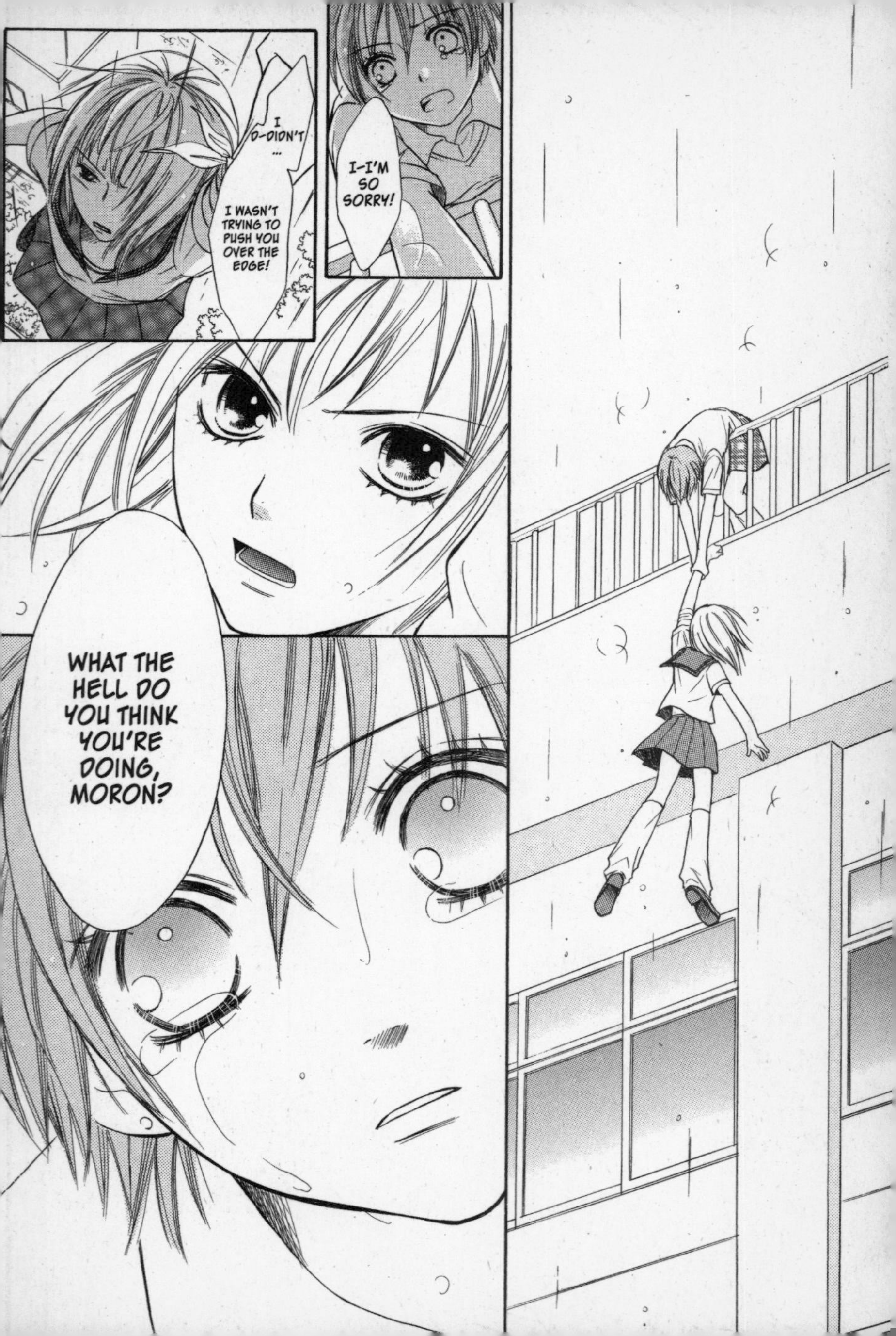
I-I'M SO SORRY!
I D-DIDN'T ...
I WASN'T TRYING TO PUSH YOU OVER THE EDGE!
WHAT THE HELL DO YOU THINK YOU'RE DOING, MORON?

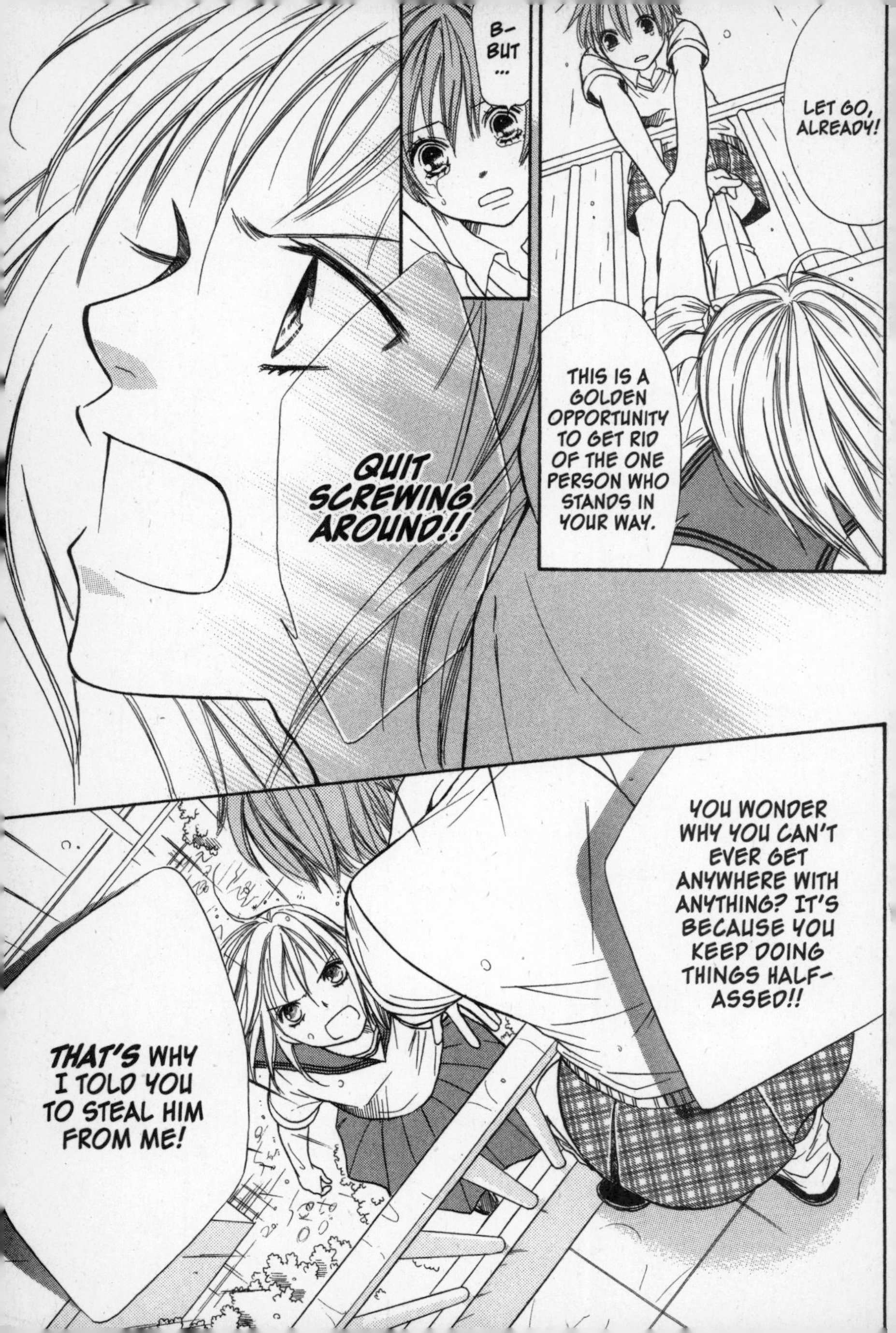
LET GO, ALREADY!
THIS IS A GOLDEN OPPORTUNITY TO GET RID OF THE ONE PERSON WHO STANDS IN YOUR WAY.
B-BUT ...
QUIT SCREWING AROUND!!
YOU WONDER WHY YOU CAN'T EVER GET ANYWHERE WITH ANYTHING? IT'S BECAUSE YOU KEEP DOING THINGS HALF-ASSED!!
THAT'S WHY I TOLD YOU TO STEAL HIM FROM ME!

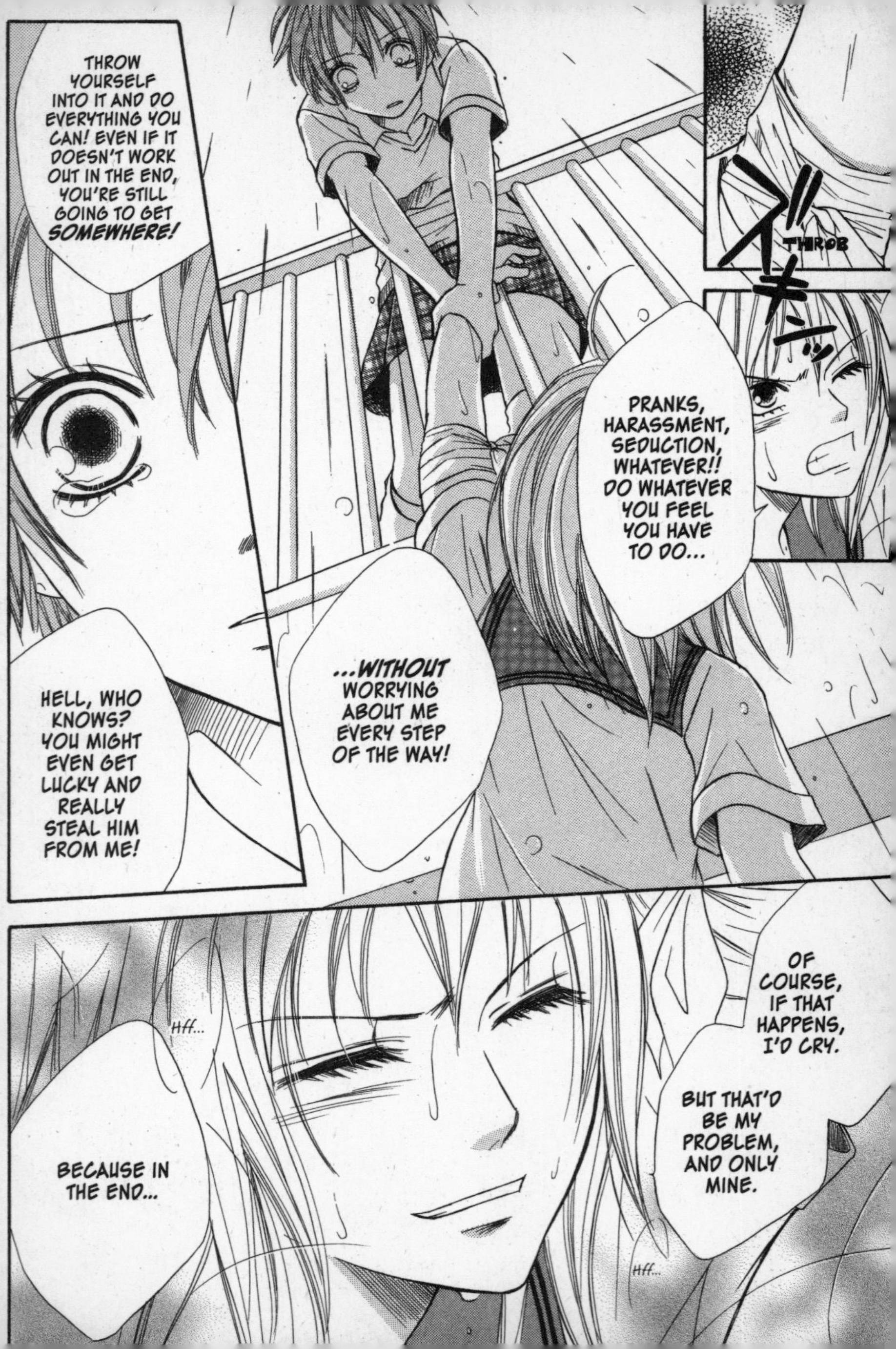
THROB
PRANKS, HARASSMENT, SEDUCTION, WHATEVER!! DO WHATEVER YOU FEEL YOU HAVE TO DO...
...WITHOUT WORRYING ABOUT ME EVERY STEP OF THE WAY!
THROW YOURSELF INTO IT AND DO EVERYTHING YOU CAN! EVEN IF IT DOESN'T WORK OUT IN THE END, YOU'RE STILL GOING TO GET SOMEWHERE!
HELL, WHO KNOWS? YOU MIGHT EVEN GET LUCKY AND REALLY STEAL HIM FROM ME!
OF COURSE, IF THAT HAPPENS, I'D CRY.
BUT THAT'D BE MY PROBLEM, AND ONLY MINE.
Hff...
Hff...
BECAUSE IN THE END...

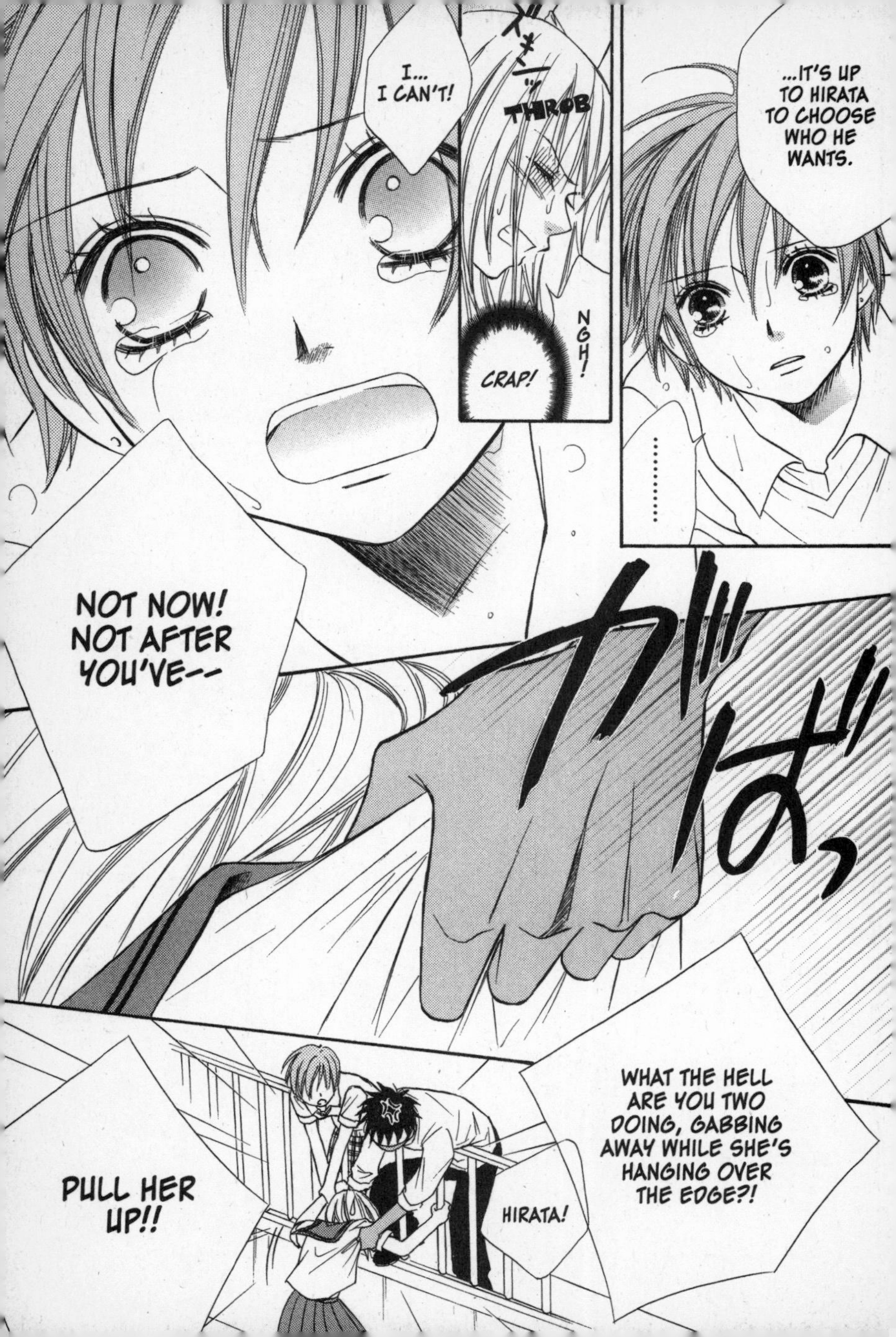

...IT'S UP TO HIRATA TO CHOOSE WHO HE WANTS.
......
THROB
NGH!
CRAP!
I... I CAN'T!
NOT NOW! NOT AFTER YOU'VE--
WHAT THE HELL ARE YOU TWO DOING, GABBING AWAY WHILE SHE'S HANGING OVER THE EDGE?!
HIRATA!
PULL HER UP!!

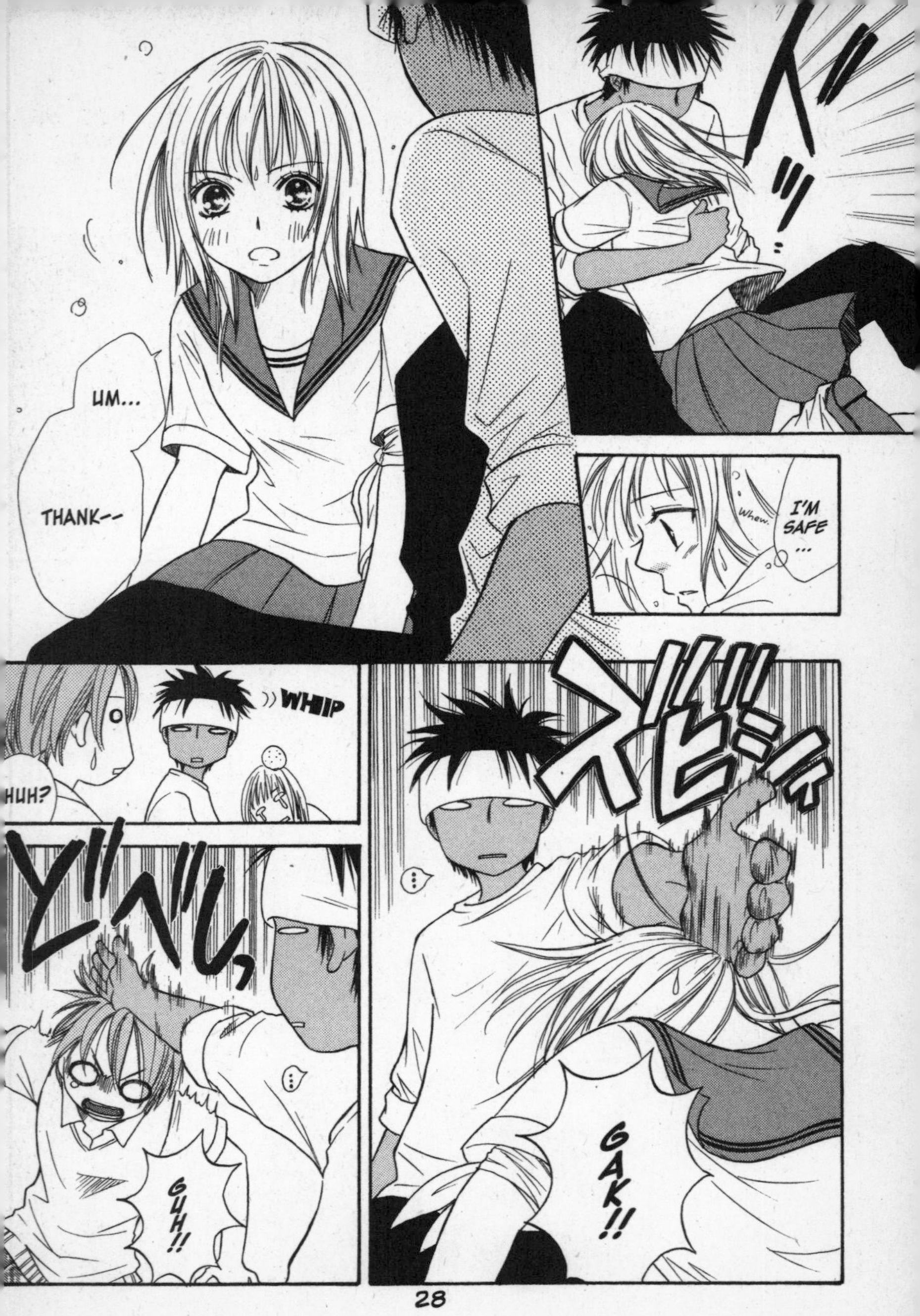
Whew.
I'M SAFE ...
UM...
THANK--
...
GAK!!
WHIP
HUH?
...
GUH!!

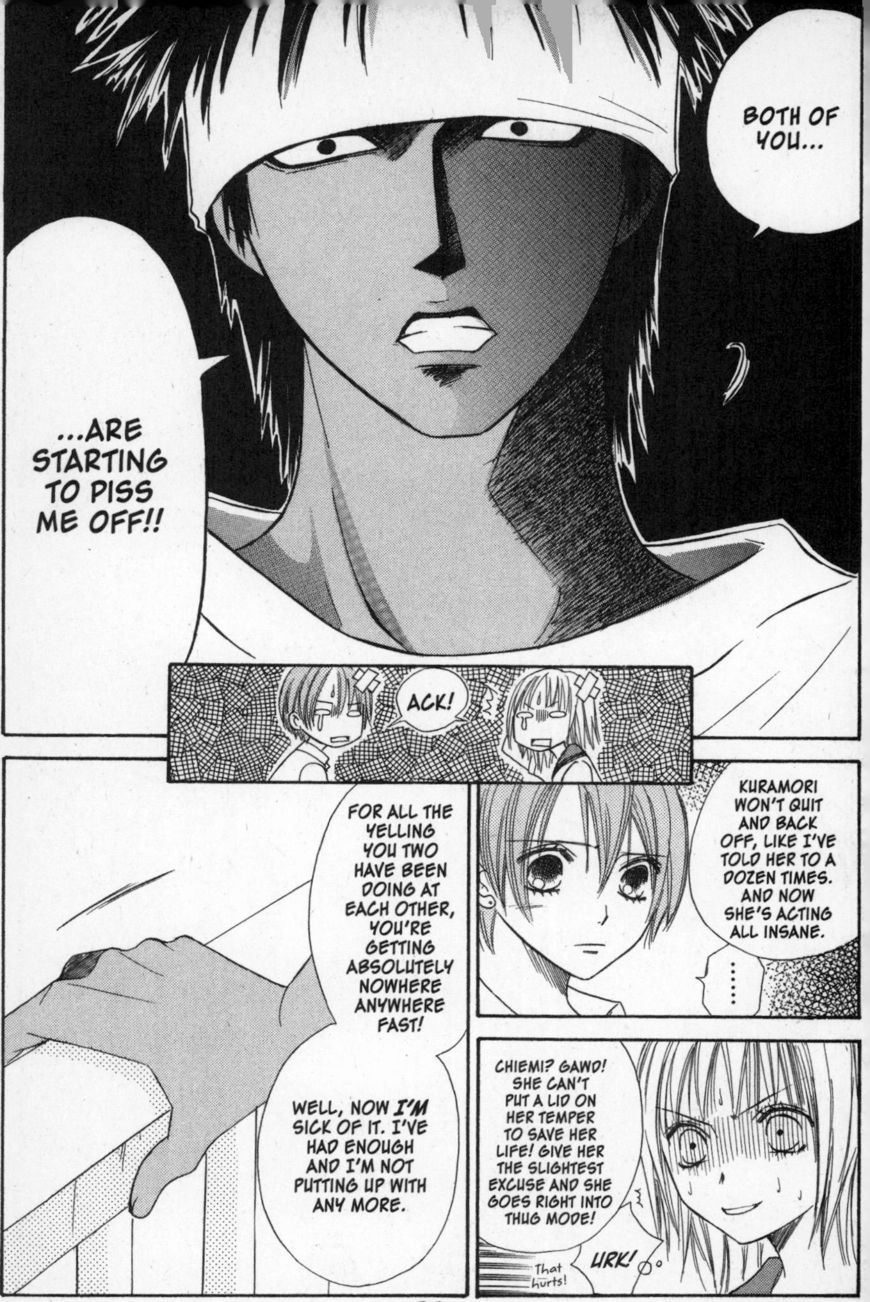
BOTH OF YOU...
...ARE STARTING TO PISS ME OFF!!
ACK!
KURAMORI WON'T QUIT AND BACK OFF, LIKE I'VE TOLD HER TO A DOZEN TIMES. AND NOW SHE'S ACTING ALL INSANE.
......
CHIEMI? GAWD! SHE CAN'T PUT A LID ON HER TEMPER TO SAVE HER LIFE! GIVE HER THE SLIGHTEST EXCUSE AND SHE GOES RIGHT INTO THUG MODE!
URK!
That hurts!
FOR ALL THE YELLING YOU TWO HAVE BEEN DOING AT EACH OTHER, YOU'RE GETTING ABSOLUTELY NOWHERE ANYWHERE FAST!
WELL, NOW I'M SICK OF IT. I'VE HAD ENOUGH AND I'M NOT PUTTING UP WITH ANY MORE.

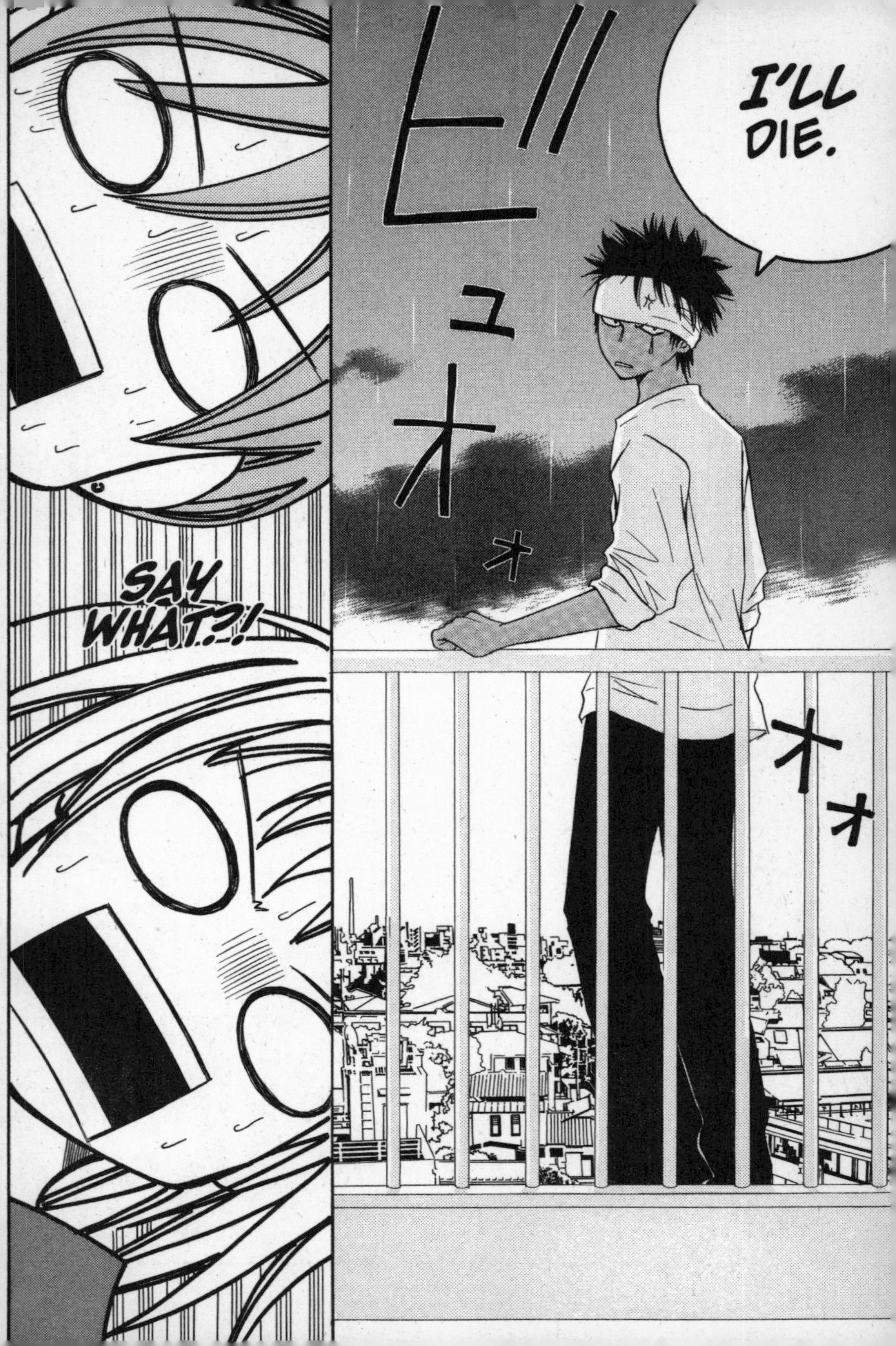
I'LL DIE.
ビュオォ
オォ
SAY WHAT?!

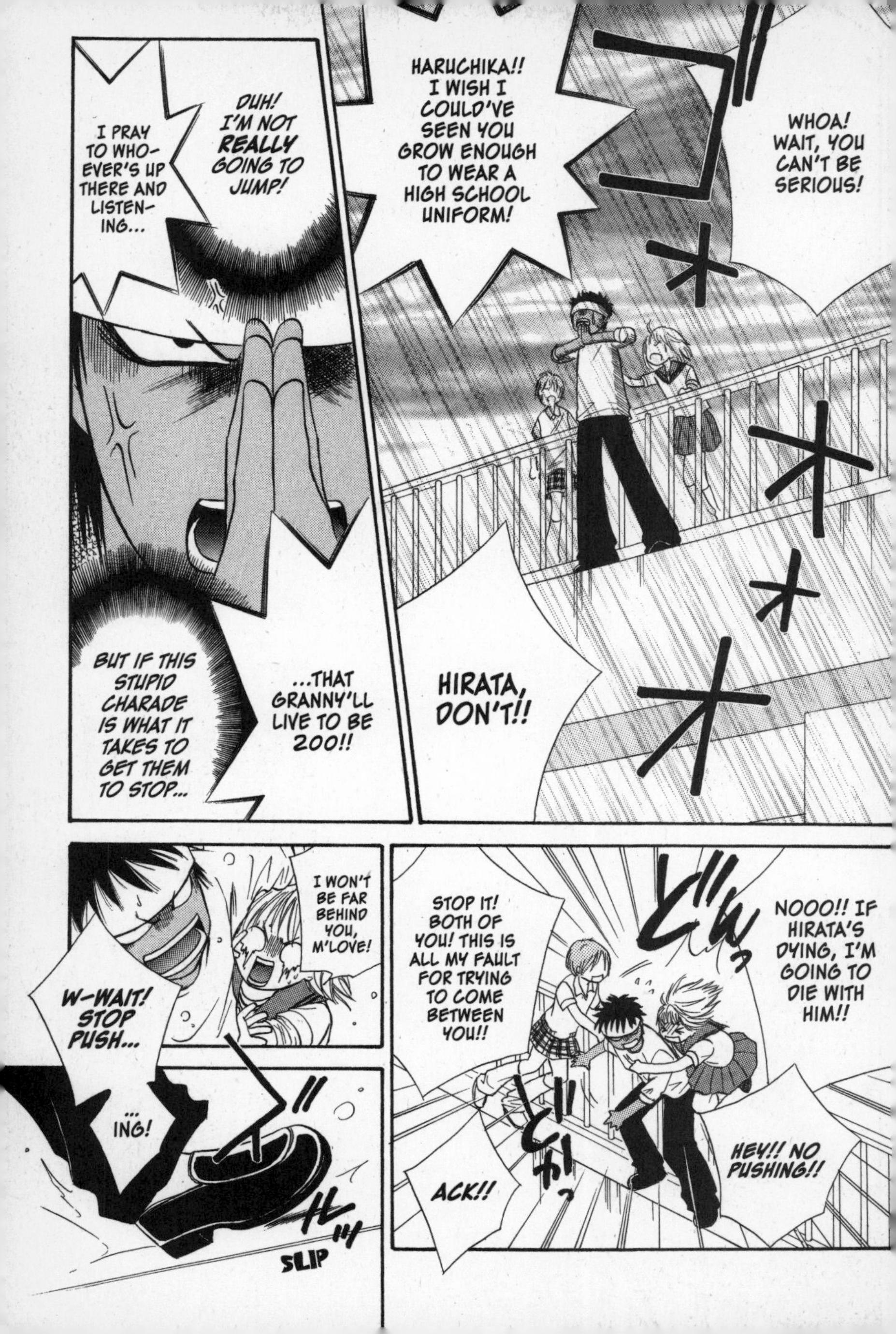
WHOA! WAIT, YOU CAN'T BE SERIOUS!
HARUCHIKA!! I WISH I COULD'VE SEEN YOU GROW ENOUGH TO WEAR A HIGH SCHOOL UNIFORM!
HIRATA, DON'T!!
DUH! I'M NOT REALLY GOING TO JUMP!
I PRAY TO WHO-EVER'S UP THERE AND LISTEN-ING...
...THAT GRANNY'LL LIVE TO BE 200!!
BUT IF THIS STUPID CHARADE IS WHAT IT TAKES TO GET THEM TO STOP...
NOOO!! IF HIRATA'S DYING, I'M GOING TO DIE WITH HIM!!
STOP IT! BOTH OF YOU! THIS IS ALL MY FAULT FOR TRYING TO COME BETWEEN YOU!!
HEY!! NO PUSHING!!
ACK!!
I WON'T BE FAR BEHIND YOU, M'LOVE!
W-WAIT! STOP PUSH...
...ING!
SLIP

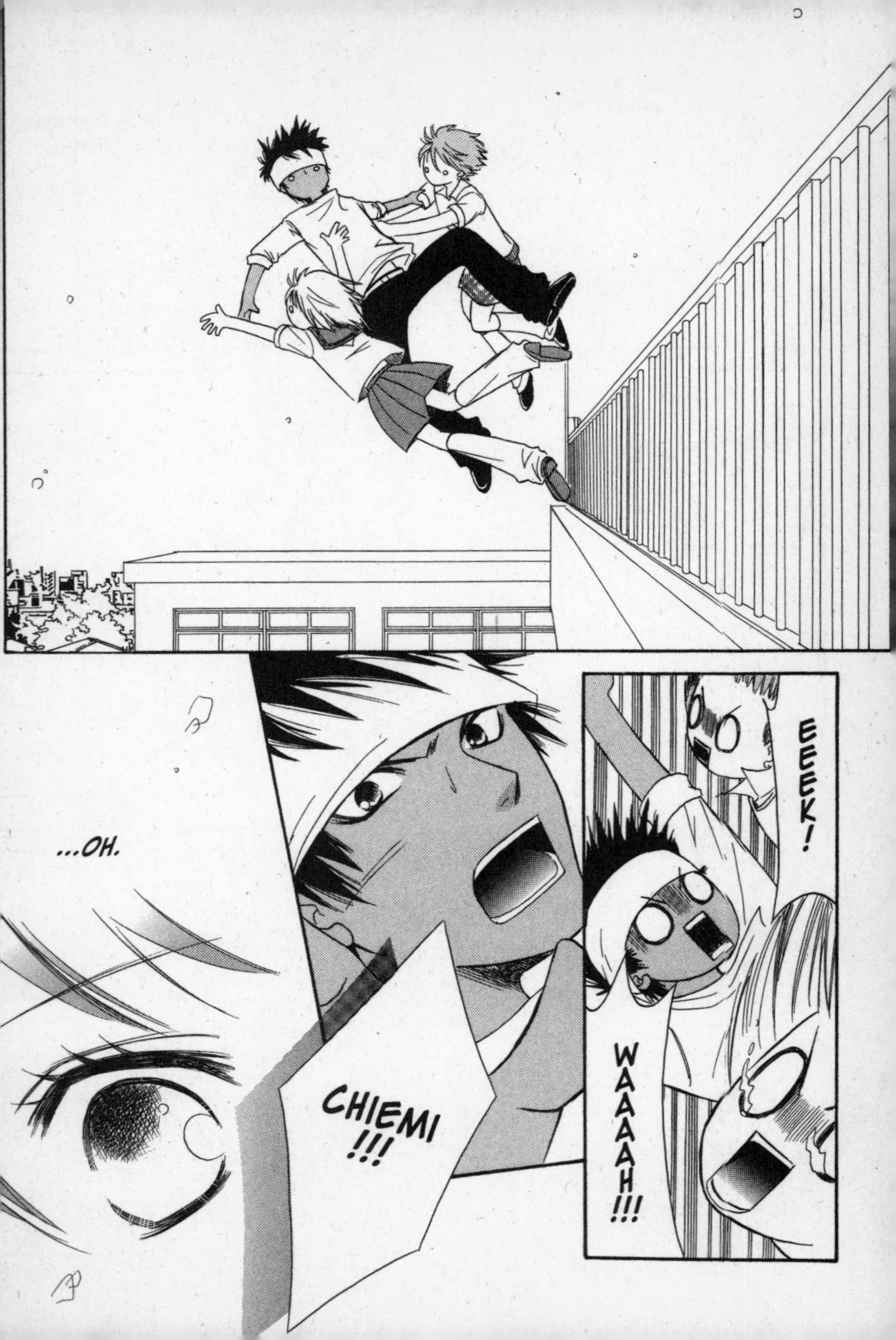
EEEK!
WAAAAH!!!
CHIEMI!!!
...OH.

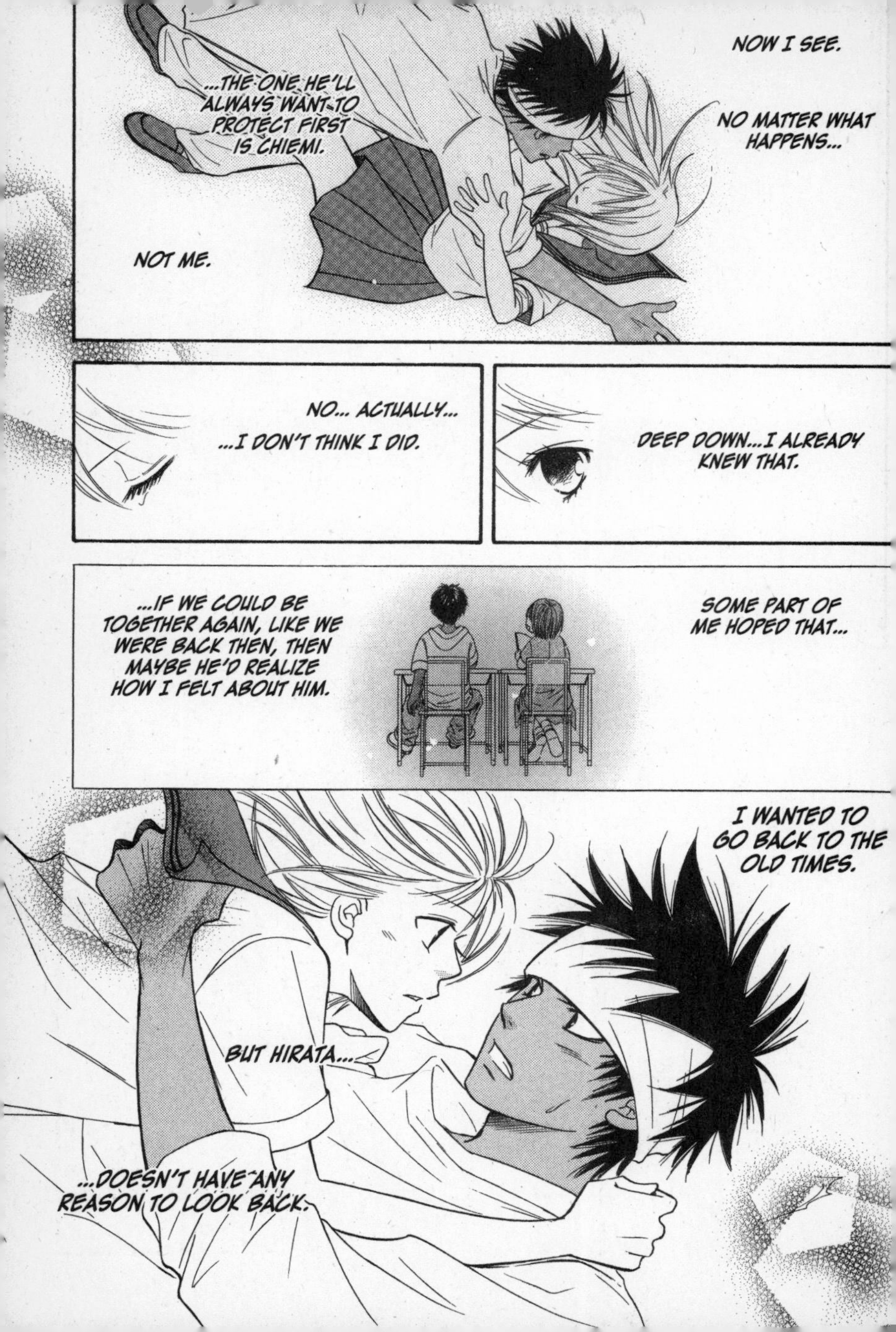
NOW I SEE.
NO MATTER WHAT HAPPENS...
...THE ONE HE'LL ALWAYS WANT TO PROTECT FIRST IS CHIEMI.
NOT ME.
DEEP DOWN...I ALREADY KNEW THAT.
NO... ACTUALLY...
...I DON'T THINK I DID.
SOME PART OF ME HOPED THAT...
...IF WE COULD BE TOGETHER AGAIN, LIKE WE WERE BACK THEN, THEN MAYBE HE'D REALIZE HOW I FELT ABOUT HIM.
I WANTED TO GO BACK TO THE OLD TIMES.
BUT HIRATA...
...DOESN'T HAVE ANY REASON TO LOOK BACK.

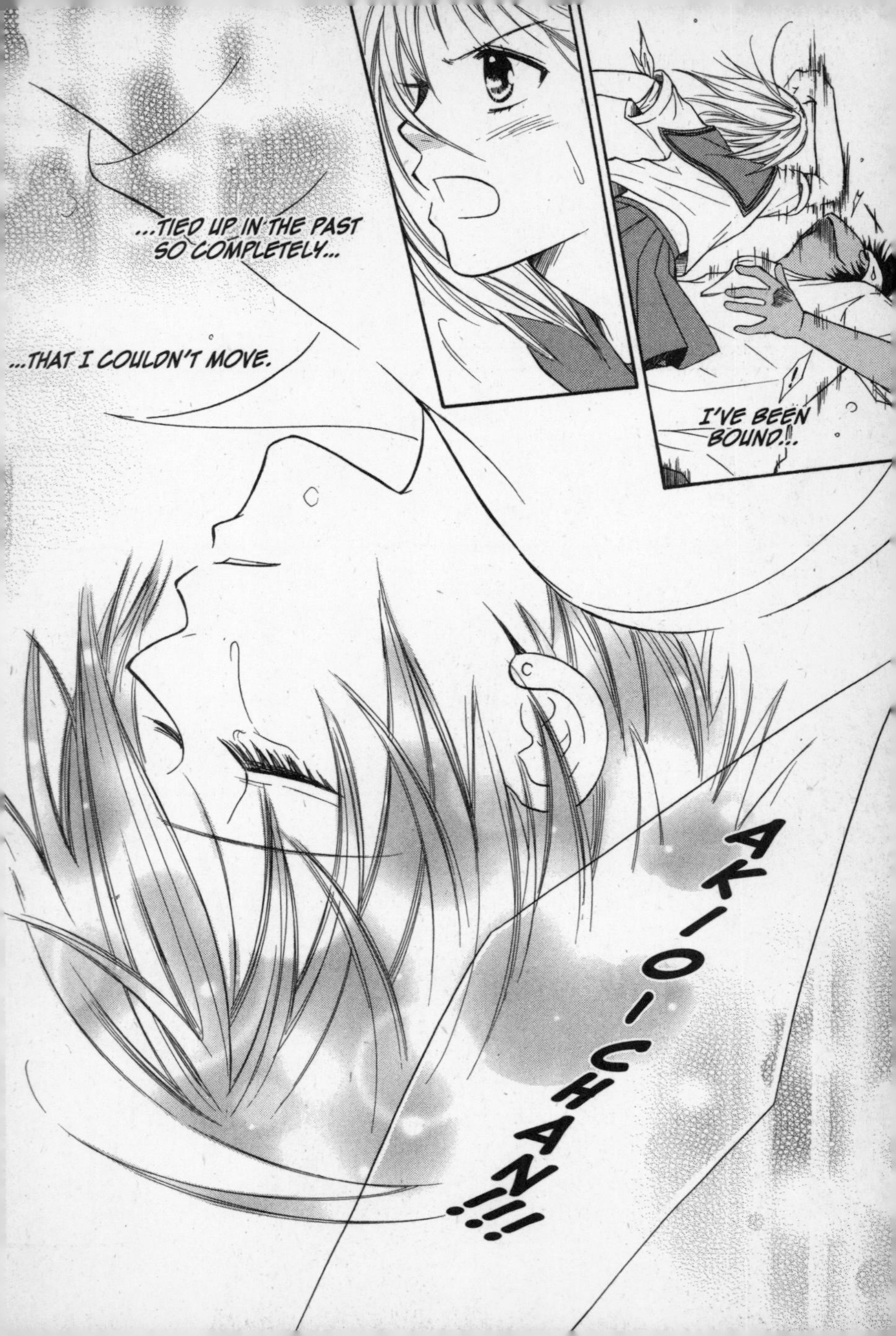
I'VE BEEN BOUND!...
...TIED UP IN THE PAST SO COMPLETELY...
...THAT I COULDN'T MOVE.
AKI-O-CHAN!!!!

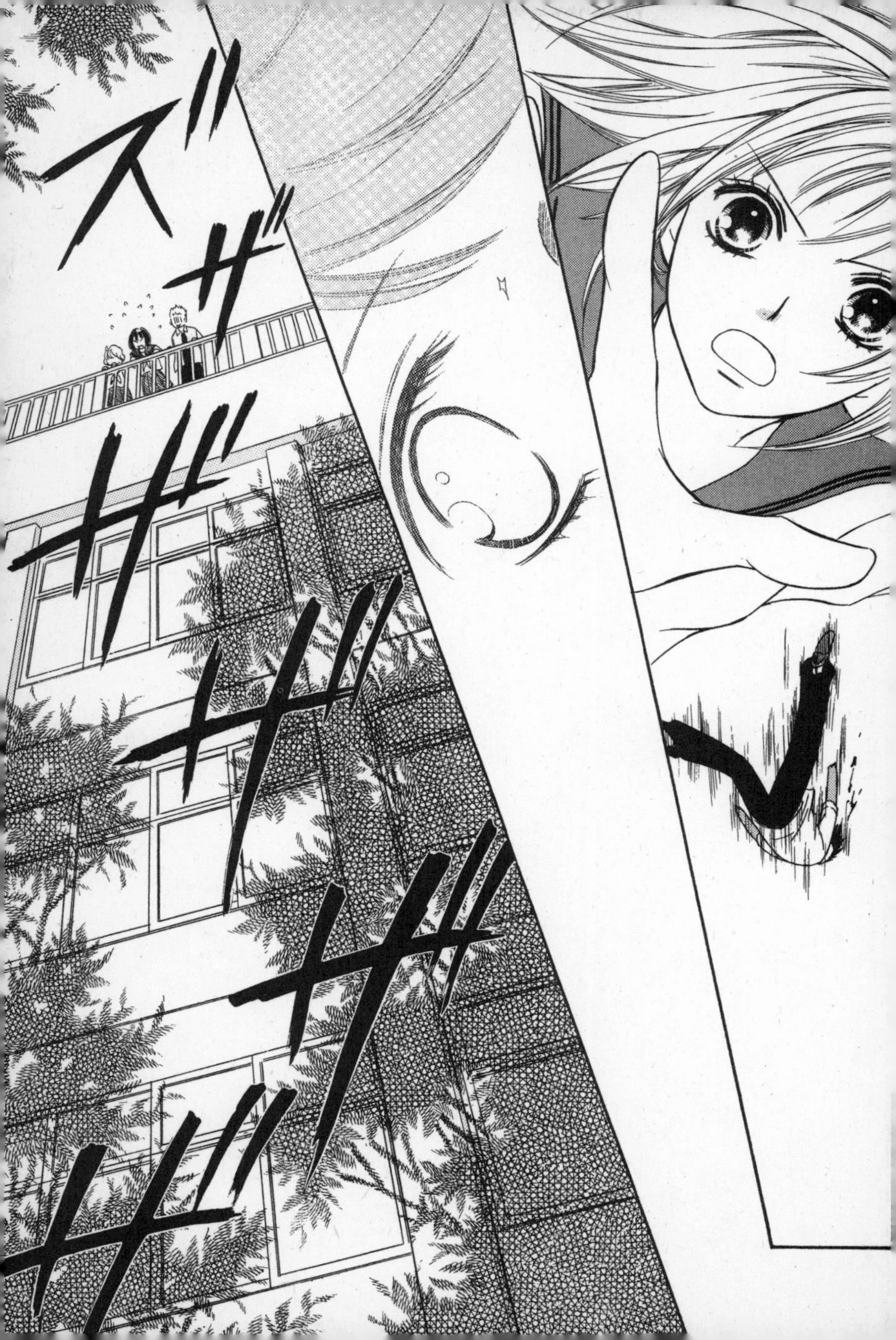
ズザザザザザ

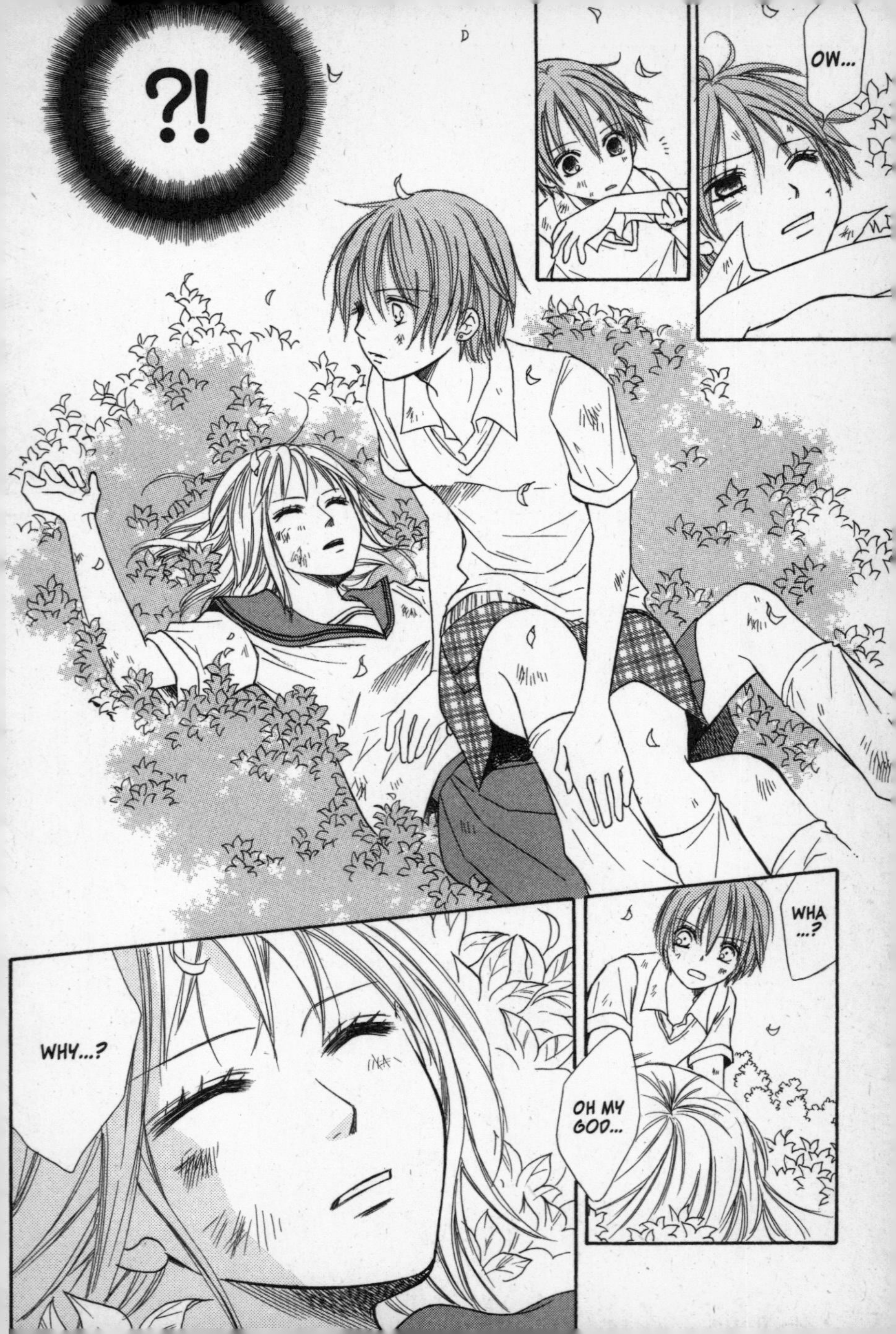
OW...
?!
WHA ...?
OH MY GOD...
WHY...?

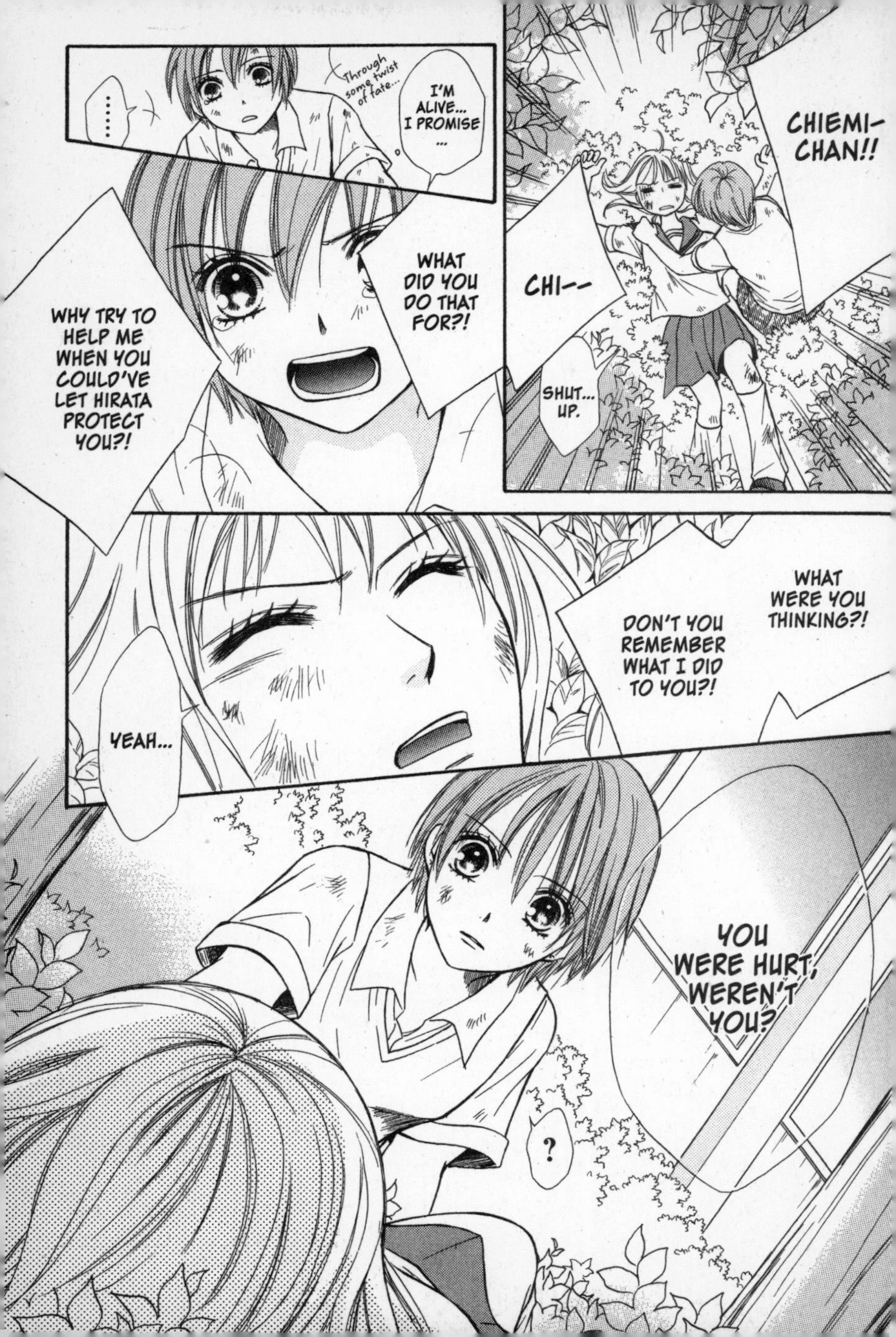
CHIEMI-CHAN!!
CHI--
SHUT... UP.
I'M ALIVE... I PROMISE ...
Through some twist of fate...
......
WHAT DID YOU DO THAT FOR?!
WHY TRY TO HELP ME WHEN YOU COULD'VE LET HIRATA PROTECT YOU?!
WHAT WERE YOU THINKING?!
DON'T YOU REMEMBER WHAT I DID TO YOU?!
YEAH...
YOU WERE HURT, WEREN'T YOU?
?

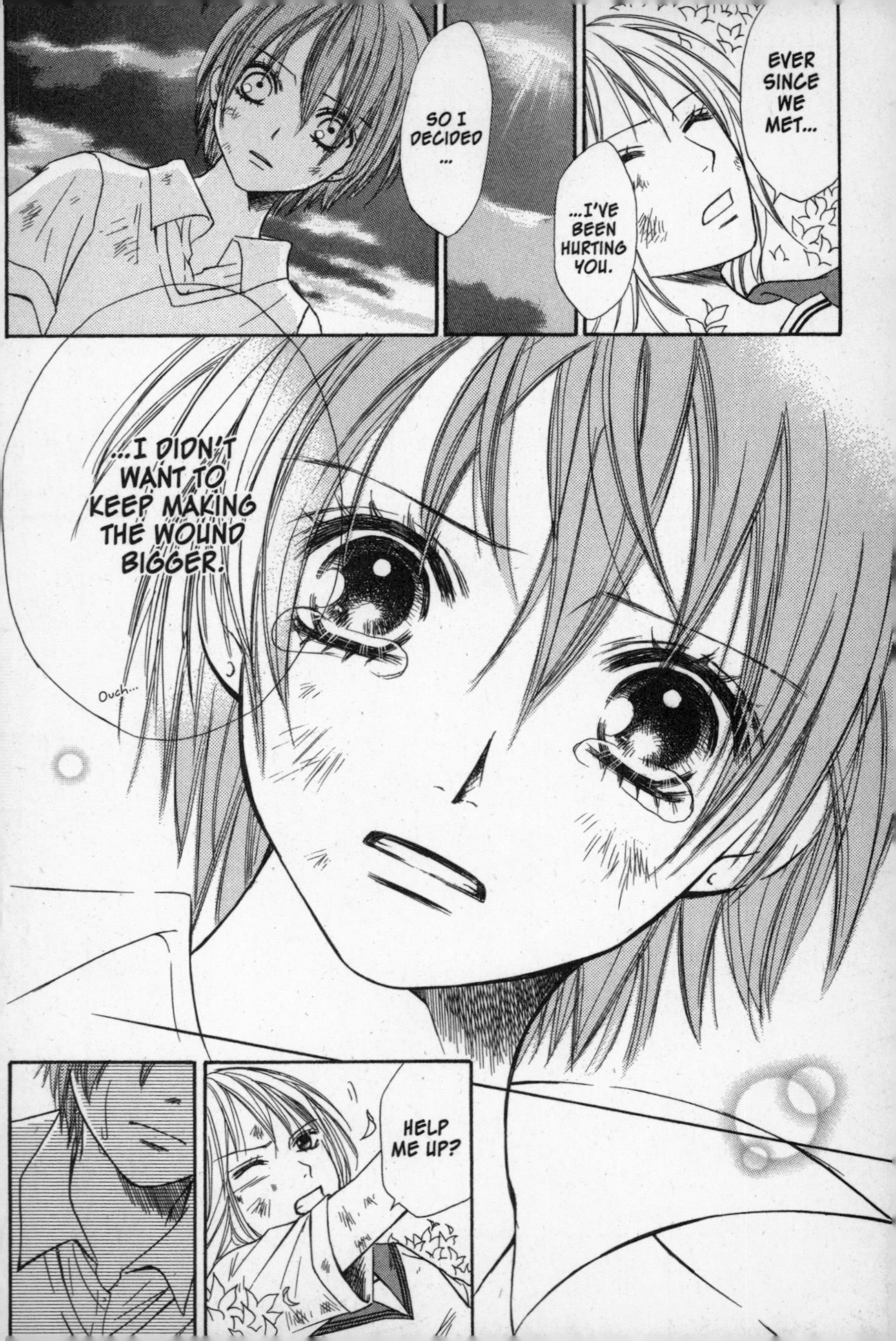
EVER SINCE WE MET...
...I'VE BEEN HURTING YOU.
SO I DECIDED ...
...I DIDN'T WANT TO KEEP MAKING THE WOUND BIGGER.
Ouch...
HELP ME UP?

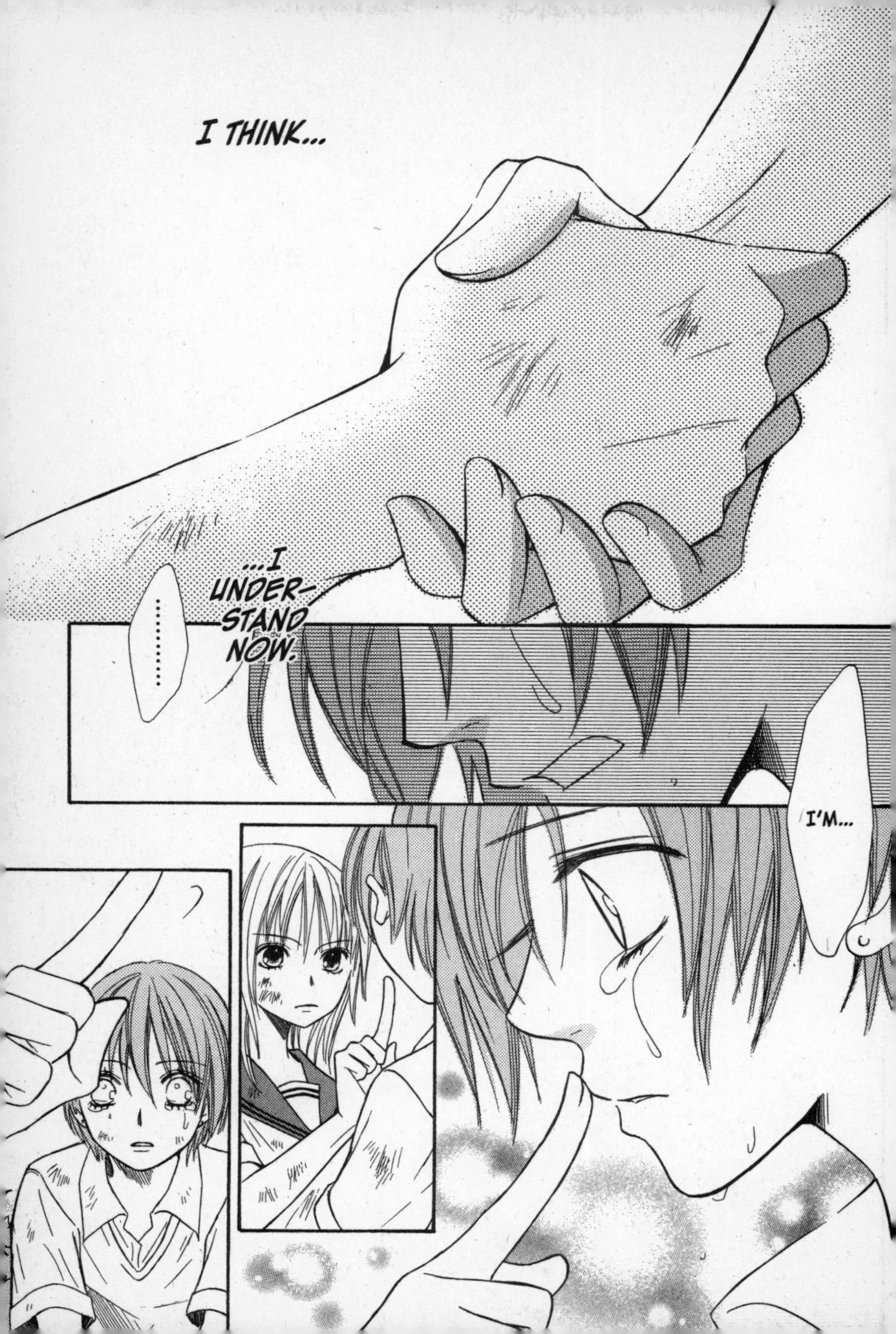
I THINK...
...I UNDER-STAND NOW.
......
I'M...

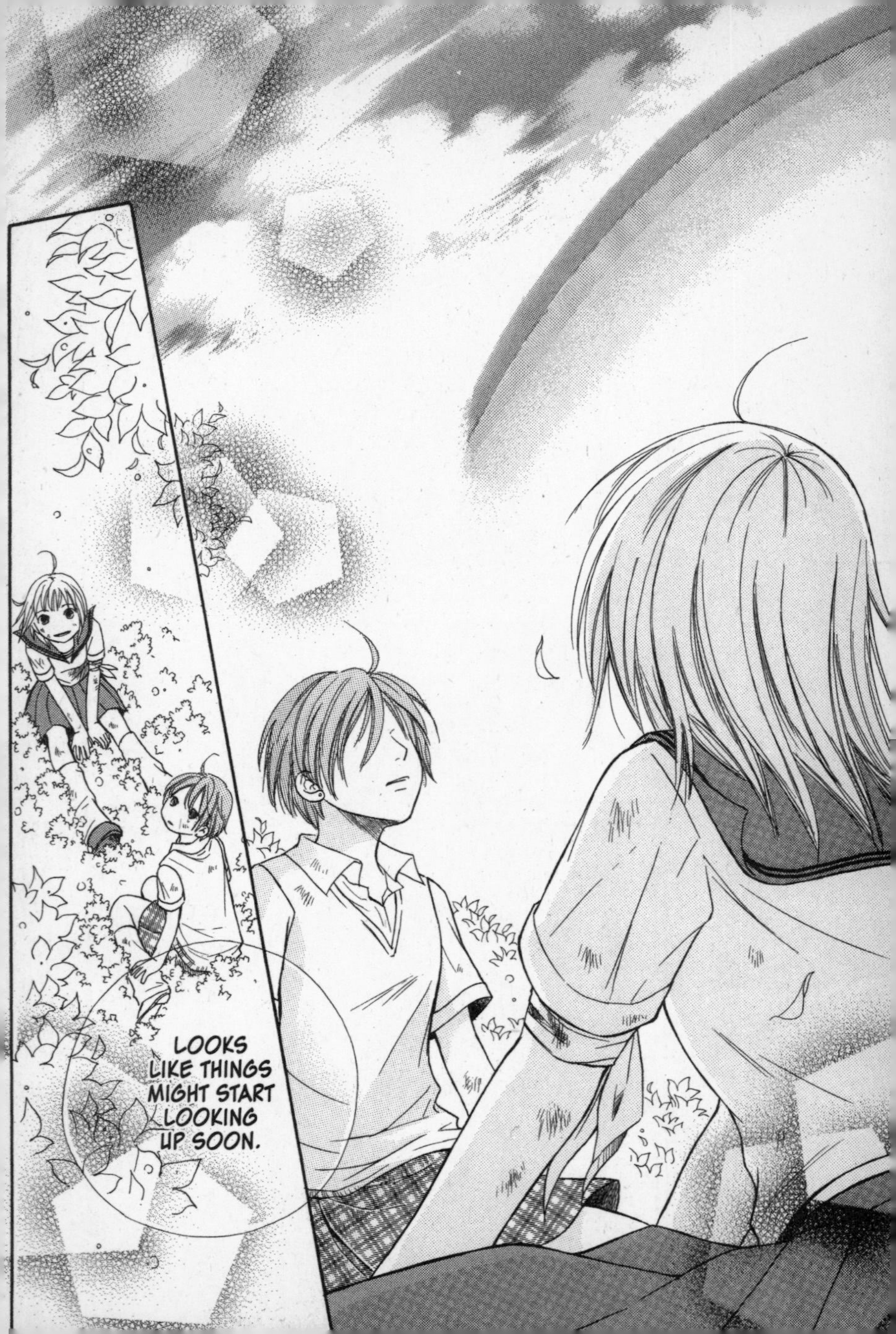
LOOKS LIKE THINGS MIGHT START LOOKING UP SOON.

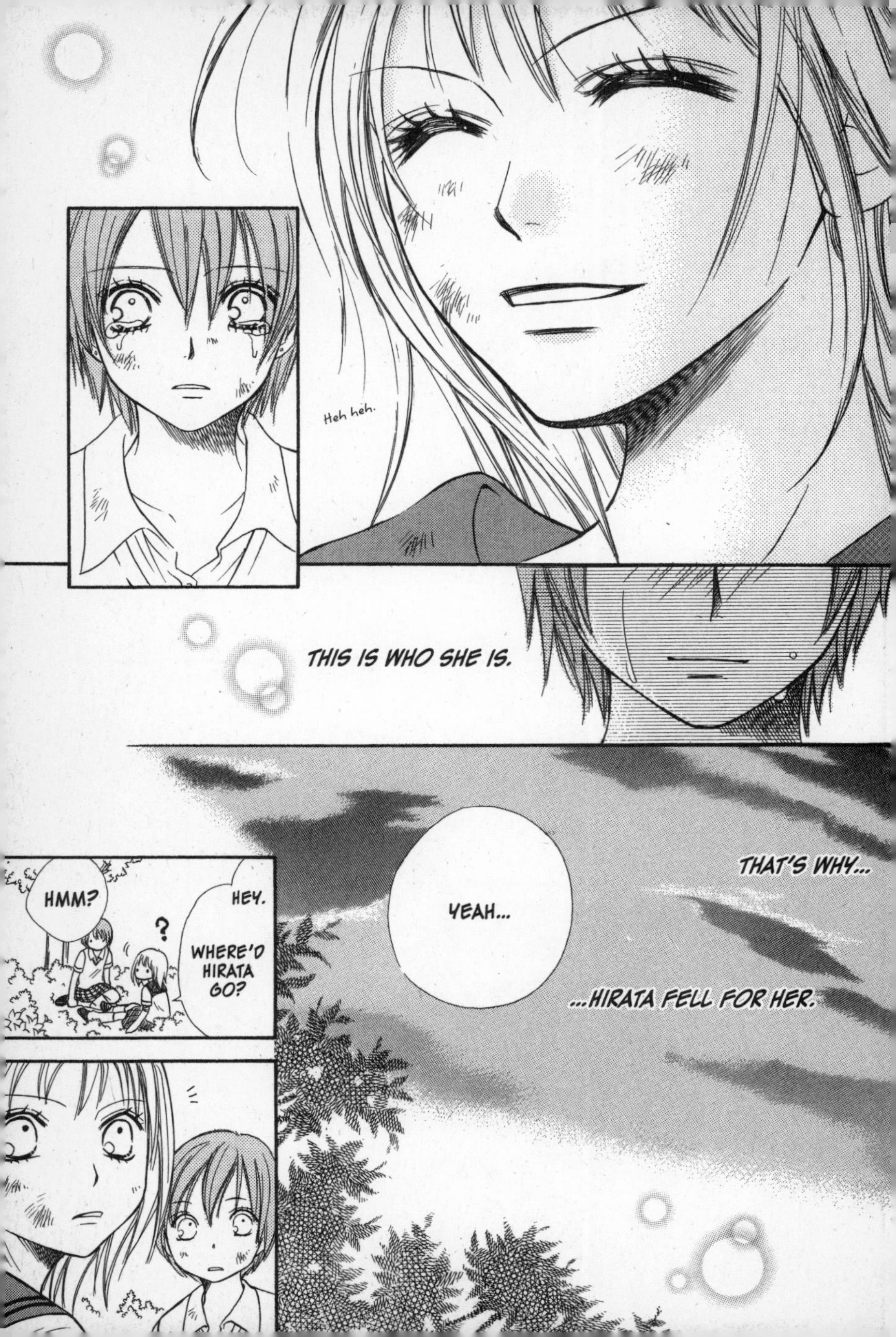
Heh heh.
THIS IS WHO SHE IS.
THAT'S WHY...
YEAH...
...HIRATA FELL FOR HER.
HEY.
WHERE'D HIRATA GO?
HMM?
?

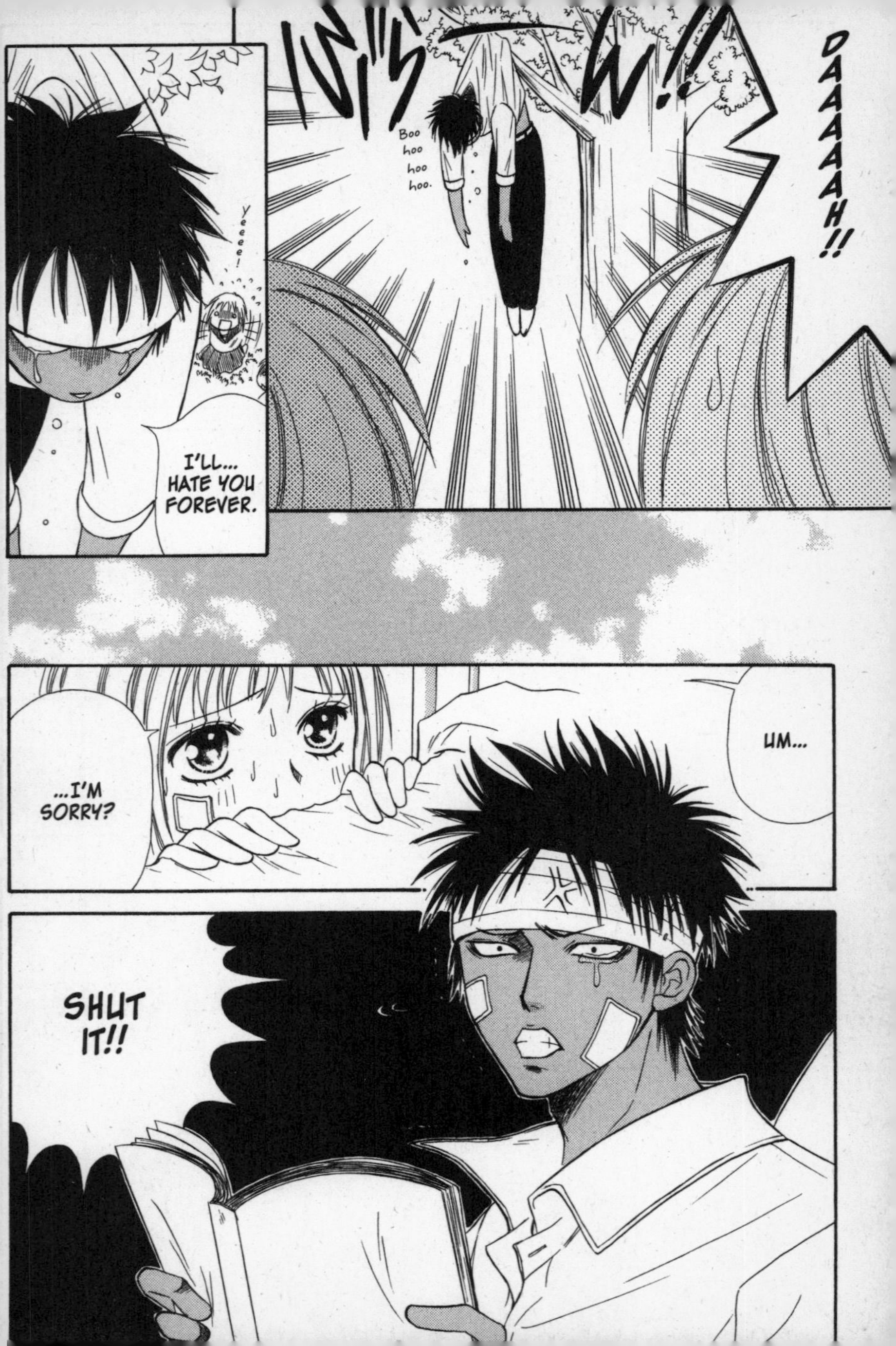
DAAAAAAH!!
Boo hoo hoo hoo.
Yeeeee!
I'LL... HATE YOU FOREVER.
UM...
...I'M SORRY?
SHUT IT!!

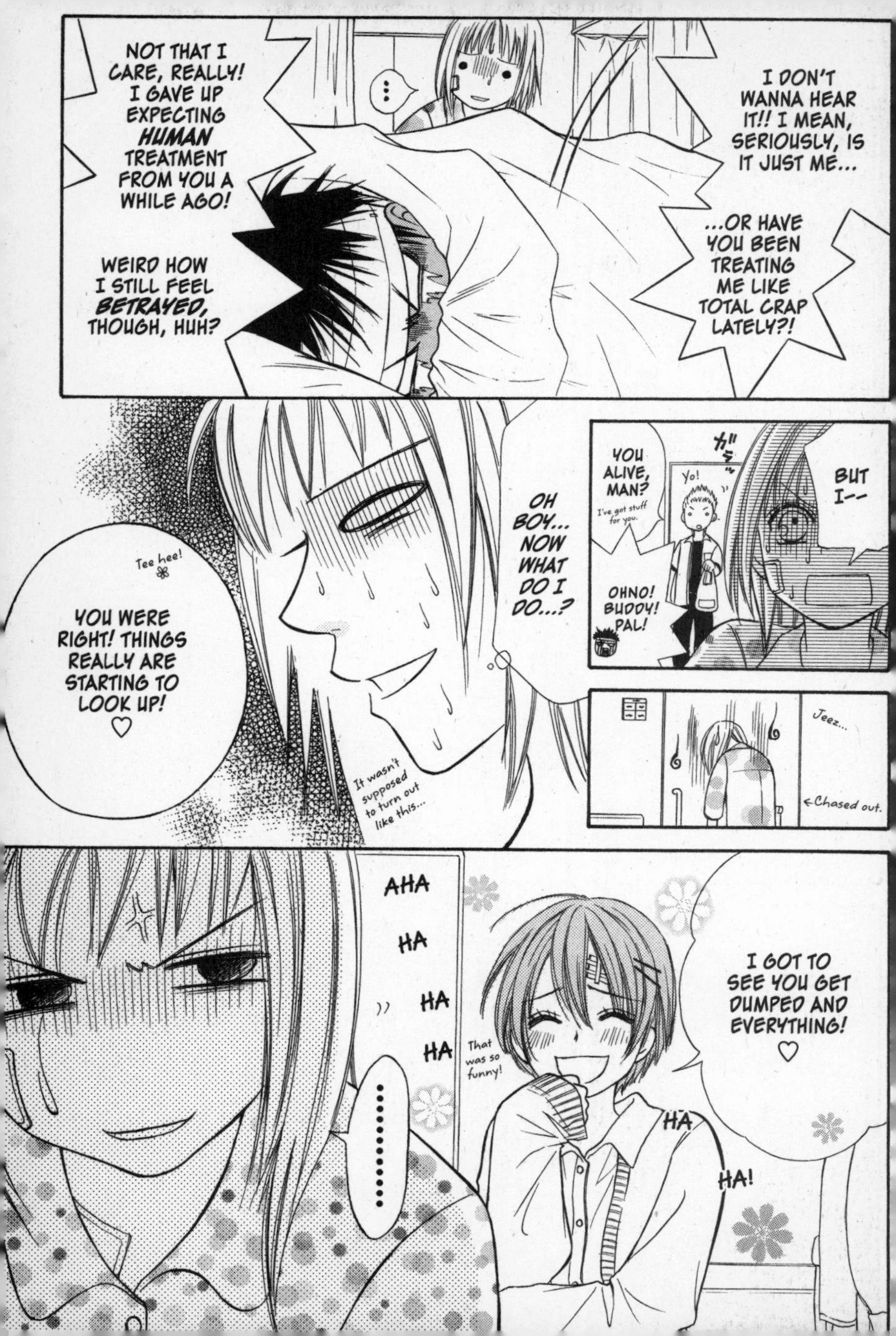
I DON'T WANNA HEAR IT!! I MEAN, SERIOUSLY, IS IT JUST ME...
...OR HAVE YOU BEEN TREATING ME LIKE TOTAL CRAP LATELY?!
...
NOT THAT I CARE, REALLY! I GAVE UP EXPECTING HUMAN TREATMENT FROM YOU A WHILE AGO!
WEIRD HOW I STILL FEEL BETRAYED, THOUGH, HUH?
BUT I--
ガラ
YOU ALIVE, MAN?
Yo!
I've got stuff for you.
OHNO! BUDDY! PAL!
Jeez...
←Chased out.
OH BOY... NOW WHAT DO I DO...?
It wasn't supposed to turn out like this...
Tee hee!
YOU WERE RIGHT! THINGS REALLY ARE STARTING TO LOOK UP! ♡
I GOT TO SEE YOU GET DUMPED AND EVERYTHING! ♡
HA
HA!
That was so funny!
AHA
HA
HA
HA
....

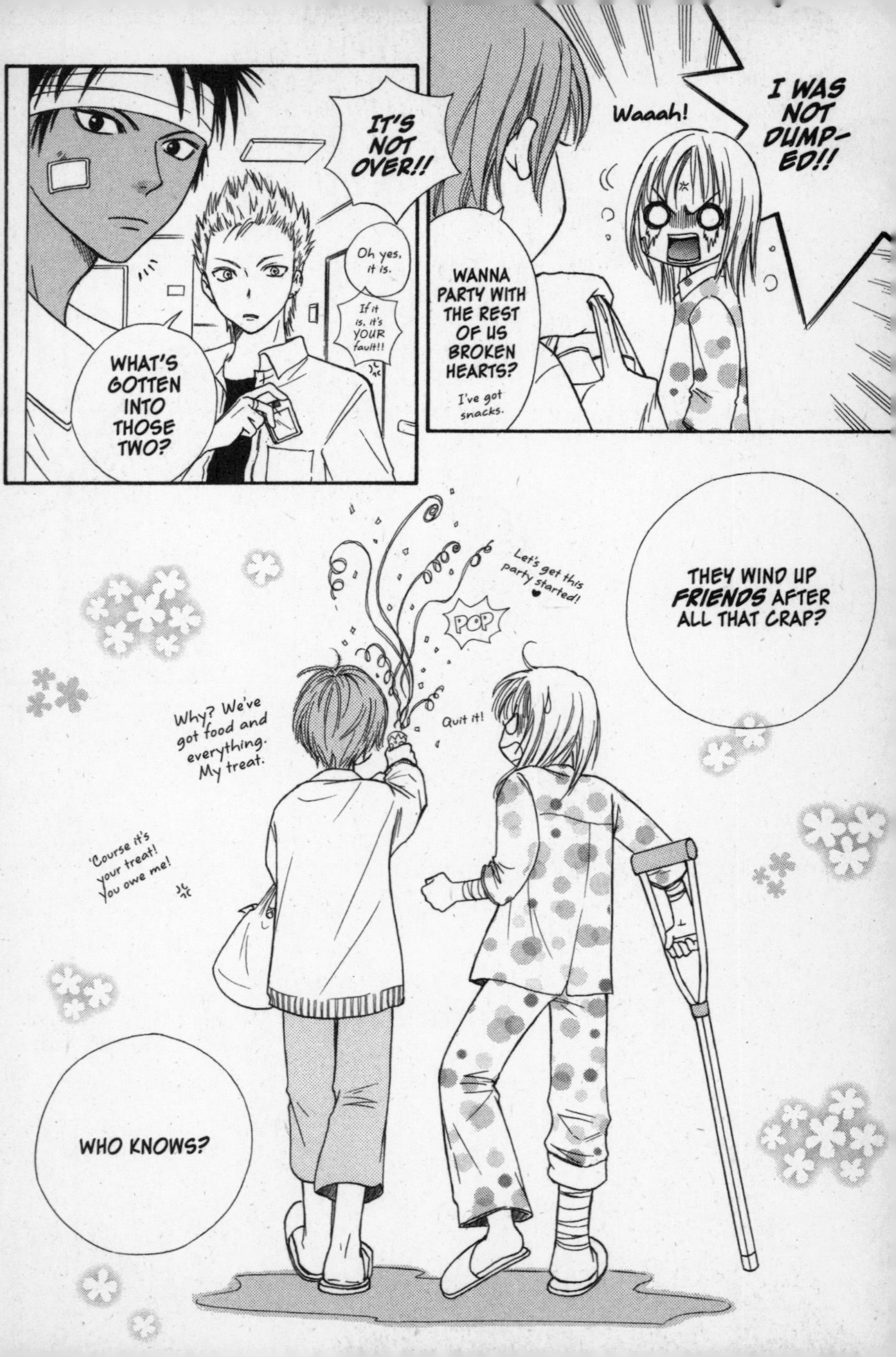
I WAS NOT DUMPED!!
Waaah!
WANNA PARTY WITH THE REST OF US BROKEN HEARTS?
I've got snacks.
IT'S NOT OVER!!
Oh yes, it is.
If it is, it's YOUR fault!!
WHAT'S GOTTEN INTO THOSE TWO?
THEY WIND UP FRIENDS AFTER ALL THAT CRAP?
Let's get this party started!
POP
Quit it!
Why? We've got food and everything. My treat.
'Course it's your treat! You owe me!
WHO KNOWS?

Ch. 8 Tough Training in Love

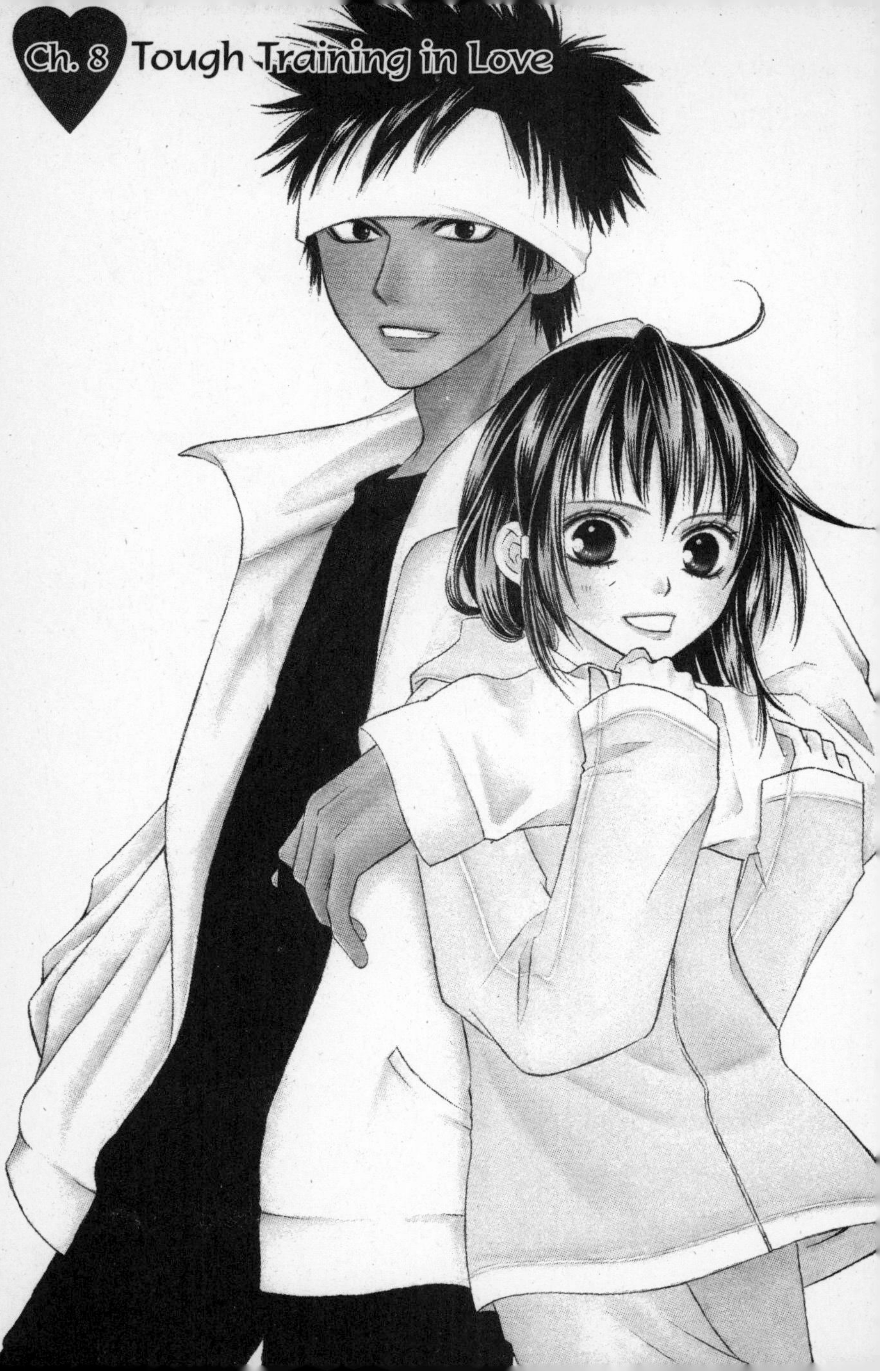

LOVE ATTACK™
JUNAi TOKKO TAiCHO!

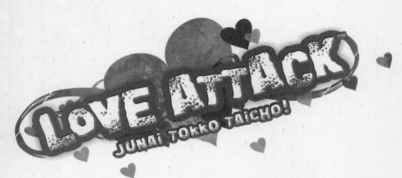

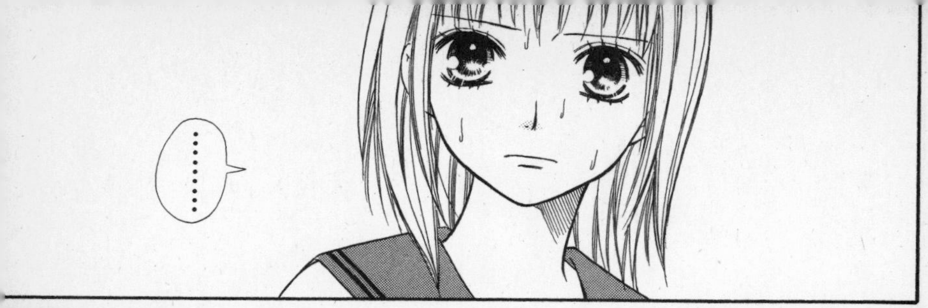
……
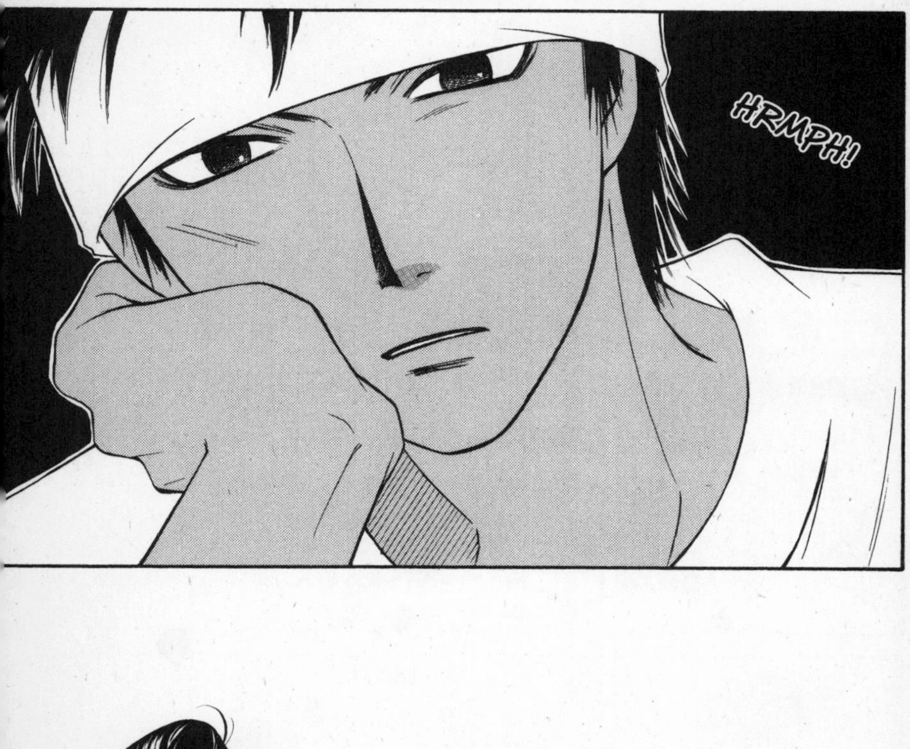
HRMPH!
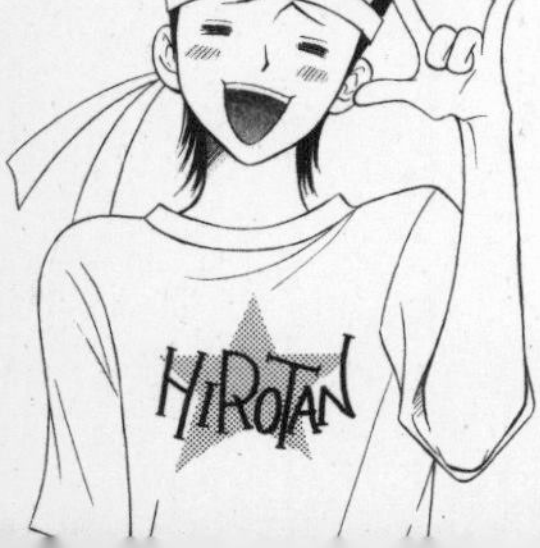
HIROTAN

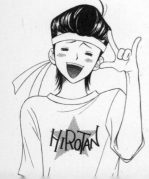

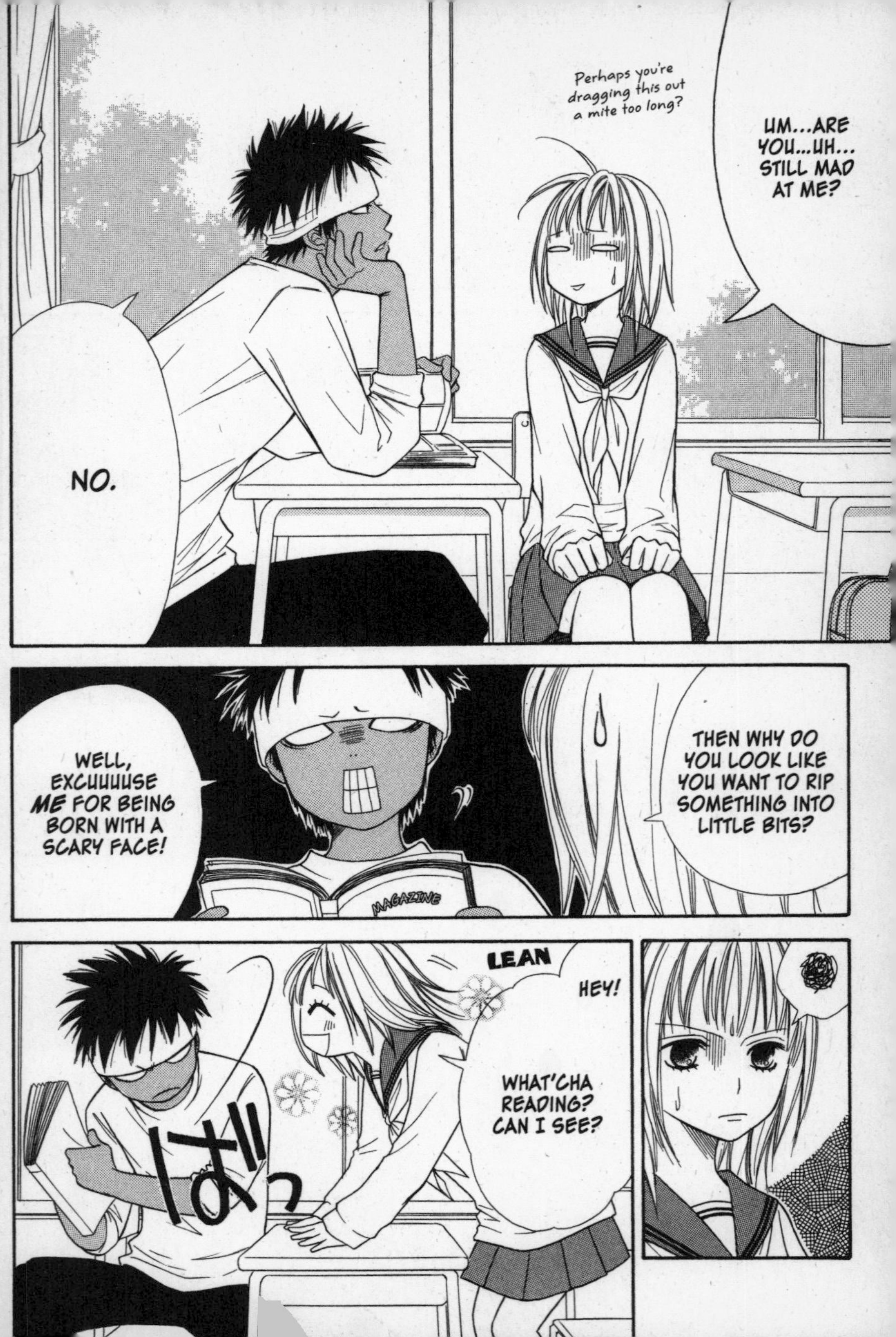
UM...ARE YOU...UH... STILL MAD AT ME?
Perhaps you're dragging this out a mite too long?
NO.
THEN WHY DO YOU LOOK LIKE YOU WANT TO RIP SOMETHING INTO LITTLE BITS?
WELL, EXCUUUUSE *ME* FOR BEING BORN WITH A SCARY FACE!
MAGAZINE
LEAN
HEY!
WHAT'CHA READING? CAN I SEE?
ばっ

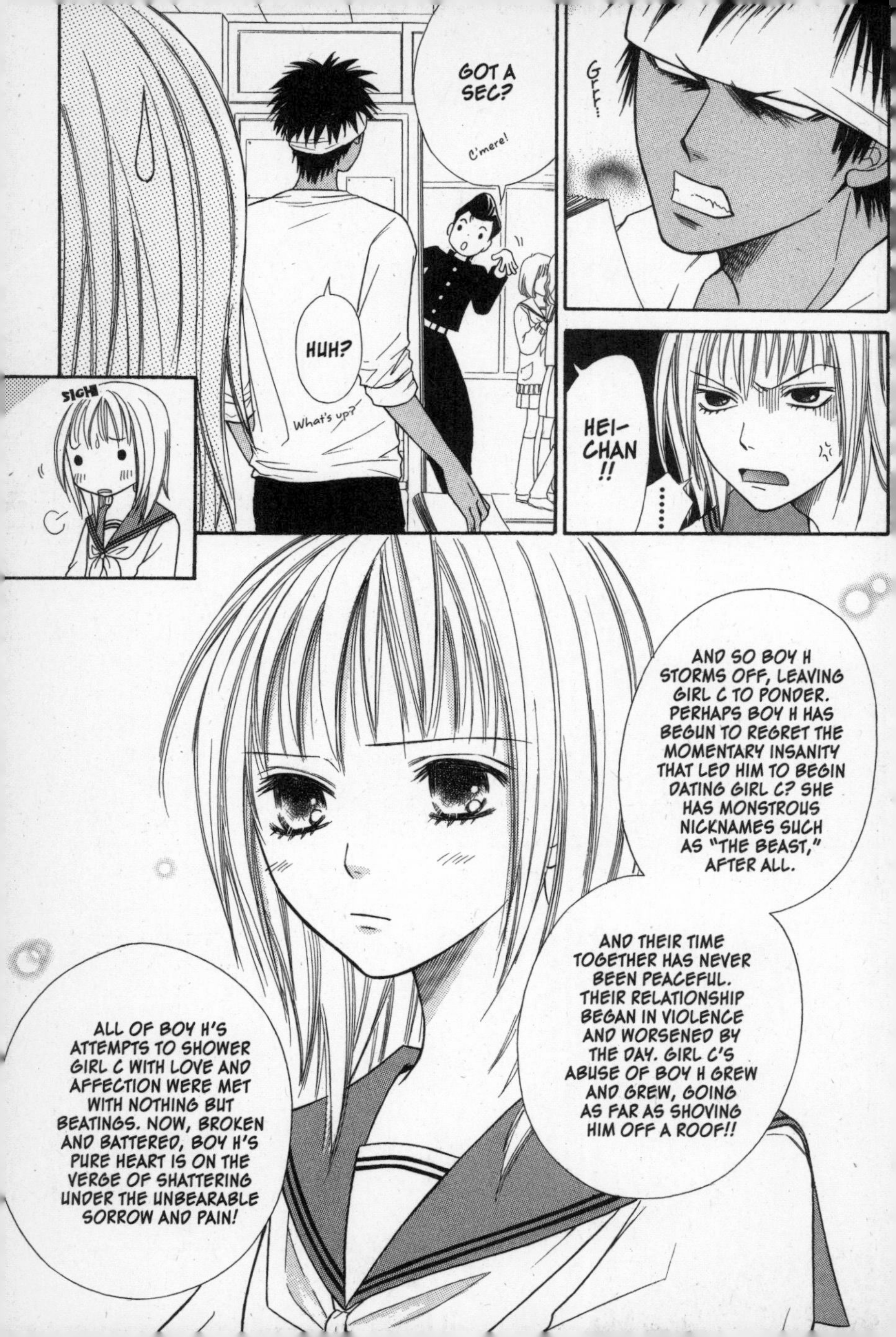
Grrr...
HEI-CHAN!!
......
GOT A SEC?
C'mere!
HUH?
What's up?
SIGH
AND SO BOY H STORMS OFF, LEAVING GIRL C TO PONDER. PERHAPS BOY H HAS BEGUN TO REGRET THE MOMENTARY INSANITY THAT LED HIM TO BEGIN DATING GIRL C? SHE HAS MONSTROUS NICKNAMES SUCH AS "THE BEAST," AFTER ALL.
AND THEIR TIME TOGETHER HAS NEVER BEEN PEACEFUL. THEIR RELATIONSHIP BEGAN IN VIOLENCE AND WORSENED BY THE DAY. GIRL C'S ABUSE OF BOY H GREW AND GREW, GOING AS FAR AS SHOVING HIM OFF A ROOF!!
ALL OF BOY H'S ATTEMPTS TO SHOWER GIRL C WITH LOVE AND AFFECTION WERE MET WITH NOTHING BUT BEATINGS. NOW, BROKEN AND BATTERED, BOY H'S PURE HEART IS ON THE VERGE OF SHATTERING UNDER THE UNBEARABLE SORROW AND PAIN!

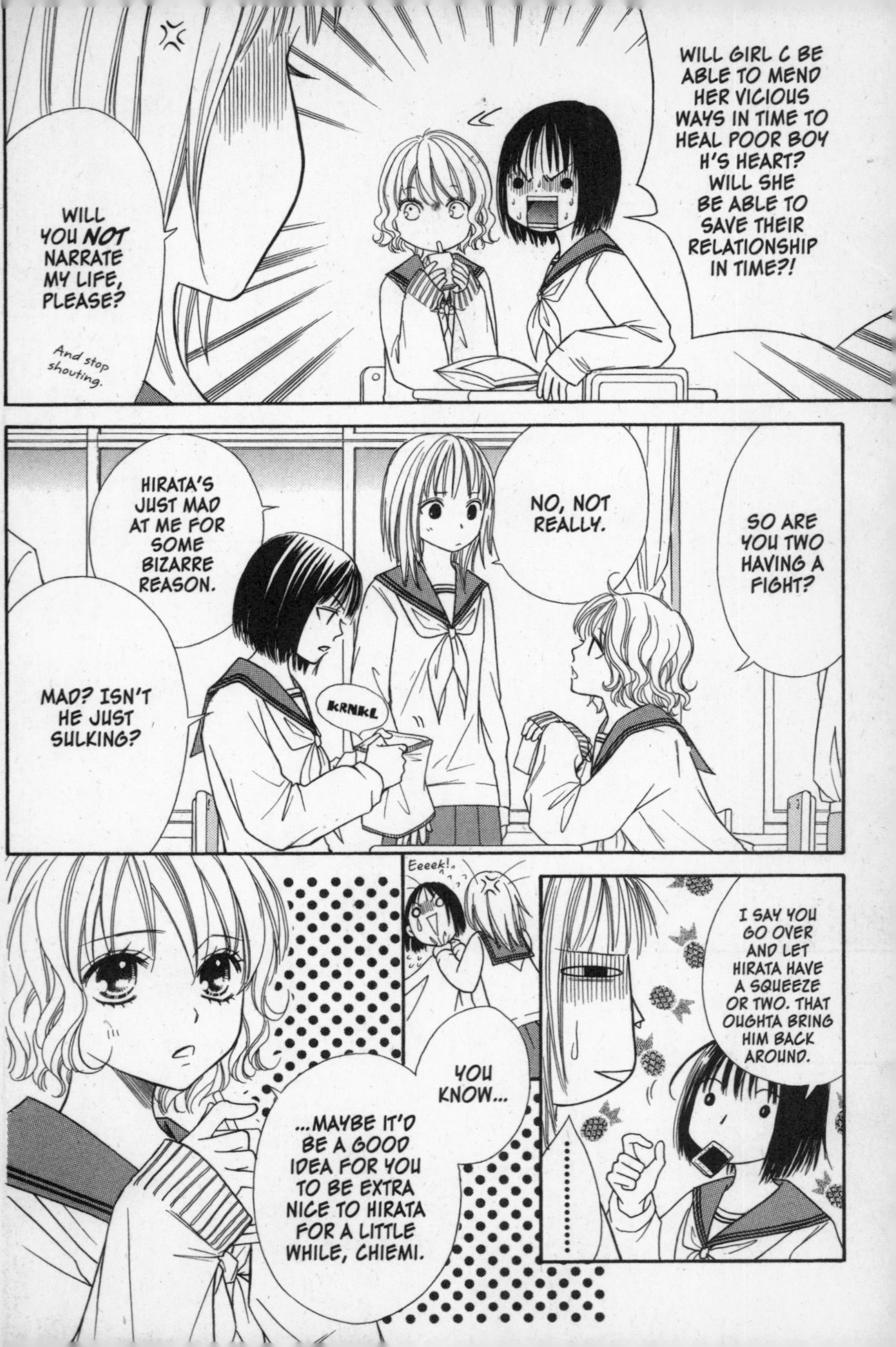
WILL GIRL C BE ABLE TO MEND HER VICIOUS WAYS IN TIME TO HEAL POOR BOY H'S HEART? WILL SHE BE ABLE TO SAVE THEIR RELATIONSHIP IN TIME?!
WILL YOU ***NOT*** NARRATE MY LIFE, PLEASE?
And stop shouting.
SO ARE YOU TWO HAVING A FIGHT?
NO, NOT REALLY.
HIRATA'S JUST MAD AT ME FOR SOME BIZARRE REASON.
KRNKL
MAD? ISN'T HE JUST SULKING?
I SAY YOU GO OVER AND LET HIRATA HAVE A SQUEEZE OR TWO. THAT OUGHTA BRING HIM BACK AROUND.
......
Eeeek!
YOU KNOW...
...MAYBE IT'D BE A GOOD IDEA FOR YOU TO BE EXTRA NICE TO HIRATA FOR A LITTLE WHILE, CHIEMI.

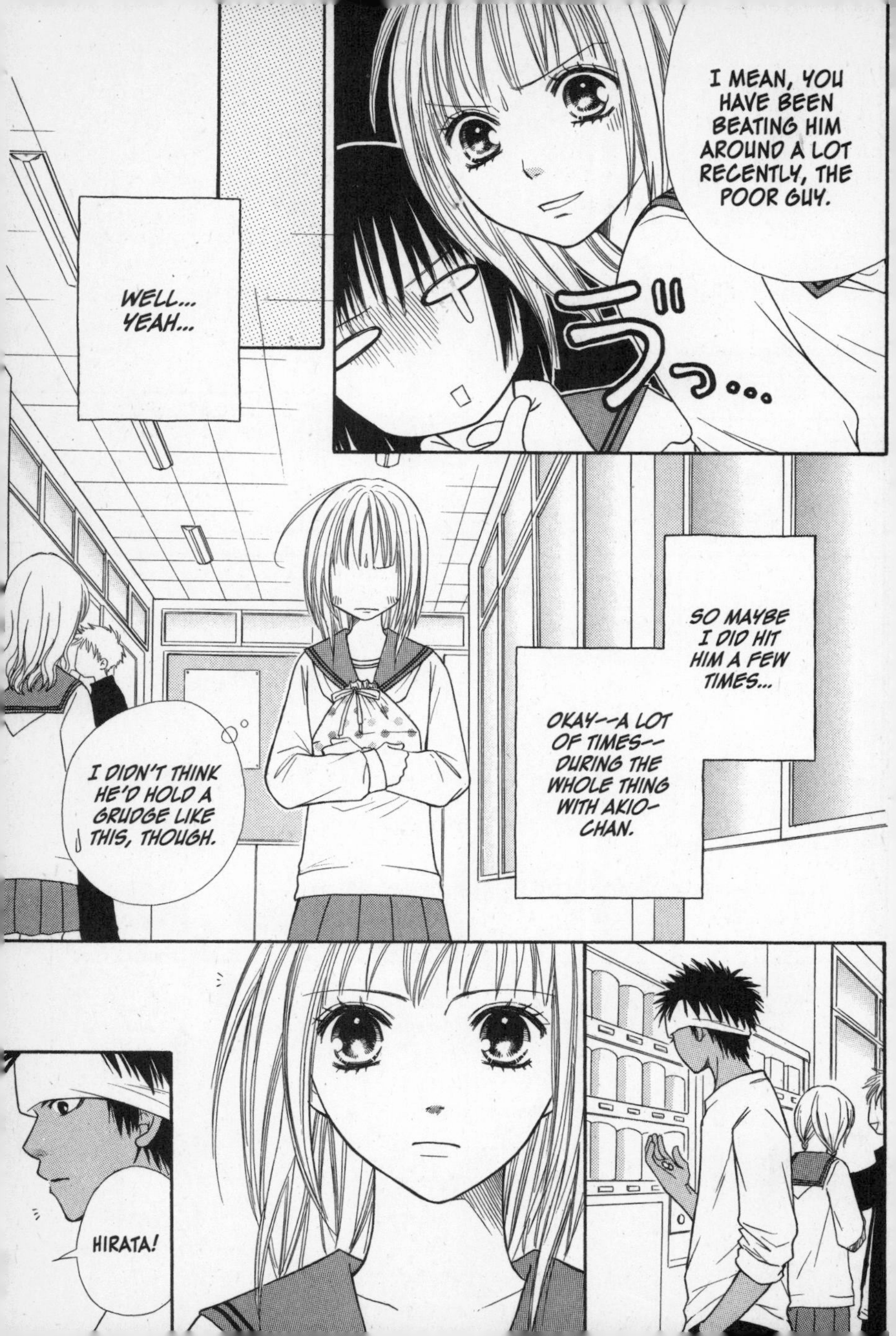
I MEAN, YOU HAVE BEEN BEATING HIM AROUND A LOT RECENTLY, THE POOR GUY.
うっ…
WELL... YEAH...
SO MAYBE I DID HIT HIM A FEW TIMES...
OKAY--A LOT OF TIMES--DURING THE WHOLE THING WITH AKIO-CHAN.
I DIDN'T THINK HE'D HOLD A GRUDGE LIKE THIS, THOUGH.
HIRATA!

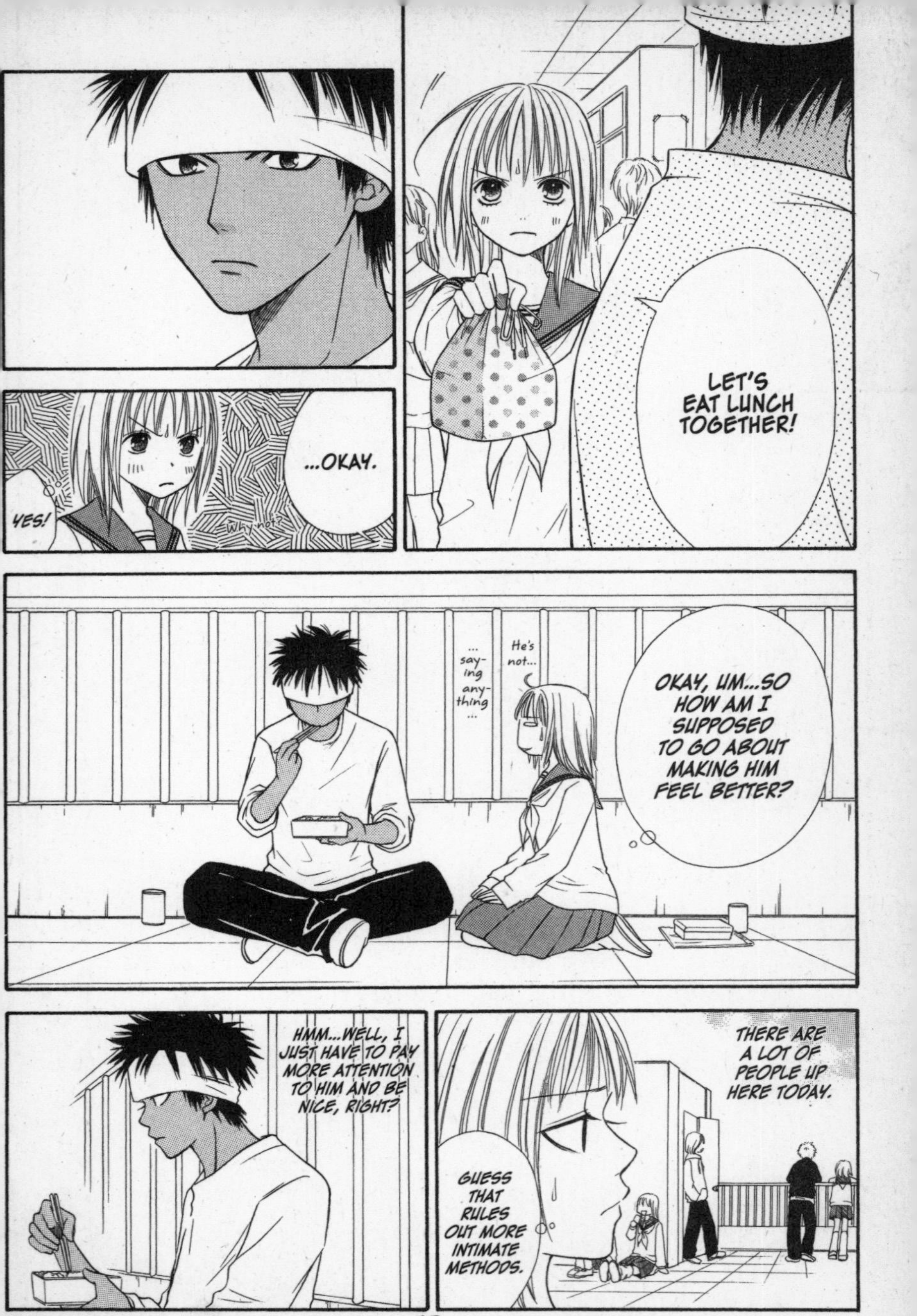
LET'S EAT LUNCH TOGETHER!
...OKAY.
Why not?
YES!
OKAY, UM...SO HOW AM I SUPPOSED TO GO ABOUT MAKING HIM FEEL BETTER?
He's not...
...saying anything...
THERE ARE A LOT OF PEOPLE UP HERE TODAY.
GUESS THAT RULES OUT MORE INTIMATE METHODS.
HMM...WELL, I JUST HAVE TO PAY MORE ATTENTION TO HIM AND BE NICE, RIGHT?

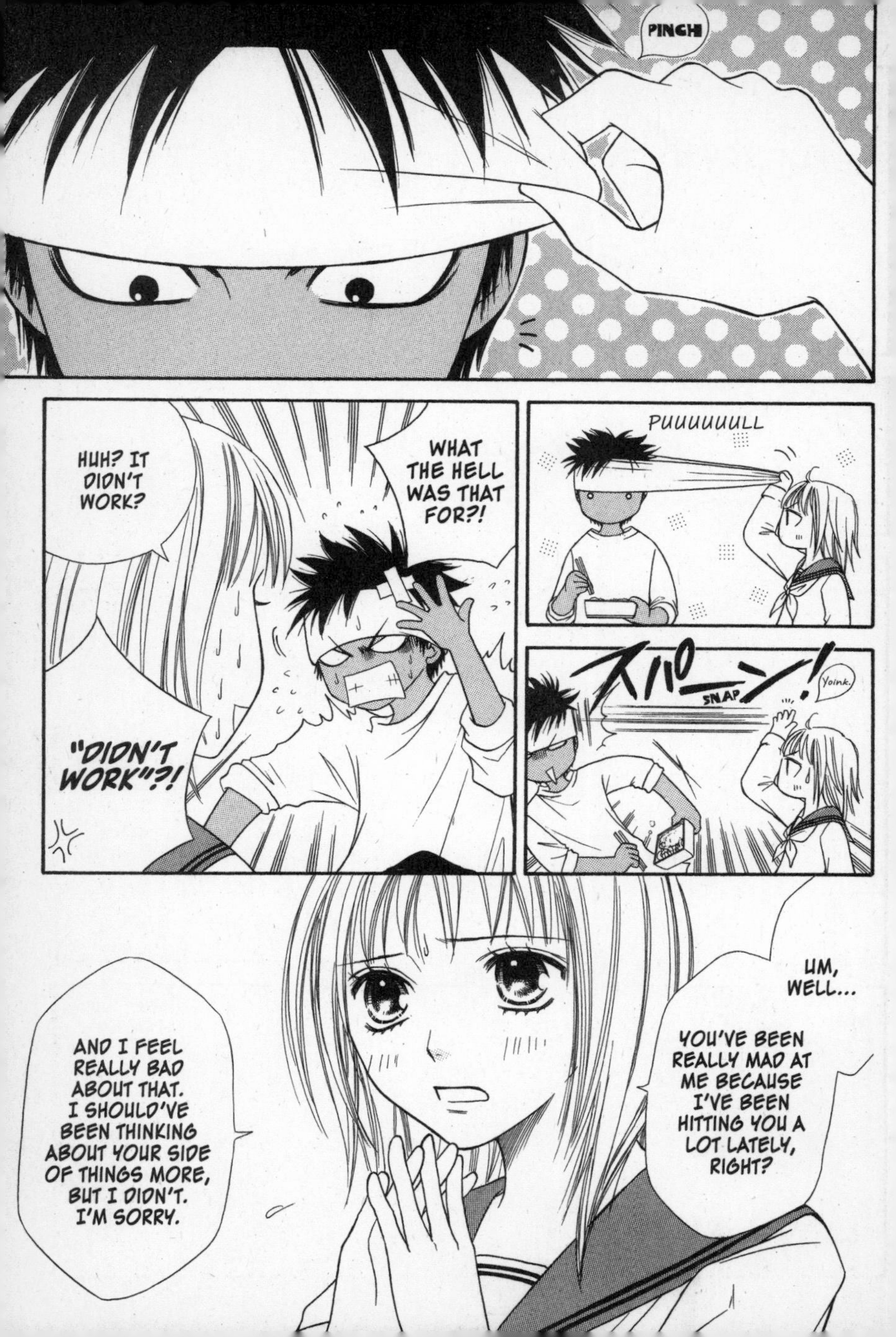
PINCH
PUUUUUULL
スパーン!
SNAP
Yoink.
WHAT THE HELL WAS THAT FOR?!
HUH? IT DIDN'T WORK?
"DIDN'T WORK"?!
UM, WELL...
YOU'VE BEEN REALLY MAD AT ME BECAUSE I'VE BEEN HITTING YOU A LOT LATELY, RIGHT?
AND I FEEL REALLY BAD ABOUT THAT. I SHOULD'VE BEEN THINKING ABOUT YOUR SIDE OF THINGS MORE, BUT I DIDN'T. I'M SORRY.

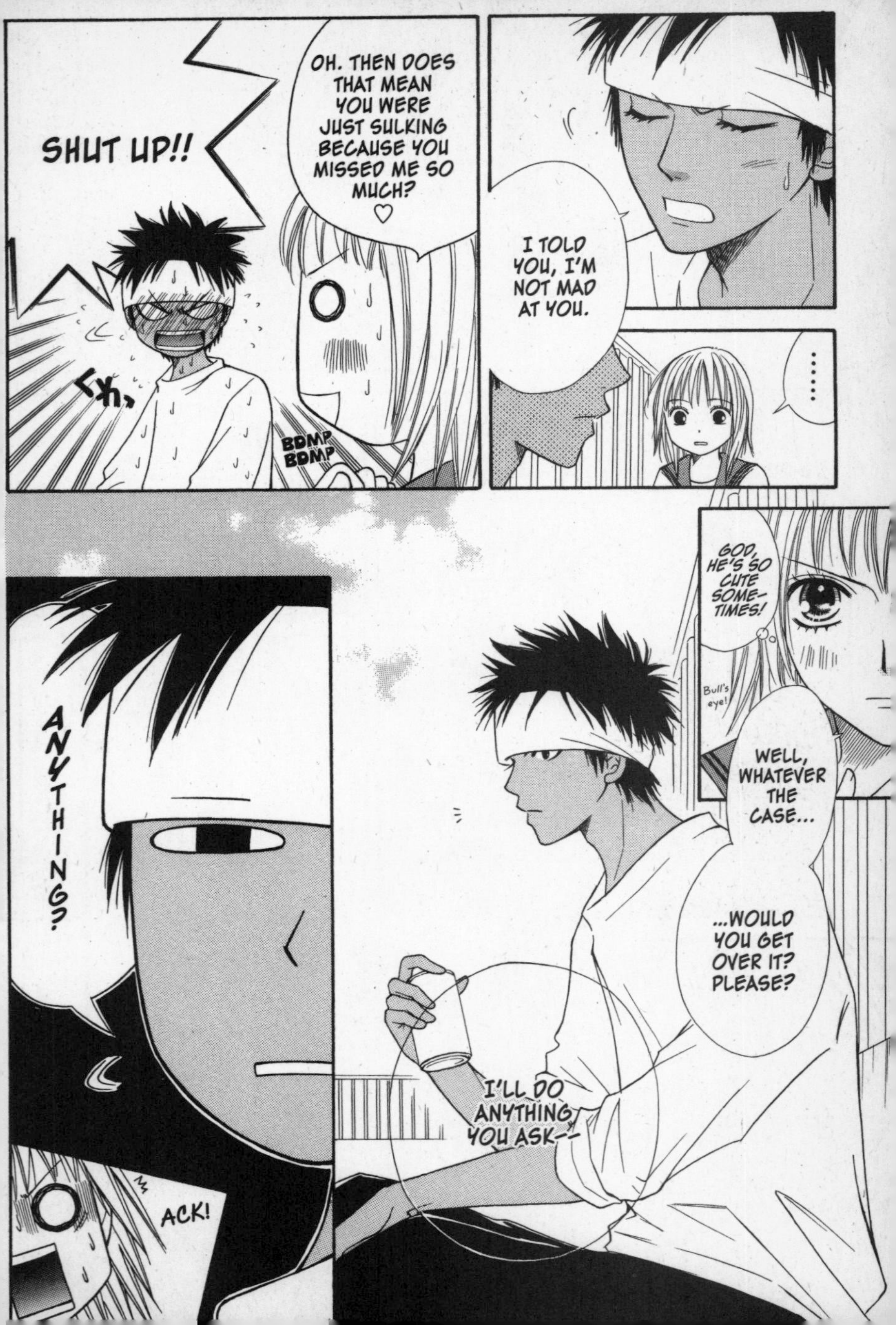
I TOLD YOU, I'M NOT MAD AT YOU.
......
OH. THEN DOES THAT MEAN YOU WERE JUST SULKING BECAUSE YOU MISSED ME SO MUCH? ♡
SHUT UP!!
BDMP BDMP
GOD, HE'S SO CUTE SOMETIMES!
Bull's eye!
WELL, WHATEVER THE CASE...
...WOULD YOU GET OVER IT? PLEASE?
I'LL DO ANYTHING YOU ASK--
ANYTHING?
ACK!

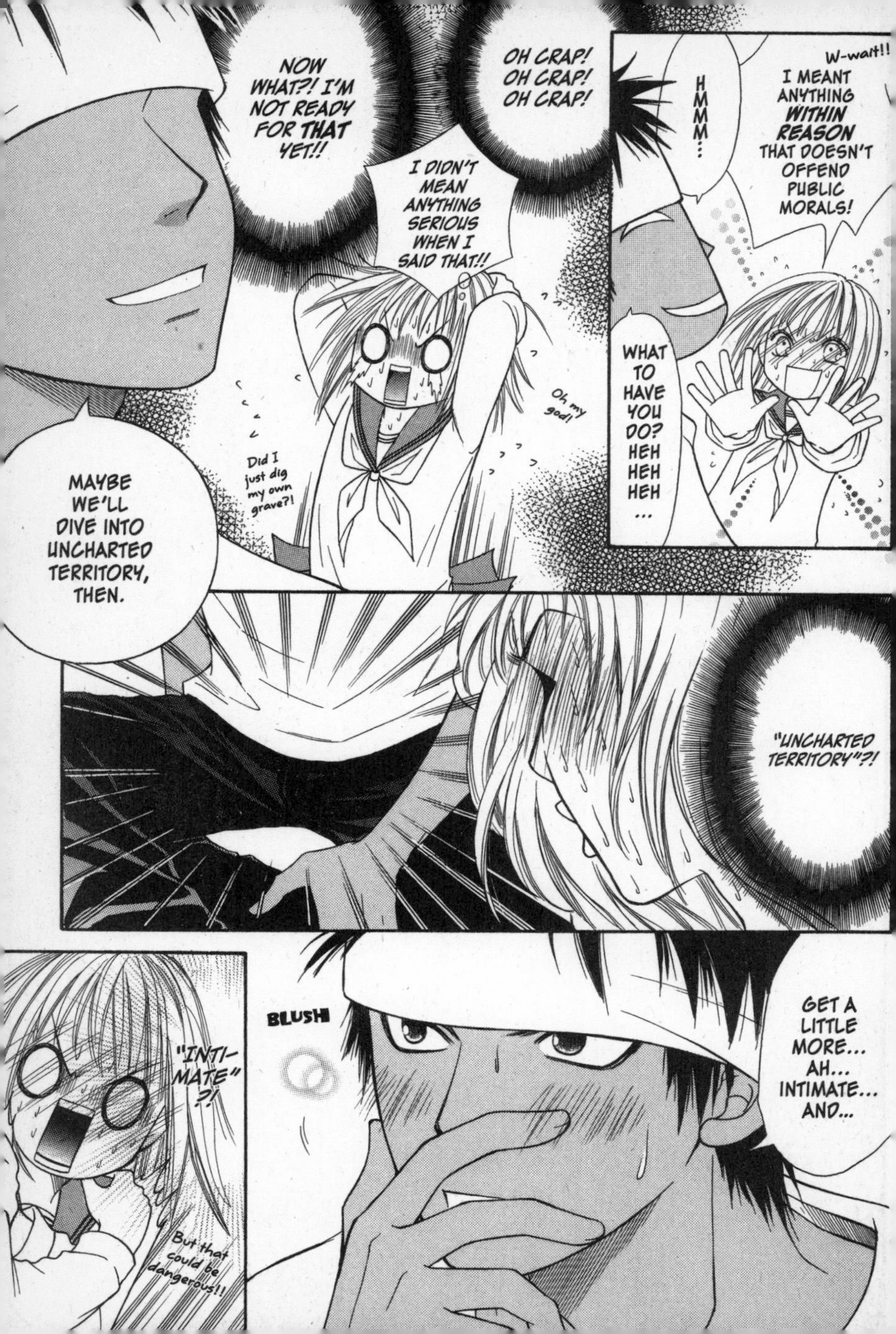
W-wait!! I MEANT ANYTHING WITHIN REASON THAT DOESN'T OFFEND PUBLIC MORALS!
HMMM...
WHAT TO HAVE YOU DO? HEH HEH HEH...
OH CRAP! OH CRAP! OH CRAP!
NOW WHAT?! I'M NOT READY FOR THAT YET!!
I DIDN'T MEAN ANYTHING SERIOUS WHEN I SAID THAT!!
Oh my god!
Did I just dig my own grave?!
MAYBE WE'LL DIVE INTO UNCHARTED TERRITORY, THEN.
"UNCHARTED TERRITORY"?!
GET A LITTLE MORE... AH... INTIMATE... AND...
BLUSH
"INTI-MATE"?!
But that could be dangerous!!

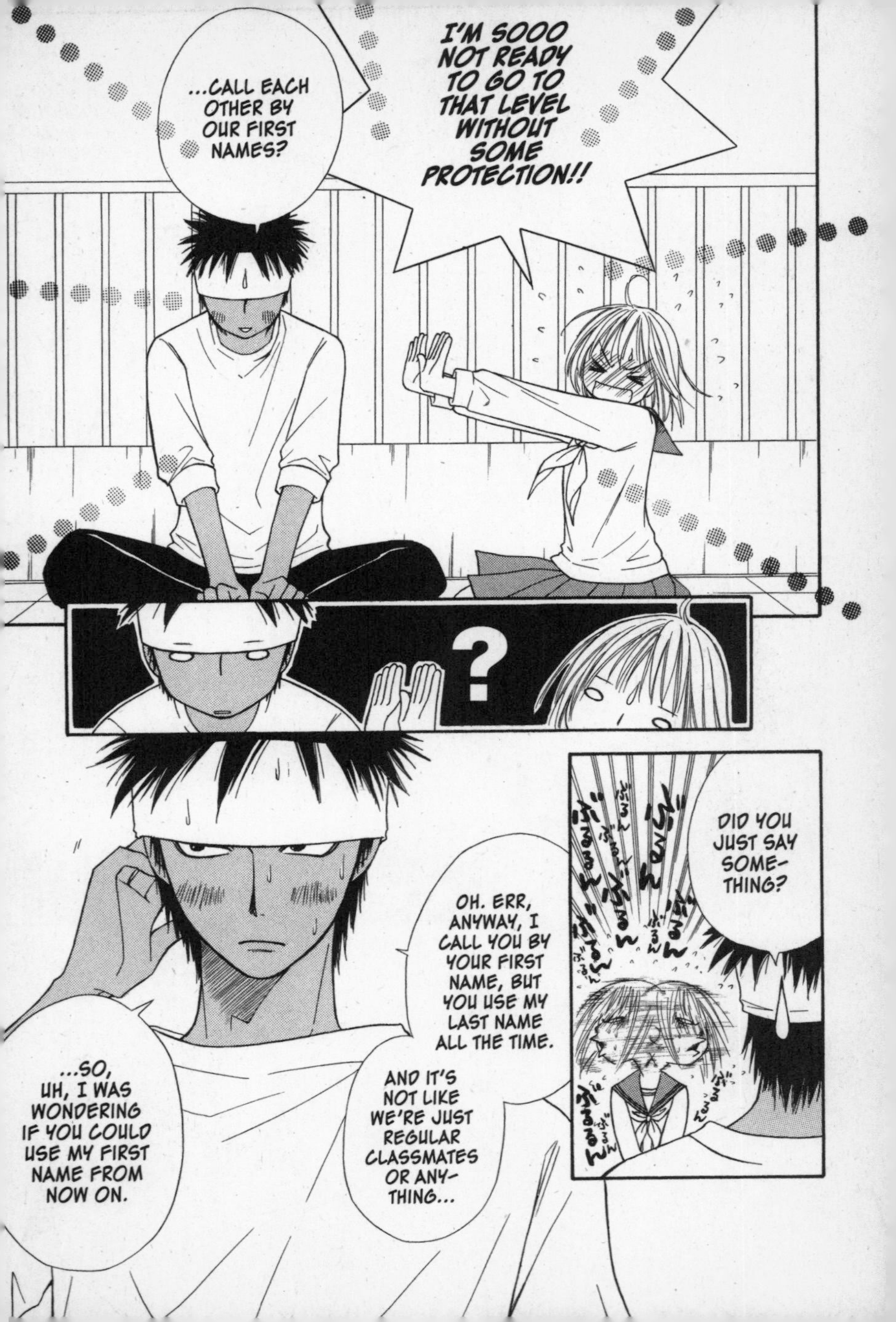
...CALL EACH OTHER BY OUR FIRST NAMES?
I'M SOOO NOT READY TO GO TO THAT LEVEL WITHOUT SOME PROTECTION!!
?
DID YOU JUST SAY SOME-THING?
OH. ERR, ANYWAY, I CALL YOU BY YOUR FIRST NAME, BUT YOU USE MY LAST NAME ALL THE TIME.
AND IT'S NOT LIKE WE'RE JUST REGULAR CLASSMATES OR ANY-THING...
...SO, UH, I WAS WONDERING IF YOU COULD USE MY FIRST NAME FROM NOW ON.

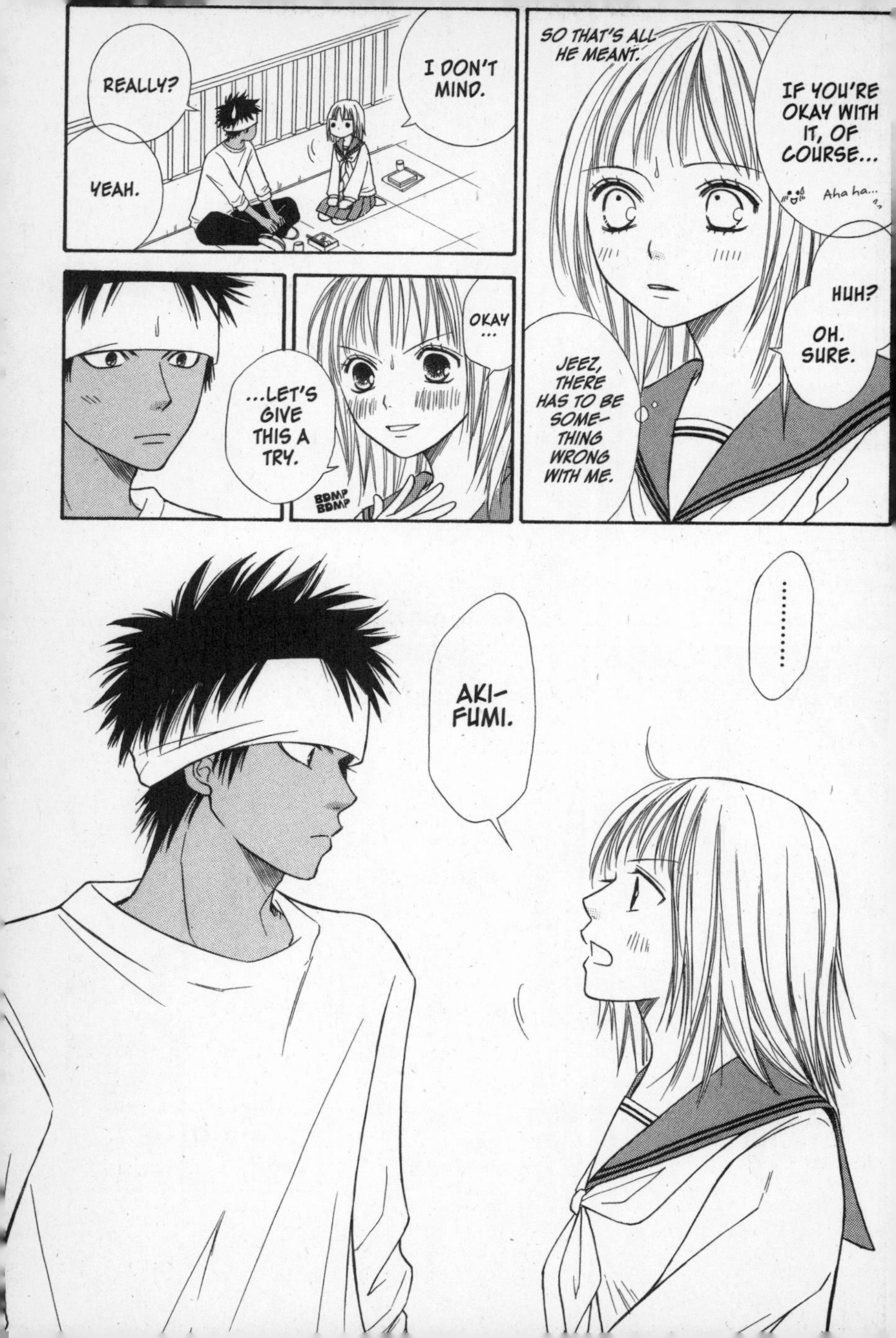
SO THAT'S ALL HE MEANT.
IF YOU'RE OKAY WITH IT, OF COURSE...
Aha ha...
HUH?
OH. SURE.
JEEZ, THERE HAS TO BE SOME-THING WRONG WITH ME.
I DON'T MIND.
REALLY?
YEAH.
OKAY ...
...LET'S GIVE THIS A TRY.
BDMP BDMP
......
AKI-FUMI.

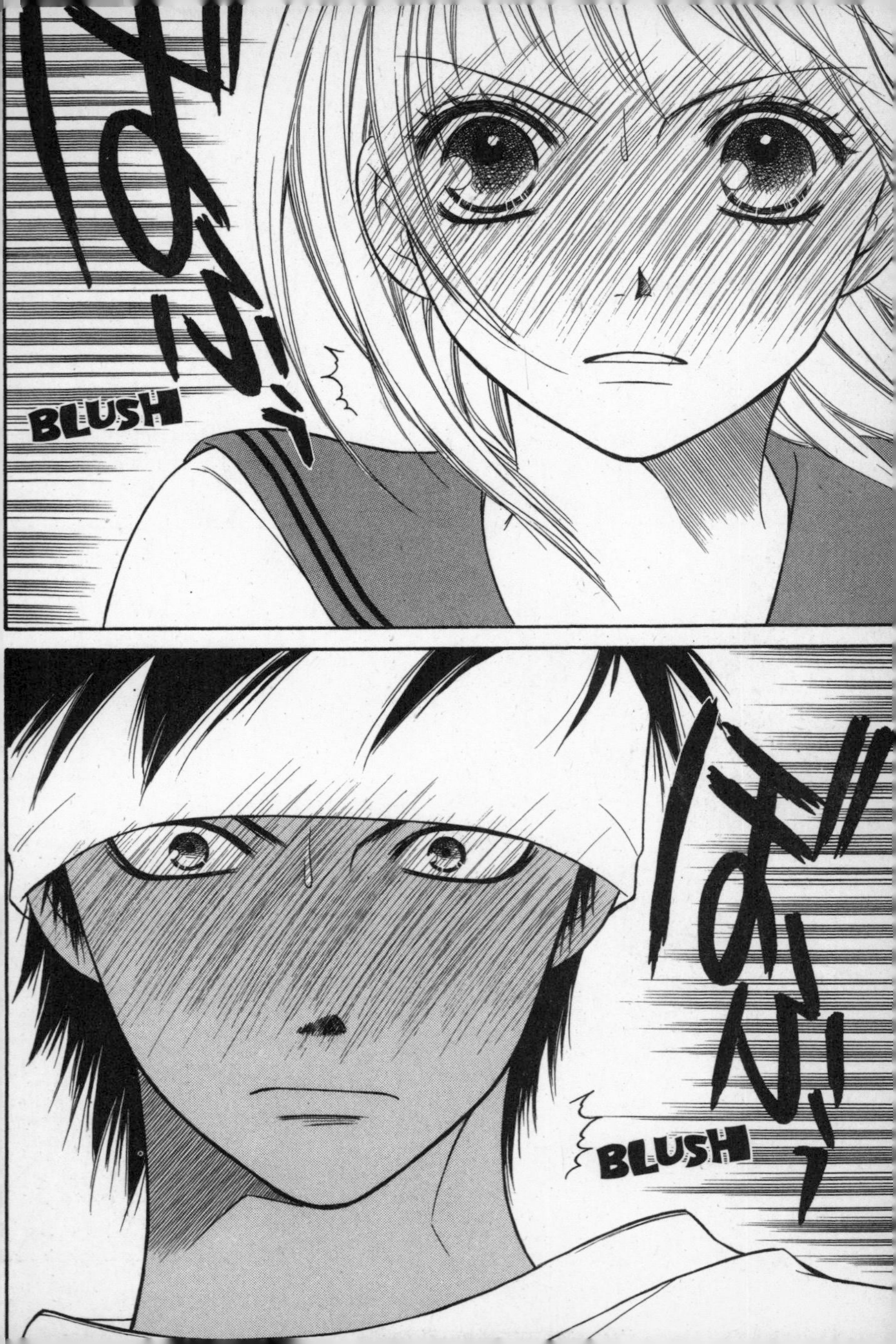
BLUSH
BLUSH

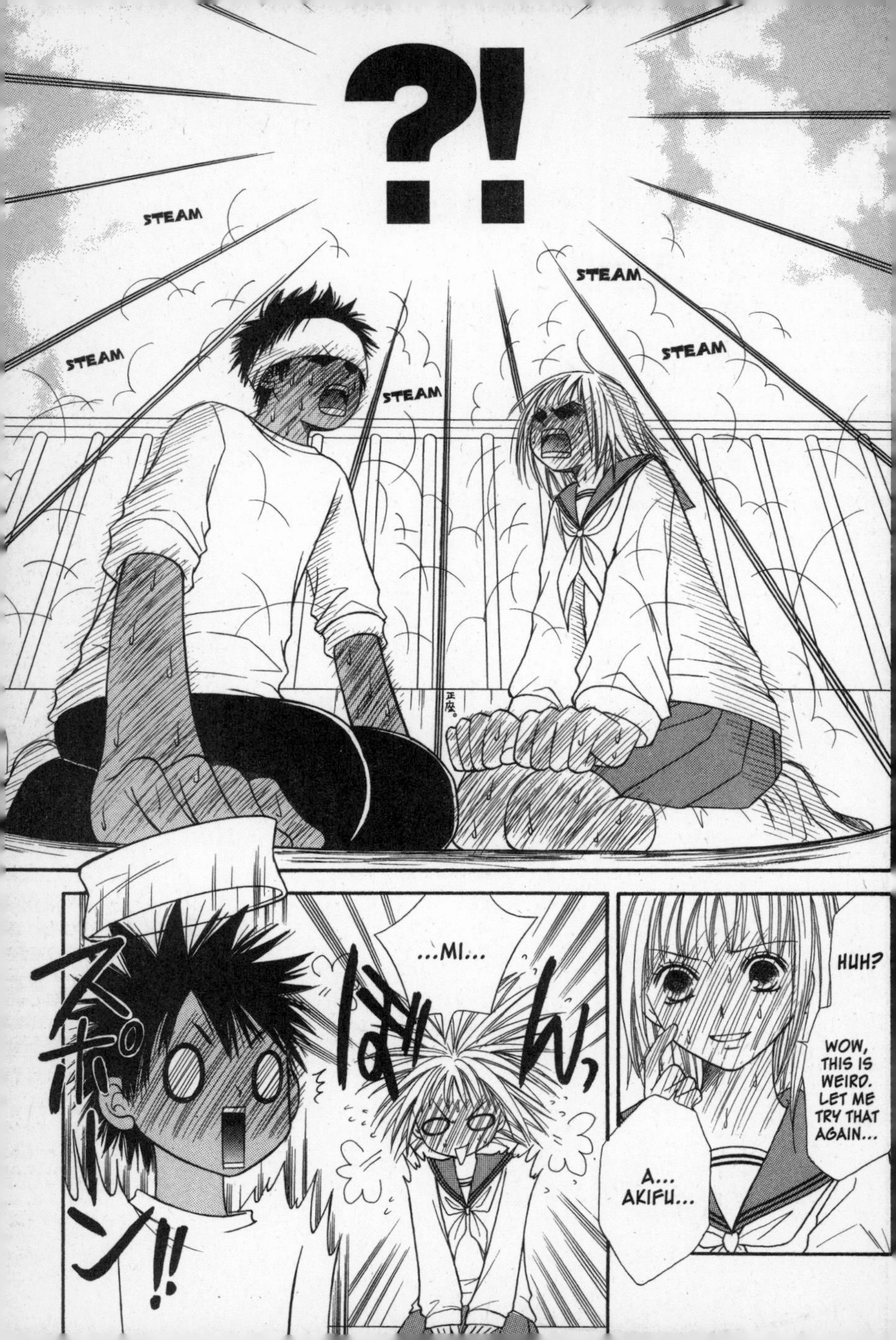
?!
STEAM
STEAM
STEAM
STEAM
STEAM
正座。
HUH?
WOW, THIS IS WEIRD. LET ME TRY THAT AGAIN...
A... AKIFU...
...MI...
ばん,
スポーン!!

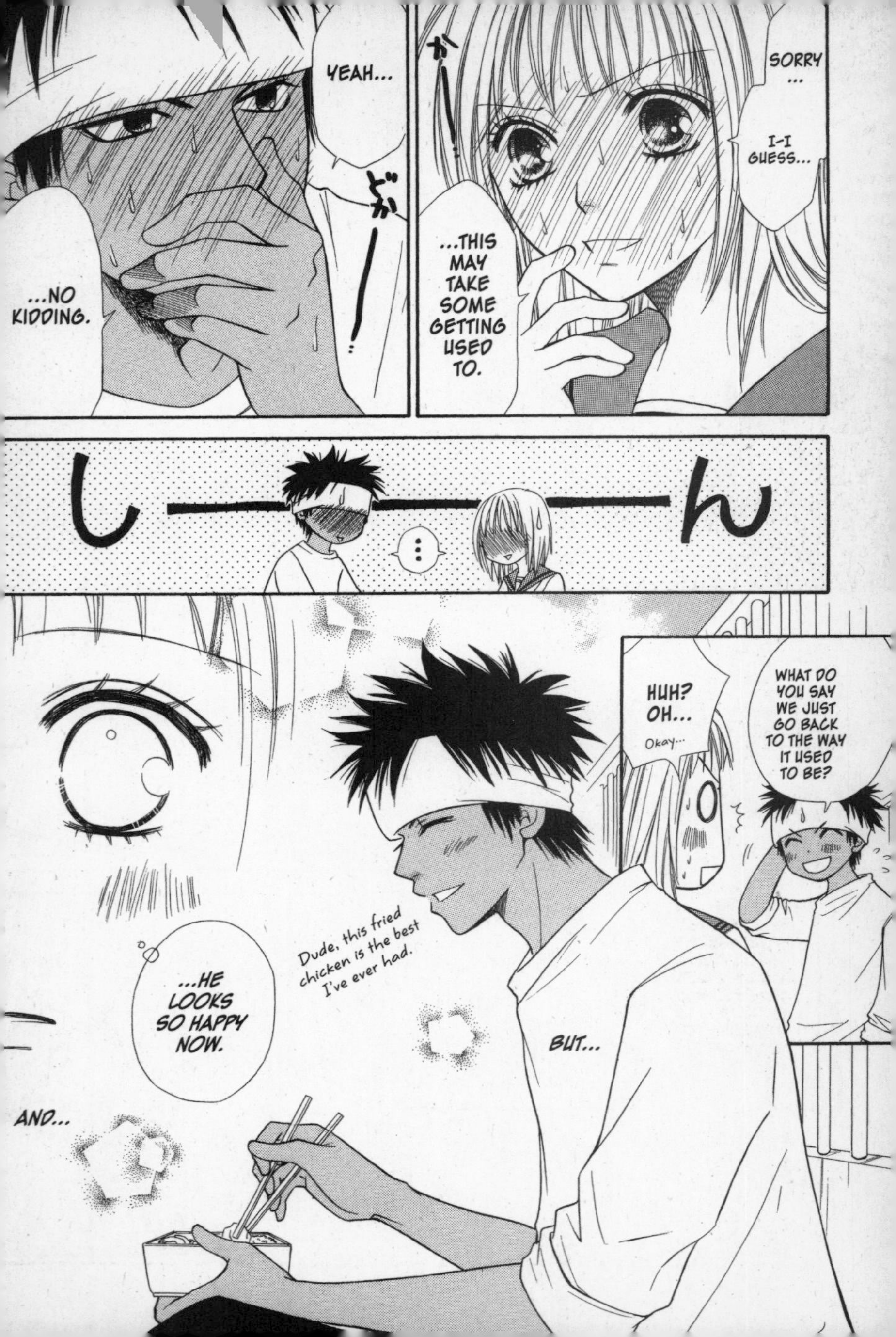
SORRY...
I-I GUESS...
がー
...THIS MAY TAKE SOME GETTING USED TO.
YEAH...
どがー!
...NO KIDDING.
しーーーん
...
WHAT DO YOU SAY WE JUST GO BACK TO THE WAY IT USED TO BE?
HUH? OH...
Okay...
BUT...
Dude, this fried chicken is the best I've ever had.
...HE LOOKS SO HAPPY NOW.
AND...

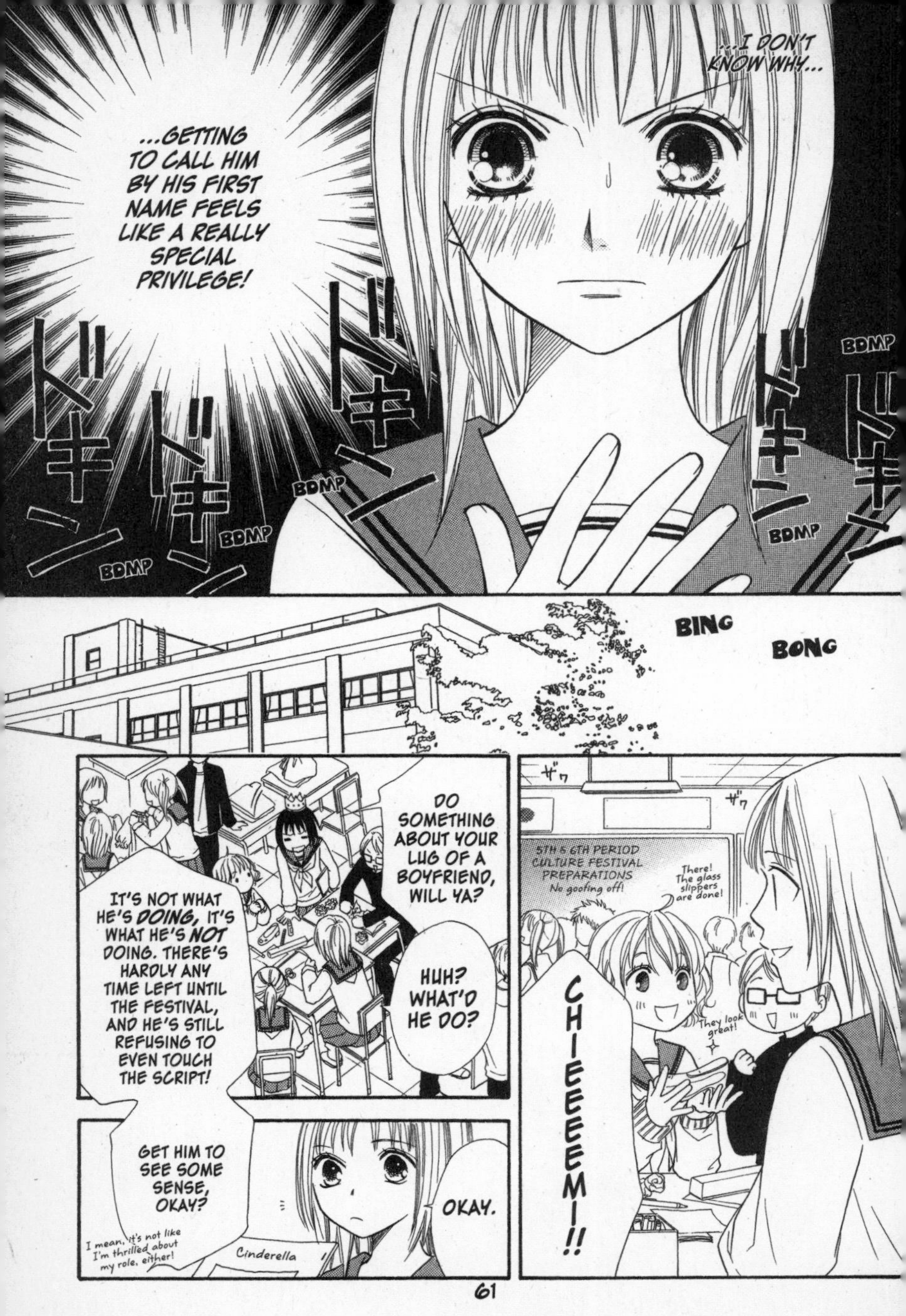
...I DON'T KNOW WHY...
...GETTING TO CALL HIM BY HIS FIRST NAME FEELS LIKE A REALLY SPECIAL PRIVILEGE!
BDMP
BDMP
BDMP
BDMP
BDMP
BING
BONG
5TH & 6TH PERIOD CULTURE FESTIVAL PREPARATIONS
No goofing off!
There! The glass slippers are done!
They look great!
CHIEEEEMI!!
DO SOMETHING ABOUT YOUR LUG OF A BOYFRIEND, WILL YA?
HUH? WHAT'D HE DO?
IT'S NOT WHAT HE'S *DOING*, IT'S WHAT HE'S *NOT* DOING. THERE'S HARDLY ANY TIME LEFT UNTIL THE FESTIVAL, AND HE'S STILL REFUSING TO EVEN TOUCH THE SCRIPT!
GET HIM TO SEE SOME SENSE, OKAY?
I mean, it's not like I'm thrilled about my role, either!
Cinderella
OKAY.

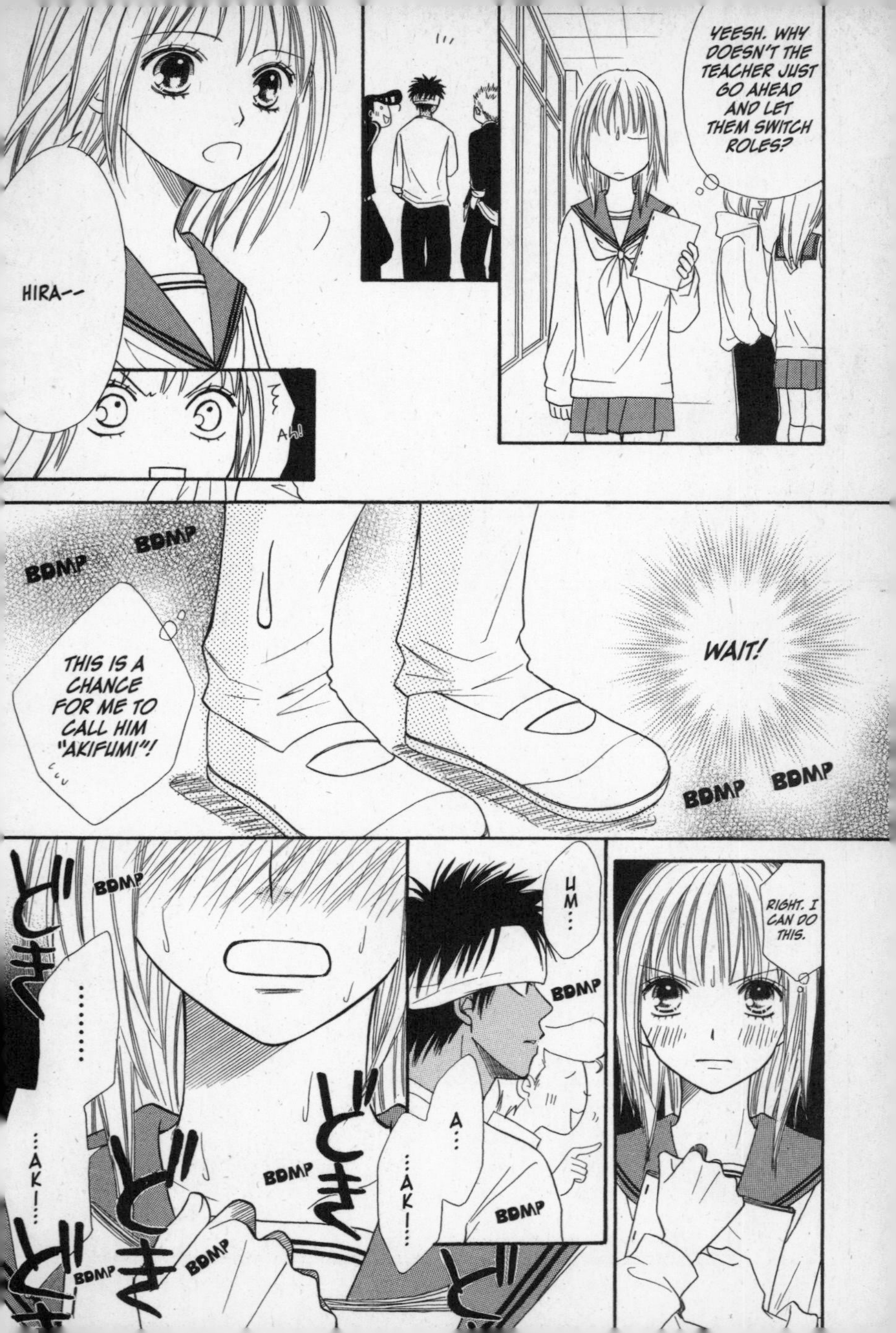
YEESH. WHY DOESN'T THE TEACHER JUST GO AHEAD AND LET THEM SWITCH ROLES?
HIRA--
AH!
WAIT!
BDMP BDMP
THIS IS A CHANCE FOR ME TO CALL HIM "AKIFUMI"!
BDMP BDMP
RIGHT. I CAN DO THIS.
UM...
BDMP
A...
...AKI...
BDMP
BDMP
BDMP
....
...AKI...
BDMP
BDMP

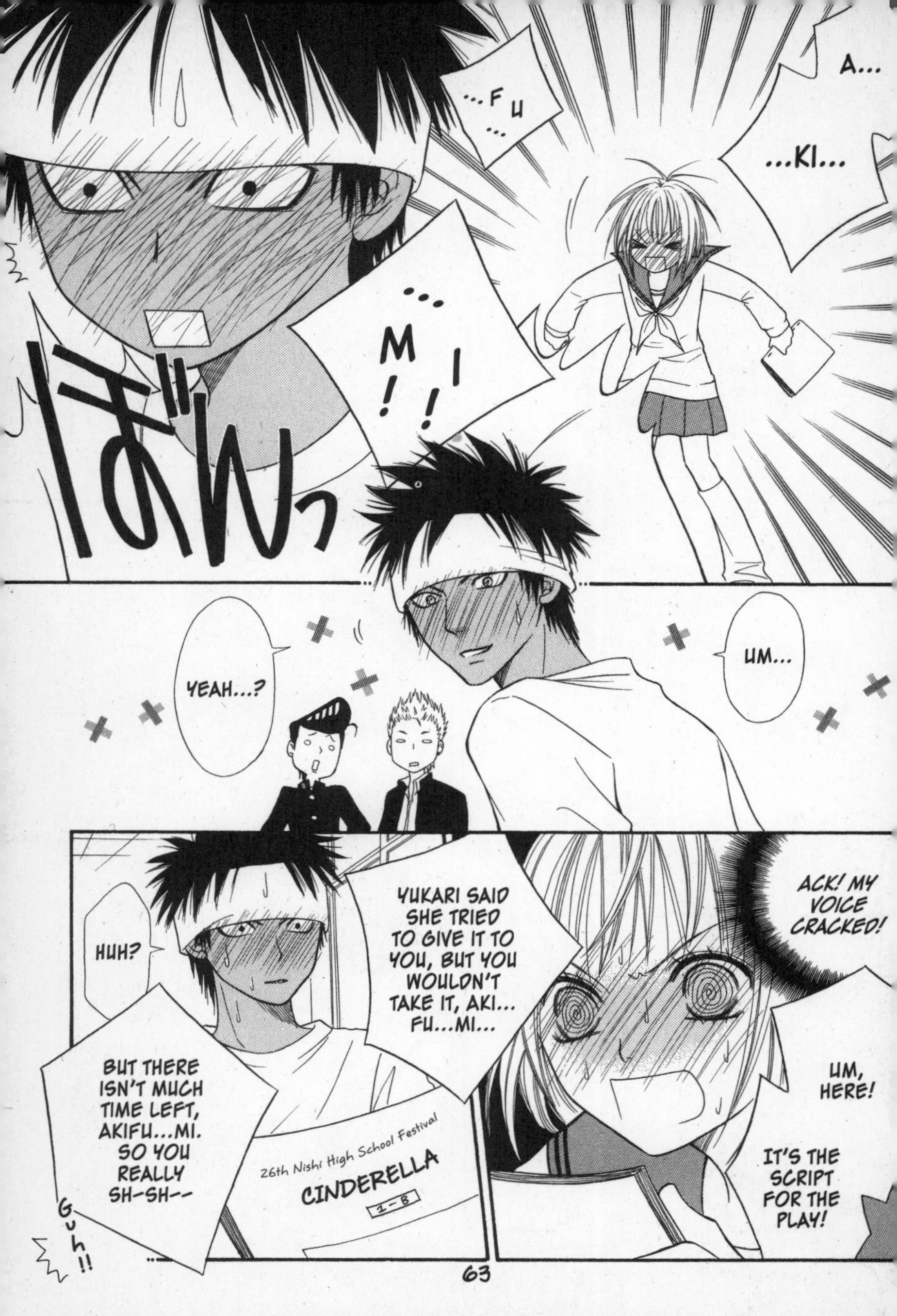

A...
...KI...
...FU...
...MI!!
ぼんっ
UM...
YEAH...?
ACK! MY VOICE CRACKED!
UM, HERE!
IT'S THE SCRIPT FOR THE PLAY!
26th Nishi High School Festival
CINDERELLA
1-B
YUKARI SAID SHE TRIED TO GIVE IT TO YOU, BUT YOU WOULDN'T TAKE IT, AKI... FU...MI...
HUH?
BUT THERE ISN'T MUCH TIME LEFT, AKIFU...MI. SO YOU REALLY SH-SH--
Guh!!

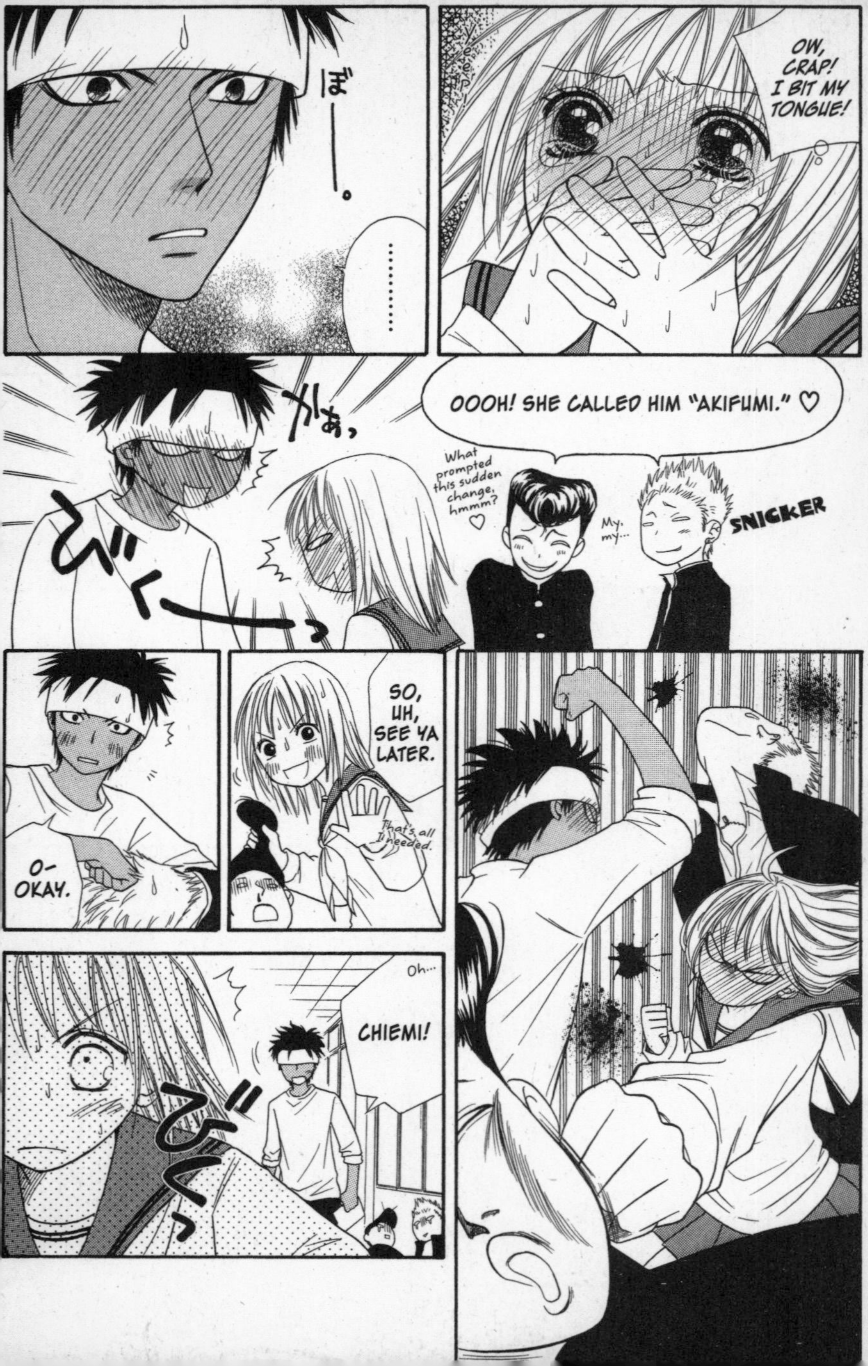
Yeep!
OW, CRAP! I BIT MY TONGUE!
ぼーー。
......
OOOH! SHE CALLED HIM "AKIFUMI." ♡
My, my...
SNICKER
What prompted this sudden change, hmmm? ♡
かあっ
びくーーっ
SO, UH, SEE YA LATER.
That's all I needed.
O-OKAY.
Oh...
CHIEMI!
びくっ

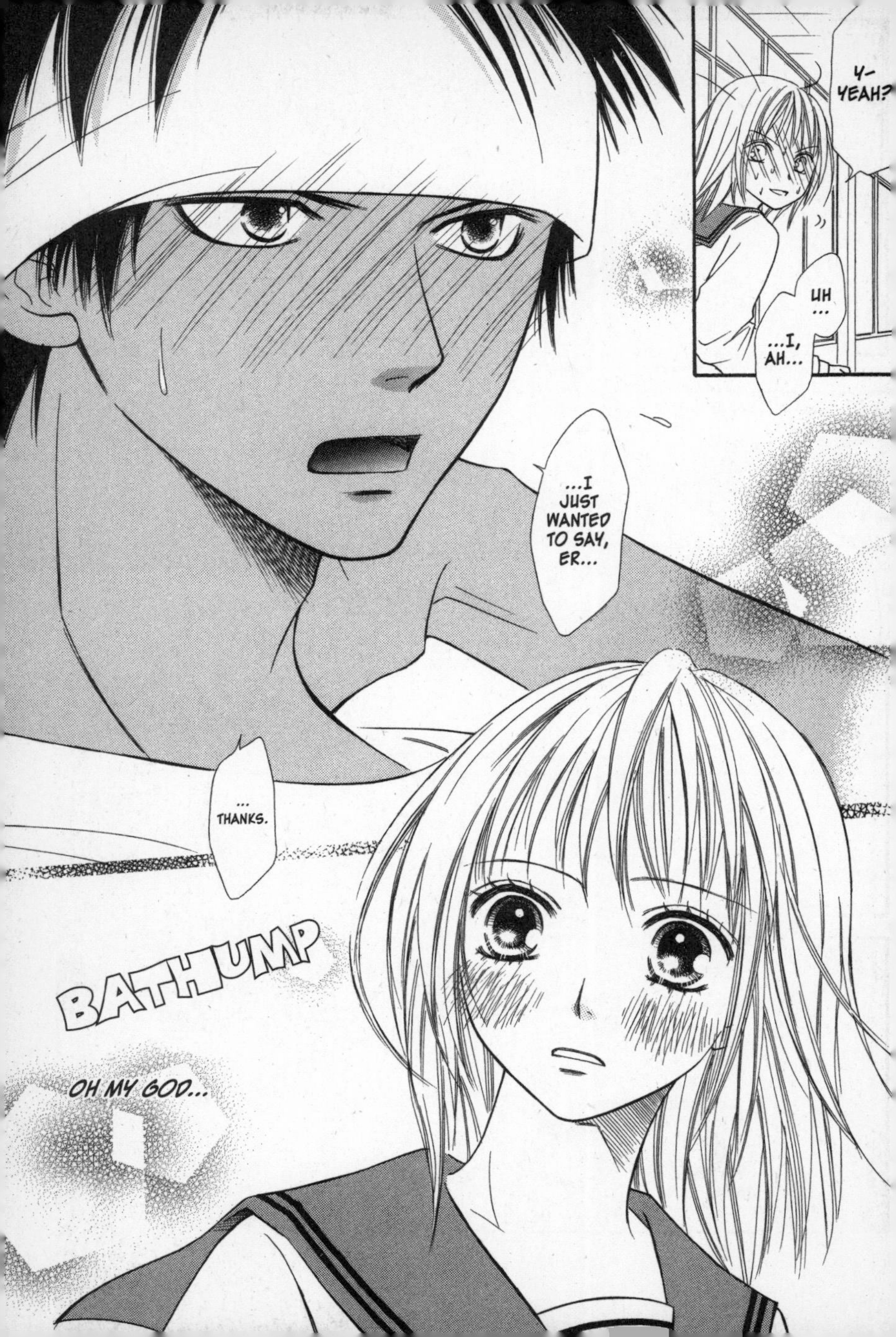
Y-YEAH?
UH ...
...I, AH...
...I JUST WANTED TO SAY, ER...
... THANKS.
BATHUMP
OH MY GOD...

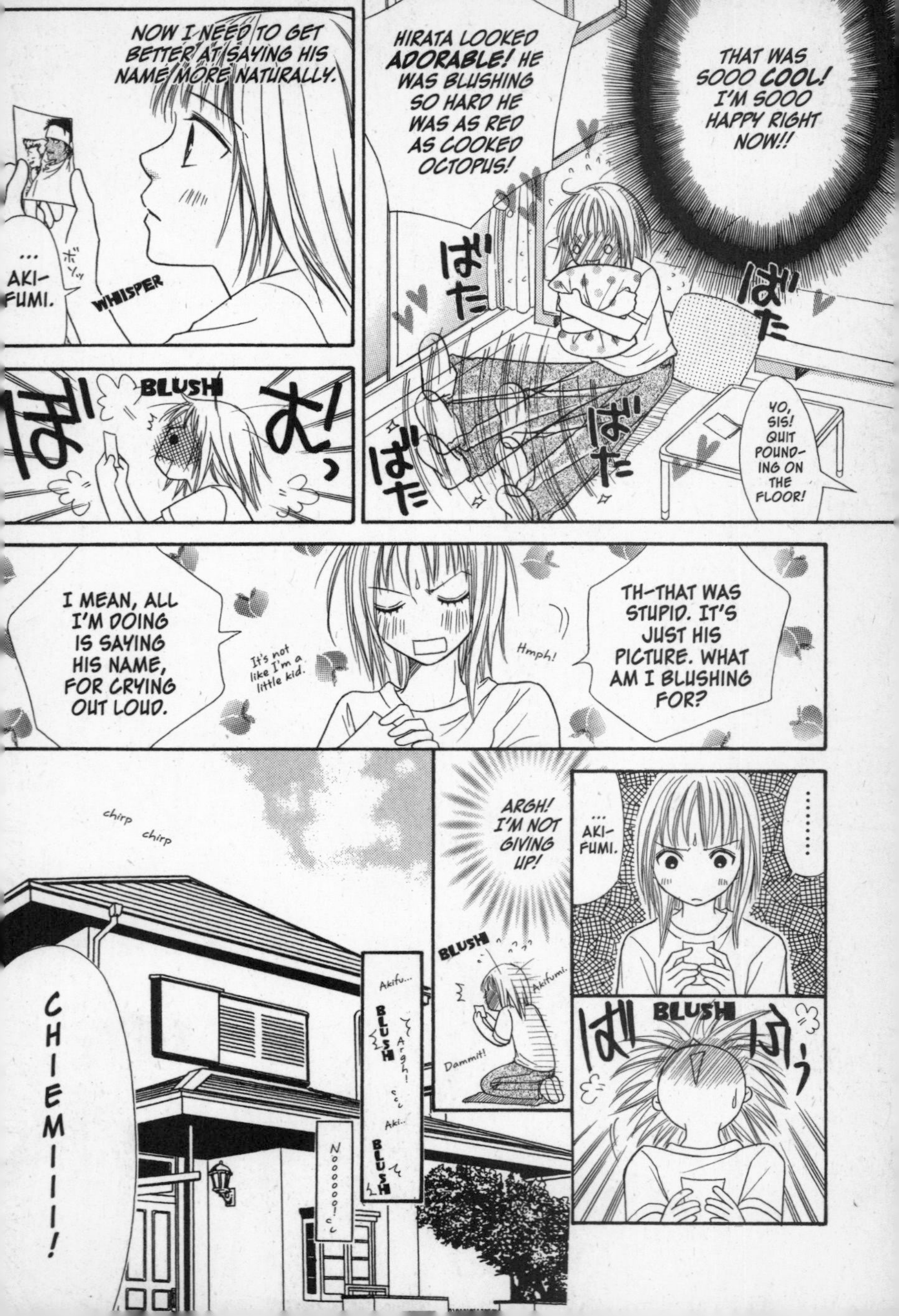
THAT WAS SOOO COOL! I'M SOOO HAPPY RIGHT NOW!!
HIRATA LOOKED ADORABLE! HE WAS BLUSHING SO HARD HE WAS AS RED AS COOKED OCTOPUS!
ばた
ばた
ばた
ばた
YO, SIS! QUIT POUNDING-ING ON THE FLOOR!
NOW I NEED TO GET BETTER AT SAYING HIS NAME MORE NATURALLY.
ボソッ
WHISPER
... AKI-FUMI.
BLUSH
ぼっ!
TH-THAT WAS STUPID. IT'S JUST HIS PICTURE. WHAT AM I BLUSHING FOR?
Hmph!
It's not like I'm a little kid.
I MEAN, ALL I'M DOING IS SAYING HIS NAME, FOR CRYING OUT LOUD.
....
... AKI-FUMI.
BLUSH
ぱふっ
ARGH! I'M NOT GIVING UP!
BLUSH
Akifumi.
Dammit!
chirp chirp
Akifu... BLUSH Argh!
Aki.. BLUSH
Noooooooo!
CHIEMIIII!

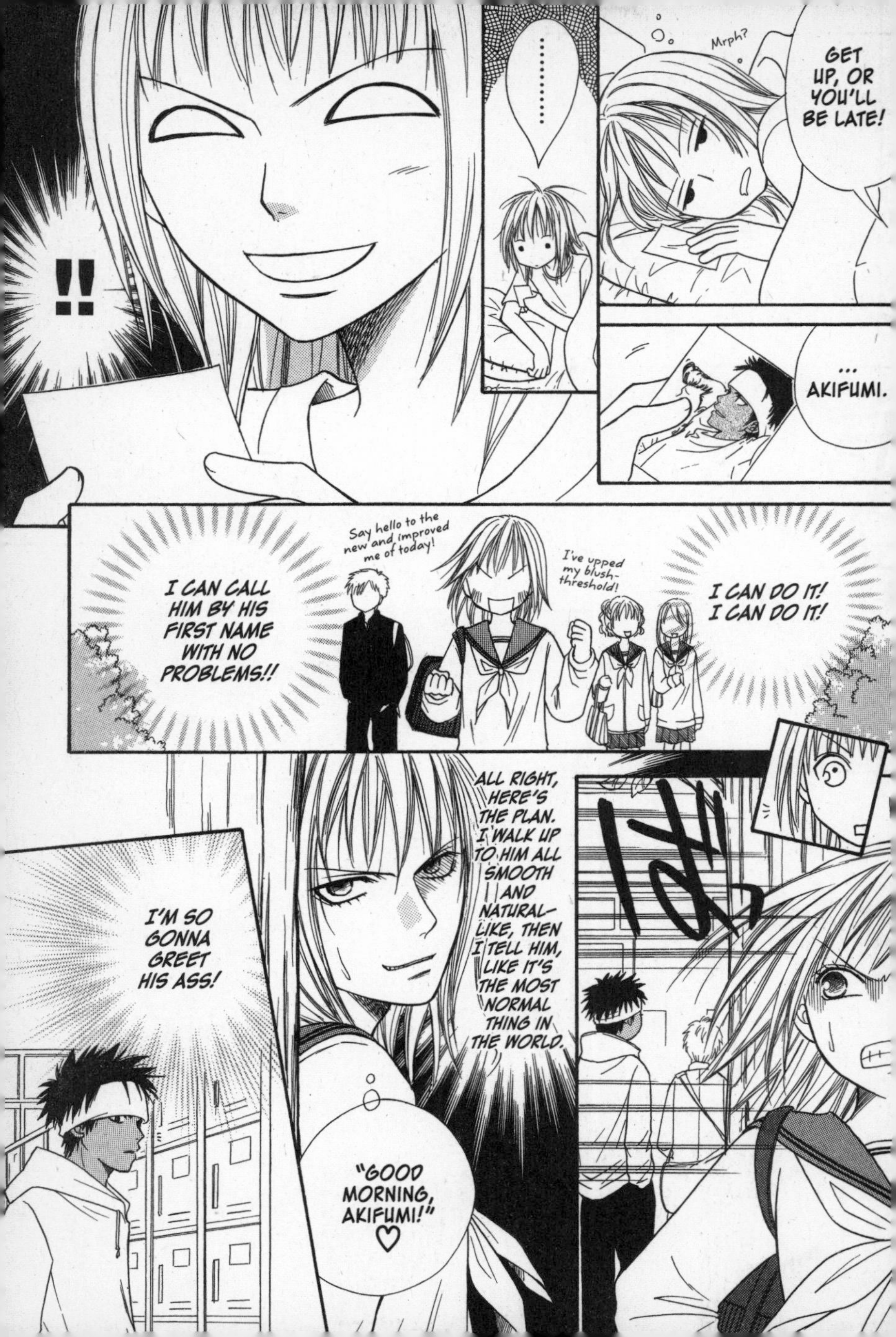
GET UP, OR YOU'LL BE LATE!
Mrph?
... AKIFUMI.
......
!!
I CAN DO IT! I CAN DO IT!
I've upped my blush-threshold!
Say hello to the new and improved me of today!
I CAN CALL HIM BY HIS FIRST NAME WITH NO PROBLEMS!!
ALL RIGHT, HERE'S THE PLAN. I WALK UP TO HIM ALL SMOOTH AND NATURAL-LIKE, THEN I TELL HIM, LIKE IT'S THE MOST NORMAL THING IN THE WORLD.
"GOOD MORNING, AKIFUMI!" ♡
I'M SO GONNA GREET HIS ASS!

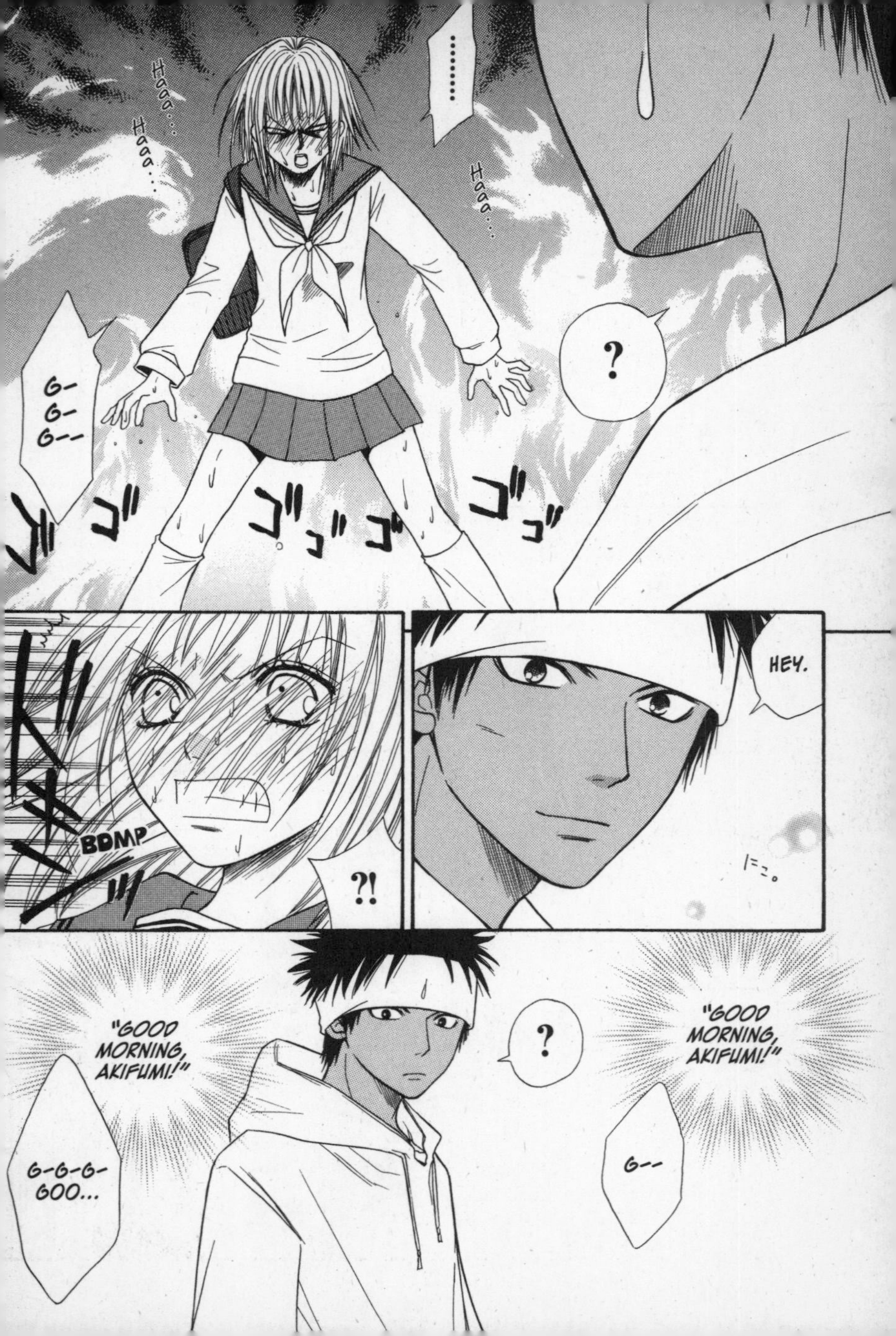
......
Haaa...
?
Haaa...
Haaa...
G- G- G--
ゴゴゴゴ
HEY.
にこ。
BDMP
?!
"GOOD MORNING, AKIFUMI!"
G--
?
"GOOD MORNING, AKIFUMI!"
G-G-G-GOO...

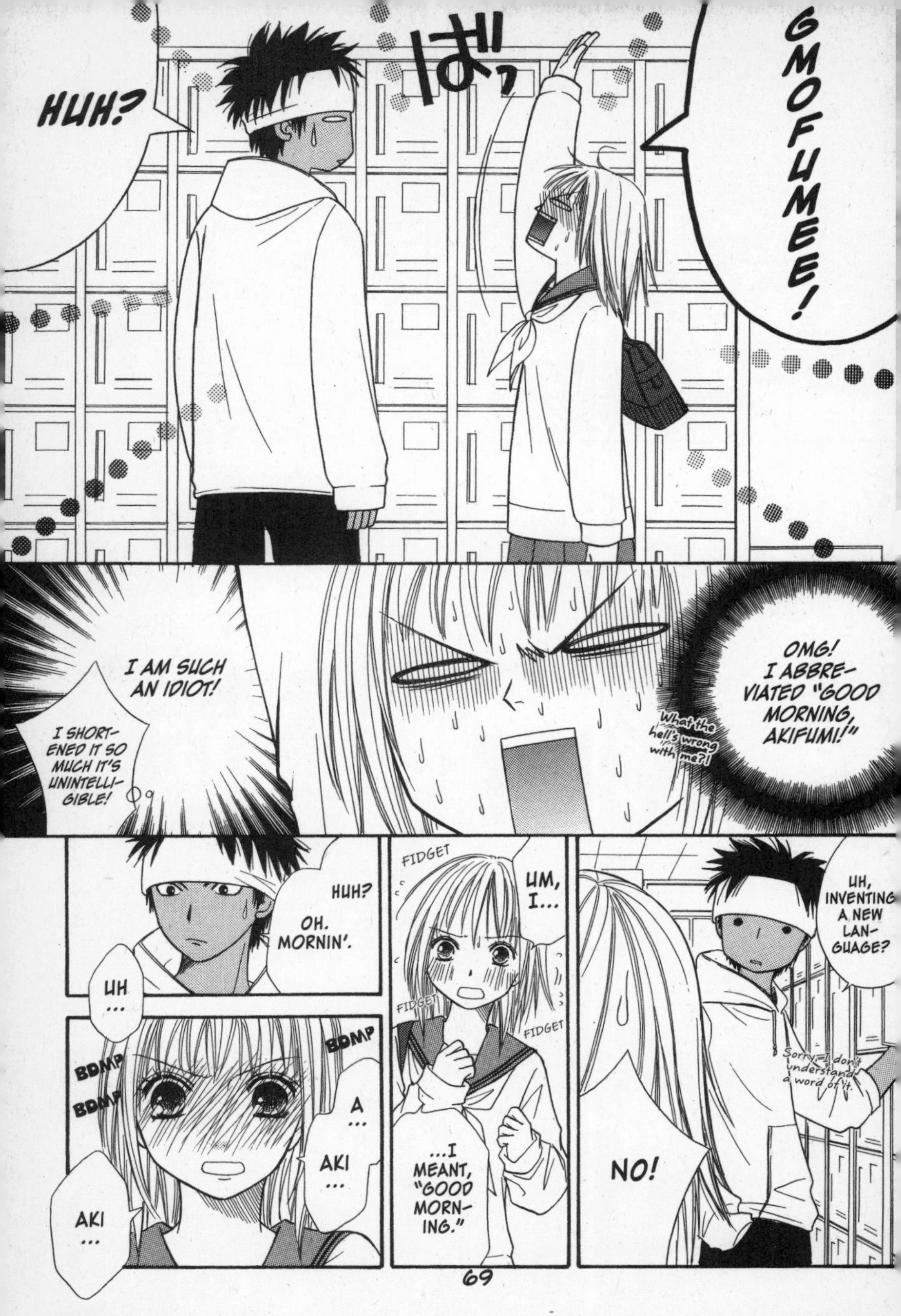

GMOFUMEE!
ばっ
HUH?
OMG! I ABBREVIATED "GOOD MORNING, AKIFUMI!"
What the hell's wrong with me?!
I AM SUCH AN IDIOT!
I SHORTENED IT SO MUCH IT'S UNINTELLIGIBLE!
UH, INVENTING A NEW LANGUAGE?
Sorry, I don't understand a word of it.
NO!
FIDGET
UM, I...
FIDGET
FIDGET
...I MEANT, "GOOD MORNING."
HUH?
OH. MORNIN'.
UH ...
BDMP
BDMP
BDMP
A ...
AKI ...
AKI ...

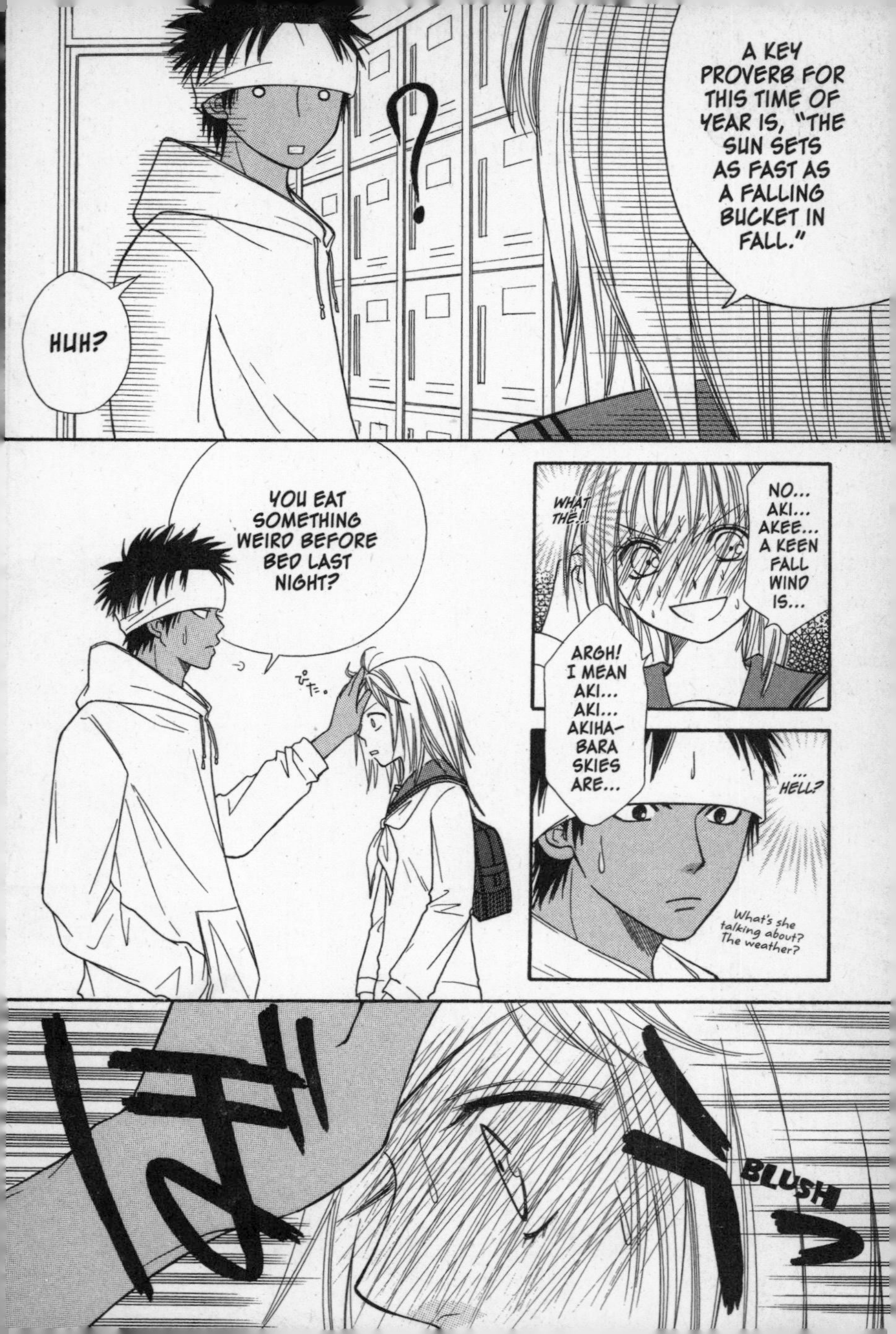
A KEY PROVERB FOR THIS TIME OF YEAR IS, "THE SUN SETS AS FAST AS A FALLING BUCKET IN FALL."
HUH?
NO... AKI... AKEE... A KEEN FALL WIND IS...
WHAT THE...!
ARGH! I MEAN AKI... AKI... AKIHA-BARA SKIES ARE...
...HELL?
What's she talking about? The weather?
YOU EAT SOMETHING WEIRD BEFORE BED LAST NIGHT?
ぴた。
BLUSH

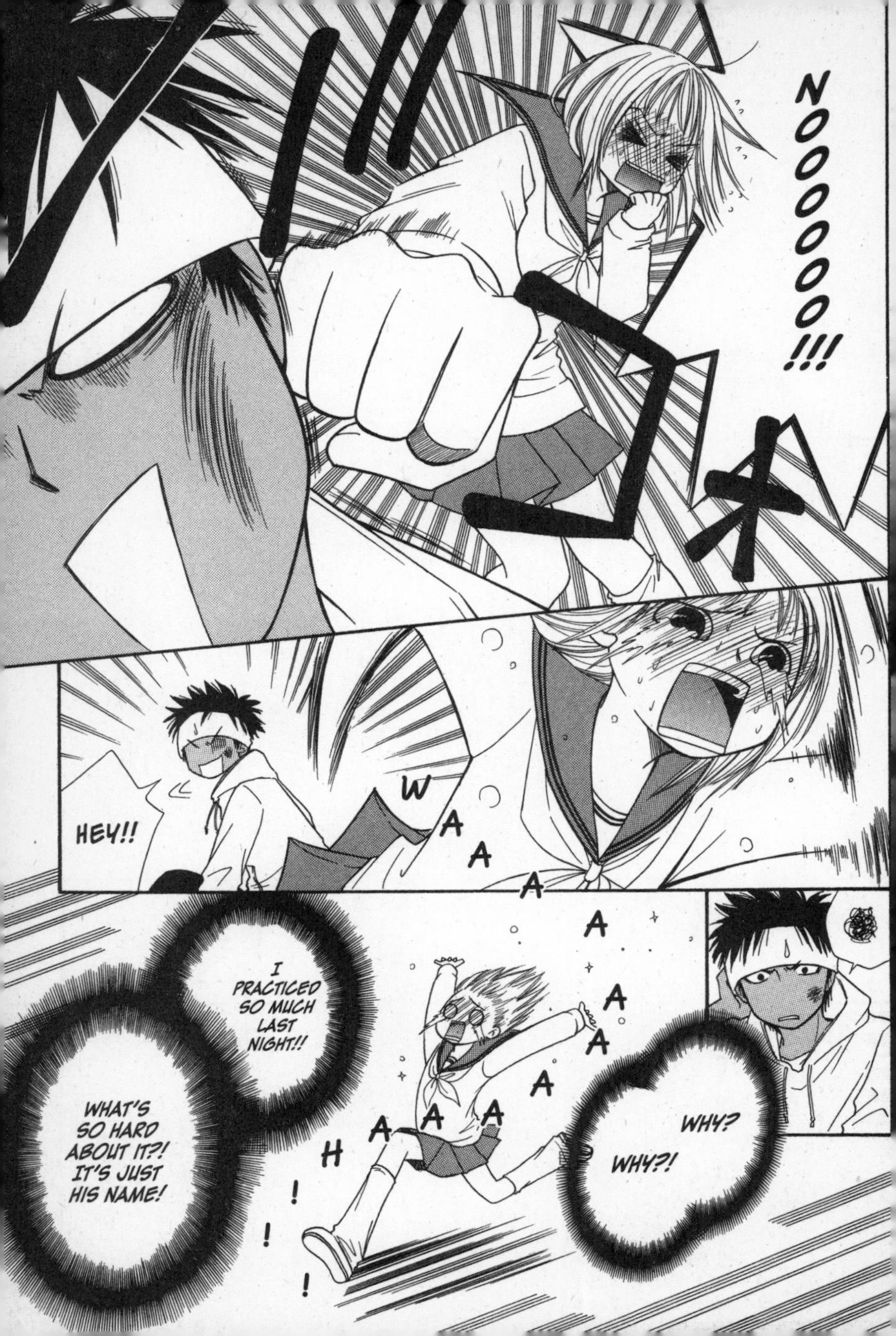
NOOOOOOOO!!!
HEY!!
WAAAAAAAAAAH!!!
WHY?
WHY?!
I PRACTICED SO MUCH LAST NIGHT!!
WHAT'S SO HARD ABOUT IT?! IT'S JUST HIS NAME!

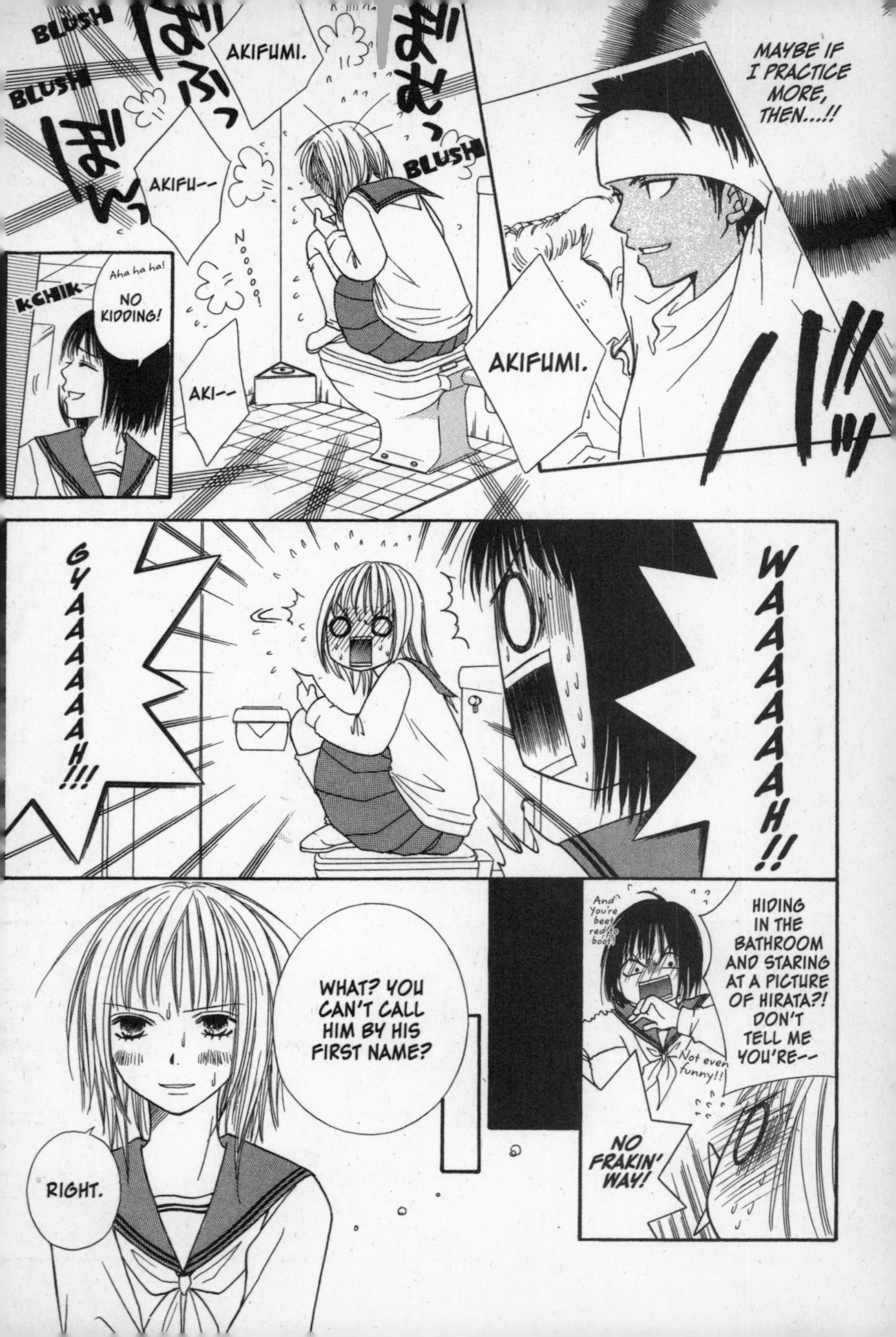
MAYBE IF I PRACTICE MORE, THEN...!!
AKIFUMI.
バッ
ぼむっ
BLUSH
AKIFUMI.
ぼふっ
BLUSH
BLUSH
ぼんっ
AKIFU--
Noooooo!
AKI--
KCHIK
Aha ha ha!
NO KIDDING!
WAAAAAAAAAH!!
GYAAAAAAAAAH!!!
HIDING IN THE BATHROOM AND STARING AT A PICTURE OF HIRATA?! DON'T TELL ME YOU'RE--
And you're beet red to boot!
Not even funny!!
NO FRAKIN' WAY!
WHAT? YOU CAN'T CALL HIM BY HIS FIRST NAME?
RIGHT.

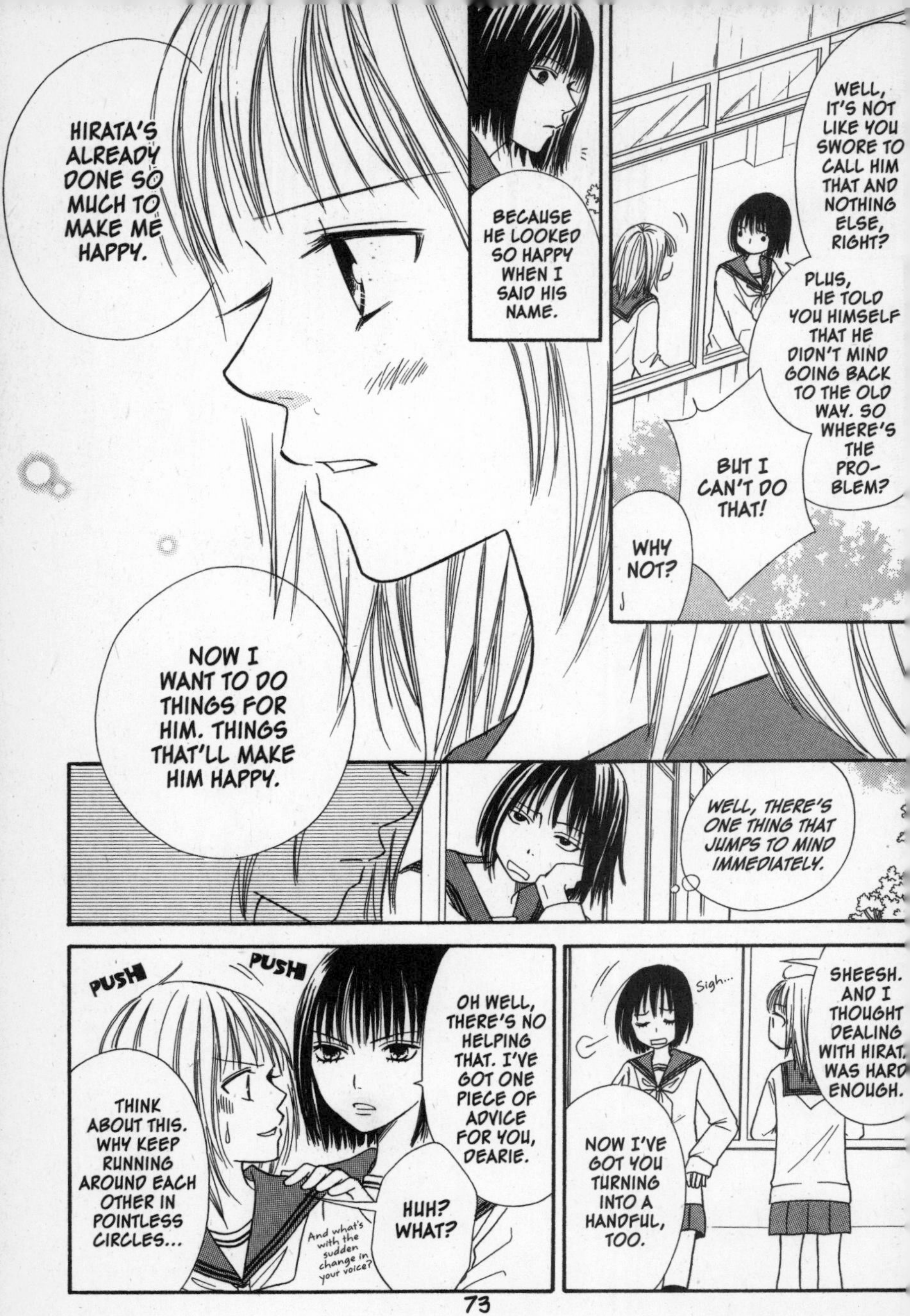

WELL, IT'S NOT LIKE YOU SWORE TO CALL HIM THAT AND NOTHING ELSE, RIGHT?
PLUS, HE TOLD YOU HIMSELF THAT HE DIDN'T MIND GOING BACK TO THE OLD WAY. SO WHERE'S THE PRO-BLEM?
BUT I CAN'T DO THAT!
WHY NOT?
BECAUSE HE LOOKED SO HAPPY WHEN I SAID HIS NAME.
HIRATA'S ALREADY DONE SO MUCH TO MAKE ME HAPPY.
NOW I WANT TO DO THINGS FOR HIM. THINGS THAT'LL MAKE HIM HAPPY.
WELL, THERE'S ONE THING THAT JUMPS TO MIND IMMEDIATELY.
SHEESH. AND I THOUGHT DEALING WITH HIRAT. WAS HARD ENOUGH.
Sigh...
NOW I'VE GOT YOU TURNING INTO A HANDFUL, TOO.
PUSH
PUSH
OH WELL, THERE'S NO HELPING THAT. I'VE GOT ONE PIECE OF ADVICE FOR YOU, DEARIE.
HUH? WHAT?
And what's with the sudden change in your voice?
THINK ABOUT THIS. WHY KEEP RUNNING AROUND EACH OTHER IN POINTLESS CIRCLES...

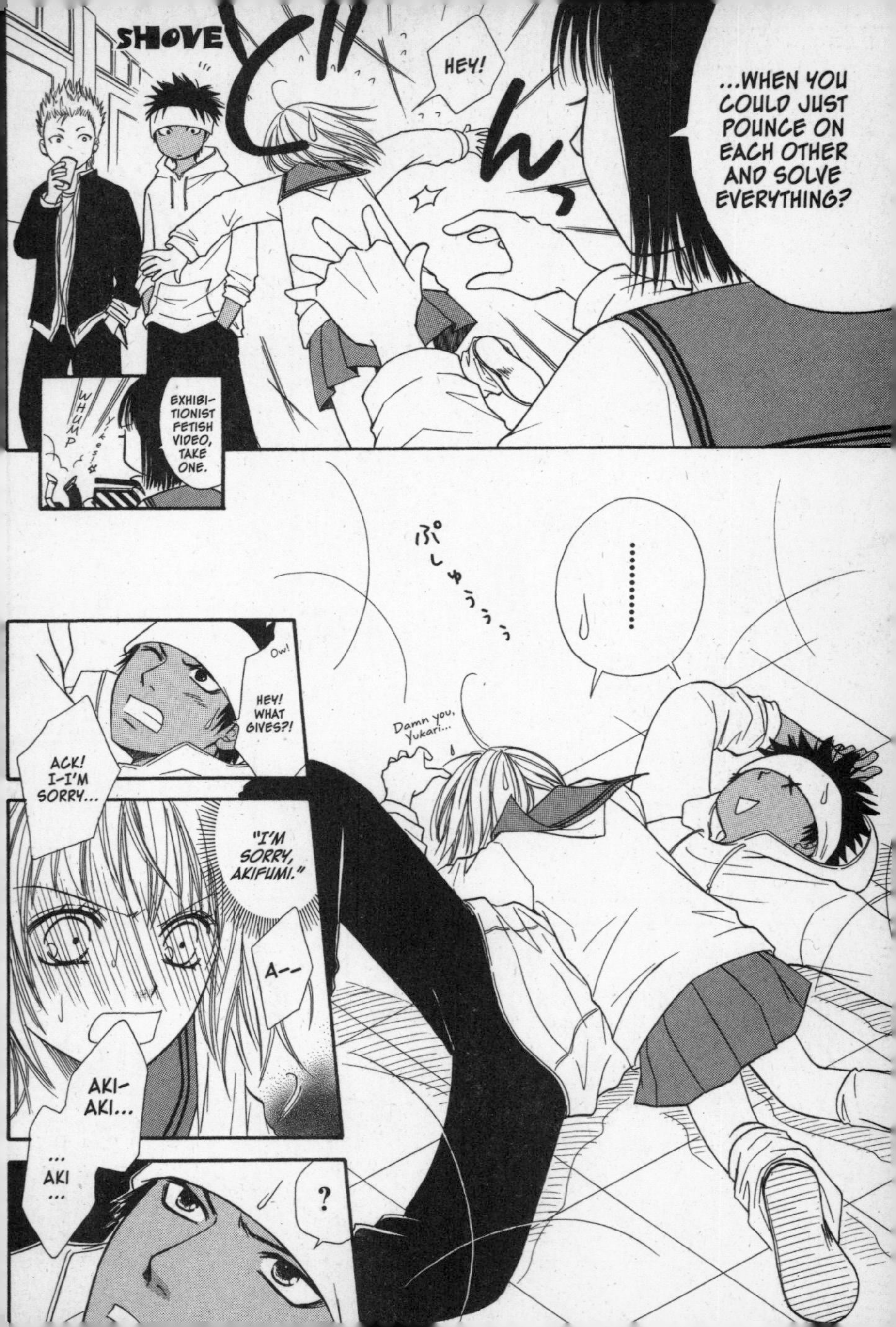

...WHEN YOU COULD JUST POUNCE ON EACH OTHER AND SOLVE EVERYTHING?
HEY!
どん
SHOVE
EXHIBITIONIST FETISH VIDEO, TAKE ONE.
WHUMP
Yikes!☆
......
ぷしゅううう
Damn you, Yukari...
Ow!
HEY! WHAT GIVES?!
ACK! I-I'M SORRY...
"I'M SORRY, AKIFUMI."
A--
AKI-AKI...
?
...AKI...

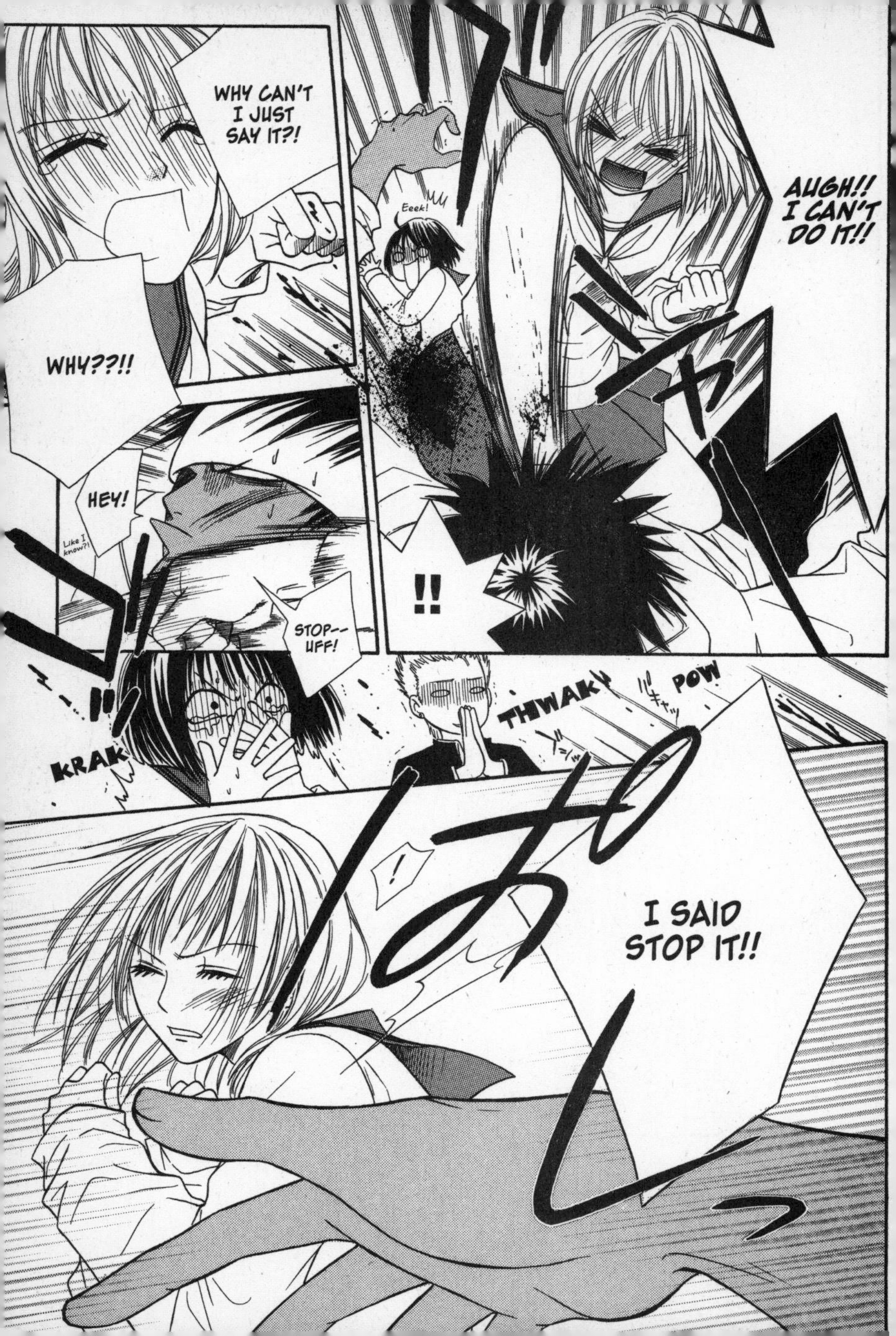
AUGH!! I CAN'T DO IT!!
Eeek!
!!
WHY CAN'T I JUST SAY IT?!
WHY??!!
HEY!
Like I know?!
STOP-- UFF!
POW
THWAK
KRAK
!
I SAID STOP IT!!

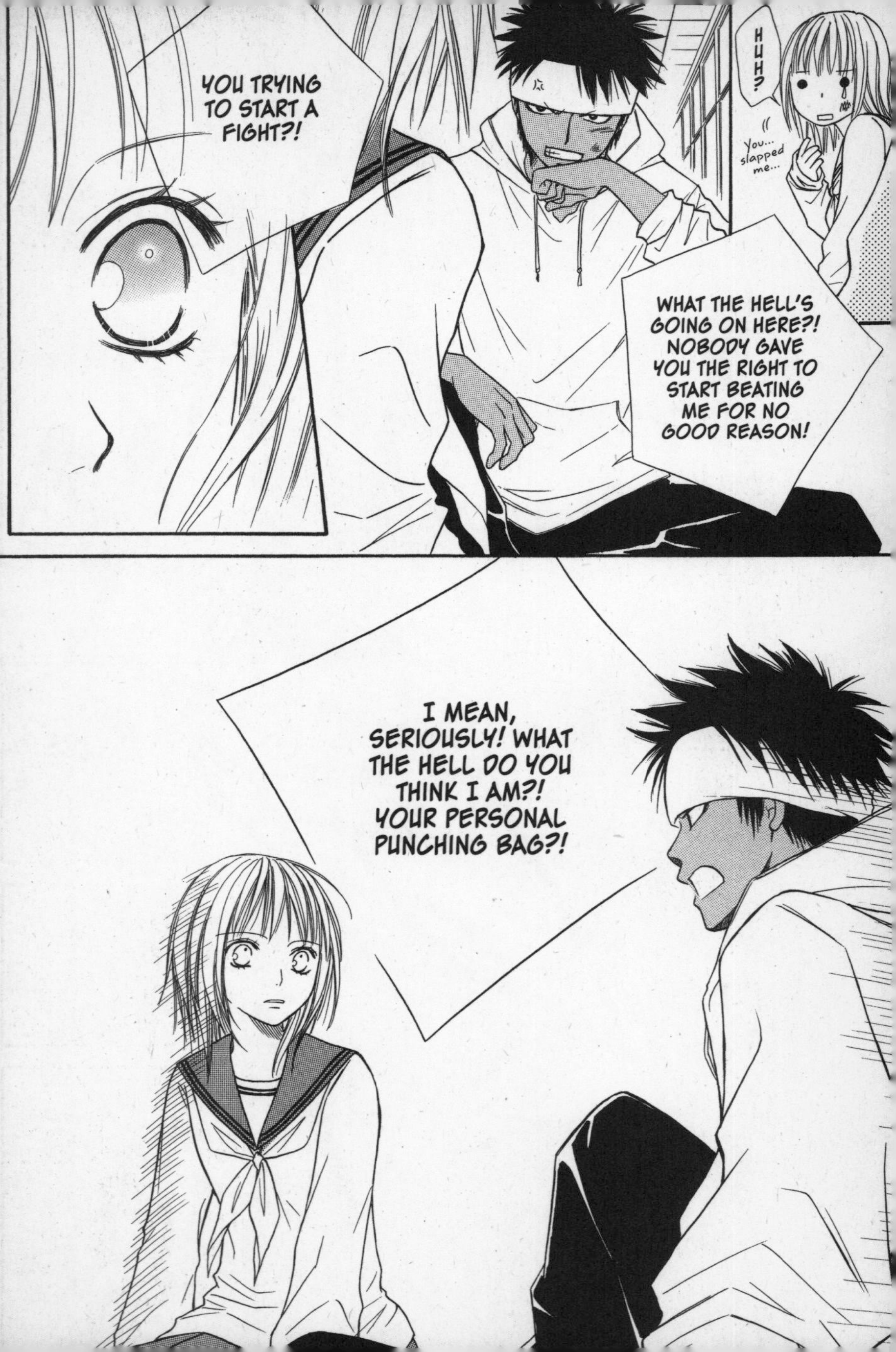
HUH?
You... slapped me...
YOU TRYING TO START A FIGHT?!
WHAT THE HELL'S GOING ON HERE?! NOBODY GAVE YOU THE RIGHT TO START BEATING ME FOR NO GOOD REASON!
I MEAN, SERIOUSLY! WHAT THE HELL DO YOU THINK I AM?! YOUR PERSONAL PUNCHING BAG?!

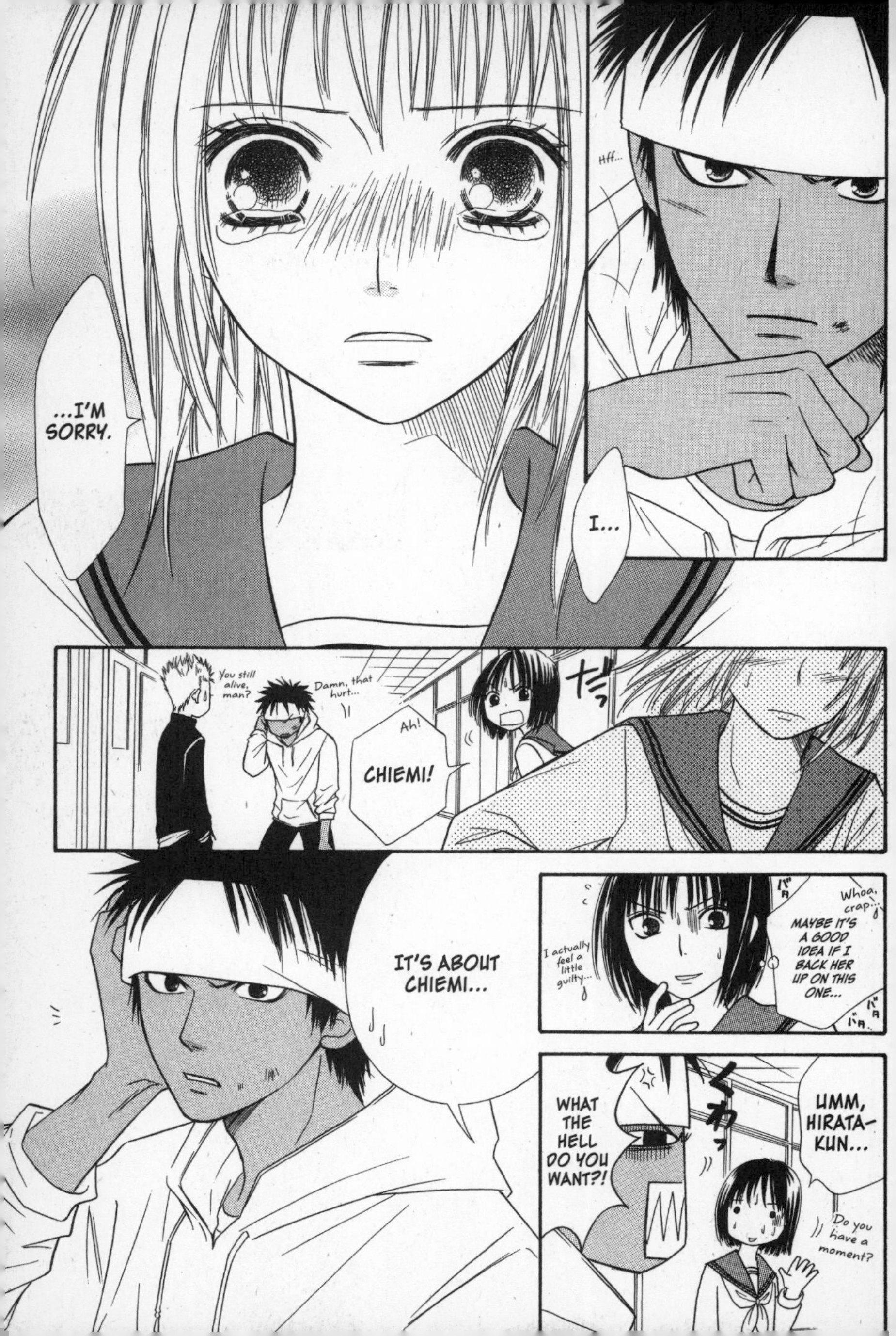
Hff...
I...
...I'M SORRY.
Ah!
CHIEMI!
Damn, that hurt...
You still alive, man?
Whoa, crap...
MAYBE IT'S A GOOD IDEA IF I BACK HER UP ON THIS ONE...
I actually feel a little guilty...
UMM, HIRATA-KUN...
Do you have a moment?
WHAT THE HELL DO YOU WANT?!
IT'S ABOUT CHIEMI...

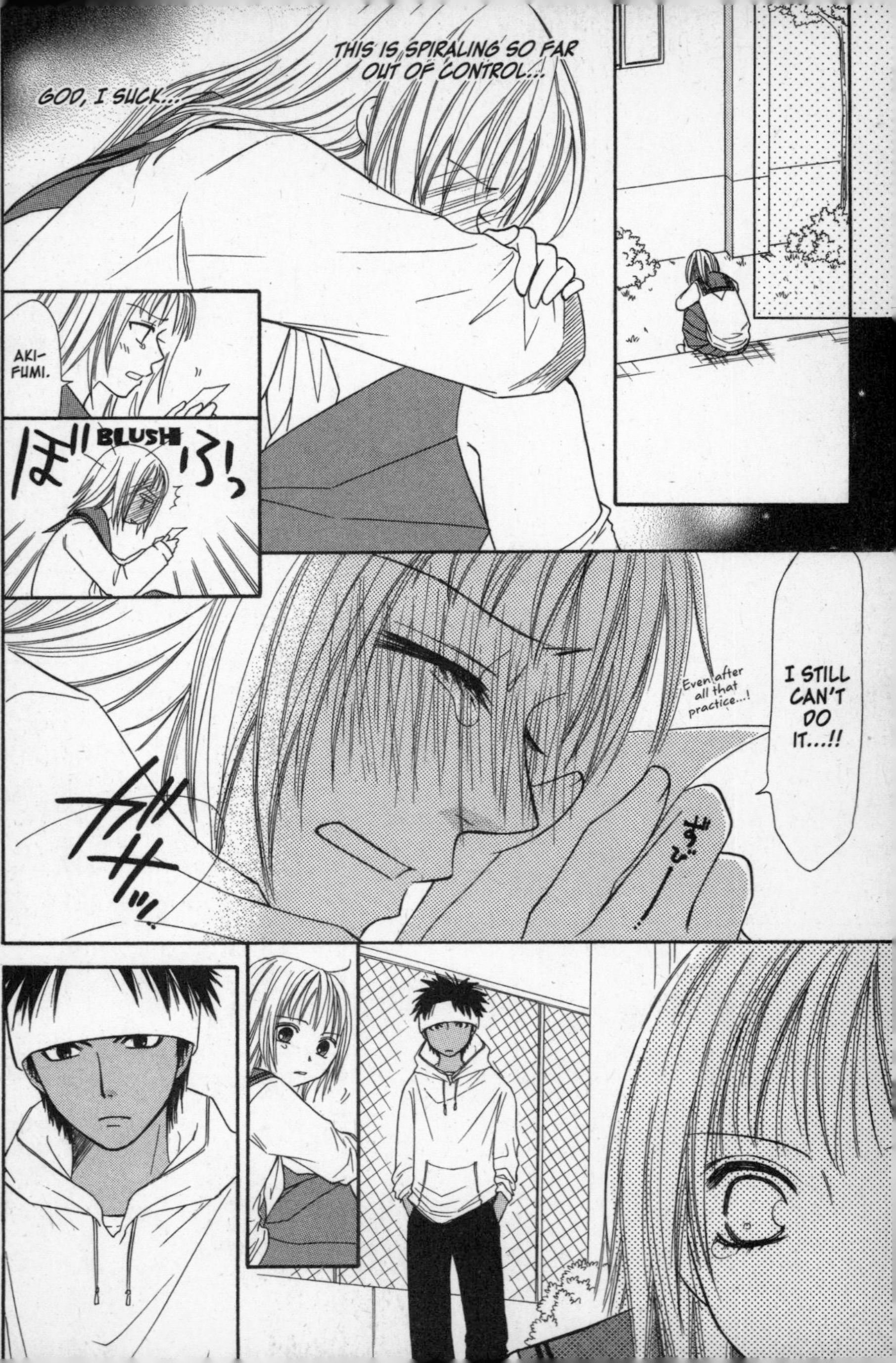
THIS IS SPIRALING SO FAR OUT OF CONTROL...
GOD, I SUCK...
AKI-FUMI.
ぼふ!っ
BLUSH
I STILL CAN'T DO IT...!!
Even after all that practice...!
ガバッ

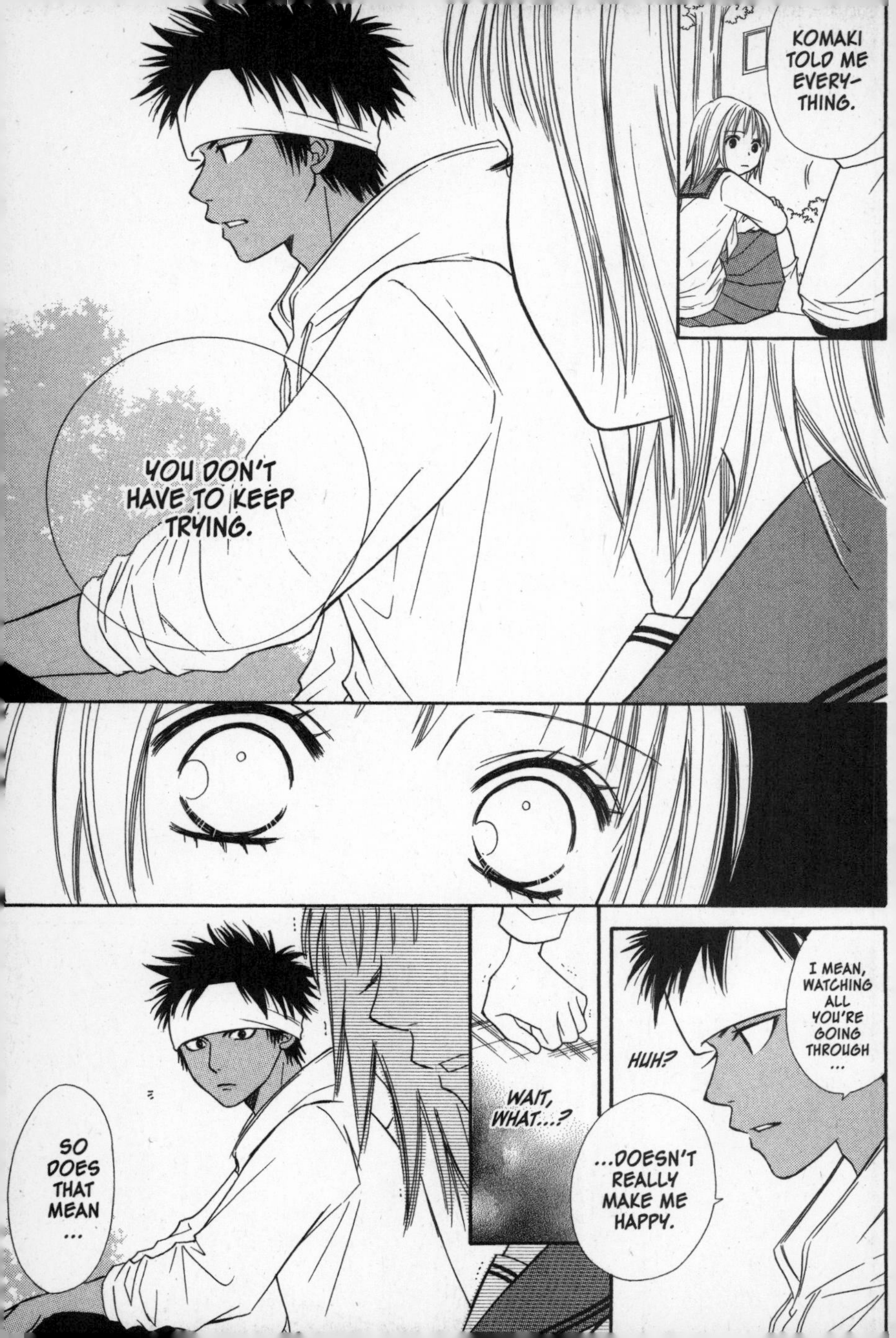
KOMAKI TOLD ME EVERY-THING.
YOU DON'T HAVE TO KEEP TRYING.
I MEAN, WATCHING ALL YOU'RE GOING THROUGH ...
HUH?
...DOESN'T REALLY MAKE ME HAPPY.
WAIT, WHAT...?
SO DOES THAT MEAN ...

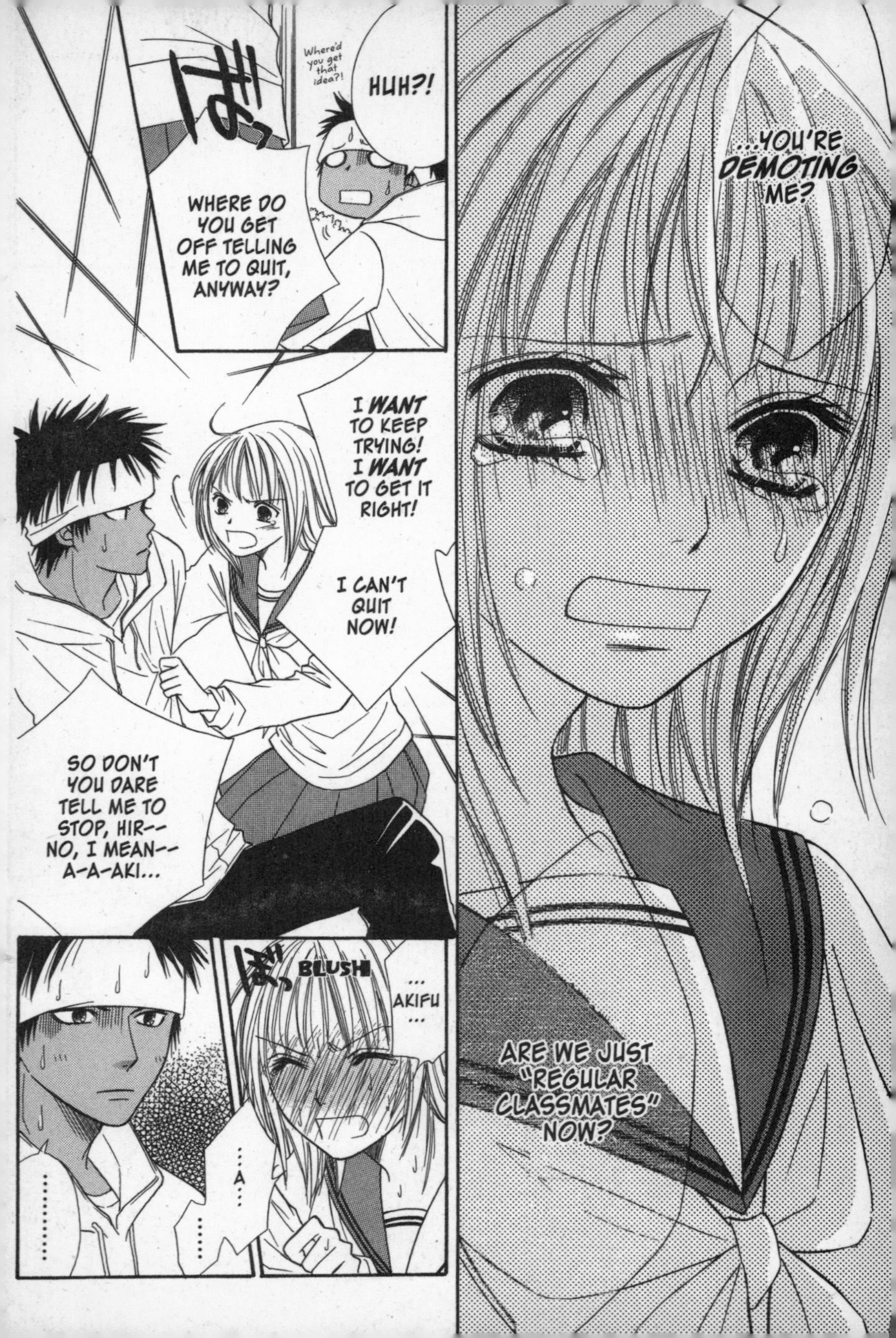
...YOU'RE DEMOTING ME?
ARE WE JUST "REGULAR CLASSMATES" NOW?
HUH?!
Where'd you get that idea?!
WHERE DO YOU GET OFF TELLING ME TO QUIT, ANYWAY?
I WANT TO KEEP TRYING! I WANT TO GET IT RIGHT!
I CAN'T QUIT NOW!
SO DON'T YOU DARE TELL ME TO STOP, HIR-- NO, I MEAN-- A-A-AKI...
BLUSH
...AKIFU...
...A...
......
......

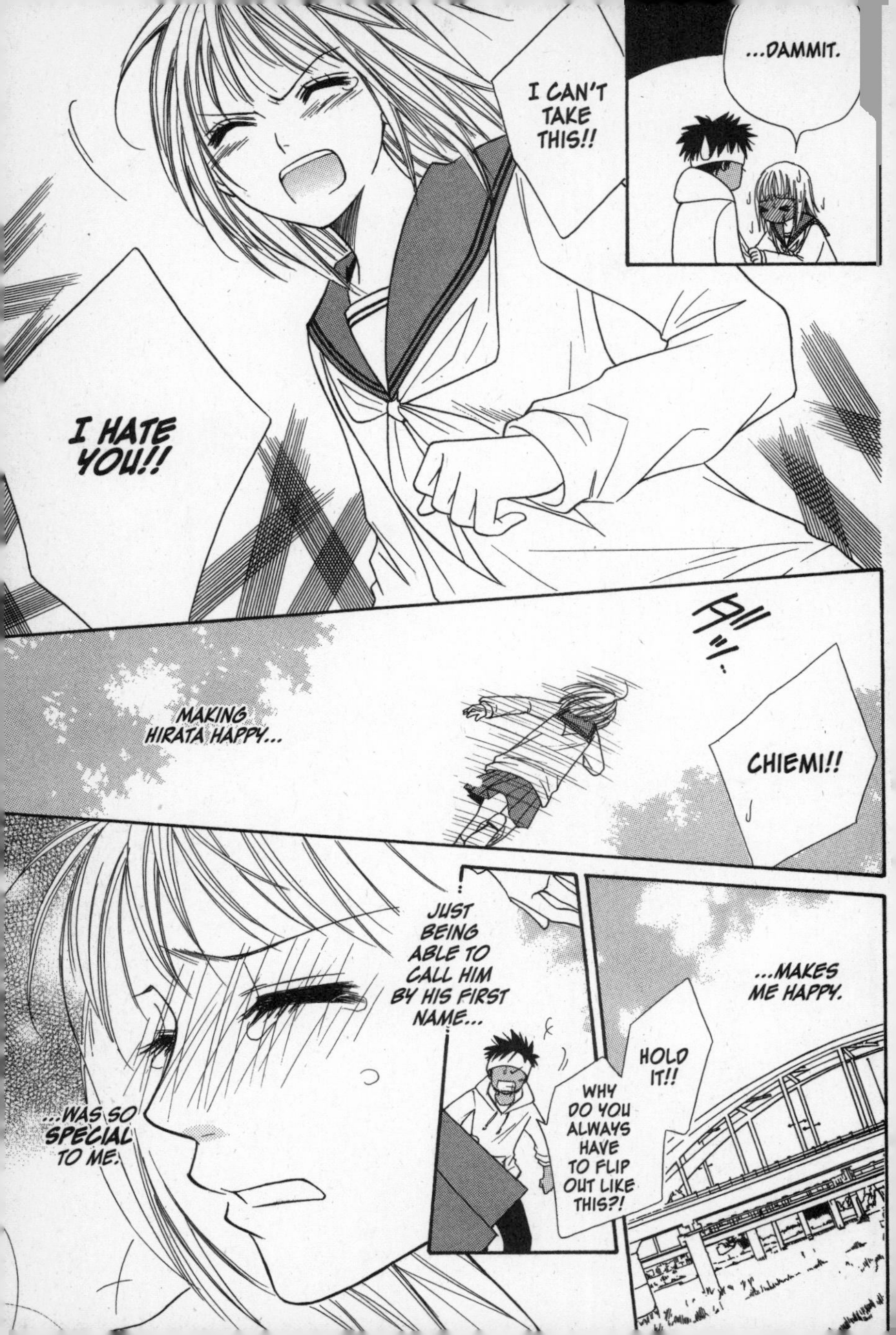
...DAMMIT.
I CAN'T TAKE THIS!!
I HATE YOU!!
CHIEMI!!
MAKING HIRATA HAPPY...
...MAKES ME HAPPY.
HOLD IT!!
WHY DO YOU ALWAYS HAVE TO FLIP OUT LIKE THIS?!
JUST BEING ABLE TO CALL HIM BY HIS FIRST NAME...
...WAS SO SPECIAL TO ME.

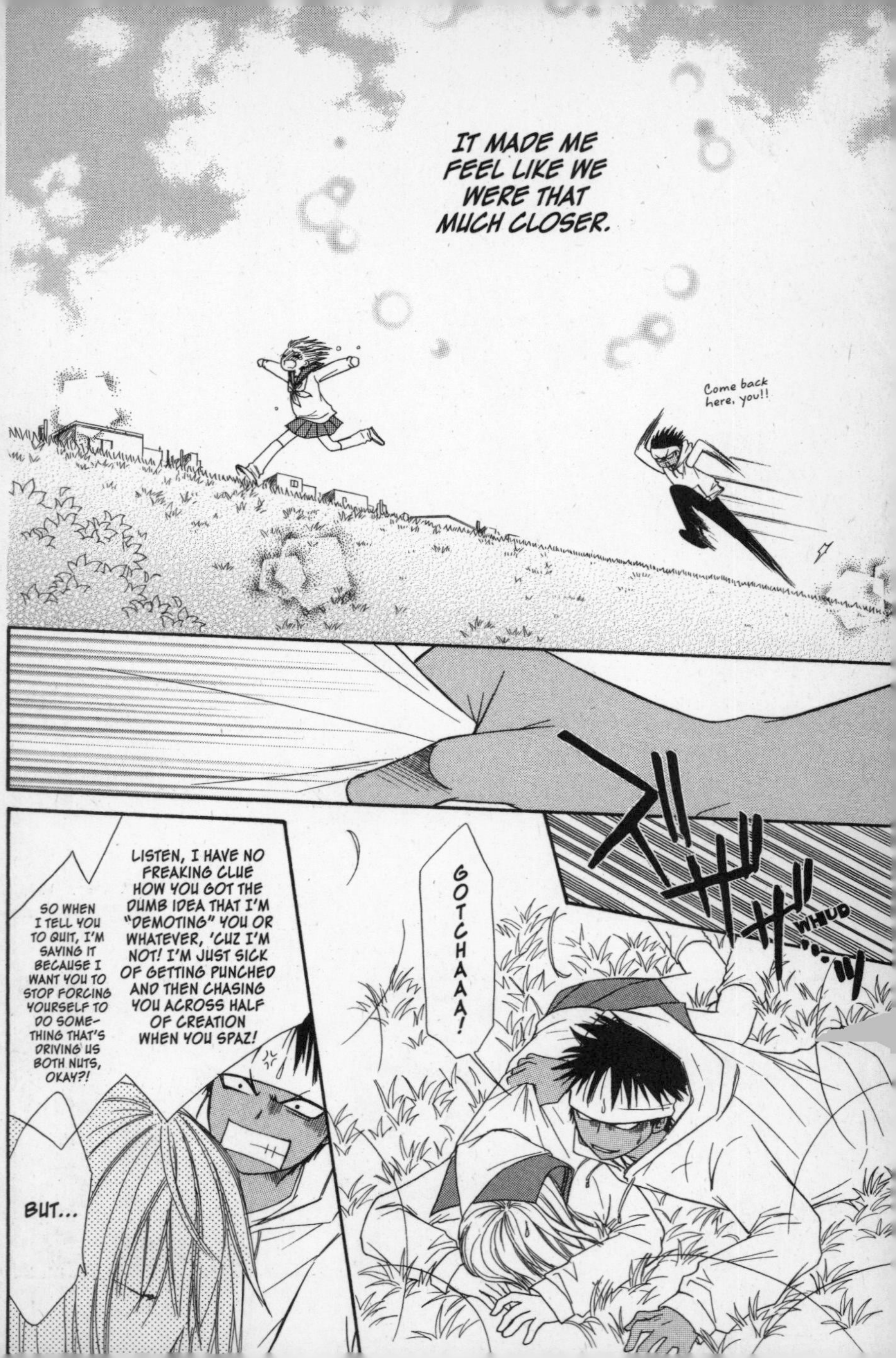
IT MADE ME FEEL LIKE WE WERE THAT MUCH CLOSER.
Come back here, you!!
GOTCHAAA!
WHUD
LISTEN, I HAVE NO FREAKING CLUE HOW YOU GOT THE DUMB IDEA THAT I'M "DEMOTING" YOU OR WHATEVER, 'CUZ I'M NOT! I'M JUST SICK OF GETTING PUNCHED AND THEN CHASING YOU ACROSS HALF OF CREATION WHEN YOU SPAZ!
SO WHEN I TELL YOU TO QUIT, I'M SAYING IT BECAUSE I WANT YOU TO STOP FORCING YOURSELF TO DO SOMETHING THAT'S DRIVING US BOTH NUTS, OKAY?!
BUT...

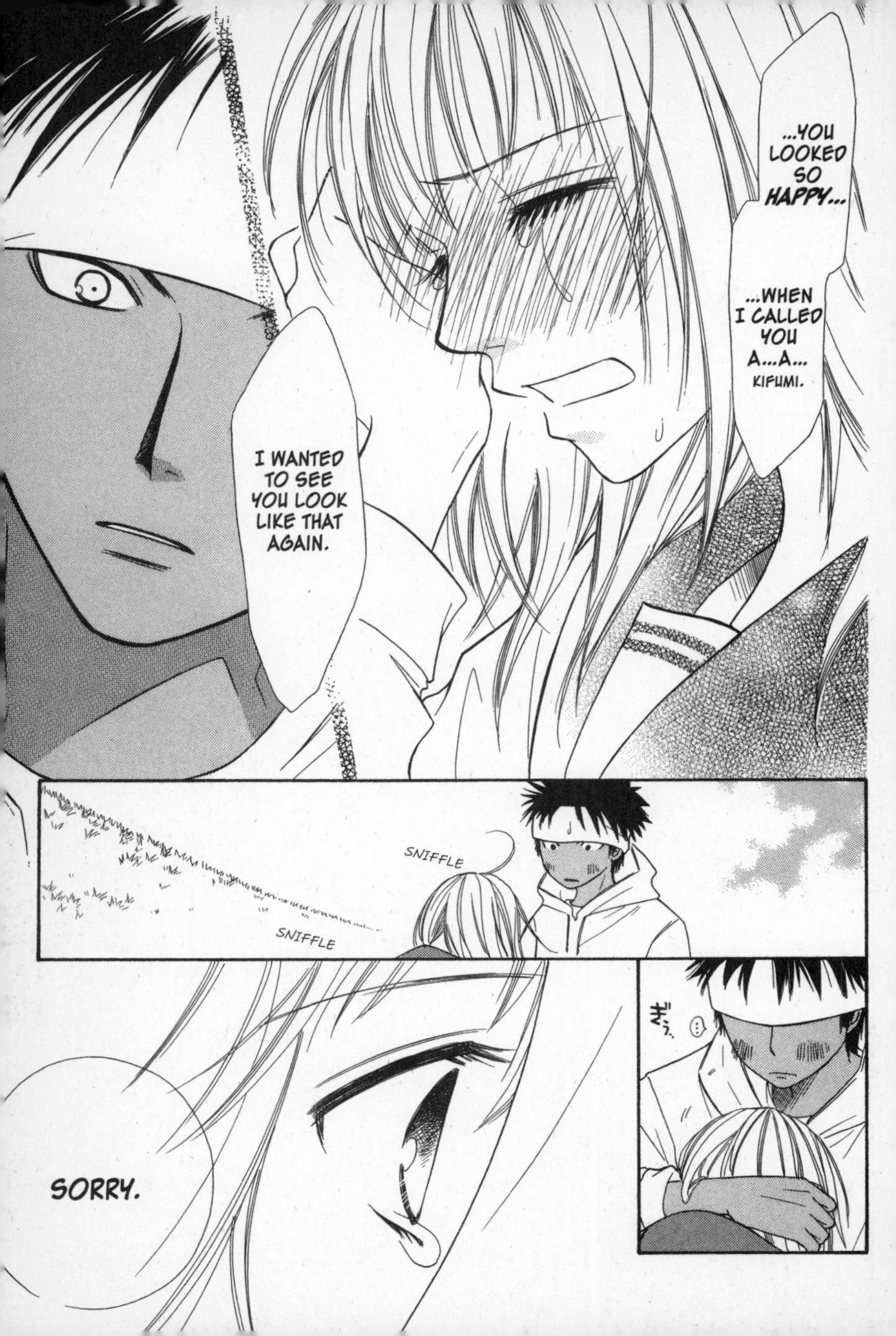
...YOU LOOKED SO HAPPY...
...WHEN I CALLED YOU A...A... KIFUMI.
I WANTED TO SEE YOU LOOK LIKE THAT AGAIN.
SNIFFLE
SNIFFLE
...
SORRY.

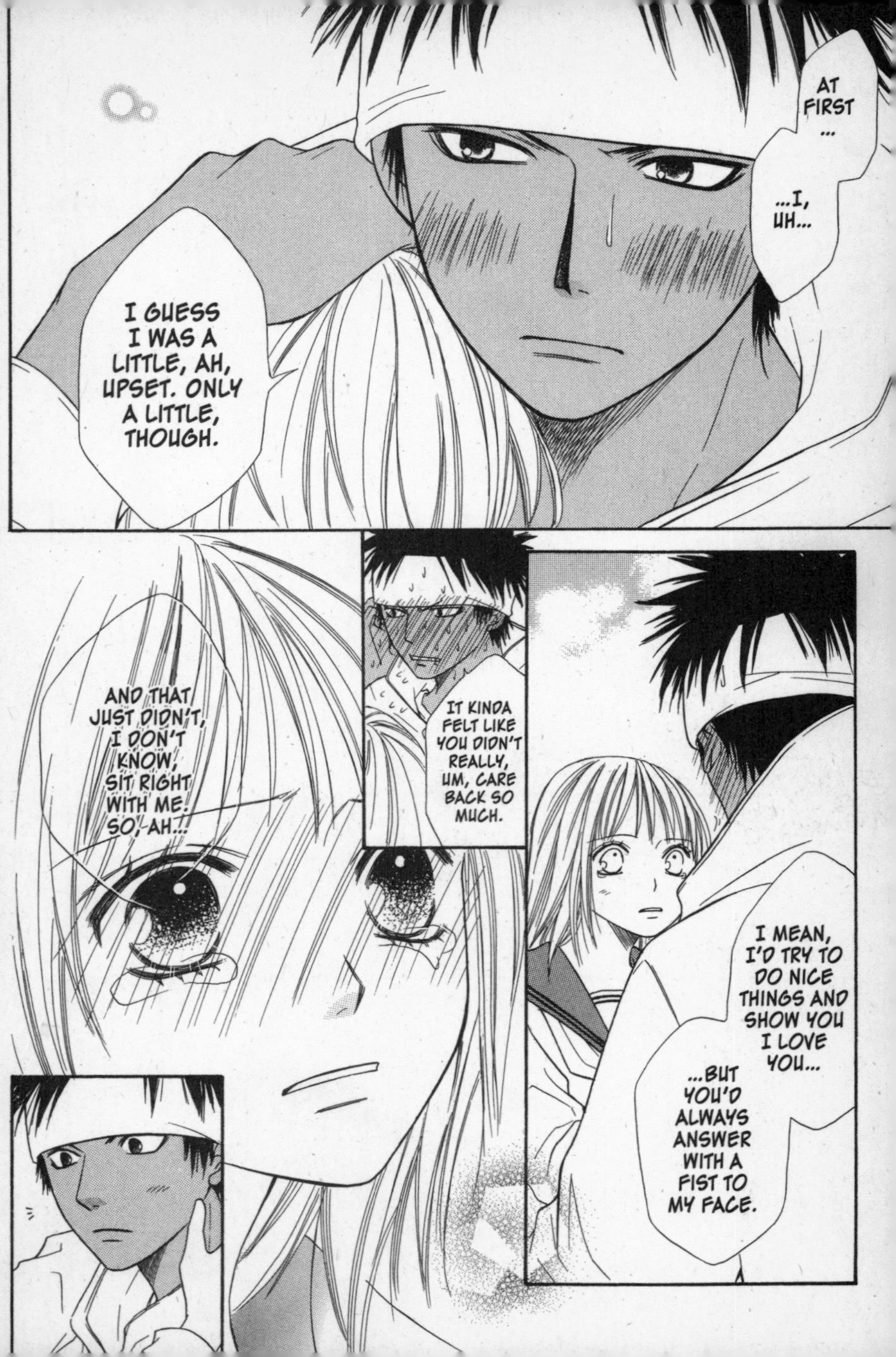
AT FIRST ...
...I, UH...
I GUESS I WAS A LITTLE, AH, UPSET. ONLY A LITTLE, THOUGH.
I MEAN, I'D TRY TO DO NICE THINGS AND SHOW YOU I LOVE YOU...
...BUT YOU'D ALWAYS ANSWER WITH A FIST TO MY FACE.
IT KINDA FELT LIKE YOU DIDN'T REALLY, UM, CARE BACK SO MUCH.
AND THAT JUST DIDN'T, I DON'T KNOW, SIT RIGHT WITH ME. SO, AH...

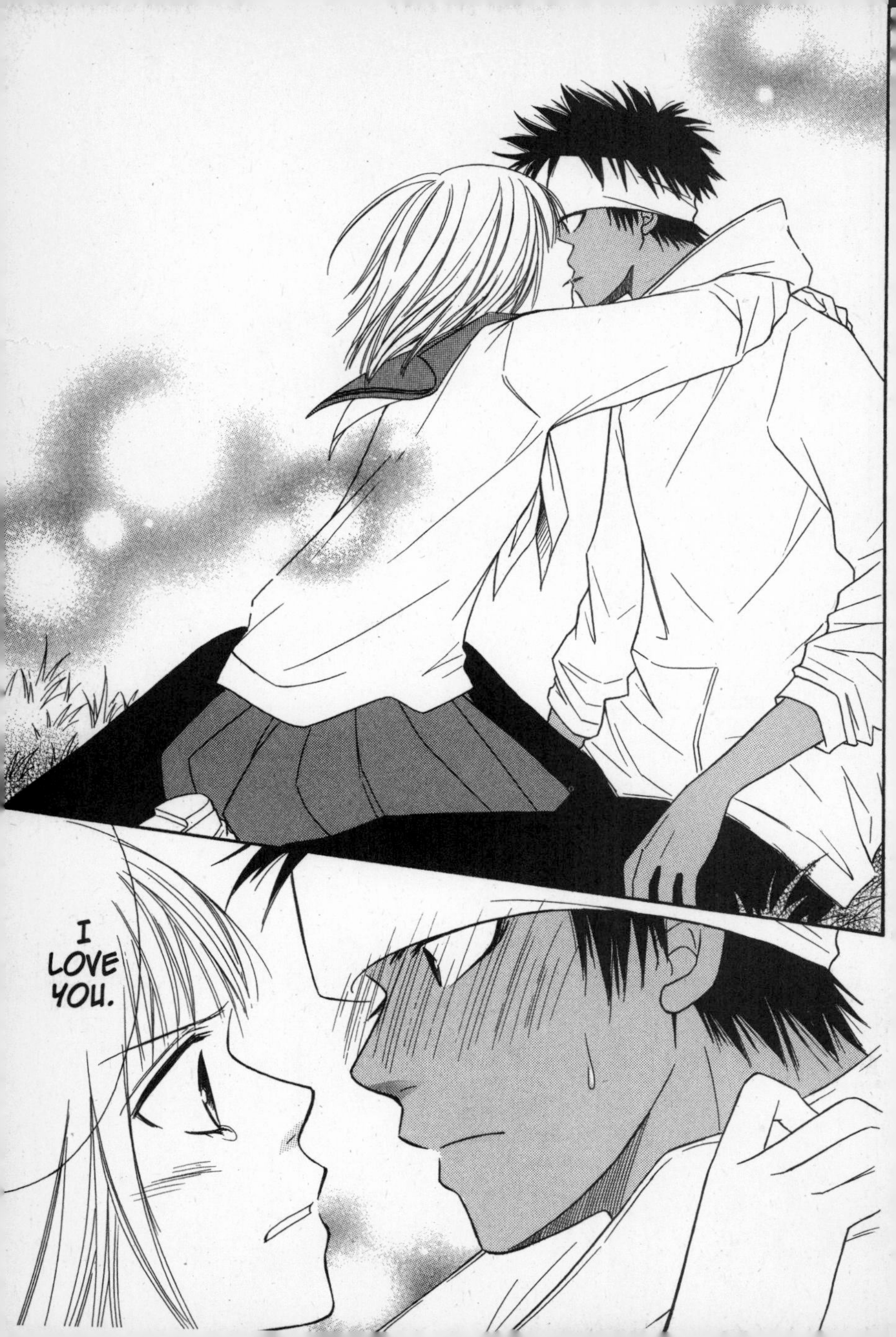
I LOVE YOU.

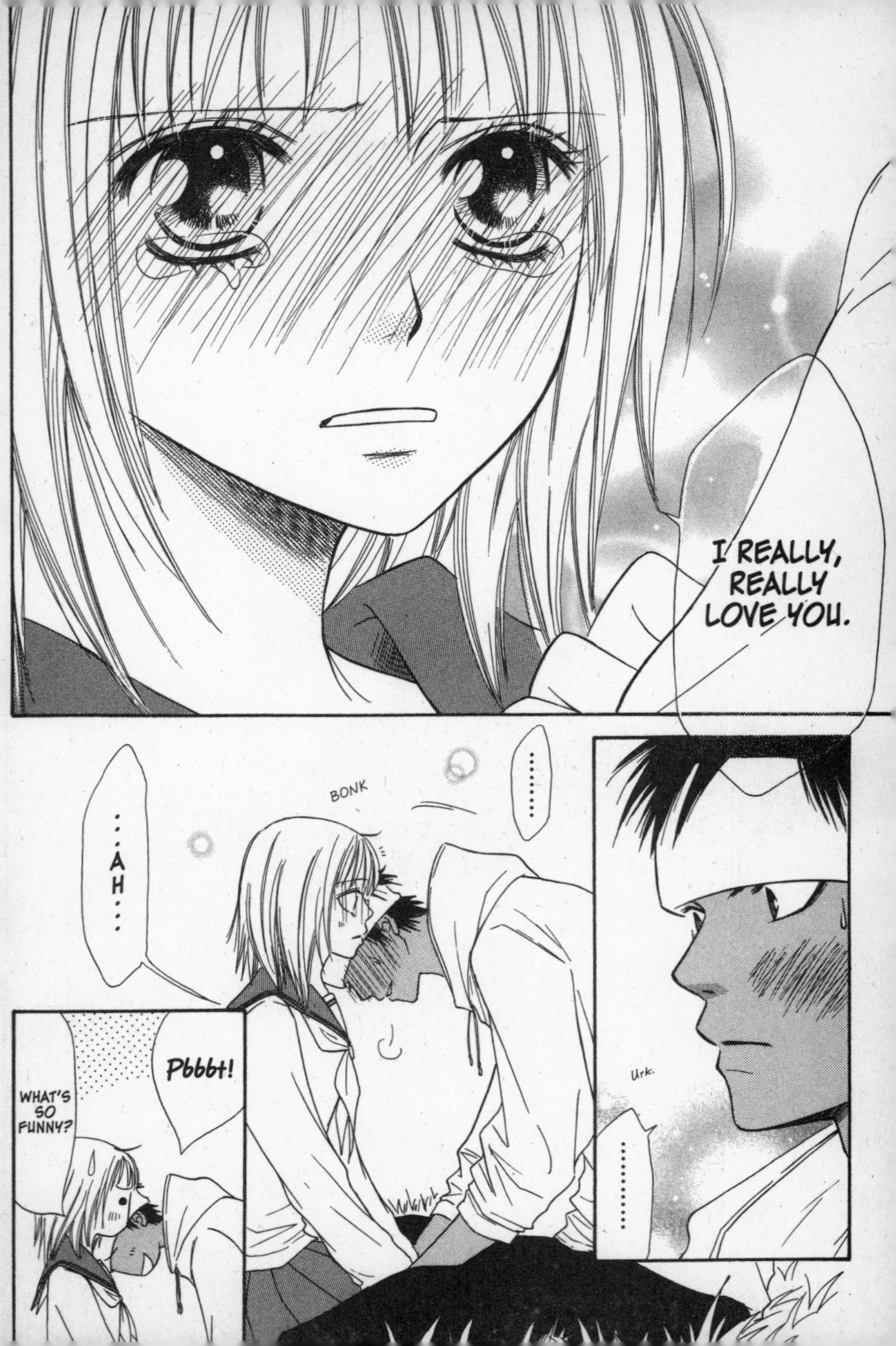
I REALLY, REALLY LOVE YOU.
Urk.
......
......
BONK
...AH...
Pbbbt!
WHAT'S SO FUNNY?

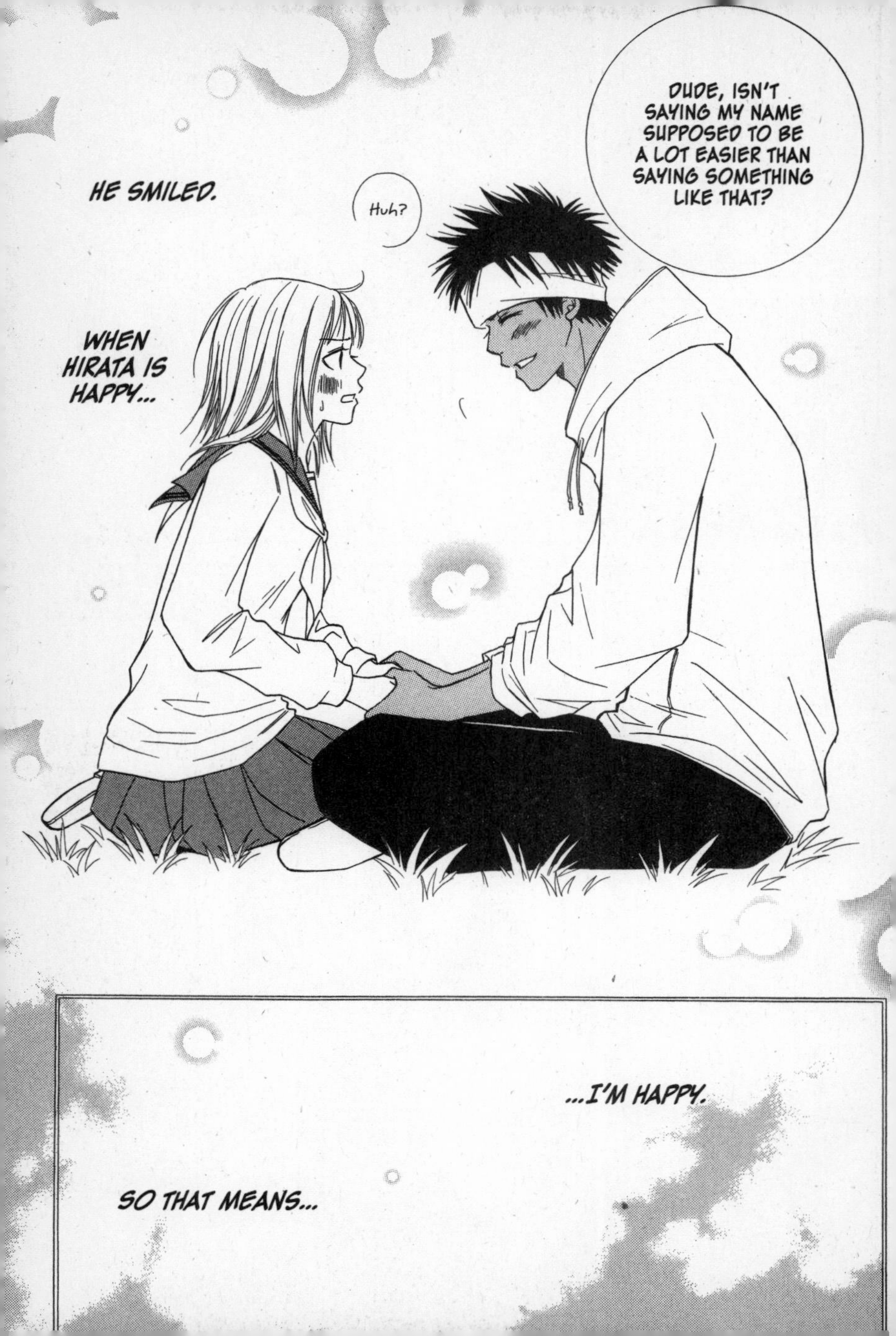
DUDE, ISN'T SAYING MY NAME SUPPOSED TO BE A LOT EASIER THAN SAYING SOMETHING LIKE THAT?
Huh?
HE SMILED.
WHEN HIRATA IS HAPPY...
...I'M HAPPY.
SO THAT MEANS...

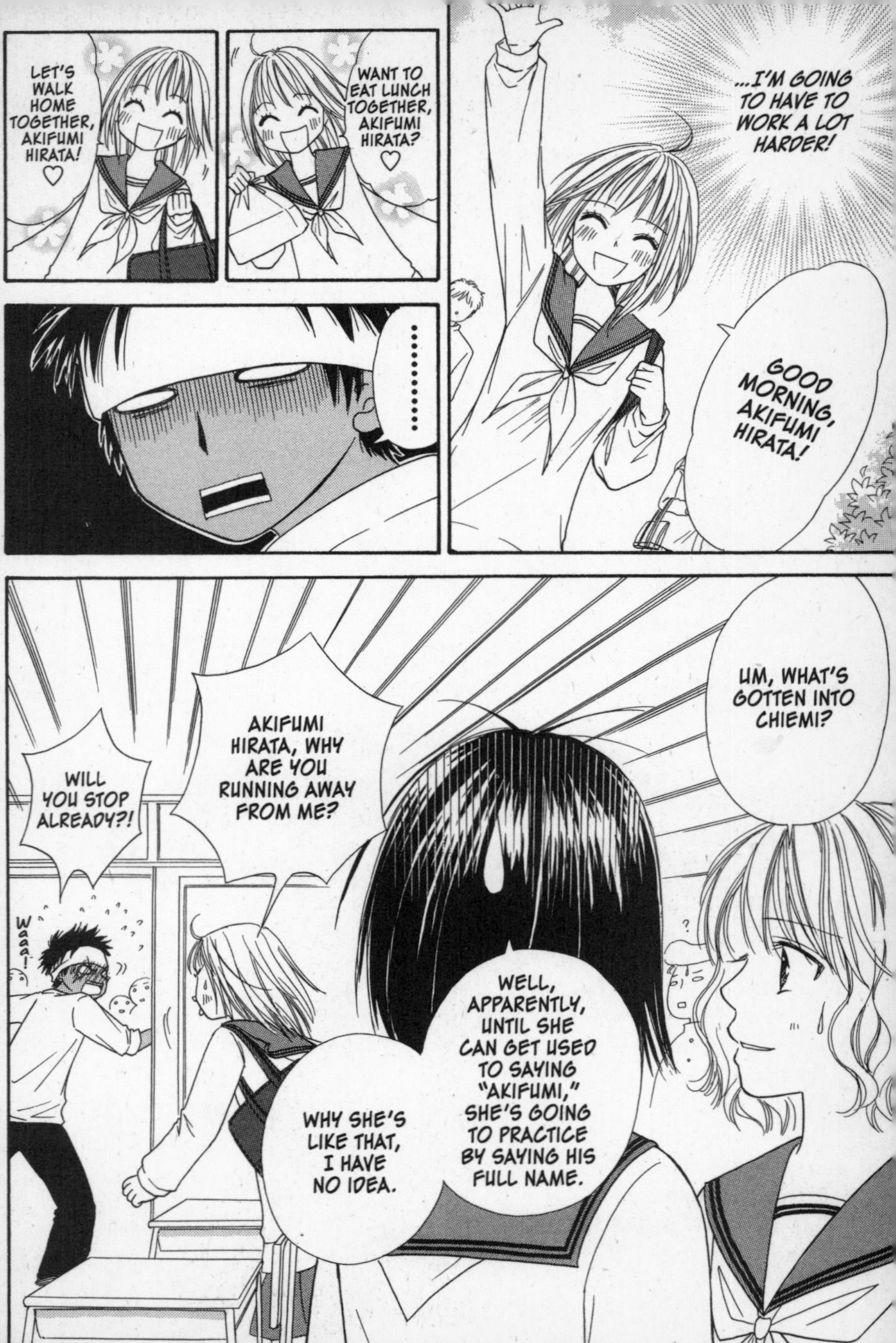
...I'M GOING TO HAVE TO WORK A LOT HARDER!
GOOD MORNING, AKIFUMI HIRATA!
WANT TO EAT LUNCH TOGETHER, AKIFUMI HIRATA? ♡
LET'S WALK HOME TOGETHER, AKIFUMI HIRATA! ♡
....
UM, WHAT'S GOTTEN INTO CHIEMI?
AKIFUMI HIRATA, WHY ARE YOU RUNNING AWAY FROM ME?
WILL YOU STOP ALREADY?!
Waaa!
WELL, APPARENTLY, UNTIL SHE CAN GET USED TO SAYING "AKIFUMI," SHE'S GOING TO PRACTICE BY SAYING HIS FULL NAME.
WHY SHE'S LIKE THAT, I HAVE NO IDEA.

Ch. 9 My Precious Cinderella

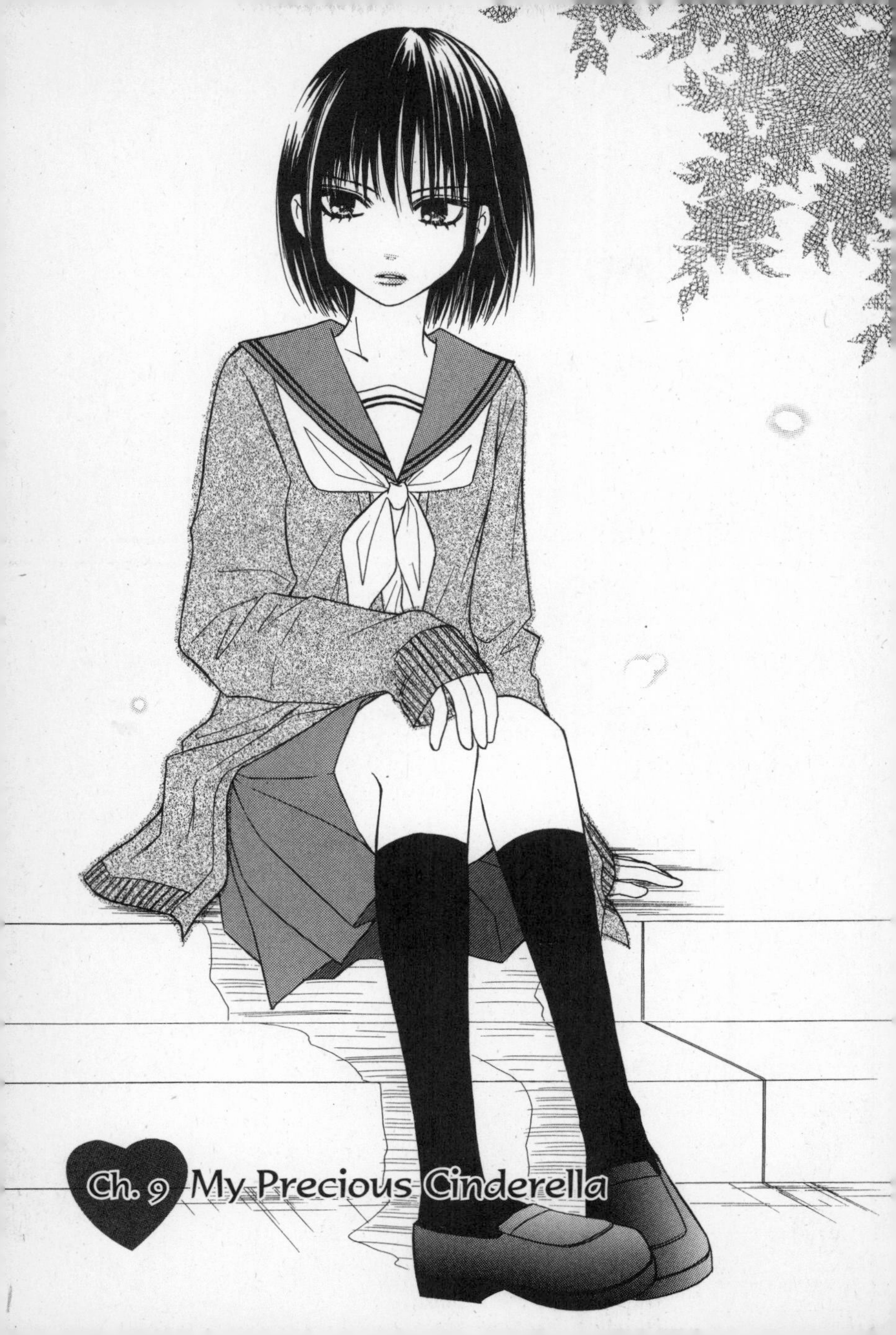

LOVE ATTACK™

JUNAI TOKKO TAICHO!

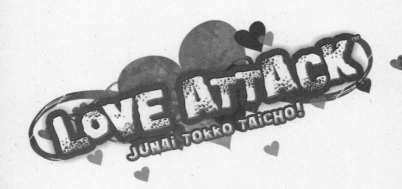

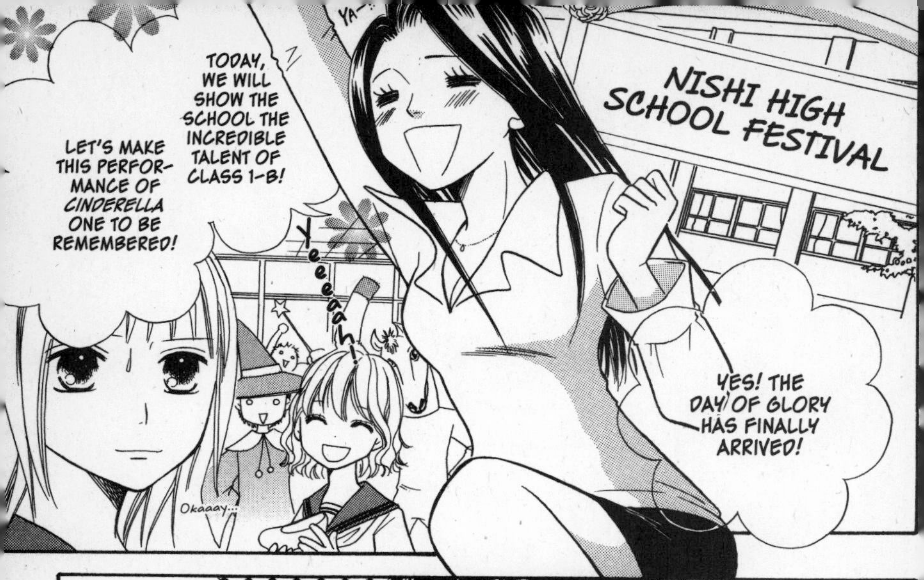
NISHI HIGH SCHOOL FESTIVAL
YA—
YES! THE DAY OF GLORY HAS FINALLY ARRIVED!
TODAY, WE WILL SHOW THE SCHOOL THE INCREDIBLE TALENT OF CLASS 1-B!
LET'S MAKE THIS PERFORMANCE OF CINDERELLA ONE TO BE REMEMBERED!
Yeeeaah!
Okaaay...

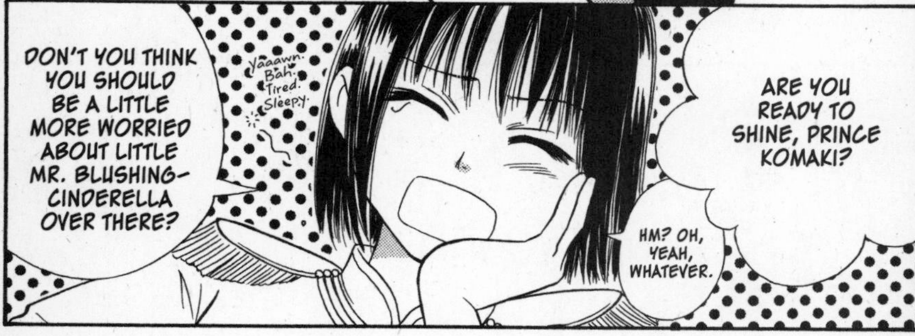
ARE YOU READY TO SHINE, PRINCE KOMAKI?
HM? OH, YEAH, WHATEVER.
Yaaawn. Bah. Tired. Sleepy.
DON'T YOU THINK YOU SHOULD BE A LITTLE MORE WORRIED ABOUT LITTLE MR. BLUSHING-CINDERELLA OVER THERE?

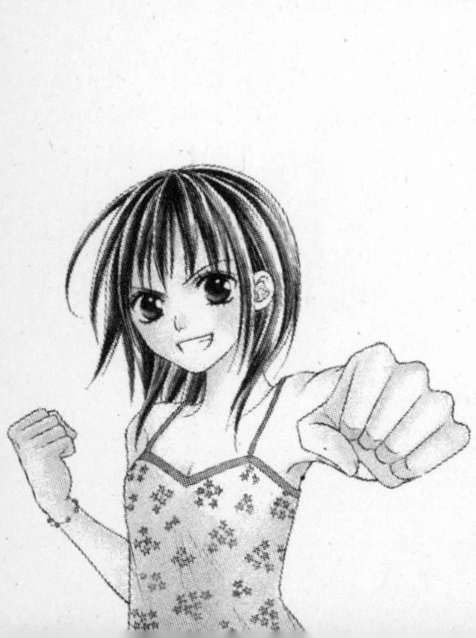

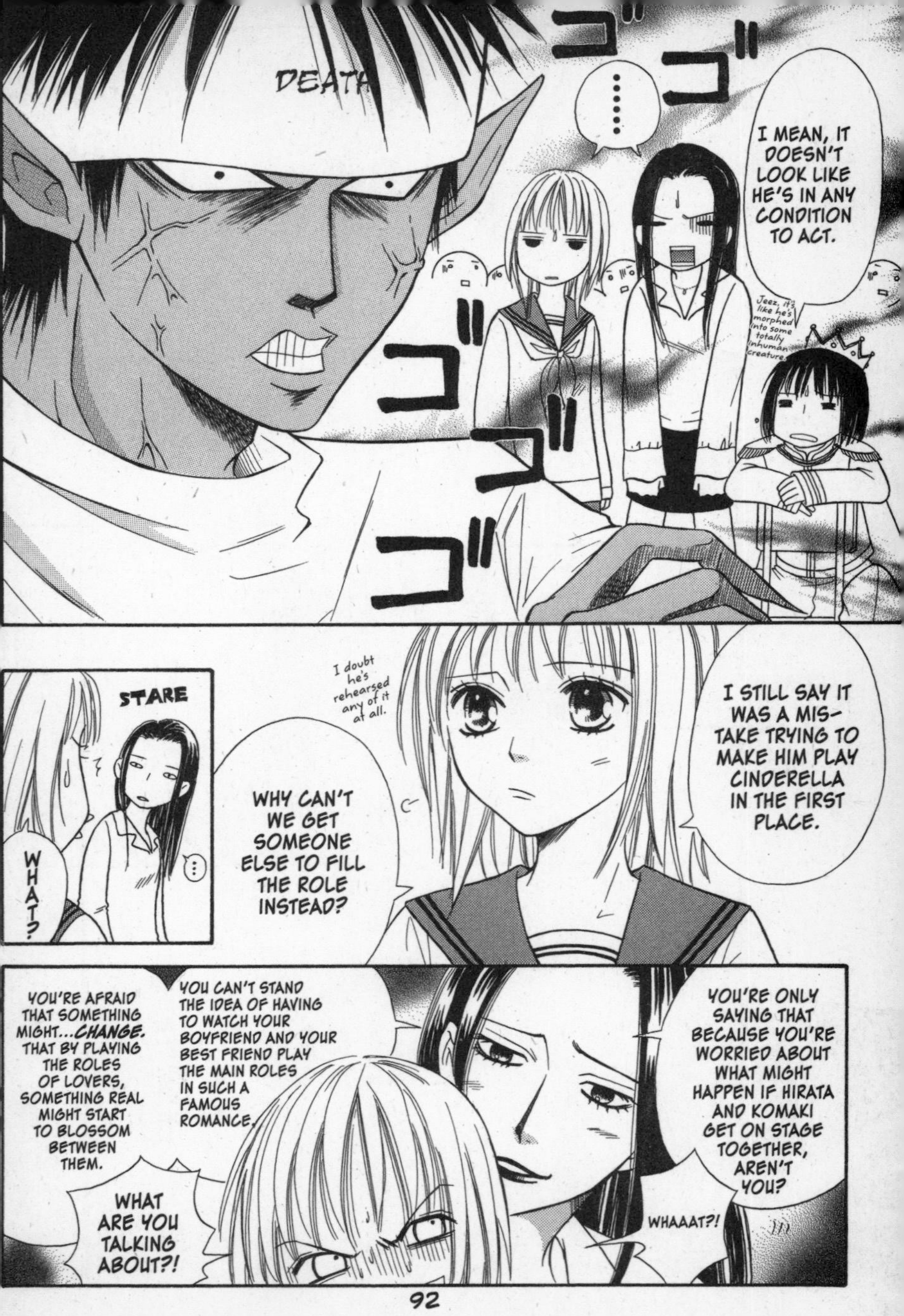
ゴゴ
I MEAN, IT DOESN'T LOOK LIKE HE'S IN ANY CONDITION TO ACT.
......
DEATH
Jeez, it's like he's morphed into some totally inhuman creature.
ゴゴゴ
I STILL SAY IT WAS A MIS-TAKE TRYING TO MAKE HIM PLAY CINDERELLA IN THE FIRST PLACE.
I doubt he's rehearsed any of it at all.
WHY CAN'T WE GET SOMEONE ELSE TO FILL THE ROLE INSTEAD?
STARE
...
WHAT?
YOU'RE ONLY SAYING THAT BECAUSE YOU'RE WORRIED ABOUT WHAT MIGHT HAPPEN IF HIRATA AND KOMAKI GET ON STAGE TOGETHER, AREN'T YOU?
YOU CAN'T STAND THE IDEA OF HAVING TO WATCH YOUR BOYFRIEND AND YOUR BEST FRIEND PLAY THE MAIN ROLES IN SUCH A FAMOUS ROMANCE.
YOU'RE AFRAID THAT SOMETHING MIGHT...CHANGE. THAT BY PLAYING THE ROLES OF LOVERS, SOMETHING REAL MIGHT START TO BLOSSOM BETWEEN THEM.
WHAAAT?!
WHAT ARE YOU TALKING ABOUT?!

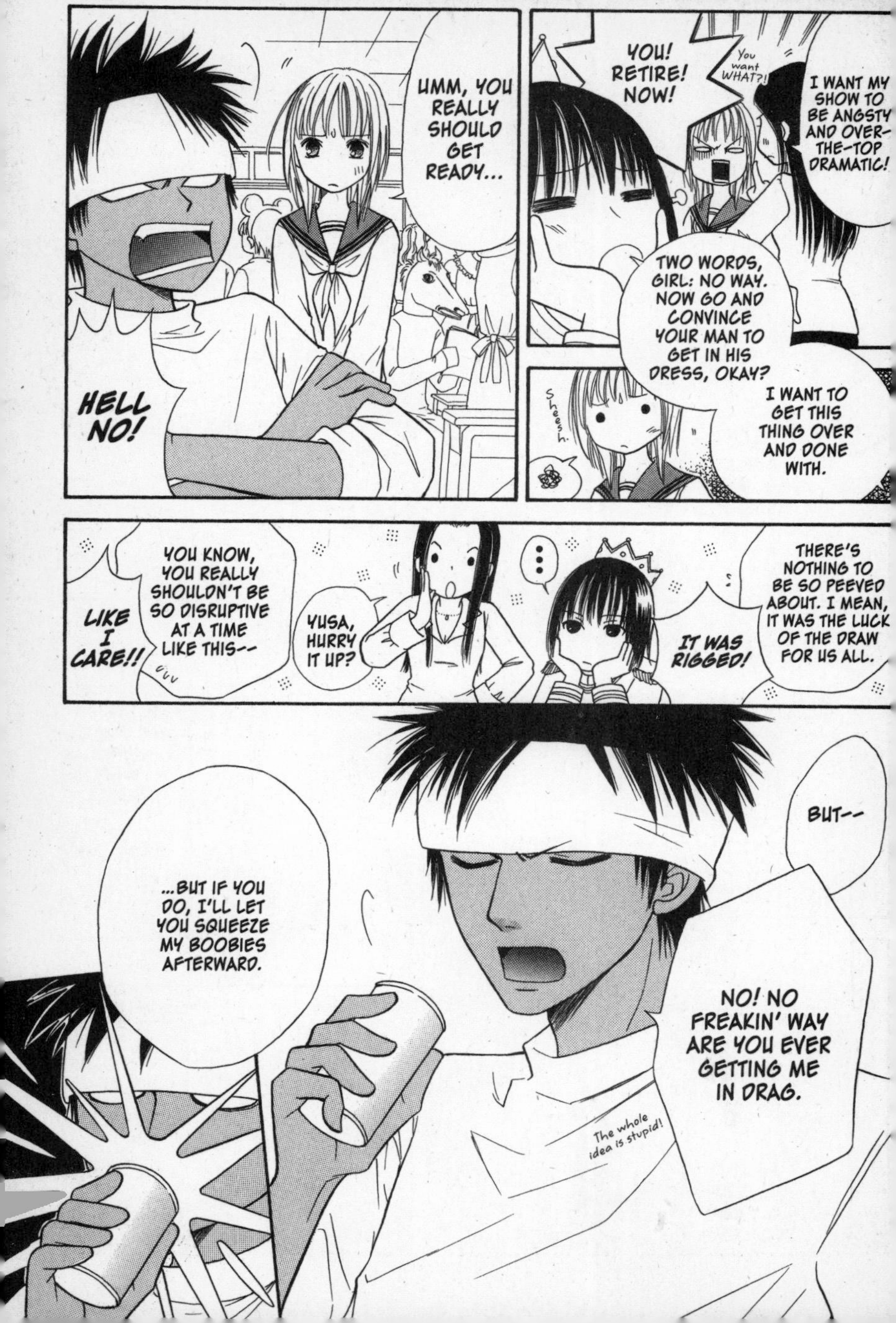
I WANT MY SHOW TO BE ANGSTY AND OVER-THE-TOP DRAMATIC!
You want WHAT?!
YOU! RETIRE! NOW!
TWO WORDS, GIRL: NO WAY. NOW GO AND CONVINCE YOUR MAN TO GET IN HIS DRESS, OKAY?
I WANT TO GET THIS THING OVER AND DONE WITH.
Sheesh.
UMM, YOU REALLY SHOULD GET READY...
HELL NO!
THERE'S NOTHING TO BE SO PEEVED ABOUT. I MEAN, IT WAS THE LUCK OF THE DRAW FOR US ALL.
IT WAS RIGGED!
YUSA, HURRY IT UP?
YOU KNOW, YOU REALLY SHOULDN'T BE SO DISRUPTIVE AT A TIME LIKE THIS--
LIKE I CARE!!
BUT--
NO! NO FREAKIN' WAY ARE YOU EVER GETTING ME IN DRAG.
The whole idea is stupid!
...BUT IF YOU DO, I'LL LET YOU SQUEEZE MY BOOBIES AFTERWARD.

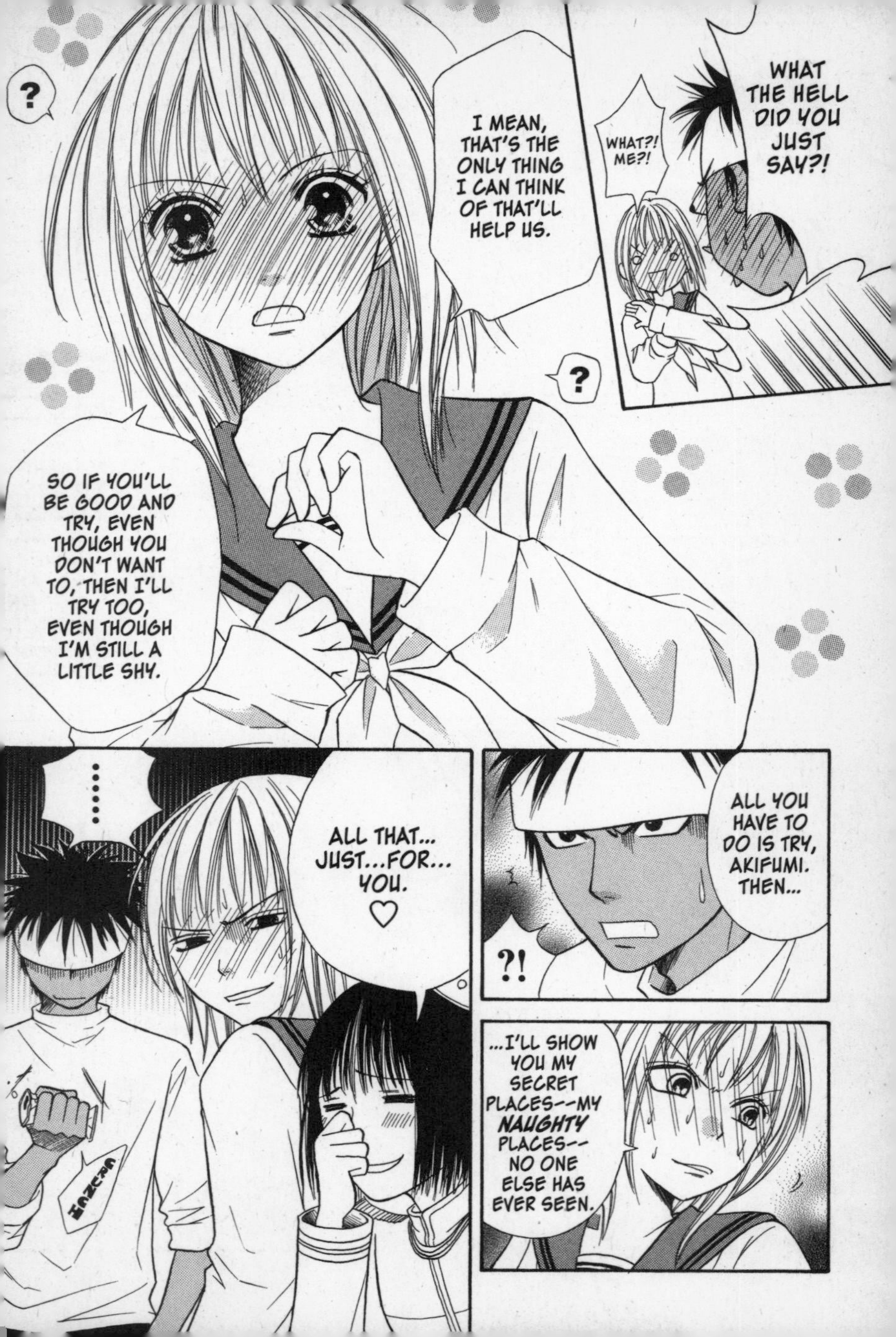
WHAT THE HELL DID YOU JUST SAY?!
WHAT?! ME?!
I MEAN, THAT'S THE ONLY THING I CAN THINK OF THAT'LL HELP US.
?
?
SO IF YOU'LL BE GOOD AND TRY, EVEN THOUGH YOU DON'T WANT TO, THEN I'LL TRY TOO, EVEN THOUGH I'M STILL A LITTLE SHY.
ALL YOU HAVE TO DO IS TRY, AKIFUMI. THEN...
?!
...I'LL SHOW YOU MY SECRET PLACES--MY *NAUGHTY* PLACES--NO ONE ELSE HAS EVER SEEN.
......
ALL THAT... JUST...FOR... YOU. ♥

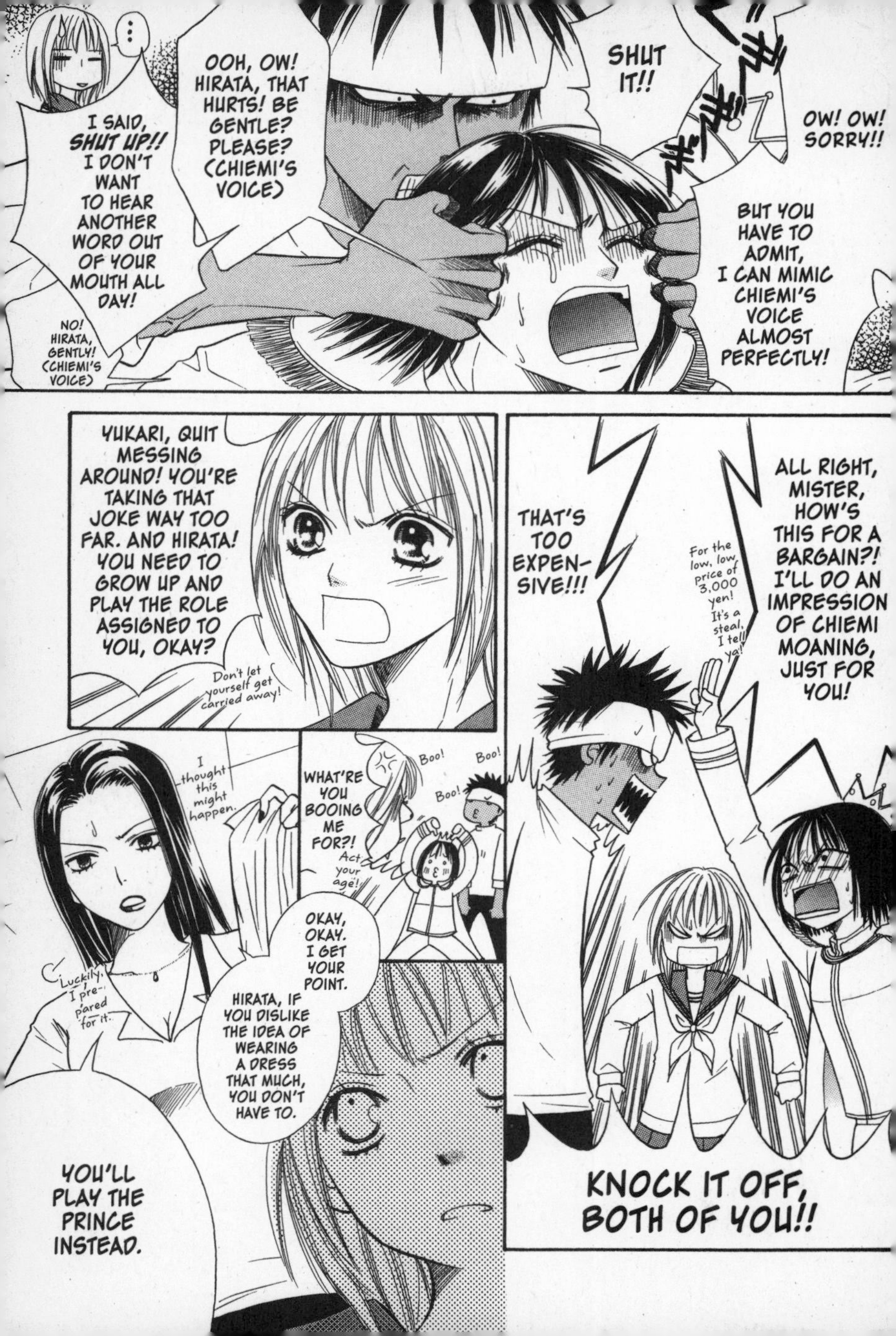
SHUT IT!!
OW! OW! SORRY!!
BUT YOU HAVE TO ADMIT, I CAN MIMIC CHIEMI'S VOICE ALMOST PERFECTLY!
OOH, OW! HIRATA, THAT HURTS! BE GENTLE? PLEASE? (CHIEMI'S VOICE)
...
I SAID, SHUT UP!! I DON'T WANT TO HEAR ANOTHER WORD OUT OF YOUR MOUTH ALL DAY!
NO! HIRATA, GENTLY! (CHIEMI'S VOICE)
ALL RIGHT, MISTER, HOW'S THIS FOR A BARGAIN?! I'LL DO AN IMPRESSION OF CHIEMI MOANING, JUST FOR YOU!
For the low, low price of 3,000 yen! It's a steal, I tell ya!
THAT'S TOO EXPEN-SIVE!!!
KNOCK IT OFF, BOTH OF YOU!!
YUKARI, QUIT MESSING AROUND! YOU'RE TAKING THAT JOKE WAY TOO FAR. AND HIRATA! YOU NEED TO GROW UP AND PLAY THE ROLE ASSIGNED TO YOU, OKAY?
Don't let yourself get carried away!
Boo!
Boo!
Boo!
WHAT'RE YOU BOOING ME FOR?!
Act your age!
I thought this might happen.
OKAY, OKAY. I GET YOUR POINT.
Luckily, I pre-pared for it.
HIRATA, IF YOU DISLIKE THE IDEA OF WEARING A DRESS THAT MUCH, YOU DON'T HAVE TO.
YOU'LL PLAY THE PRINCE INSTEAD.

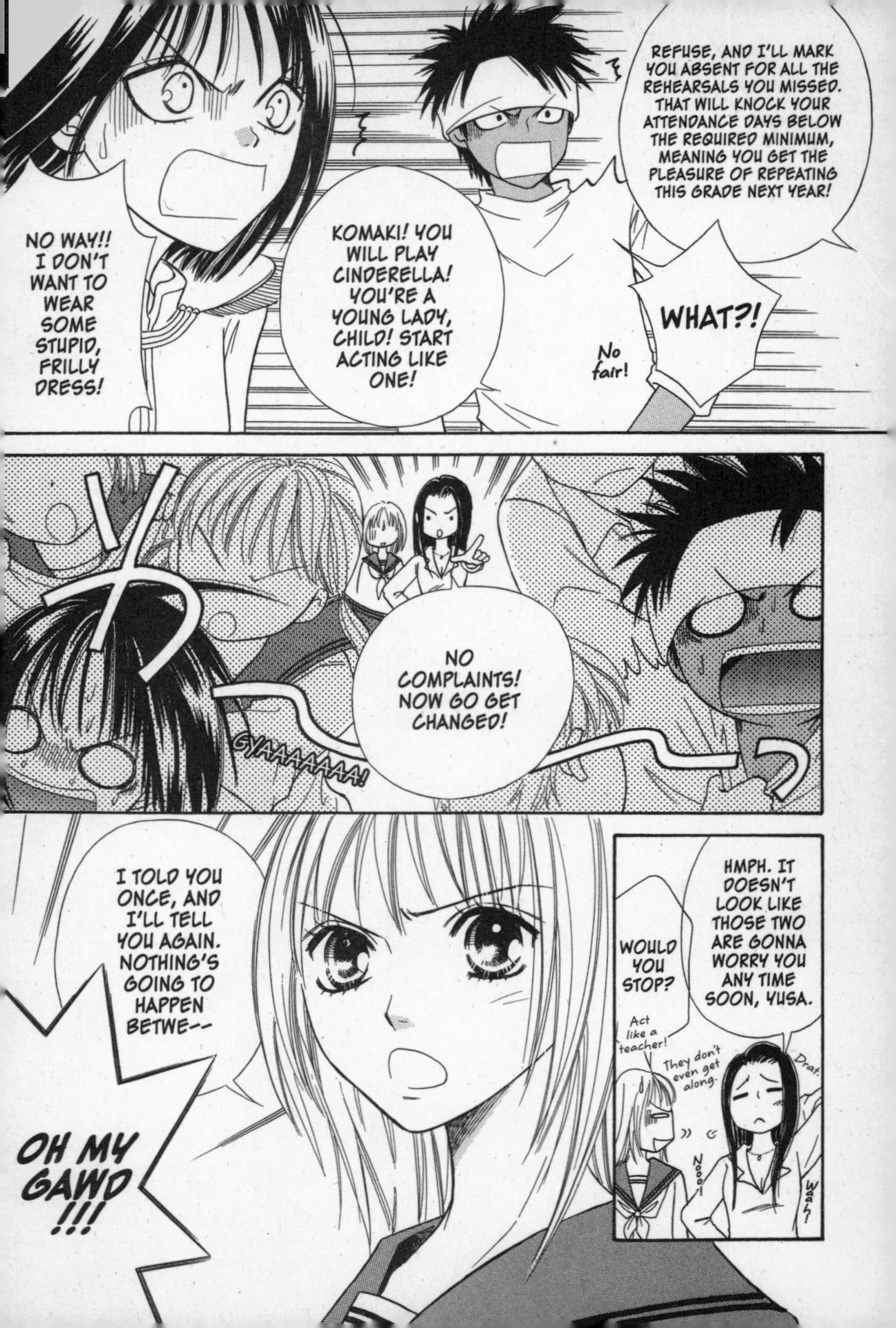
REFUSE, AND I'LL MARK YOU ABSENT FOR ALL THE REHEARSALS YOU MISSED. THAT WILL KNOCK YOUR ATTENDANCE DAYS BELOW THE REQUIRED MINIMUM, MEANING YOU GET THE PLEASURE OF REPEATING THIS GRADE NEXT YEAR!
KOMAKI! YOU WILL PLAY CINDERELLA! YOU'RE A YOUNG LADY, CHILD! START ACTING LIKE ONE!
WHAT?!
No fair!
NO WAY!! I DON'T WANT TO WEAR SOME STUPID, FRILLY DRESS!
NO COMPLAINTS! NOW GO GET CHANGED!
GYAAAAAAAA!
HMPH. IT DOESN'T LOOK LIKE THOSE TWO ARE GONNA WORRY YOU ANY TIME SOON, YUSA.
WOULD YOU STOP?
Act like a teacher!
They don't even get along.
Drat.
Nooo!
Waah!
I TOLD YOU ONCE, AND I'LL TELL YOU AGAIN. NOTHING'S GOING TO HAPPEN BETWE--
OH MY GAWD!!!

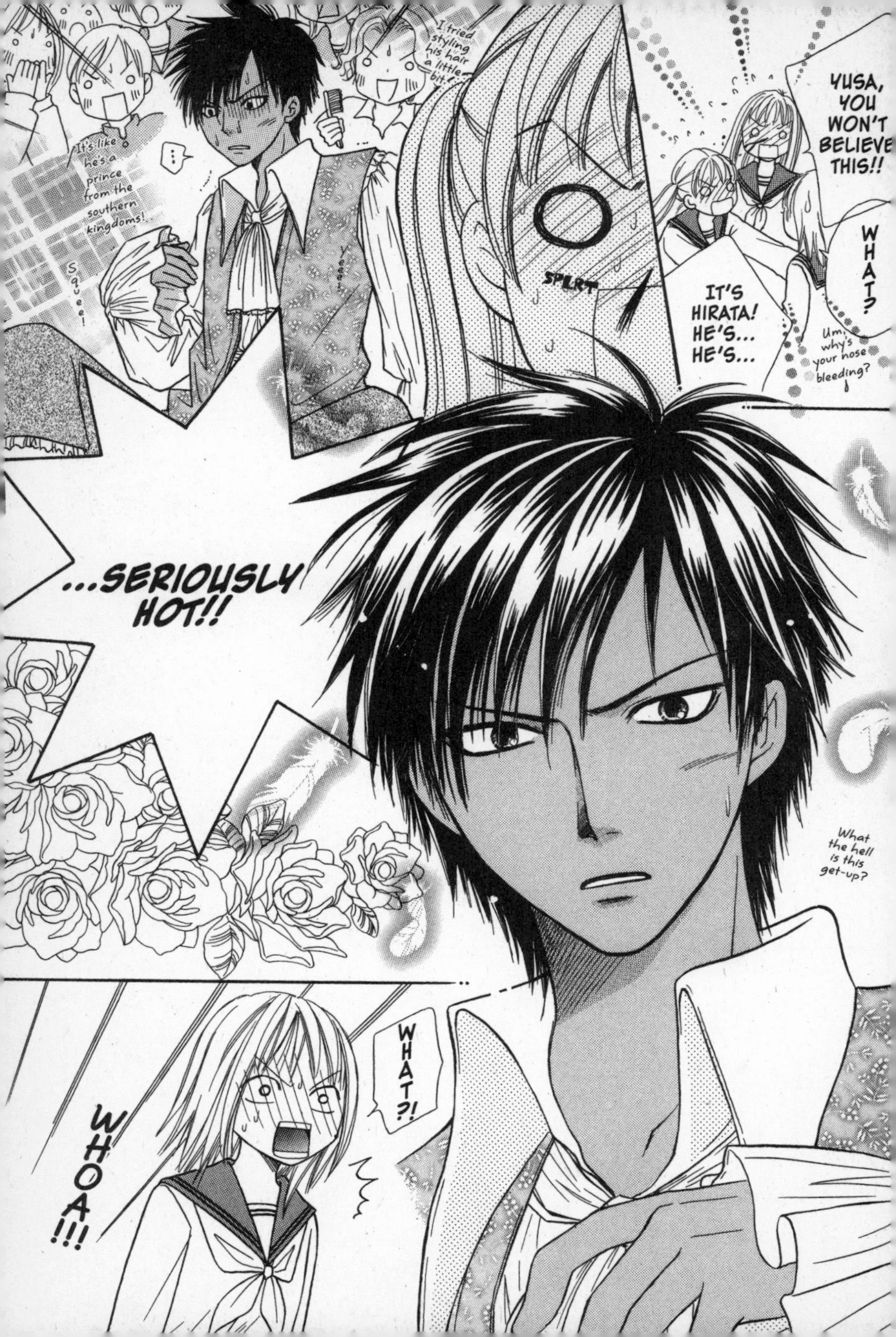
YUSA, YOU WON'T BELIEVE THIS!!
WHAT?
IT'S HIRATA! HE'S... HE'S...
Um, why's your nose bleeding?
SPLRT
I tried styling his hair a little bit...
...
It's like he's a prince from the southern kingdoms!
...
Yeee!
Squee!
...SERIOUSLY HOT!!
What the hell is this get-up?
WHAT?!
WHOA!!!

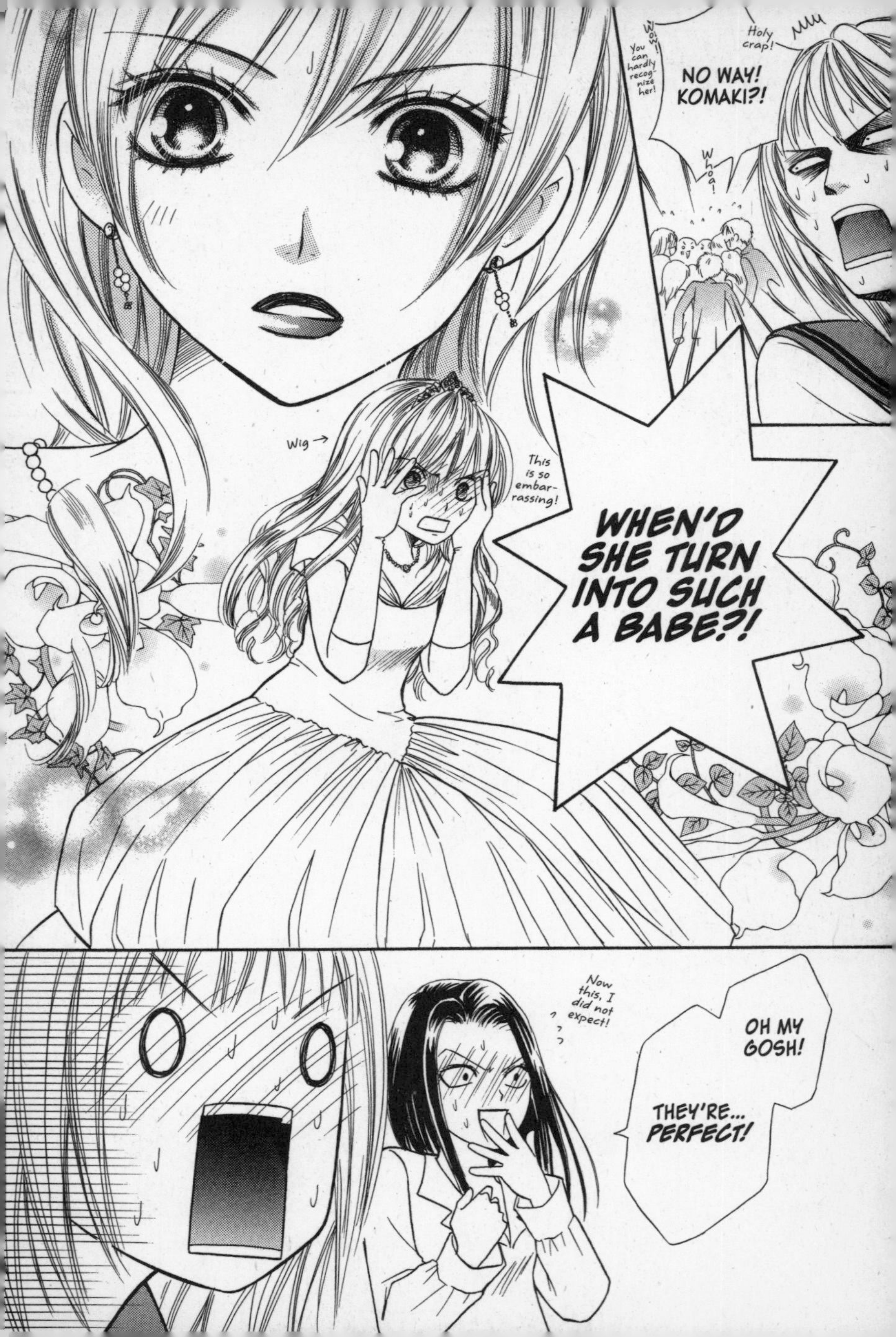
Holy crap!
Wow!
You can hardly recognize her!
NO WAY! KOMAKI?!
Whoa!
WHEN'D SHE TURN INTO SUCH A BABE?!
This is so embarrassing!
Wig →
OH MY GOSH!
THEY'RE... PERFECT!
Now this, I did not expect!

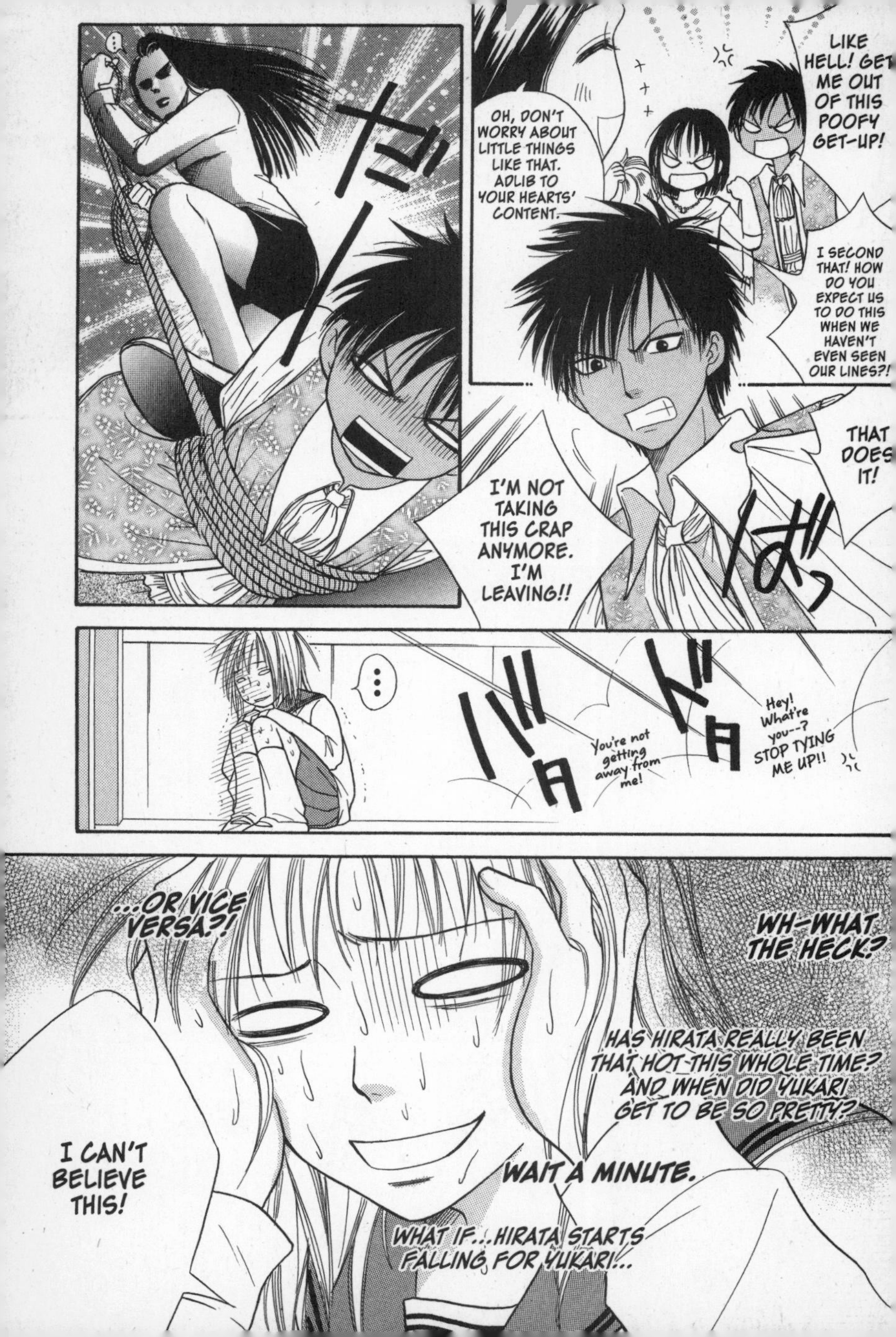
LIKE HELL! GET ME OUT OF THIS POOFY GET-UP!
I SECOND THAT! HOW DO YOU EXPECT US TO DO THIS WHEN WE HAVEN'T EVEN SEEN OUR LINES?!
OH, DON'T WORRY ABOUT LITTLE THINGS LIKE THAT. ADLIB TO YOUR HEARTS' CONTENT.
THAT DOES IT!
I'M NOT TAKING THIS CRAP ANYMORE. I'M LEAVING!!
...
Hey! What're you--? STOP TYING ME UP!!
You're not getting away from me!
...
WH-WHAT THE HECK?
HAS HIRATA REALLY BEEN THAT HOT THIS WHOLE TIME? AND WHEN DID YUKARI GET TO BE SO PRETTY?
WAIT A MINUTE.
WHAT IF...HIRATA STARTS FALLING FOR YUKARI...
...OR VICE VERSA?!
I CAN'T BELIEVE THIS!

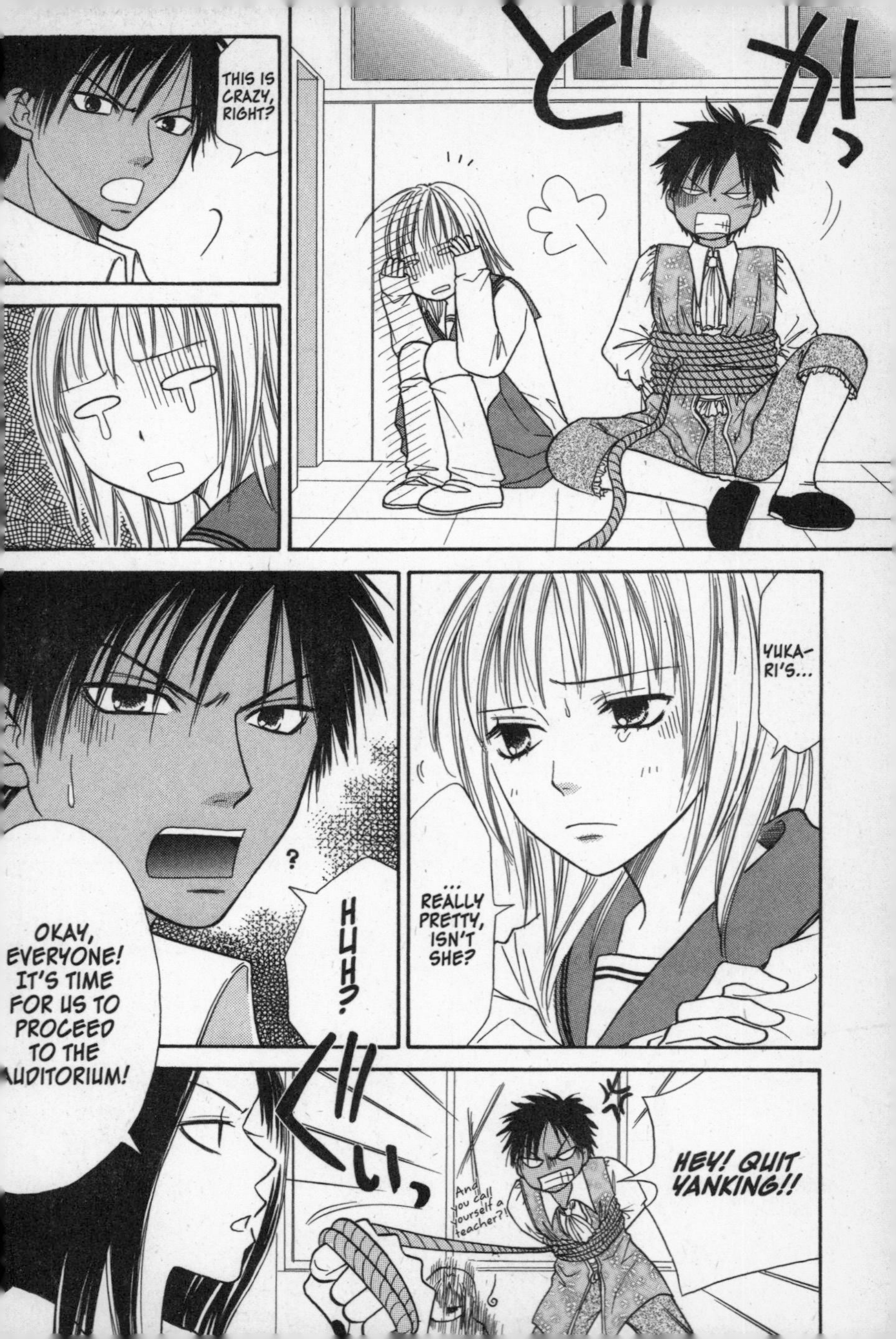
どかっ
THIS IS CRAZY, RIGHT?
YUKA-RI'S...
... REALLY PRETTY, ISN'T SHE?
?
HUH?
HEY! QUIT YANKING!!
And you call yourself a teacher?!
ぐいっ
OKAY, EVERYONE! IT'S TIME FOR US TO PROCEED TO THE AUDITORIUM!

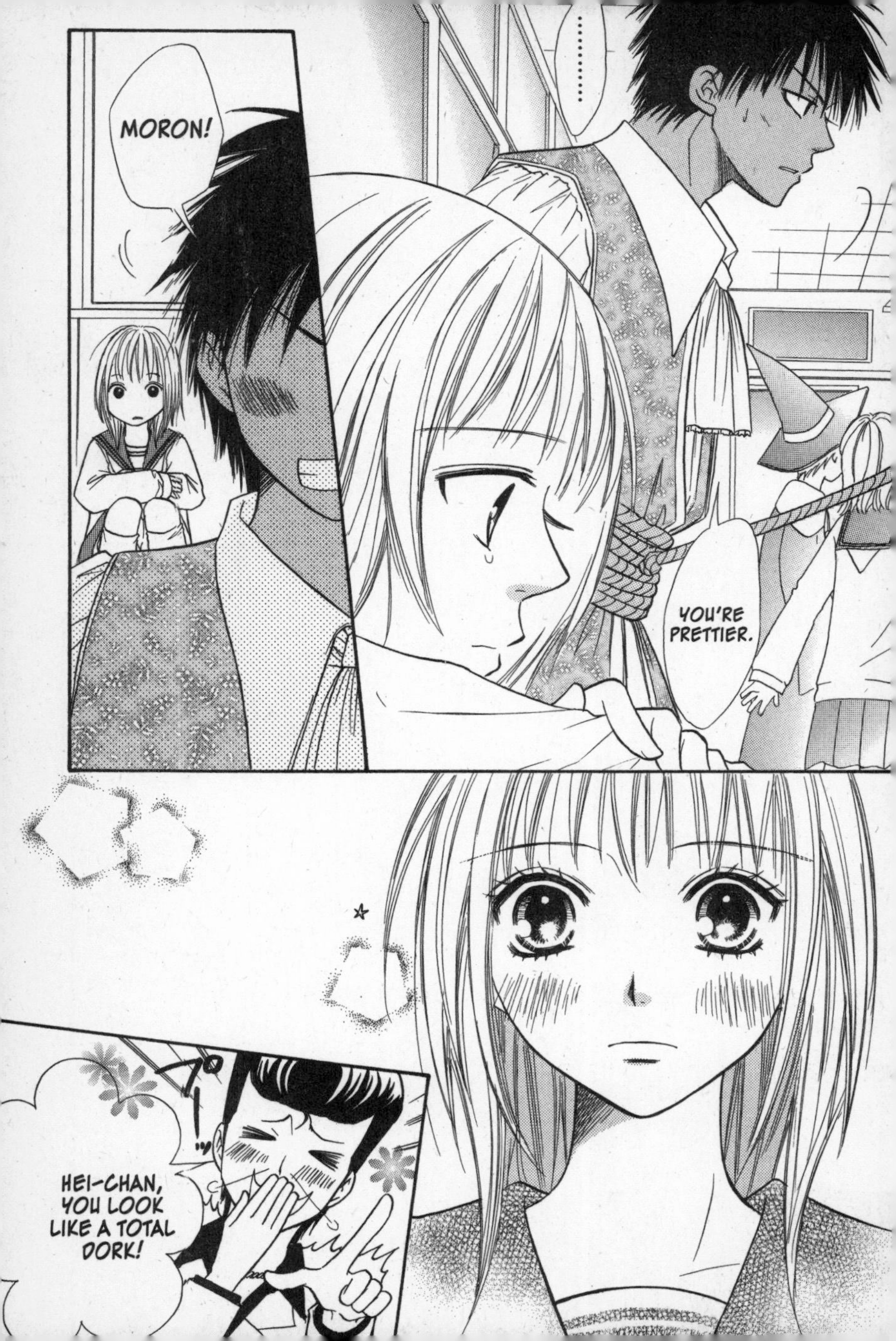
......
YOU'RE PRETTIER.
MORON!
HEI-CHAN, YOU LOOK LIKE A TOTAL DORK!

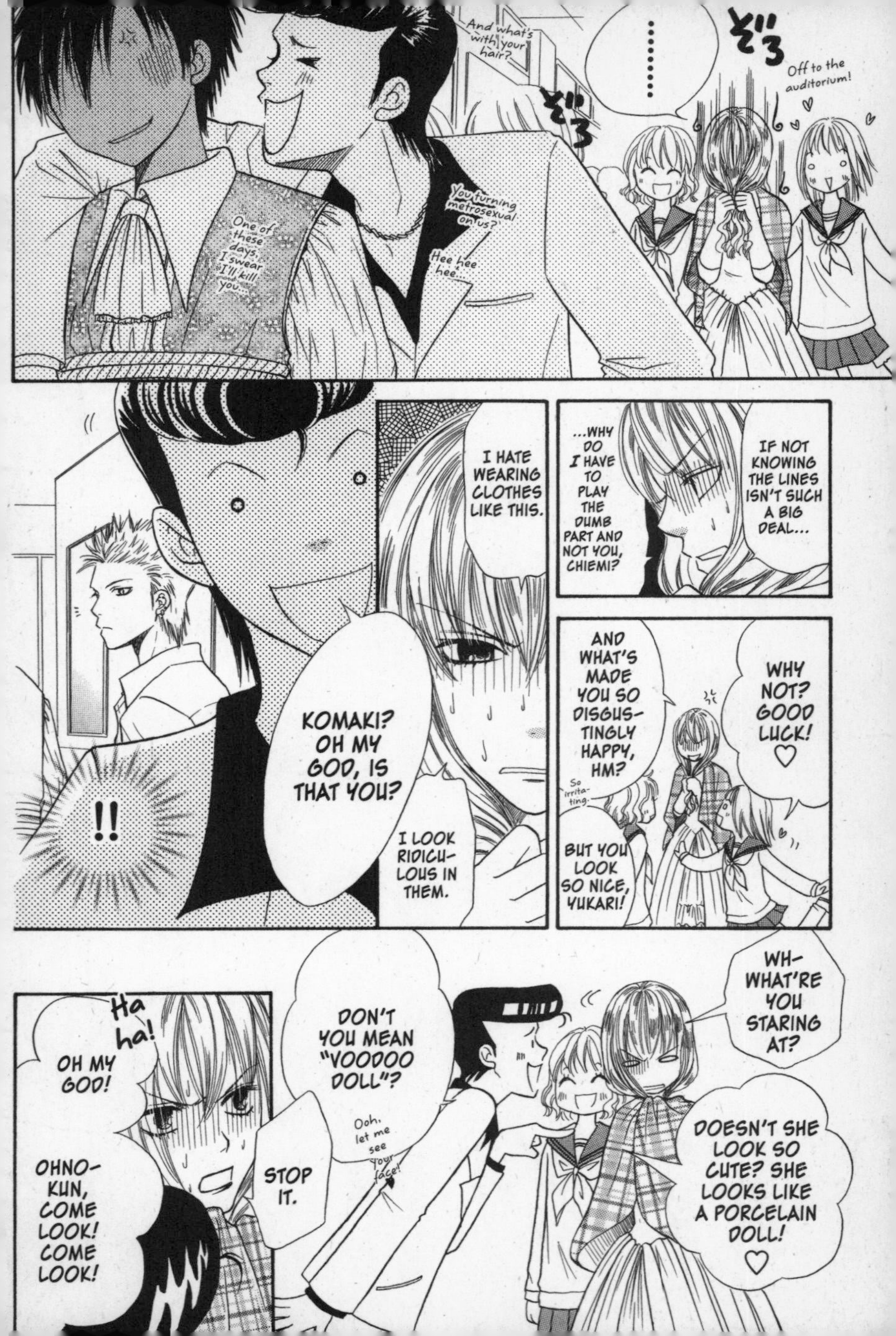
Off to the auditorium!
......
And what's with your hair?
You turning metrosexual on us?
Hee hee hee...
One of these days, I swear I'll kill you...
If not knowing the lines isn't such a big deal...
...Why do I have to play the dumb part and not you, Chiemi?
Why not? Good luck! ♥
And what's made you so disgustingly happy, hm?
So irritating.
But you look so nice, Yukari!
I hate wearing clothes like this.
I look ridiculous in them.
Komaki? Oh my god, is that you?
!!
Wh-what're you staring at?
Doesn't she look so cute? She looks like a porcelain doll! ♥
Don't you mean "voodoo doll"?
Ooh, let me see your face!
Ha ha!
Oh my god!
Stop it.
Ohno-kun, come look! Come look!

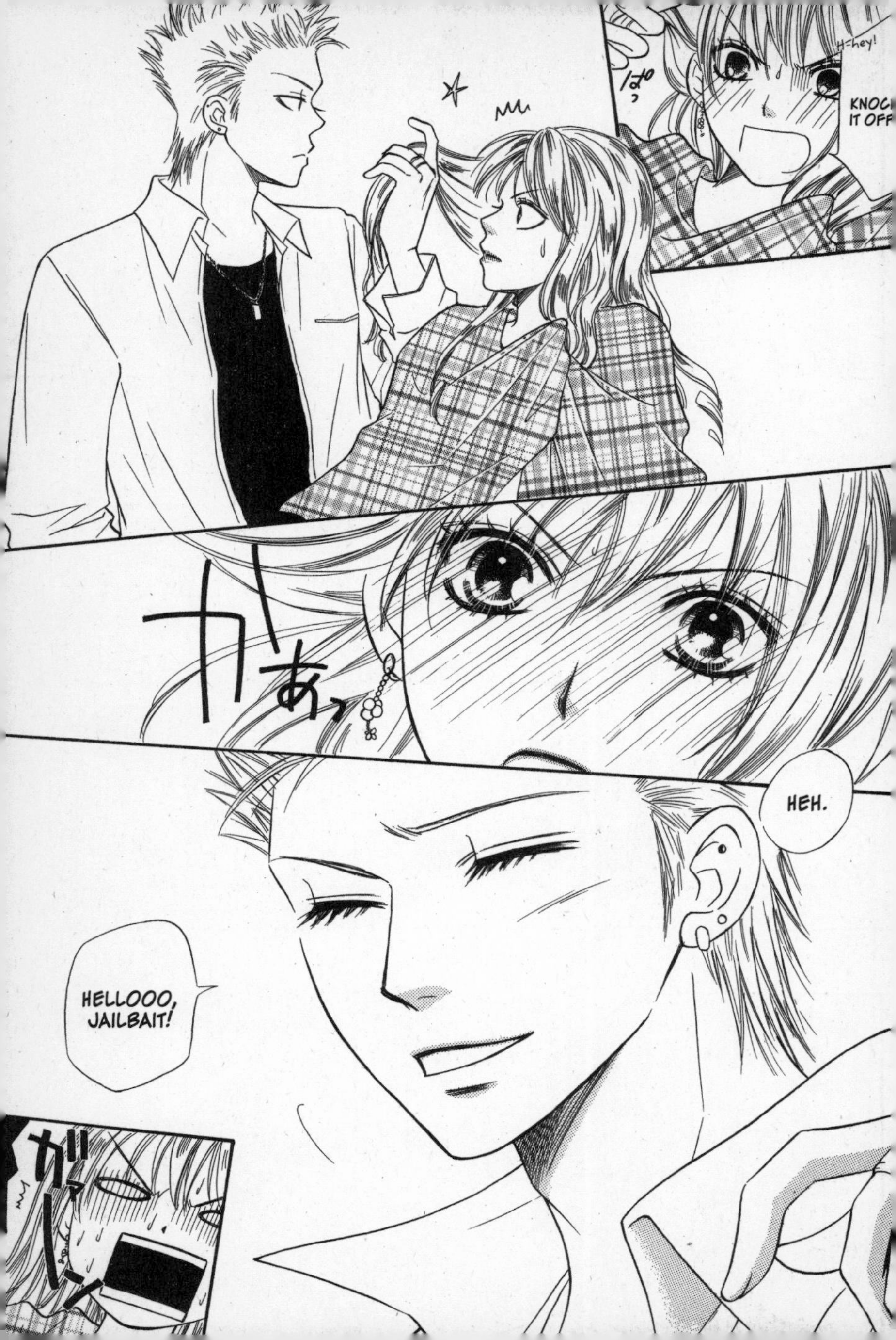
H-hey!
KNOC
IT OFF
かあっ
HEH.
HELLOOO, JAILBAIT!

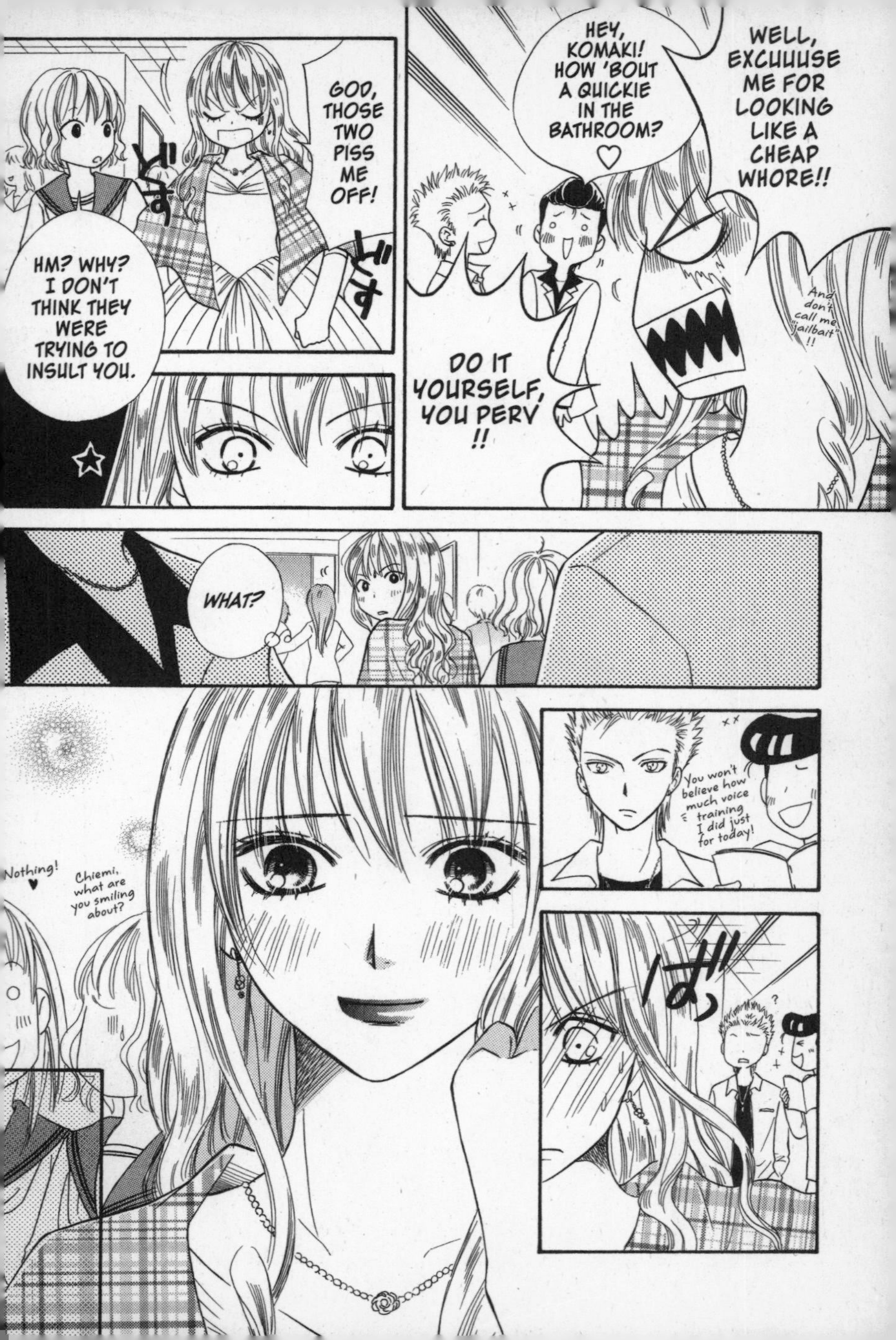
WELL, EXCUUUSE ME FOR LOOKING LIKE A CHEAP WHORE!!
HEY, KOMAKI! HOW 'BOUT A QUICKIE IN THE BATHROOM? ♡
And don't call me "jailbait"!!
DO IT YOURSELF, YOU PERV!!
GOD, THOSE TWO PISS ME OFF!
どす
どす
HM? WHY? I DON'T THINK THEY WERE TRYING TO INSULT YOU.
WHAT?
You won't believe how much voice training I did just for today!
ぱっ
Chiemi, what are you smiling about?
Nothing! ♥

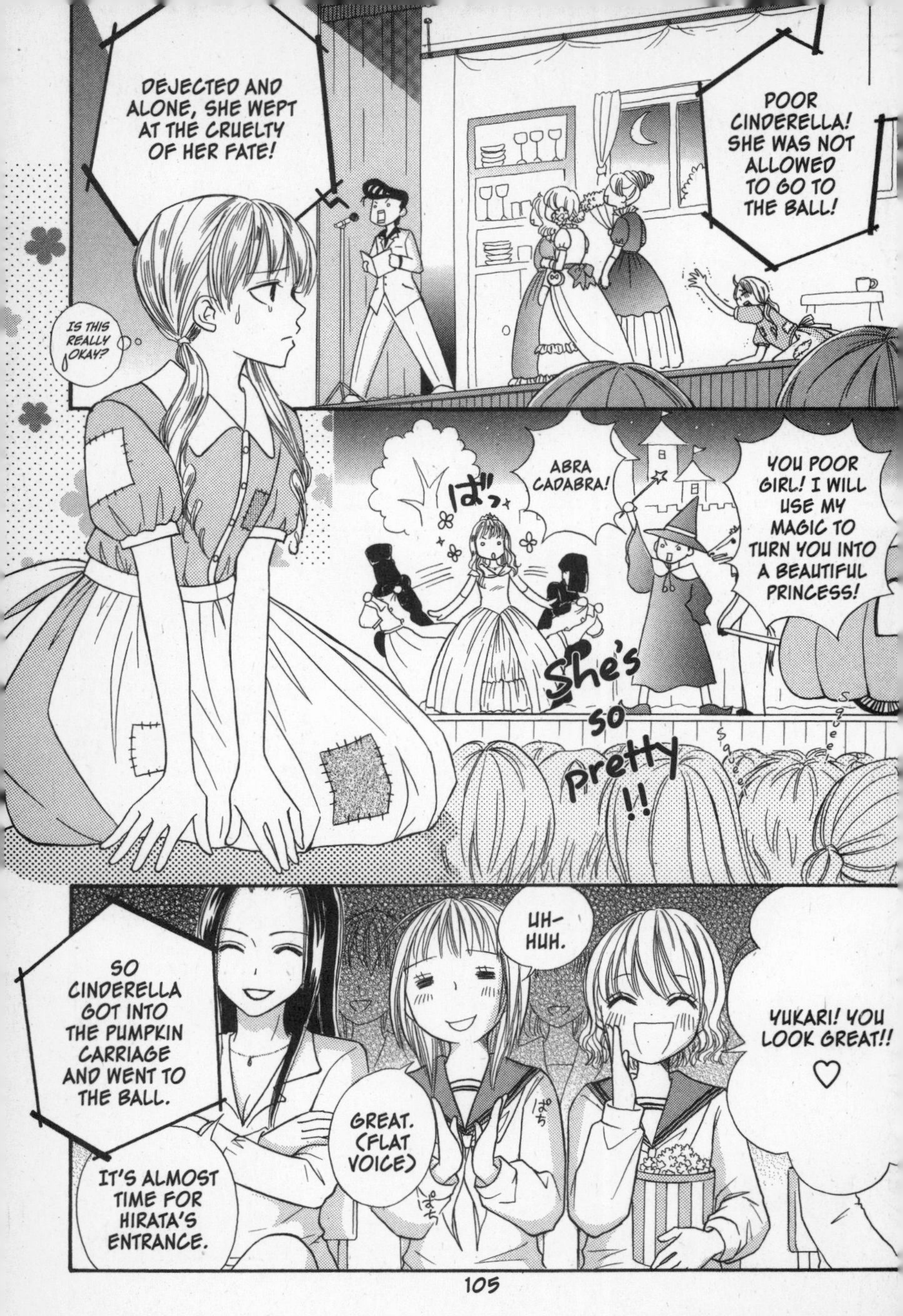
POOR CINDERELLA! SHE WAS NOT ALLOWED TO GO TO THE BALL!
DEJECTED AND ALONE, SHE WEPT AT THE CRUELTY OF HER FATE!
IS THIS REALLY OKAY?
YOU POOR GIRL! I WILL USE MY MAGIC TO TURN YOU INTO A BEAUTIFUL PRINCESS!
ABRA CADABRA!
ぱっ
Squeee
Squeee
She's so pretty!!
YUKARI! YOU LOOK GREAT!! ♡
UH-HUH.
ぱち
GREAT. (FLAT VOICE)
ぱち
SO CINDERELLA GOT INTO THE PUMPKIN CARRIAGE AND WENT TO THE BALL.
IT'S ALMOST TIME FOR HIRATA'S ENTRANCE.

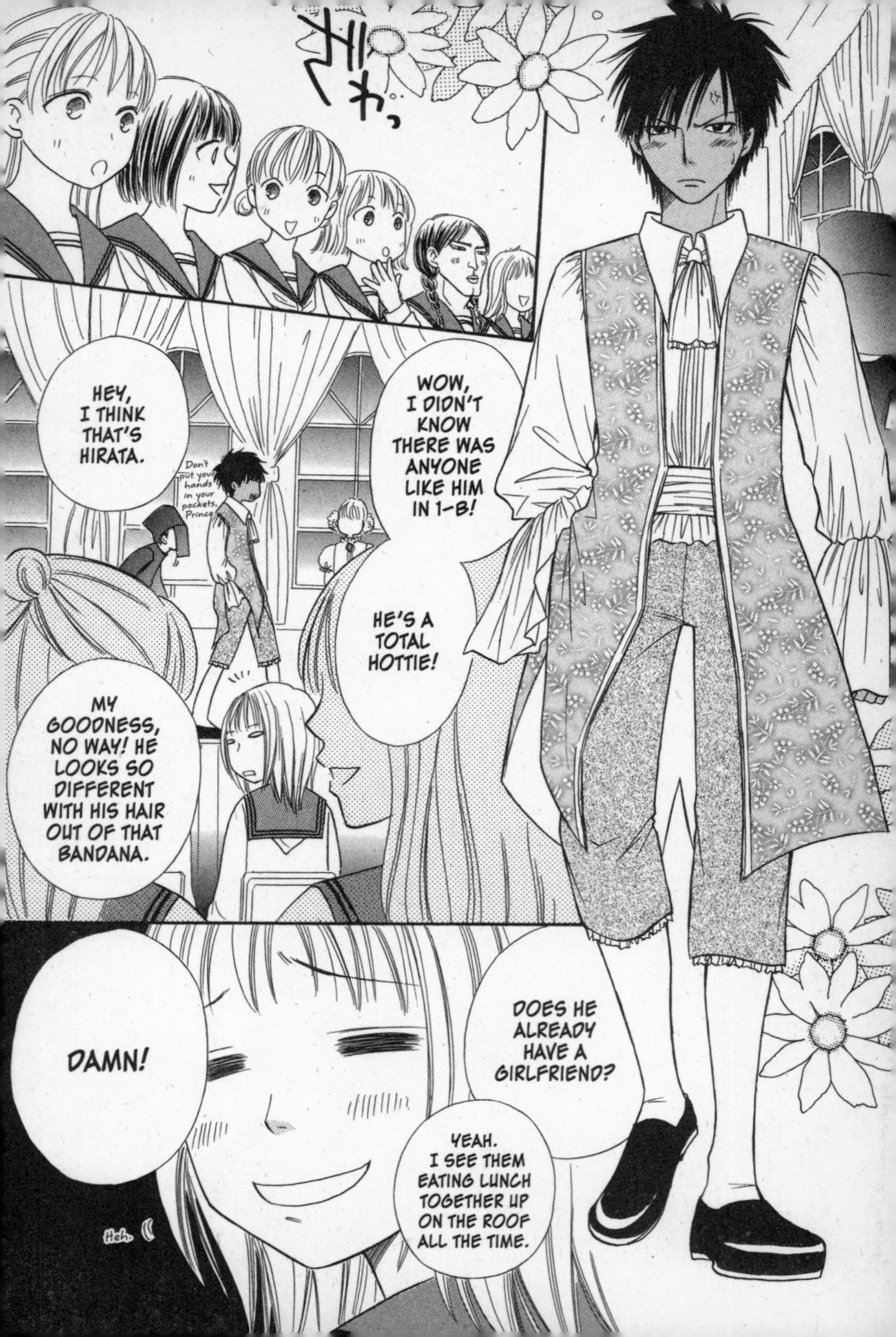
ざわっ
WOW, I DIDN'T KNOW THERE WAS ANYONE LIKE HIM IN 1-B!
HEY, I THINK THAT'S HIRATA.
Don't put your hands in your pockets, Prince.
HE'S A TOTAL HOTTIE!
MY GOODNESS, NO WAY! HE LOOKS SO DIFFERENT WITH HIS HAIR OUT OF THAT BANDANA.
DOES HE ALREADY HAVE A GIRLFRIEND?
DAMN!
YEAH. I SEE THEM EATING LUNCH TOGETHER UP ON THE ROOF ALL THE TIME.
Heh.

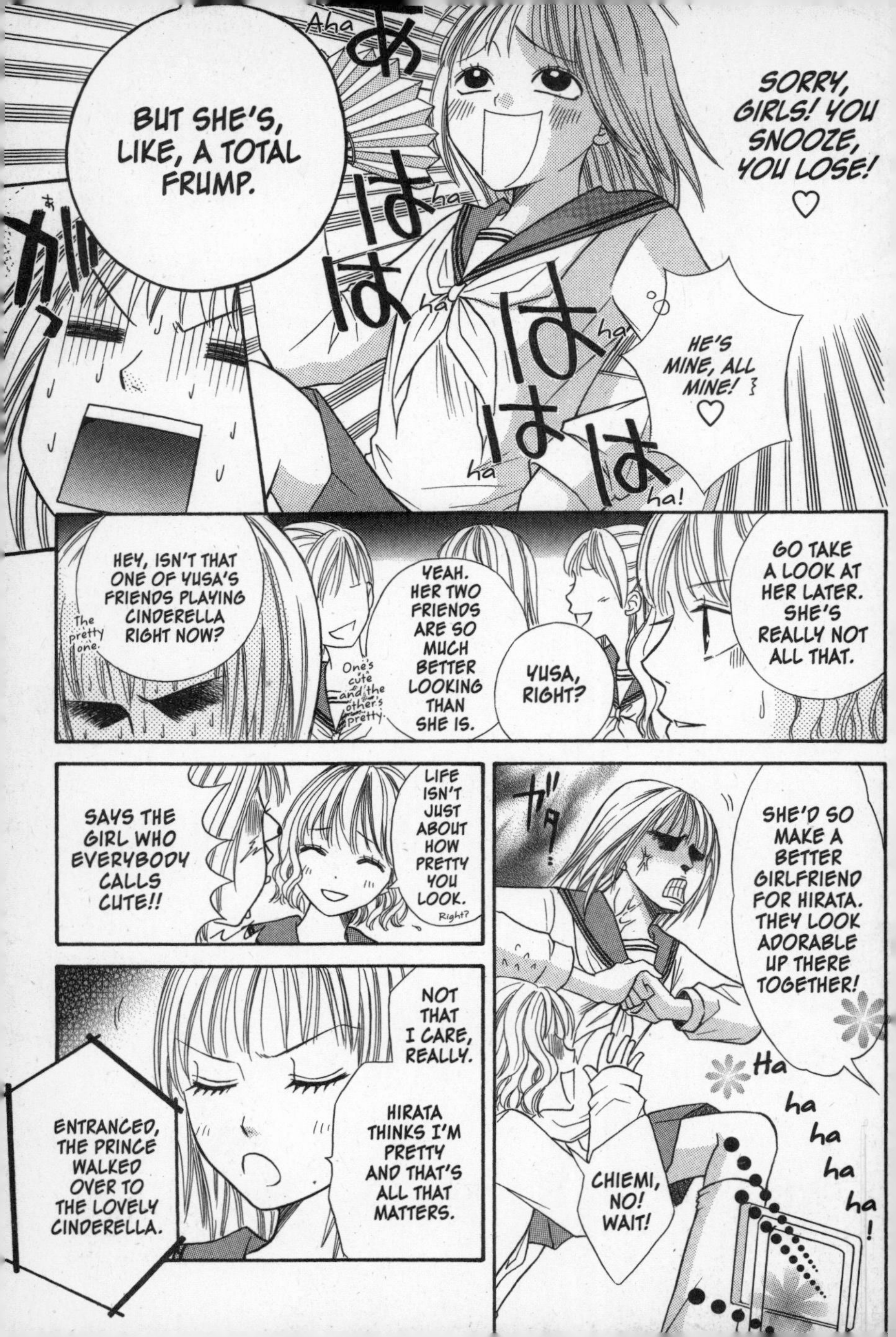
SORRY, GIRLS! YOU SNOOZE, YOU LOSE! ♡
HE'S MINE, ALL MINE! ♡
Aha ha ha ha ha!
BUT SHE'S, LIKE, A TOTAL FRUMP.
GO TAKE A LOOK AT HER LATER. SHE'S REALLY NOT ALL THAT.
YUSA, RIGHT?
YEAH. HER TWO FRIENDS ARE SO MUCH BETTER LOOKING THAN SHE IS.
One's cute and the other's pretty.
HEY, ISN'T THAT ONE OF YUSA'S FRIENDS PLAYING CINDERELLA RIGHT NOW?
The pretty one.
SHE'D SO MAKE A BETTER GIRLFRIEND FOR HIRATA. THEY LOOK ADORABLE UP THERE TOGETHER!
Ha ha ha ha ha!
CHIEMI, NO! WAIT!
LIFE ISN'T JUST ABOUT HOW PRETTY YOU LOOK.
Right?
SAYS THE GIRL WHO EVERYBODY CALLS CUTE!!
NOT THAT I CARE, REALLY.
HIRATA THINKS I'M PRETTY AND THAT'S ALL THAT MATTERS.
ENTRANCED, THE PRINCE WALKED OVER TO THE LOVELY CINDERELLA.

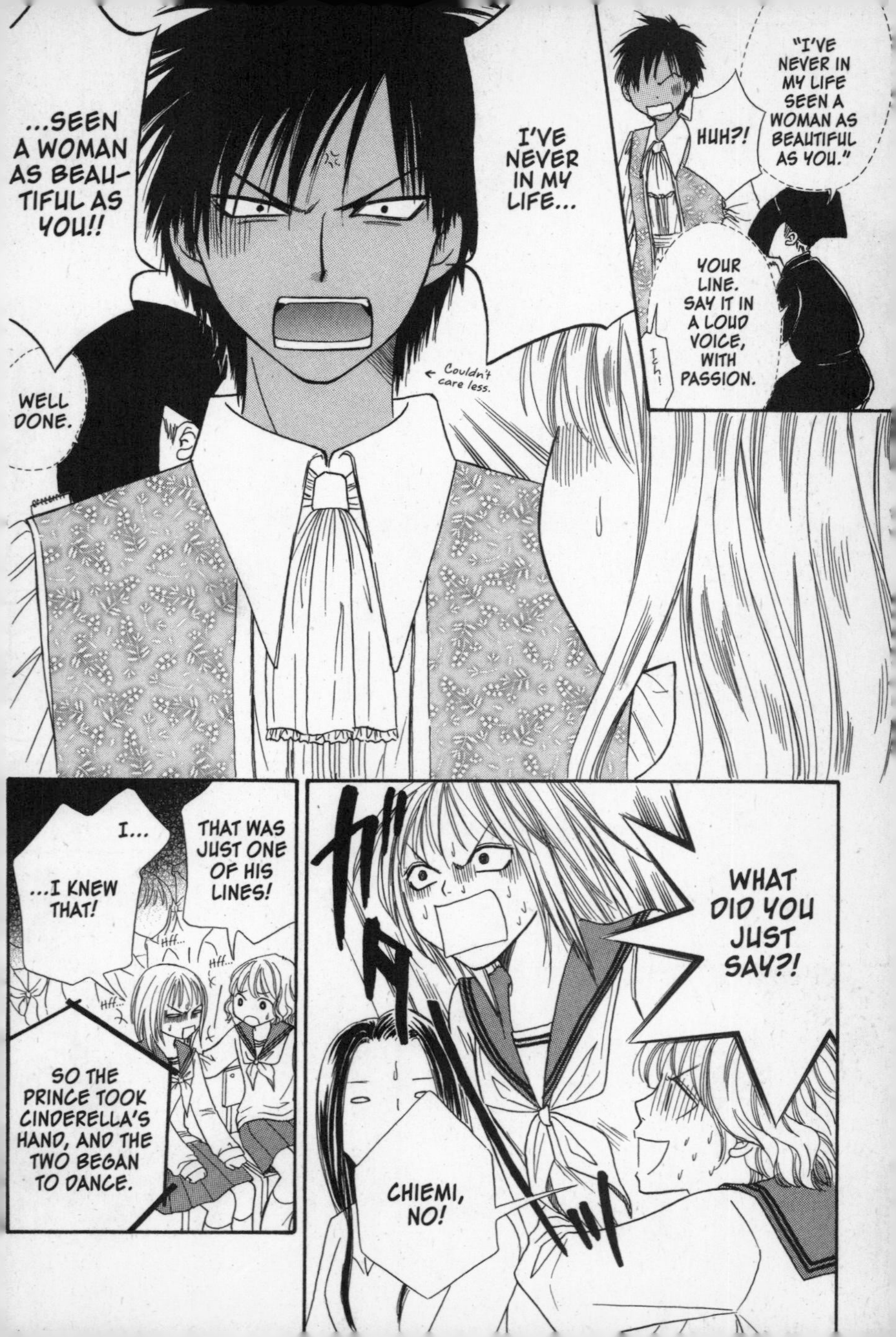
"I'VE NEVER IN MY LIFE SEEN A WOMAN AS BEAUTIFUL AS YOU."
HUH?!
YOUR LINE. SAY IT IN A LOUD VOICE, WITH PASSION.
Tch!
I'VE NEVER IN MY LIFE...
...SEEN A WOMAN AS BEAU-TIFUL AS YOU!!
Couldn't care less.
WELL DONE.
WHAT DID YOU JUST SAY?!
CHIEMI, NO!
THAT WAS JUST ONE OF HIS LINES!
I...
...I KNEW THAT!
Hff...
Hff...
Hff...
SO THE PRINCE TOOK CINDERELLA'S HAND, AND THE TWO BEGAN TO DANCE.

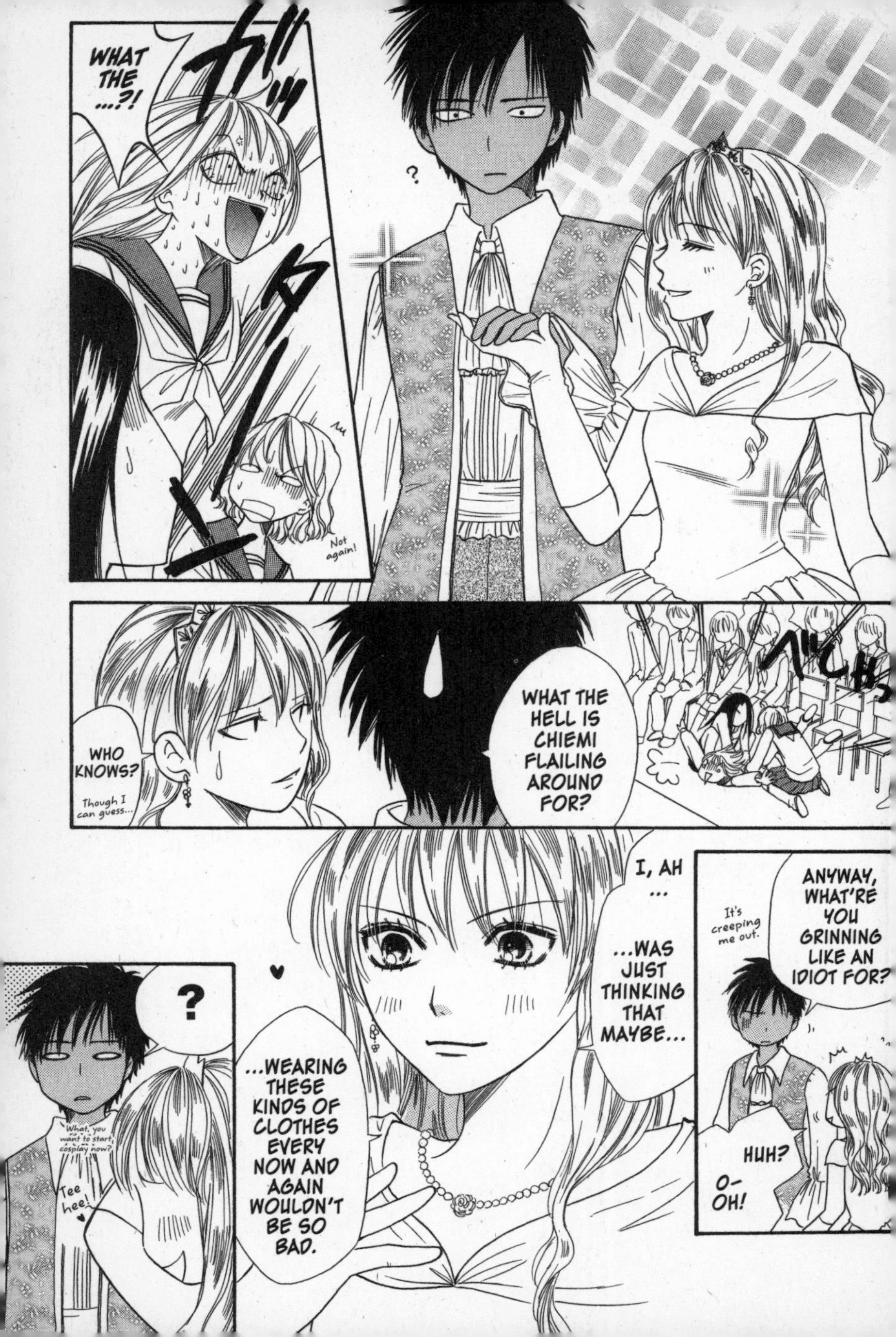
?
WHAT THE ...?!
Not again!
WHAT THE HELL IS CHIEMI FLAILING AROUND FOR?
WHO KNOWS?
Though I can guess...
ANYWAY, WHAT'RE YOU GRINNING LIKE AN IDIOT FOR?
It's creeping me out.
HUH?
O-OH!
I, AH ...
...WAS JUST THINKING THAT MAYBE...
...WEARING THESE KINDS OF CLOTHES EVERY NOW AND AGAIN WOULDN'T BE SO BAD.
?
What, you want to start cosplay now?
Tee hee!

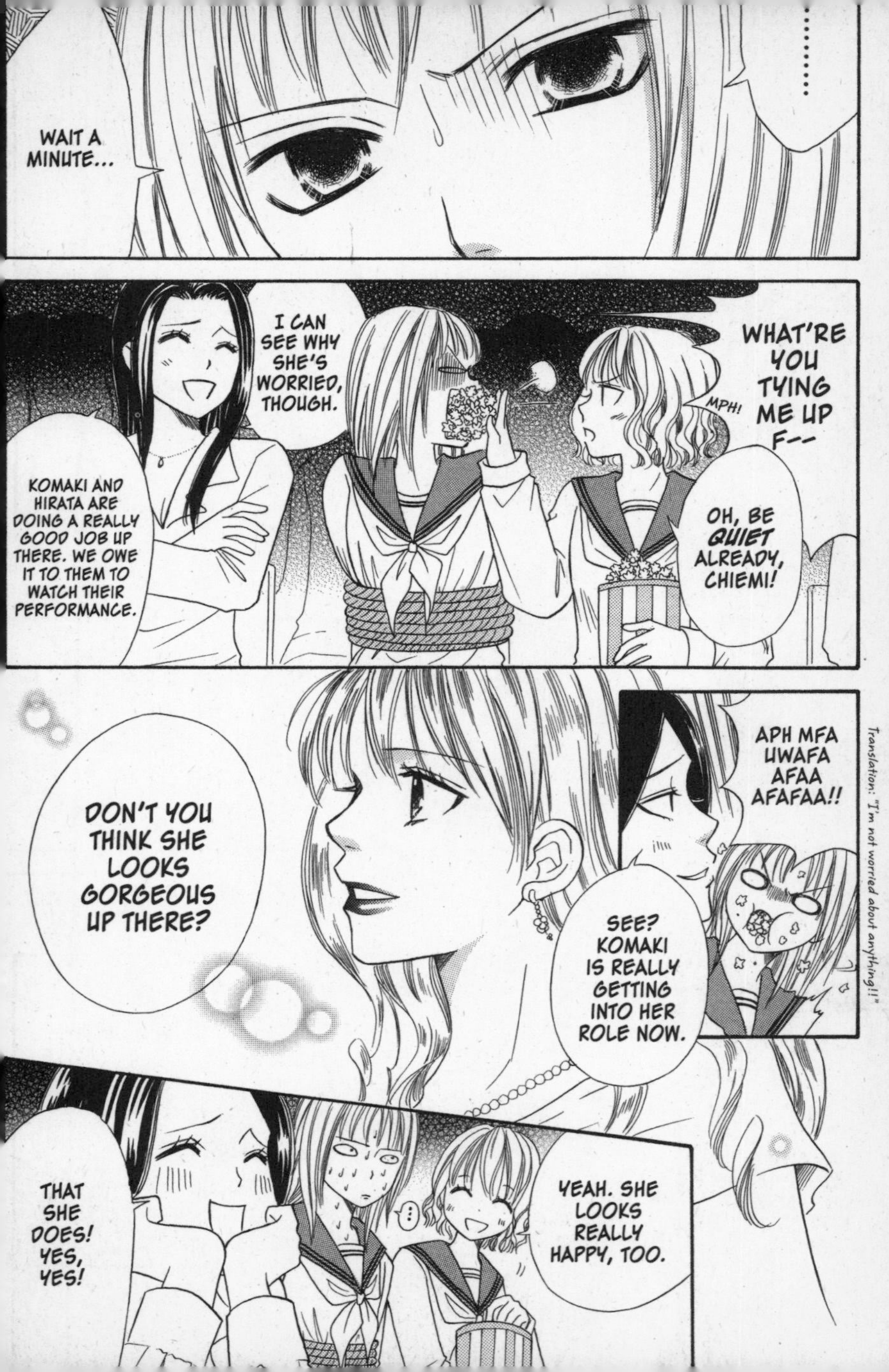
WAIT A MINUTE...
WHAT'RE YOU TYING ME UP F--
MPH!
OH, BE QUIET ALREADY, CHIEMI!
I CAN SEE WHY SHE'S WORRIED, THOUGH.
KOMAKI AND HIRATA ARE DOING A REALLY GOOD JOB UP THERE. WE OWE IT TO THEM TO WATCH THEIR PERFORMANCE.
APH MFA UWAFA AFAA AFAFAA!!
SEE? KOMAKI IS REALLY GETTING INTO HER ROLE NOW.
DON'T YOU THINK SHE LOOKS GORGEOUS UP THERE?
YEAH. SHE LOOKS REALLY HAPPY, TOO.
...
THAT SHE DOES! YES, YES!

Translation: "I'm not worried about anything!!"

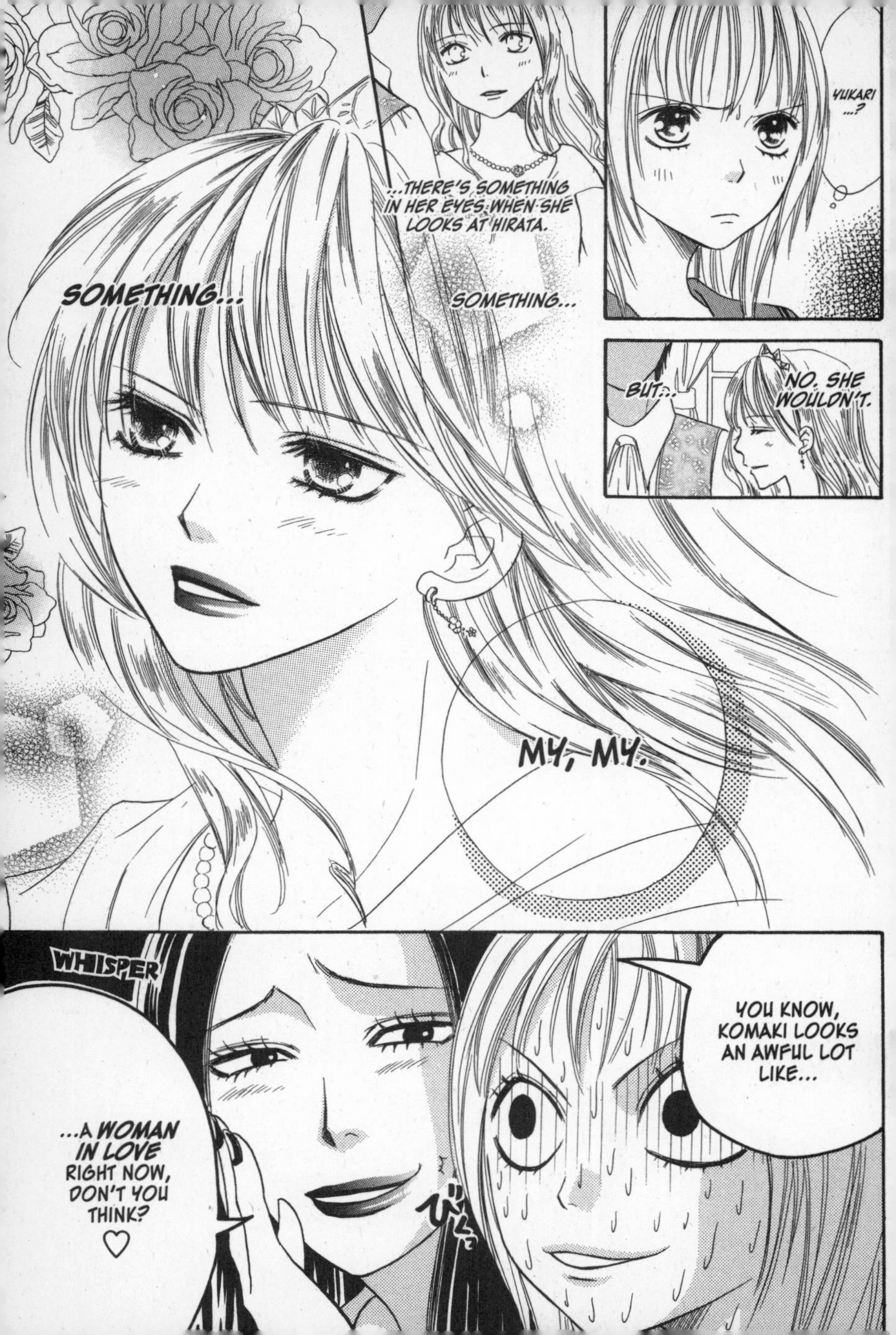
YUKARI ...?
NO. SHE WOULDN'T.
BUT...
...THERE'S SOMETHING IN HER EYES WHEN SHE LOOKS AT HIRATA.
SOMETHING...
SOMETHING...
MY, MY.
YOU KNOW, KOMAKI LOOKS AN AWFUL LOT LIKE...
WHISPER
...A *WOMAN IN LOVE* RIGHT NOW, DON'T YOU THINK? ♡

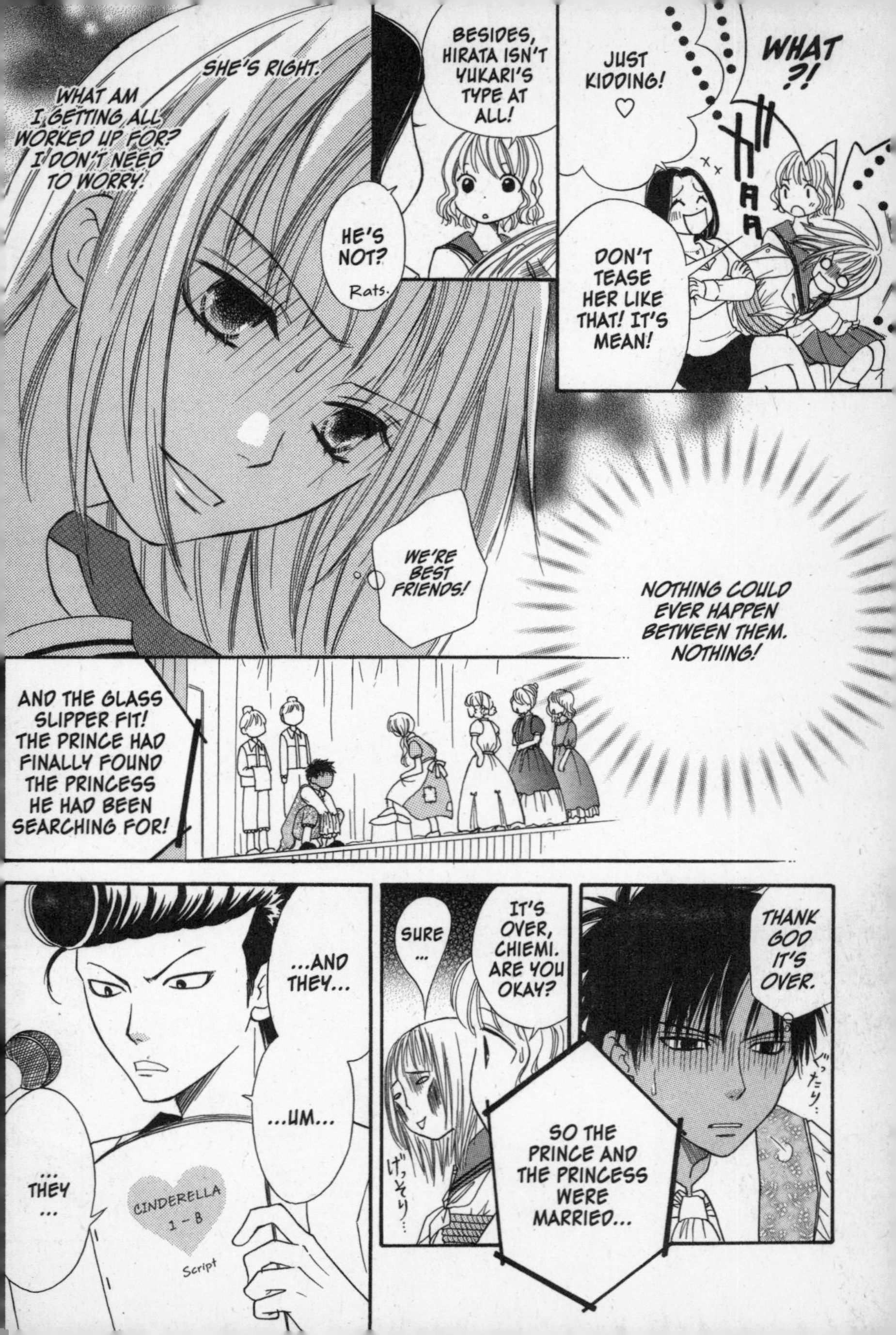
BESIDES, HIRATA ISN'T YUKARI'S TYPE AT ALL!
HE'S NOT?
Rats.
JUST KIDDING! ♡
WHAT ?!
DON'T TEASE HER LIKE THAT! IT'S MEAN!
SHE'S RIGHT.
WHAT AM I GETTING ALL WORKED UP FOR? I DON'T NEED TO WORRY.
WE'RE BEST FRIENDS!
NOTHING COULD EVER HAPPEN BETWEEN THEM. NOTHING!
AND THE GLASS SLIPPER FIT! THE PRINCE HAD FINALLY FOUND THE PRINCESS HE HAD BEEN SEARCHING FOR!
THANK GOD IT'S OVER.
ぐったり…
IT'S OVER, CHIEMI. ARE YOU OKAY?
SURE ...
げっそり…
SO THE PRINCE AND THE PRINCESS WERE MARRIED...
...AND THEY...
...UM...
... THEY ...
CINDERELLA 1-B
Script

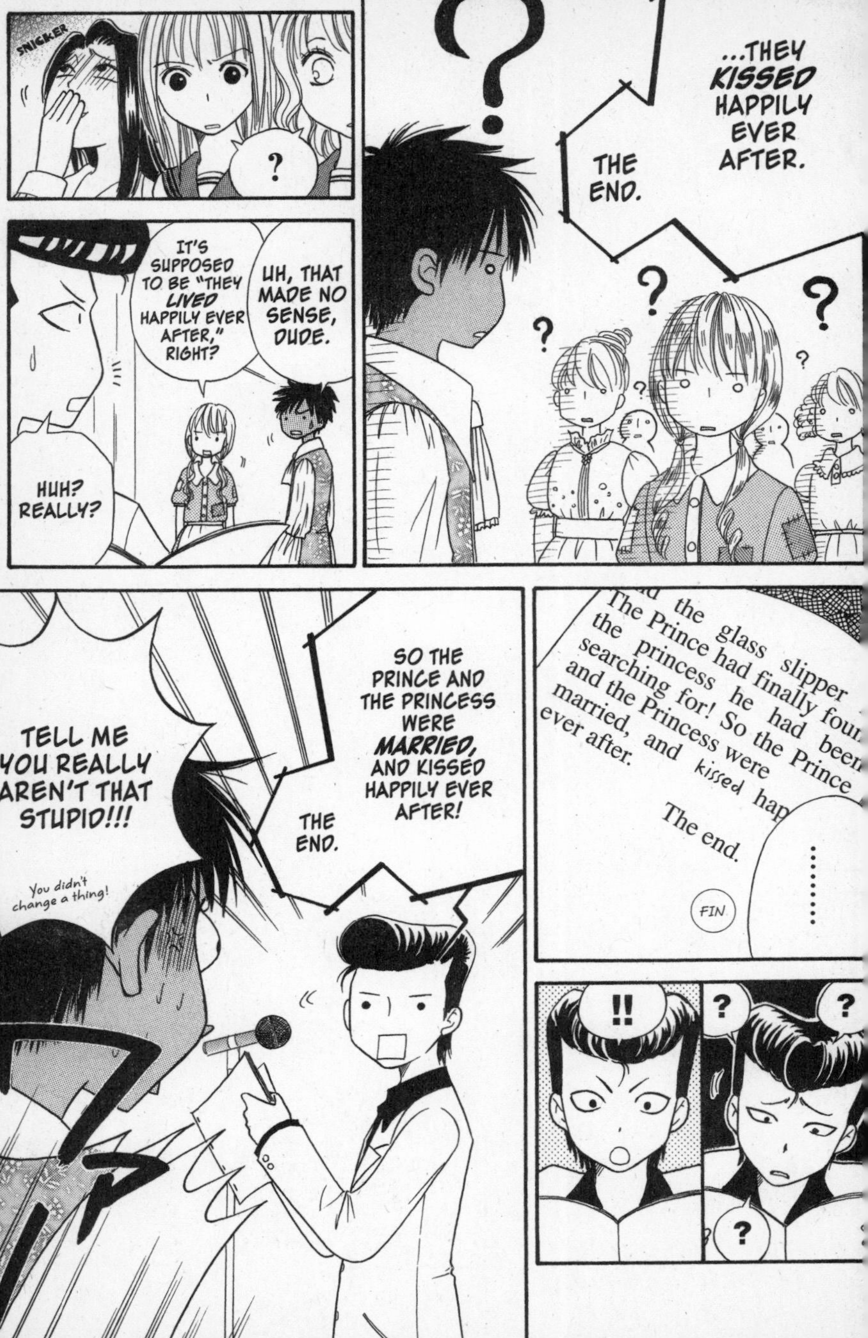
?
...THEY KISSED HAPPILY EVER AFTER.
THE END.
? ? ? ?
SNICKER
?
UH, THAT MADE NO SENSE, DUDE.
IT'S SUPPOSED TO BE "THEY LIVED HAPPILY EVER AFTER," RIGHT?
HUH? REALLY?
d the glass slipper
The Prince had finally foun
the princess he had been
searching for! So the Prince
and the Princess were
married, and kissed hap
ever after.
The end.
......
FIN
? ?
!!
?
SO THE PRINCE AND THE PRINCESS WERE MARRIED, AND KISSED HAPPILY EVER AFTER!
THE END.
TELL ME YOU REALLY AREN'T THAT STUPID!!!
You didn't change a thing!

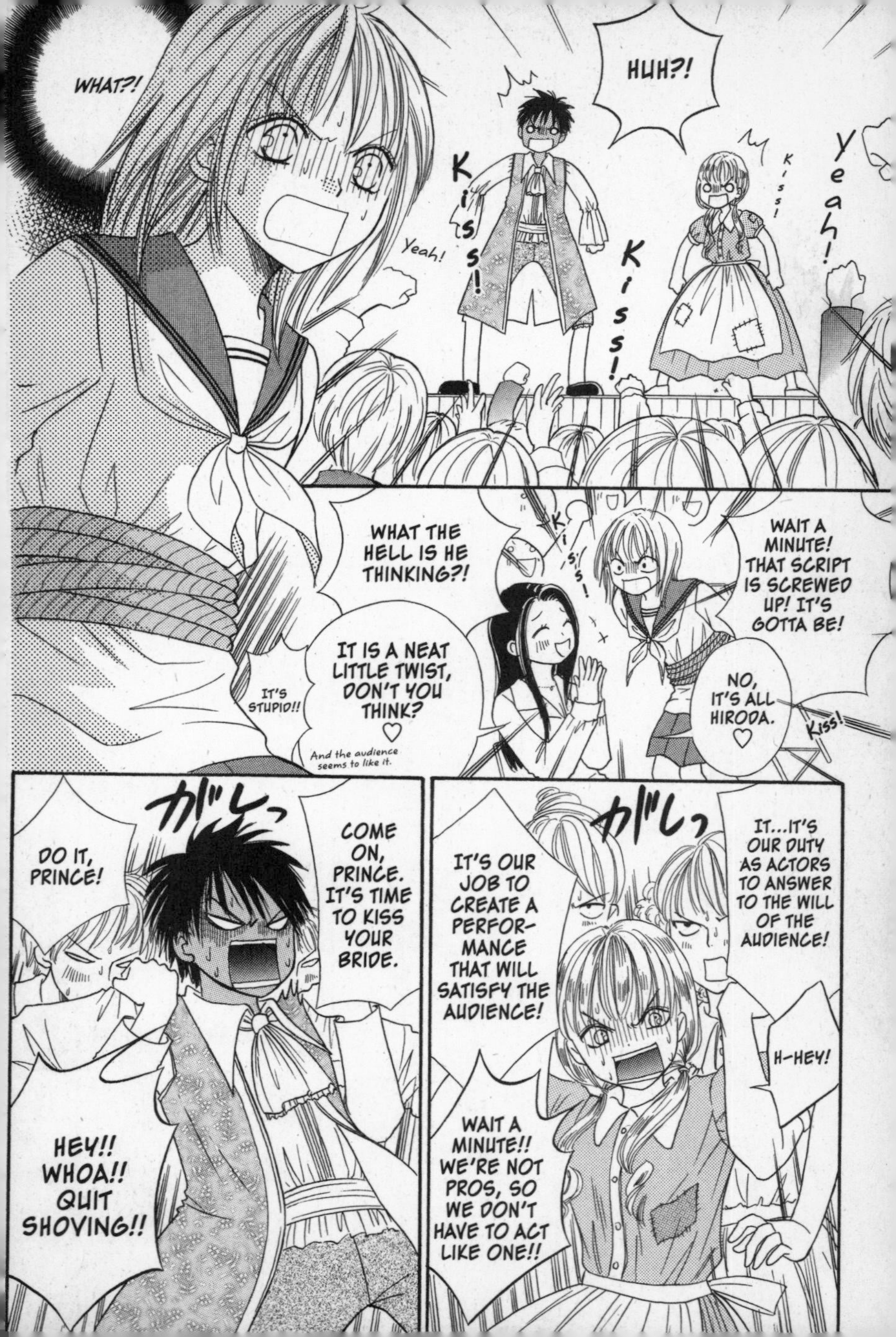
HUH?!
Kiss!
Yeah!
Kiss!
Kiss!
Yeah!
WHAT?!
WAIT A MINUTE! THAT SCRIPT IS SCREWED UP! IT'S GOTTA BE!
Kiss!
WHAT THE HELL IS HE THINKING?!
NO, IT'S ALL HIRODA. ♡
Kiss!
IT IS A NEAT LITTLE TWIST, DON'T YOU THINK? ♡
And the audience seems to like it.
IT'S STUPID!!
ガしっ
IT...IT'S OUR DUTY AS ACTORS TO ANSWER TO THE WILL OF THE AUDIENCE!
IT'S OUR JOB TO CREATE A PERFORMANCE THAT WILL SATISFY THE AUDIENCE!
H-HEY!
WAIT A MINUTE!! WE'RE NOT PROS, SO WE DON'T HAVE TO ACT LIKE ONE!!
ガしっ
COME ON, PRINCE. IT'S TIME TO KISS YOUR BRIDE.
DO IT, PRINCE!
HEY!! WHOA!! QUIT SHOVING!!

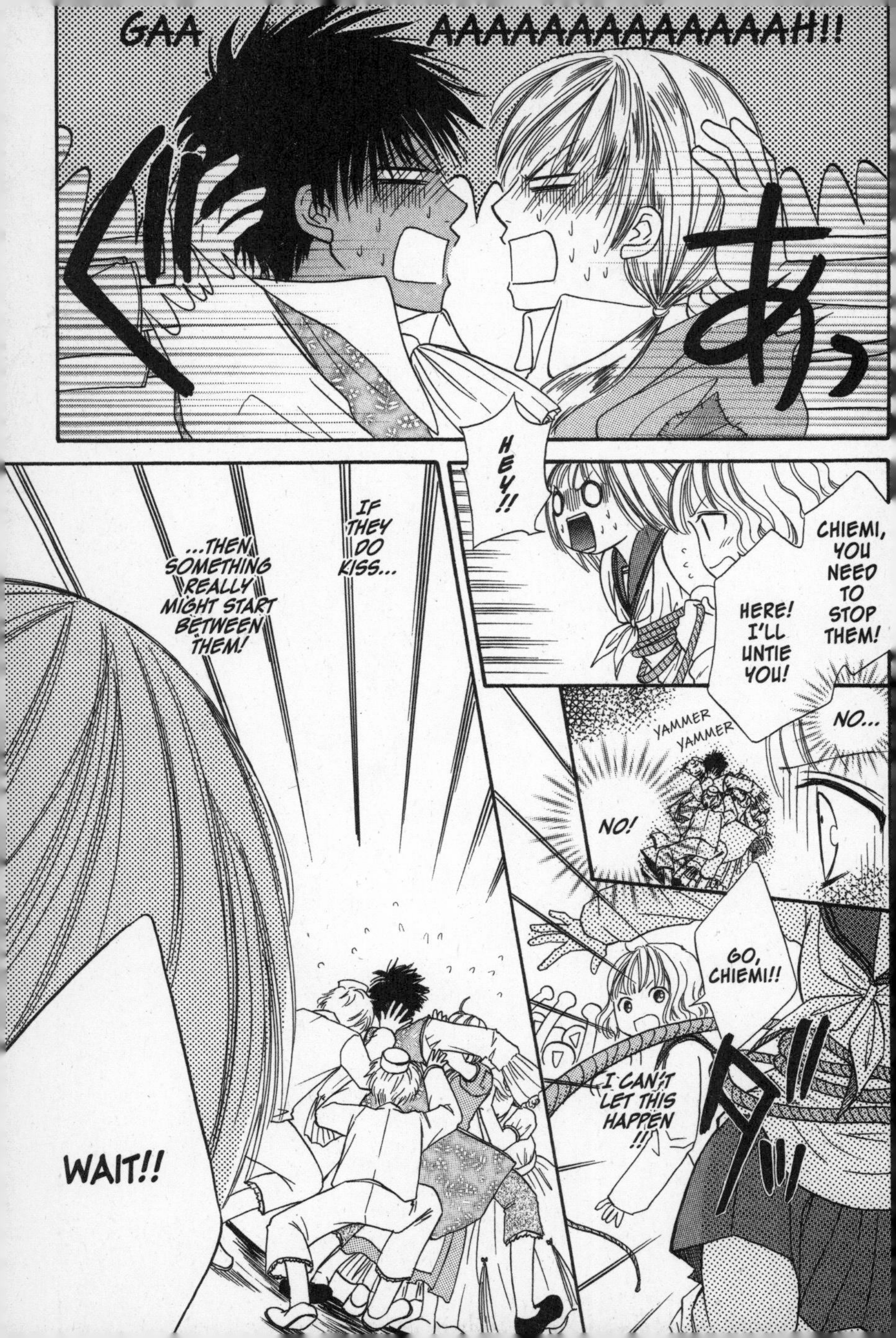
GAA AAAAAAAAAAAAAH!!
あっ
HEY!!
CHIEMI, YOU NEED TO STOP THEM!
HERE! I'LL UNTIE YOU!
NO...
YAMMER YAMMER
NO!
IF THEY DO KISS...
...THEN SOMETHING REALLY MIGHT START BETWEEN THEM!
GO, CHIEMI!!
I CAN'T LET THIS HAPPEN!!
WAIT!!

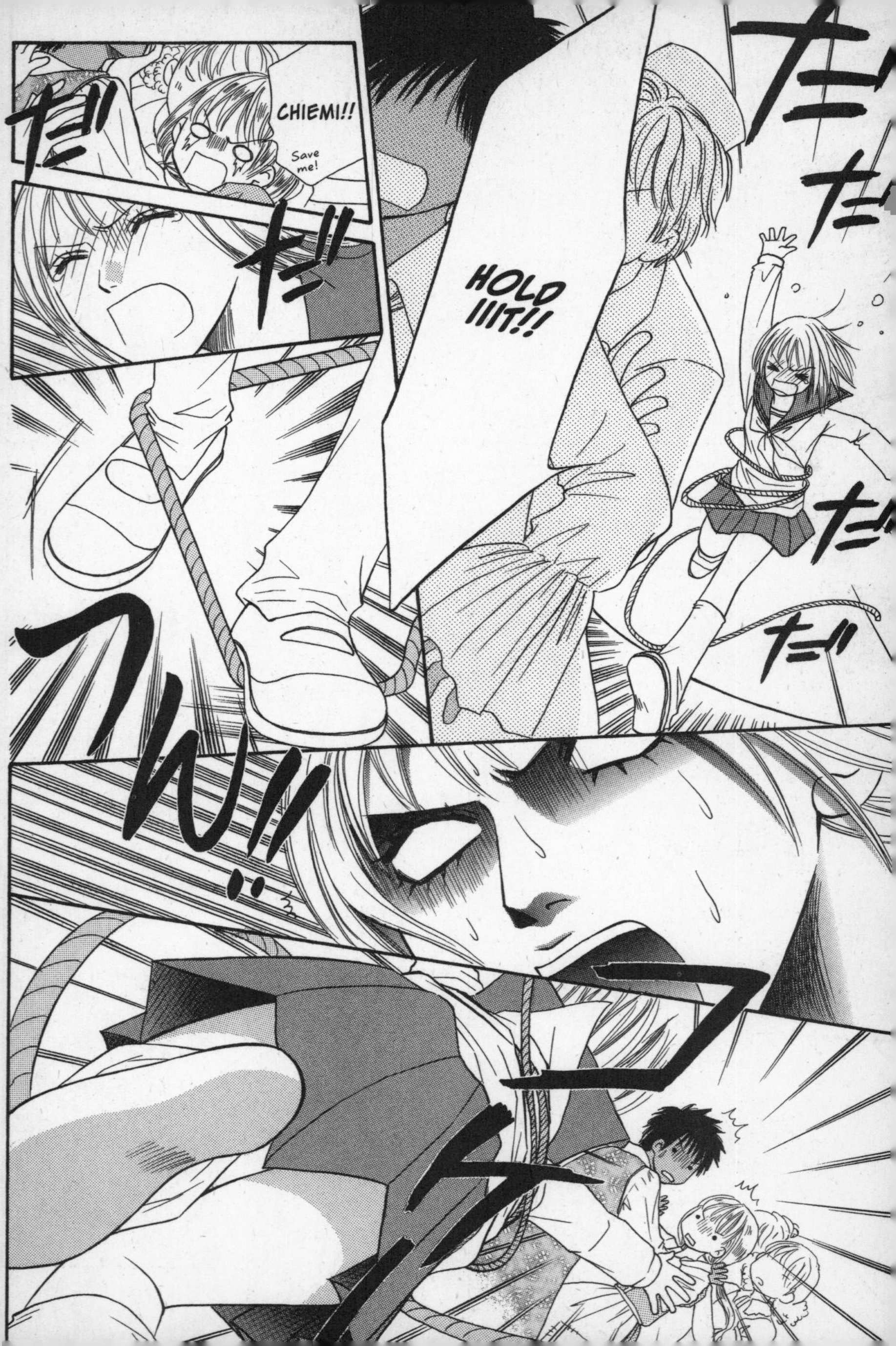
HOLD IIIT!!
CHIEMI!!
Save me!

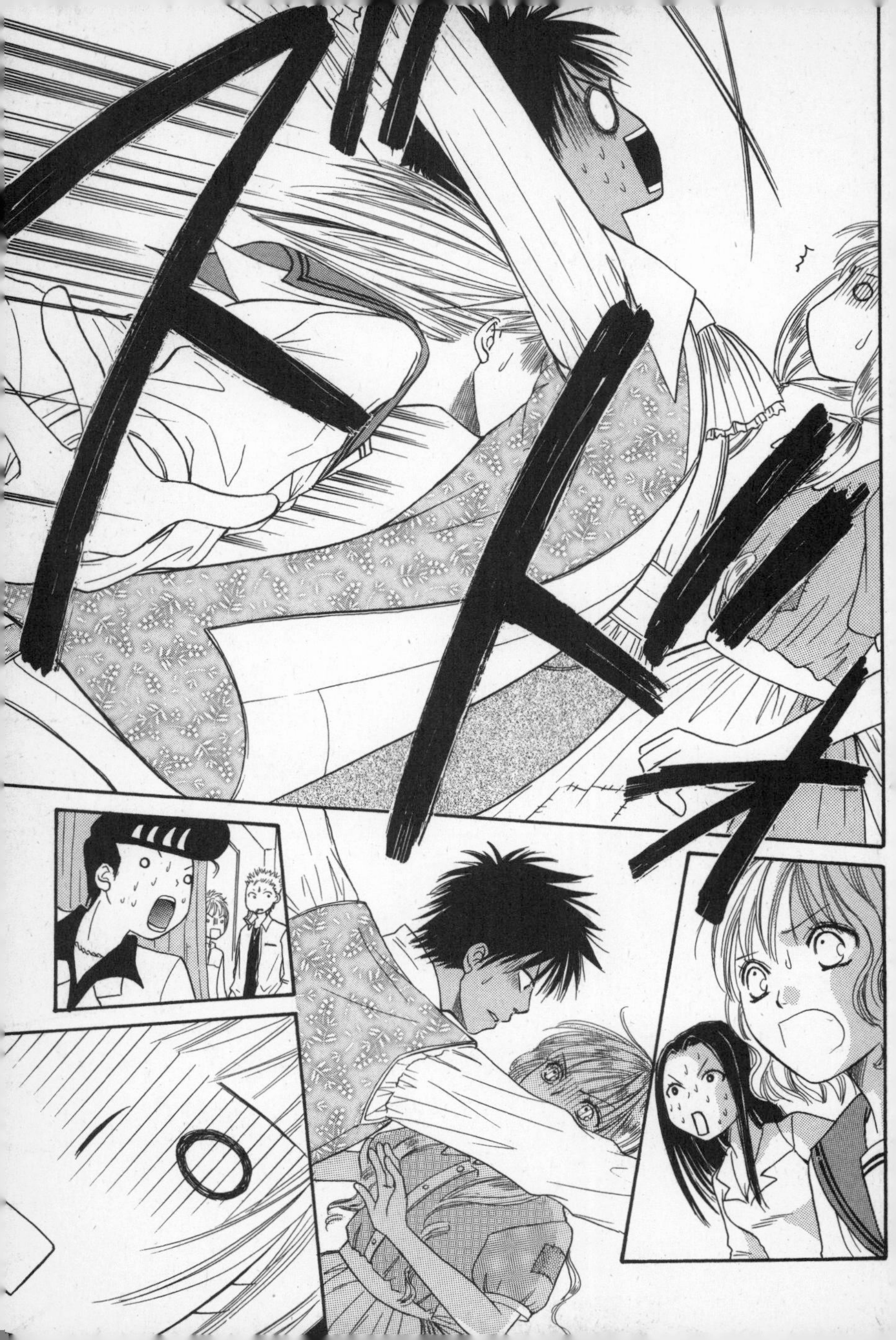

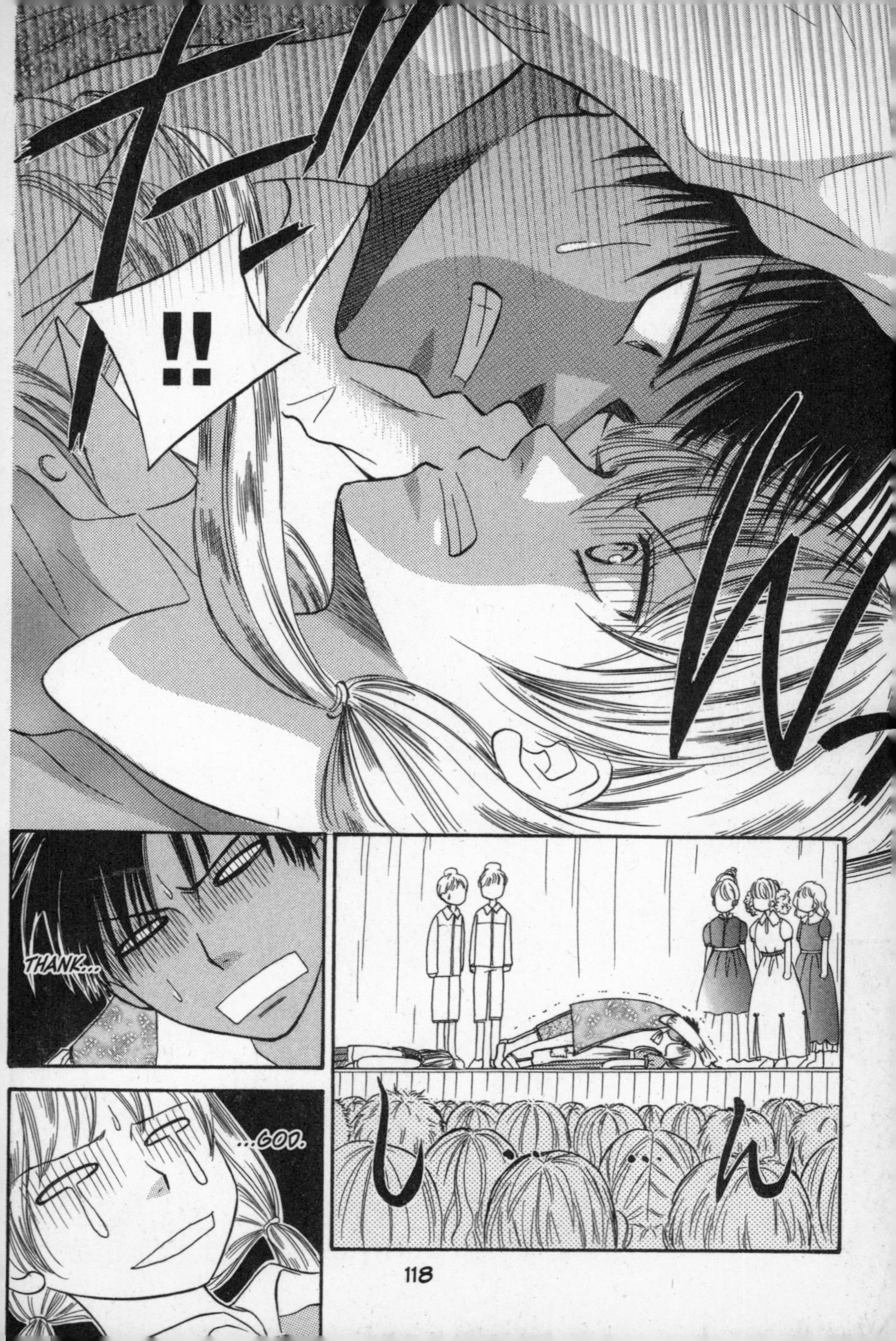
!!
しん
THANK...
...GOD.

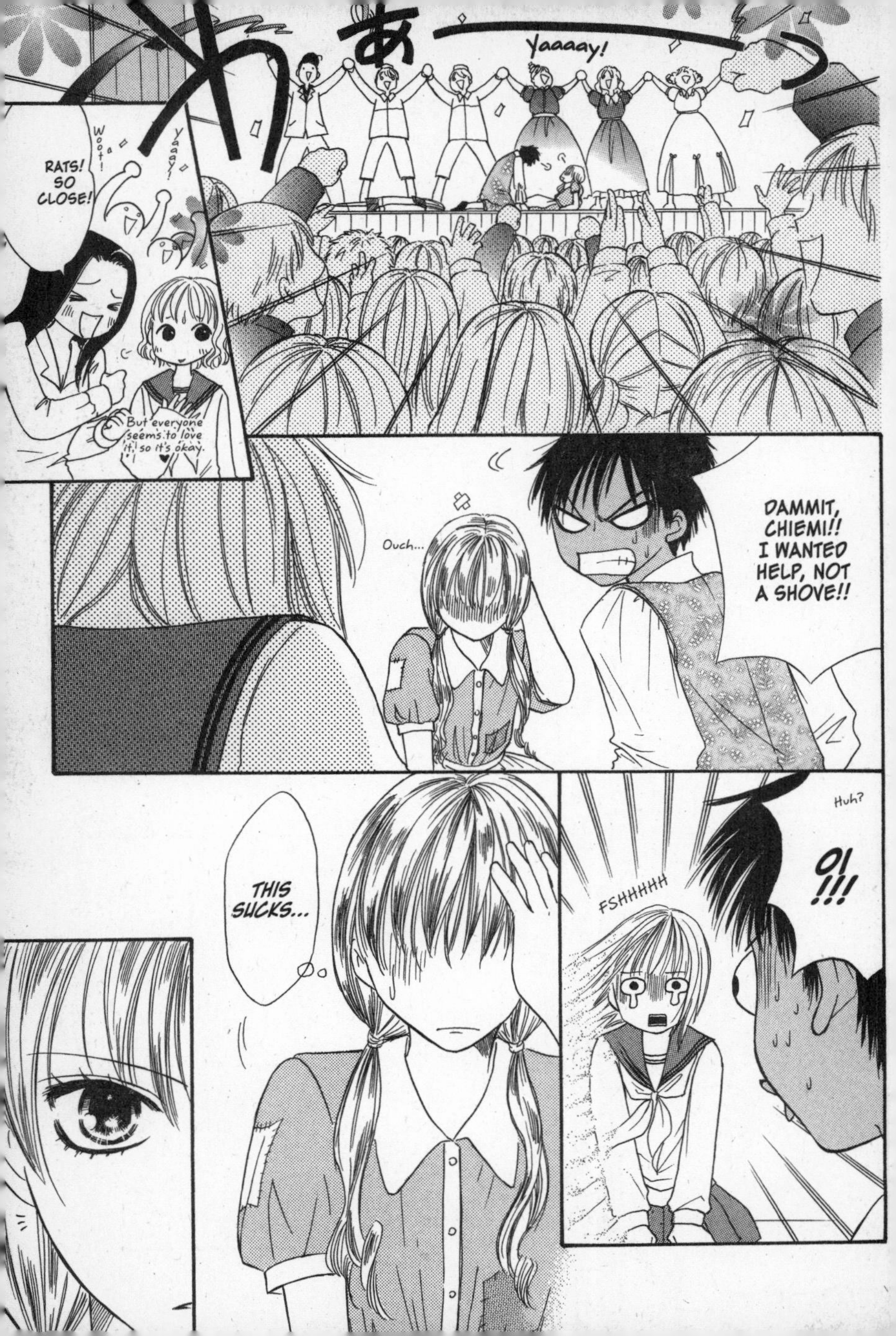
わあーー
Yaaaay!
Yaaay!
Woot!
RATS! SO CLOSE!
But everyone seems to love it, so it's okay.
DAMMIT, CHIEMI!! I WANTED HELP, NOT A SHOVE!!
Ouch...
Huh?
OI!!!
FSHHHHH
THIS SUCKS...

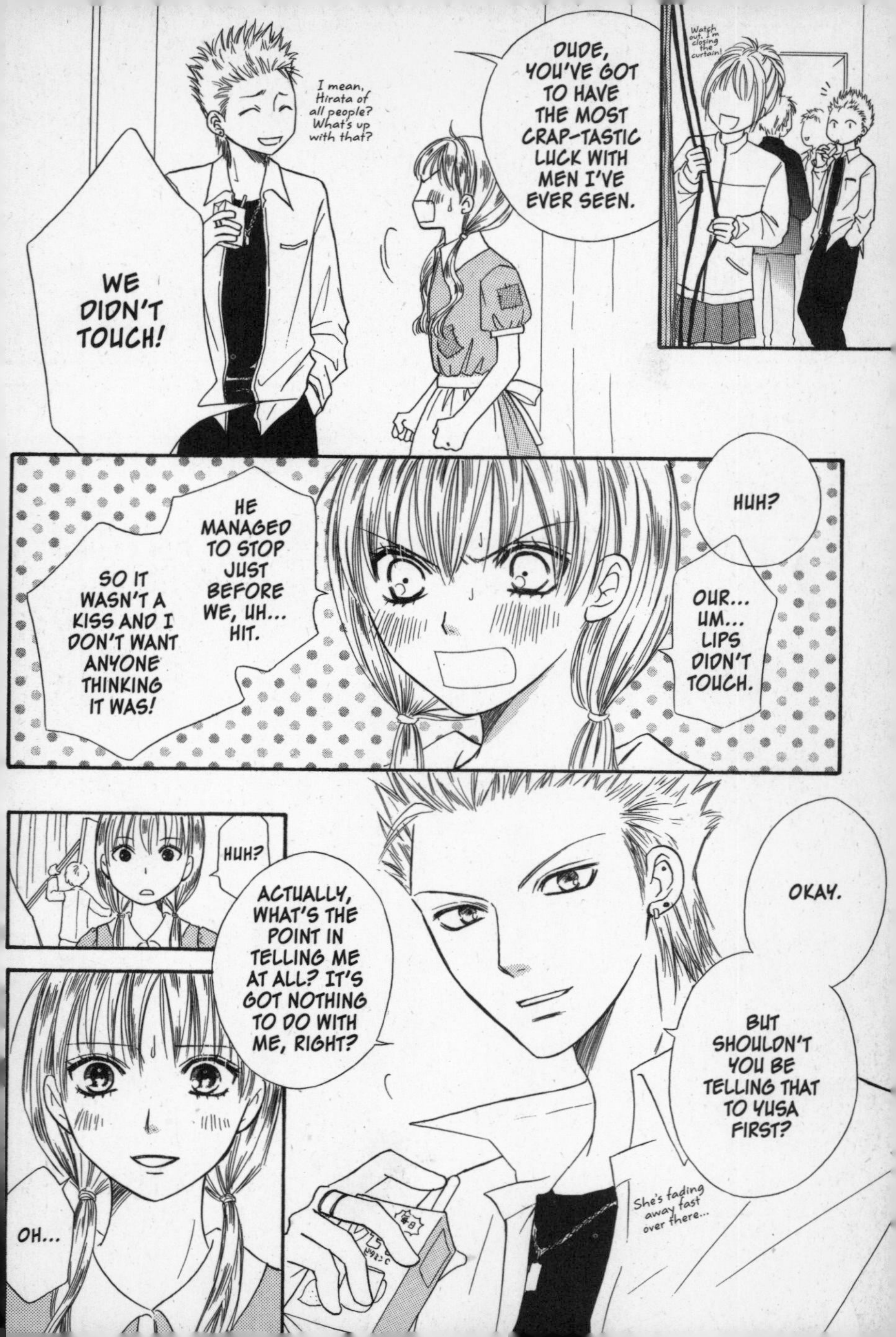
Watch out, I'm closing the curtain!
DUDE, YOU'VE GOT TO HAVE THE MOST CRAP-TASTIC LUCK WITH MEN I'VE EVER SEEN.
I mean, Hirata of all people? What's up with that?
WE DIDN'T TOUCH!
HUH?
OUR... UM... LIPS DIDN'T TOUCH.
HE MANAGED TO STOP JUST BEFORE WE, UH... HIT.
SO IT WASN'T A KISS AND I DON'T WANT ANYONE THINKING IT WAS!
OKAY.
BUT SHOULDN'T YOU BE TELLING THAT TO YUSA FIRST?
ACTUALLY, WHAT'S THE POINT IN TELLING ME AT ALL? IT'S GOT NOTHING TO DO WITH ME, RIGHT?
She's fading away fast over there...
HUH?
OH...

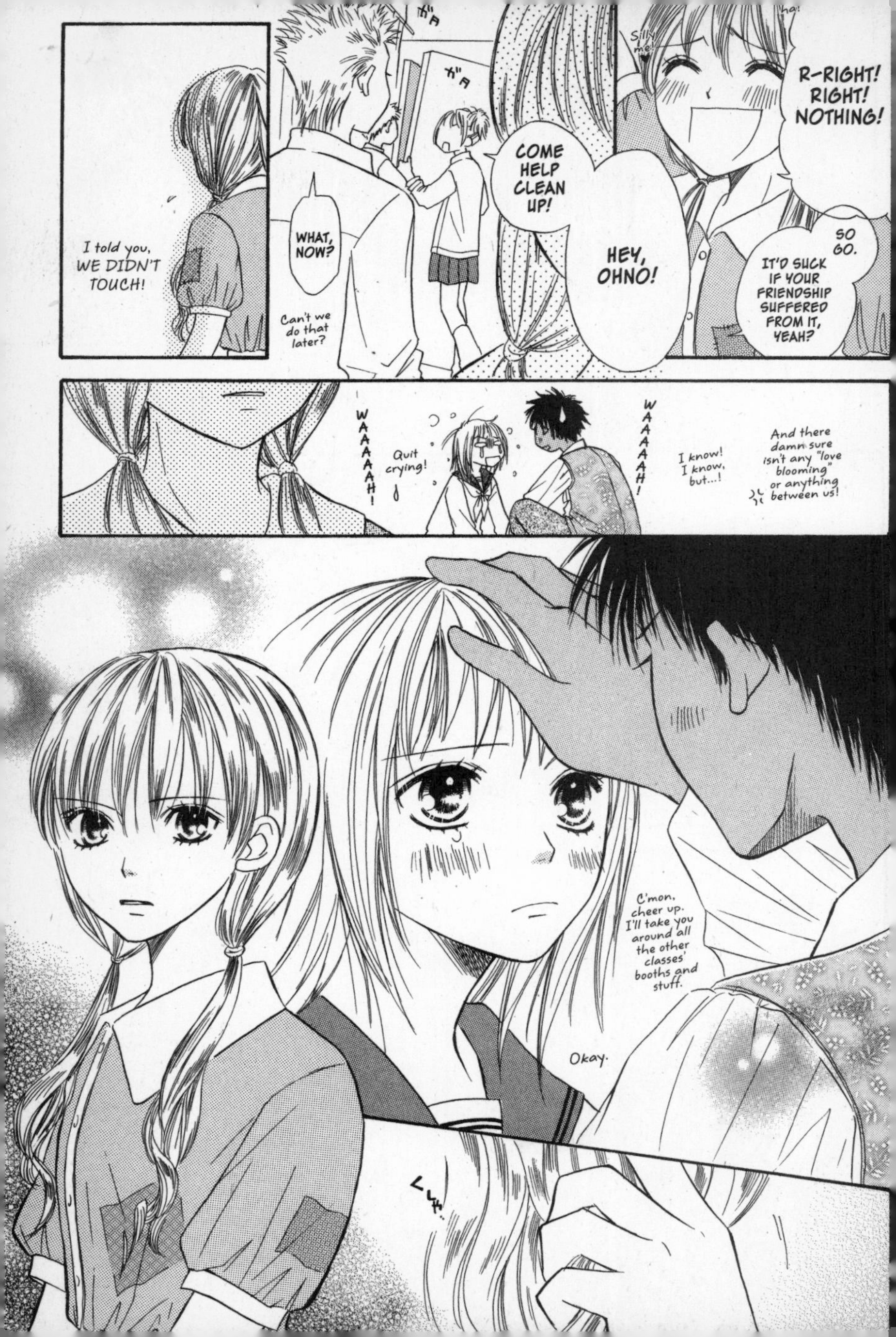
ha!
Silly me!
R-RIGHT! RIGHT! NOTHING!
SO GO.
IT'D SUCK IF YOUR FRIENDSHIP SUFFERED FROM IT, YEAH?
HEY, OHNO!
COME HELP CLEAN UP!
ガタ
ガタ
WHAT, NOW?
Can't we do that later?
I told you, WE DIDN'T TOUCH!
And there damn sure isn't any "love blooming" or anything between us!
WAAAAAAH!
I know! I know, but...!
Quit crying!
WAAAAAAH!
C'mon, cheer up. I'll take you around all the other classes' booths and stuff.
Okay.
くしゃ..

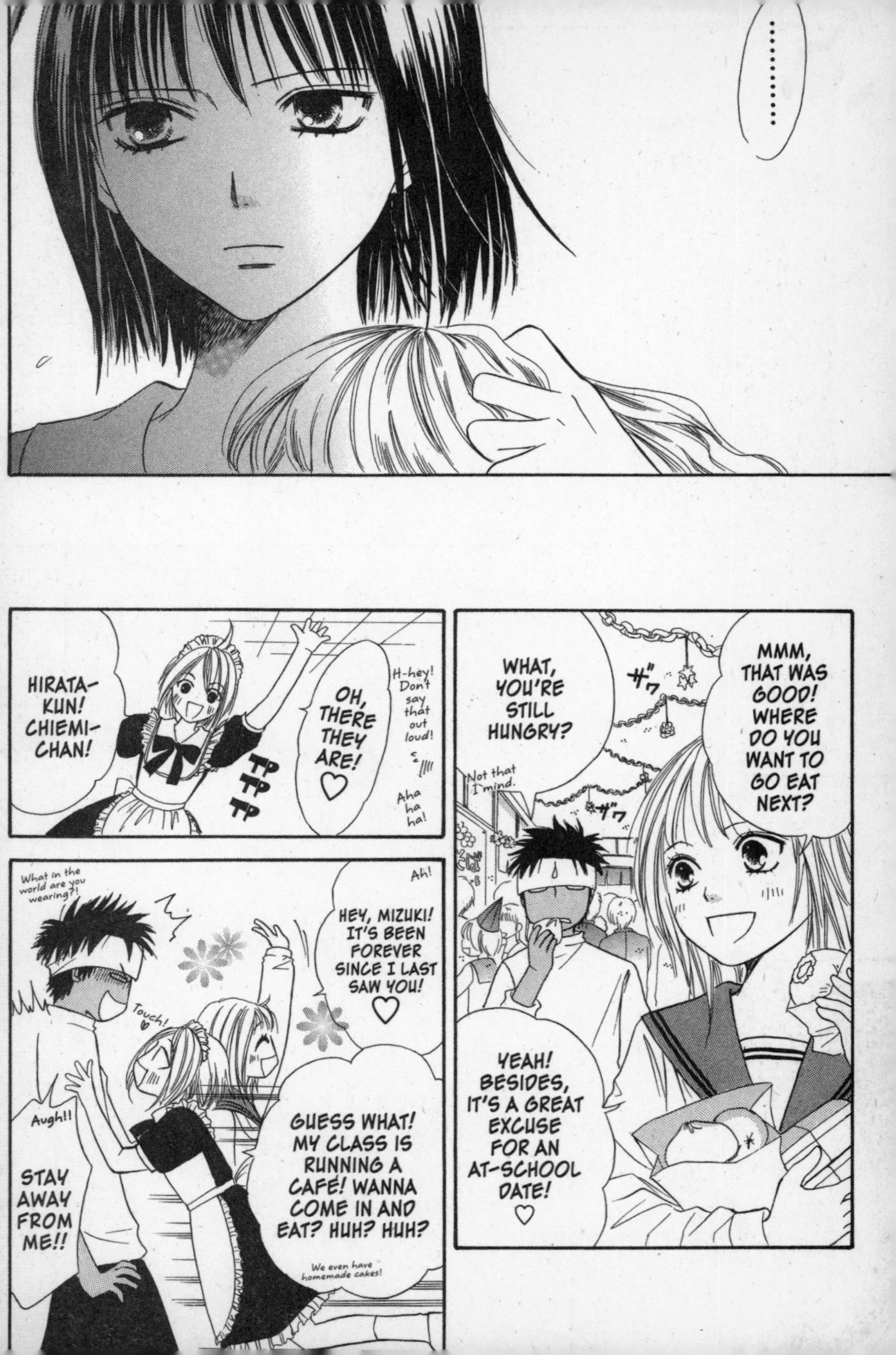
……
MMM, THAT WAS GOOD! WHERE DO YOU WANT TO GO EAT NEXT?
WHAT, YOU'RE STILL HUNGRY?
Not that I'm mind.
YEAH! BESIDES, IT'S A GREAT EXCUSE FOR AN AT-SCHOOL DATE! ♡
OH, THERE THEY ARE! ♡
H-hey! Don't say that out loud!
Aha ha ha!
HIRATA-KUN! CHIEMI-CHAN!
Ah!
HEY, MIZUKI! IT'S BEEN FOREVER SINCE I LAST SAW YOU! ♡
GUESS WHAT! MY CLASS IS RUNNING A CAFÉ! WANNA COME IN AND EAT? HUH? HUH?
We even have homemade cakes!
Touch! ♥
What in the world are you wearing?!
Augh!!
STAY AWAY FROM ME!!

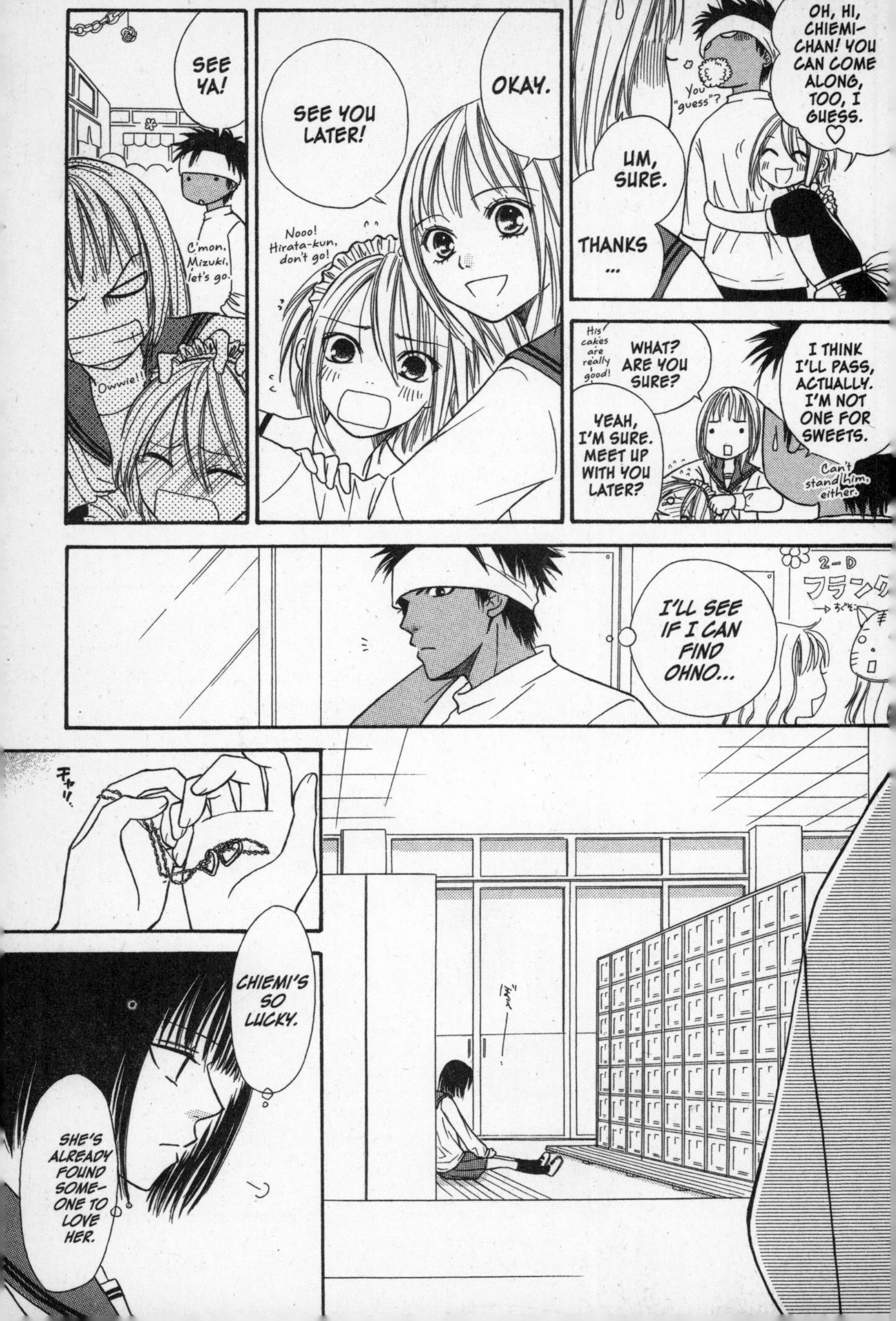
OH, HI, CHIEMI-CHAN! YOU CAN COME ALONG, TOO, I GUESS. ♡
You "guess"?
UM, SURE.
THANKS ...
I THINK I'LL PASS, ACTUALLY. I'M NOT ONE FOR SWEETS.
Can't stand him, either.
WHAT? ARE YOU SURE?
His cakes are really good!
YEAH, I'M SURE. MEET UP WITH YOU LATER?
OKAY.
SEE YOU LATER!
Nooo! Hirata-kun, don't go!
SEE YA!
C'mon, Mizuki, let's go.
Owwie!!
2-D
I'LL SEE IF I CAN FIND OHNO...
CHIEMI'S SO LUCKY.
SHE'S ALREADY FOUND SOME-ONE TO LOVE HER.

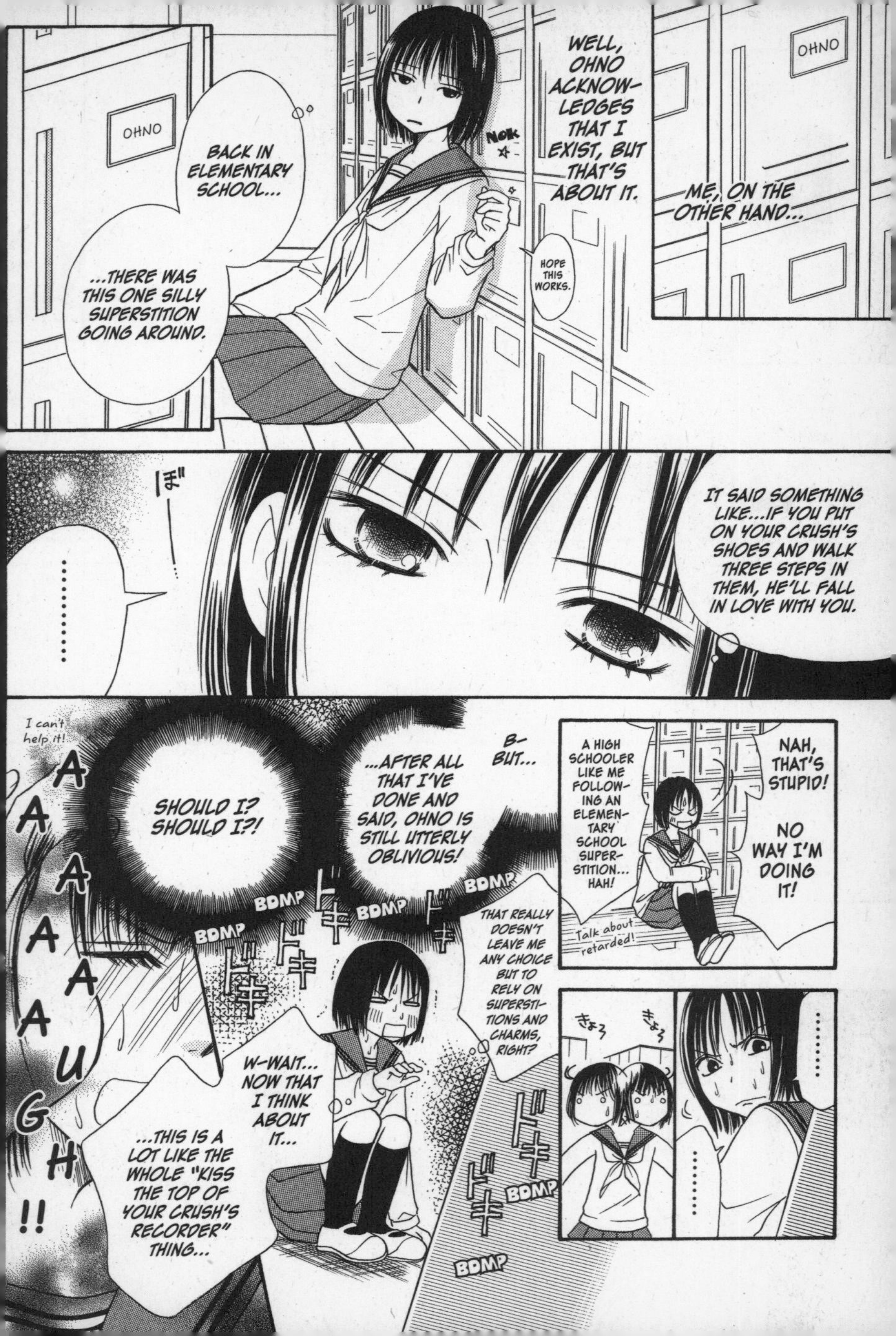
OHNO
WELL, OHNO ACKNOWLEDGES THAT I EXIST, BUT THAT'S ABOUT IT.
ME, ON THE OTHER HAND...
NOK
HOPE THIS WORKS.
OHNO
BACK IN ELEMENTARY SCHOOL...
...THERE WAS THIS ONE SILLY SUPERSTITION GOING AROUND.
IT SAID SOMETHING LIKE...IF YOU PUT ON YOUR CRUSH'S SHOES AND WALK THREE STEPS IN THEM, HE'LL FALL IN LOVE WITH YOU.
ぼー
......
NAH, THAT'S STUPID!
NO WAY I'M DOING IT!
A HIGH SCHOOLER LIKE ME FOLLOWING AN ELEMENTARY SCHOOL SUPERSTITION... HAH!
Talk about retarded!
......
きょろ
きょろ
......
B-BUT...
...AFTER ALL THAT I'VE DONE AND SAID, OHNO IS STILL UTTERLY OBLIVIOUS!
THAT REALLY DOESN'T LEAVE ME ANY CHOICE BUT TO RELY ON SUPERSTITIONS AND CHARMS, RIGHT?
SHOULD I? SHOULD I?!
BDMP
ドキ
BDMP
ドキ
BDMP
ドキ
BDMP
ドキ
W-WAIT... NOW THAT I THINK ABOUT IT...
...THIS IS A LOT LIKE THE WHOLE "KISS THE TOP OF YOUR CRUSH'S RECORDER" THING...
BDMP
ドキ
BDMP
ドキ
I can't help it!
AAAAAAAUGH!!

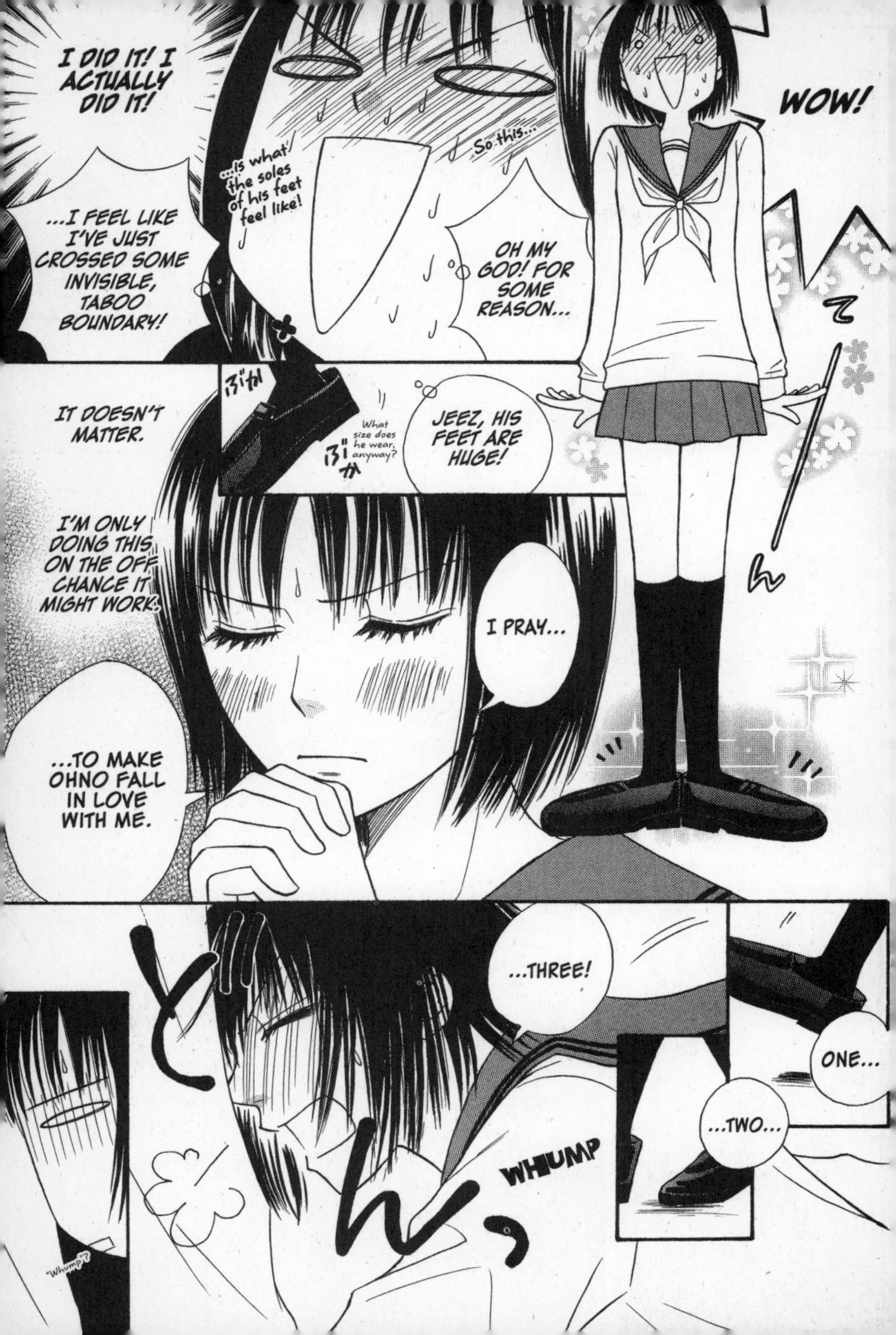
WOW!
So this...
...is what the soles of his feet feel like!
OH MY GOD! FOR SOME REASON...
...I FEEL LIKE I'VE JUST CROSSED SOME INVISIBLE, TABOO BOUNDARY!
I DID IT! I ACTUALLY DID IT!
JEEZ, HIS FEET ARE HUGE!
What size does he wear, anyway?
IT DOESN'T MATTER.
I PRAY...
I'M ONLY DOING THIS ON THE OFF CHANCE IT MIGHT WORK.
...TO MAKE OHNO FALL IN LOVE WITH ME.
ONE...
...TWO...
...THREE!
WHUMP
"Whump"?

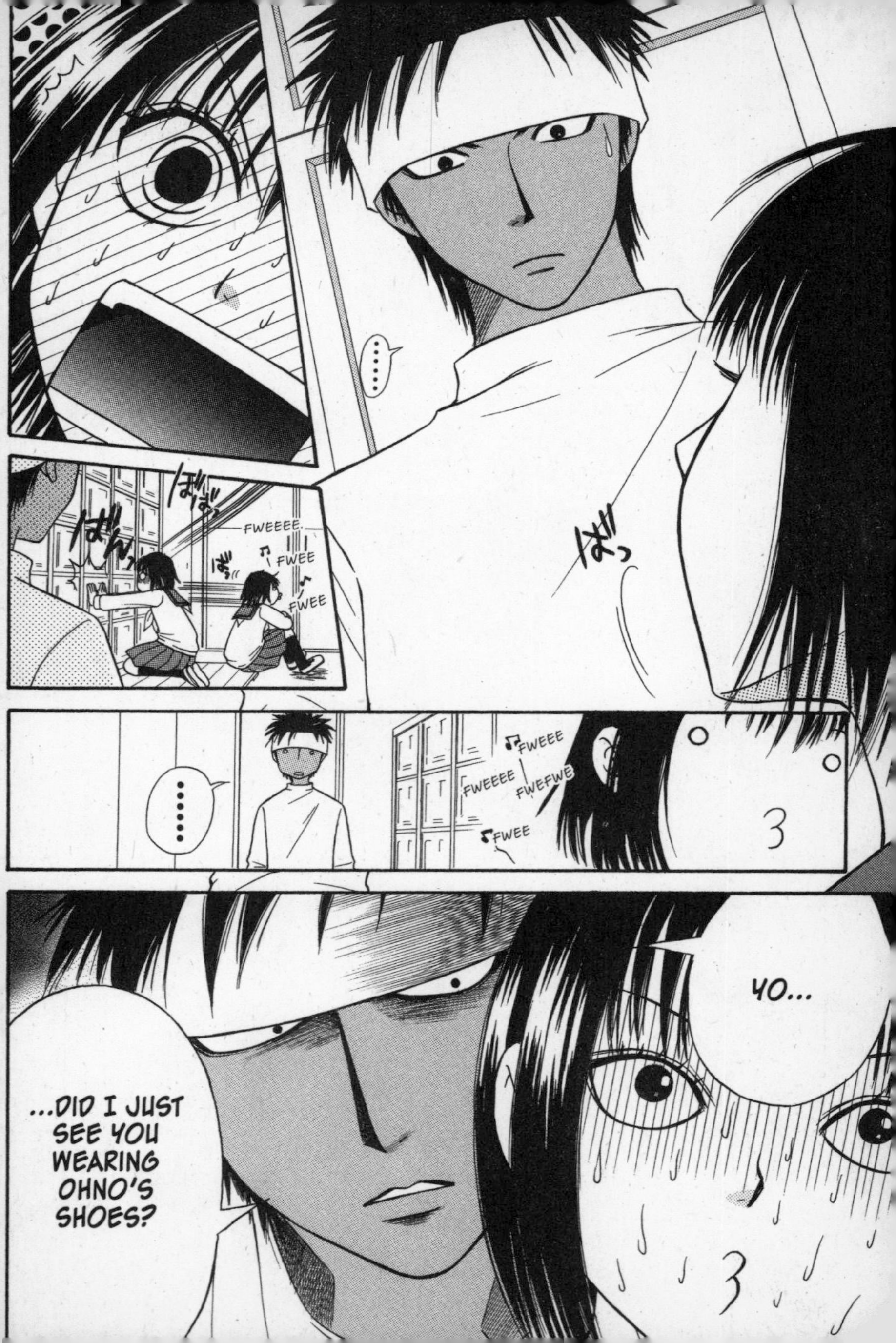
.....
FWEEEE.
FWEE
FWEE
.....
FWEEE
FWEEEE
FWEFWE
FWEE
YO...
...DID I JUST SEE YOU WEARING OHNO'S SHOES?

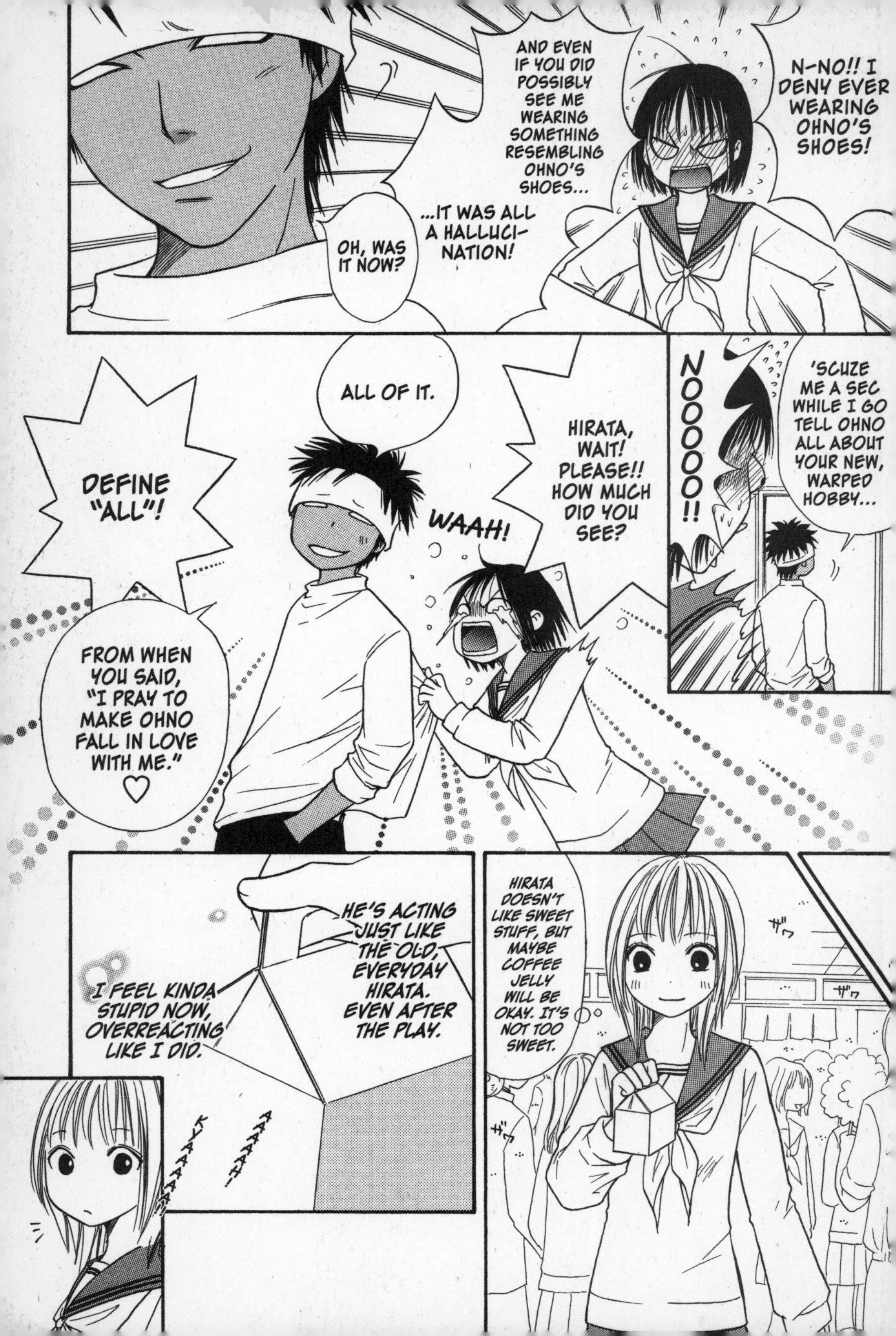

N-NO!! I DENY EVER WEARING OHNO'S SHOES!
AND EVEN IF YOU DID POSSIBLY SEE ME WEARING SOMETHING RESEMBLING OHNO'S SHOES...
...IT WAS ALL A HALLUCI-NATION!
OH, WAS IT NOW?
'SCUZE ME A SEC WHILE I GO TELL OHNO ALL ABOUT YOUR NEW, WARPED HOBBY...
NOOOOOO!!
HIRATA, WAIT! PLEASE!! HOW MUCH DID YOU SEE?
WAAH!
ALL OF IT.
DEFINE "ALL"!
FROM WHEN YOU SAID, "I PRAY TO MAKE OHNO FALL IN LOVE WITH ME." ♡
HIRATA DOESN'T LIKE SWEET STUFF, BUT MAYBE COFFEE JELLY WILL BE OKAY. IT'S NOT TOO SWEET.
HE'S ACTING JUST LIKE THE OLD, EVERYDAY HIRATA. EVEN AFTER THE PLAY.
I FEEL KINDA STUPID NOW, OVERREACTING LIKE I DID.

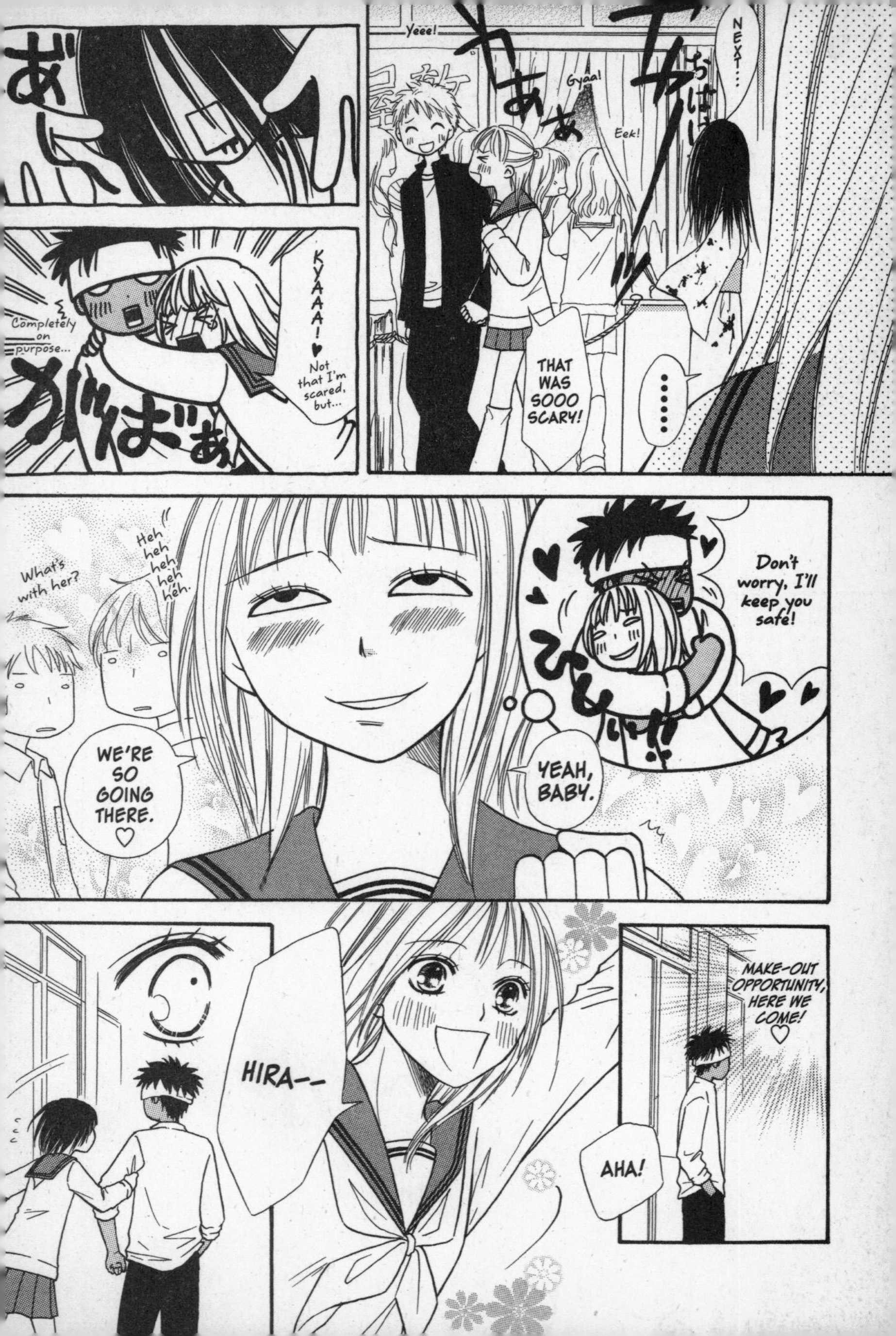
NEXT...
Yeee!
Gyaa!
Eek!
THAT WAS SOOO SCARY!
......
KYAAAA! ♥ Not that I'm scared, but...
Completely on purpose...
Don't worry, I'll keep you safe!
YEAH, BABY.
Heh heh heh heh heh.
What's with her?
WE'RE SO GOING THERE. ♡
MAKE-OUT OPPORTUNITY, HERE WE COME! ♡
AHA!
HIRA--

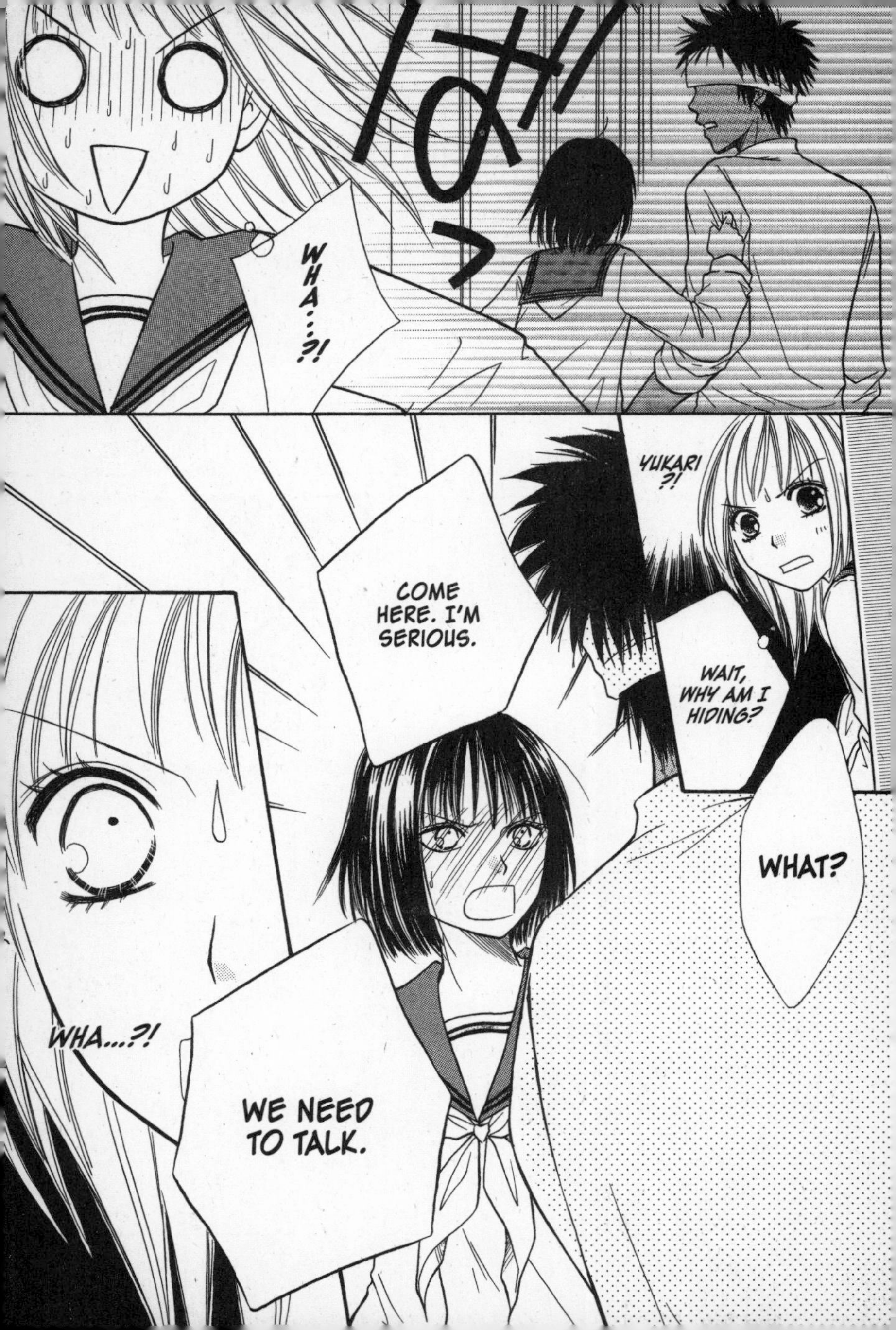
はっ
WHA...?!
YUKARI ?!
WAIT, WHY AM I HIDING?
COME HERE. I'M SERIOUS.
WHAT?
WHA...?!
WE NEED TO TALK.

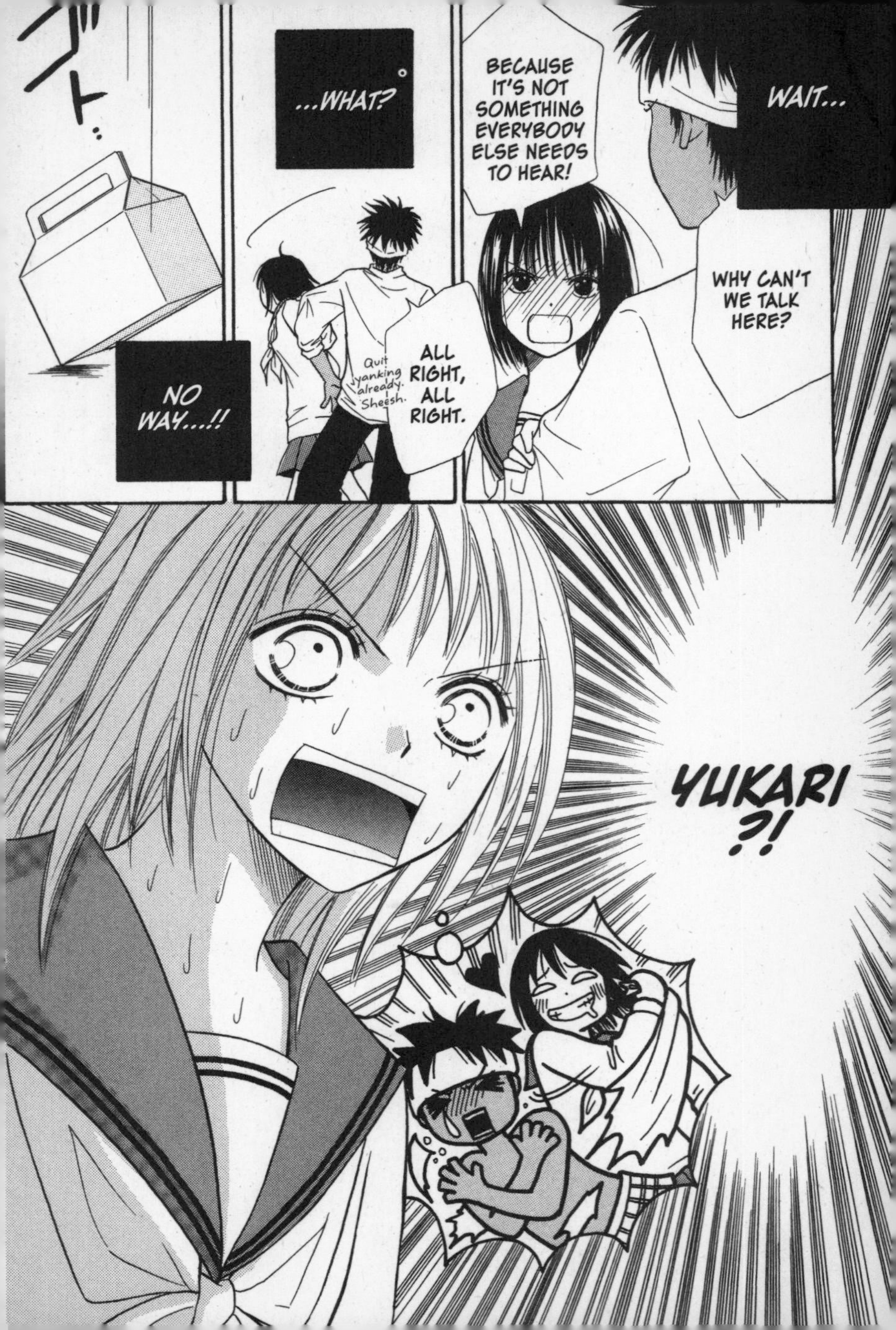
WAIT...
WHY CAN'T WE TALK HERE?
BECAUSE IT'S NOT SOMETHING EVERYBODY ELSE NEEDS TO HEAR!
...WHAT?
ALL RIGHT, ALL RIGHT.
Quit yanking already. Sheesh.
NO WAY...!!
YUKARI ?!

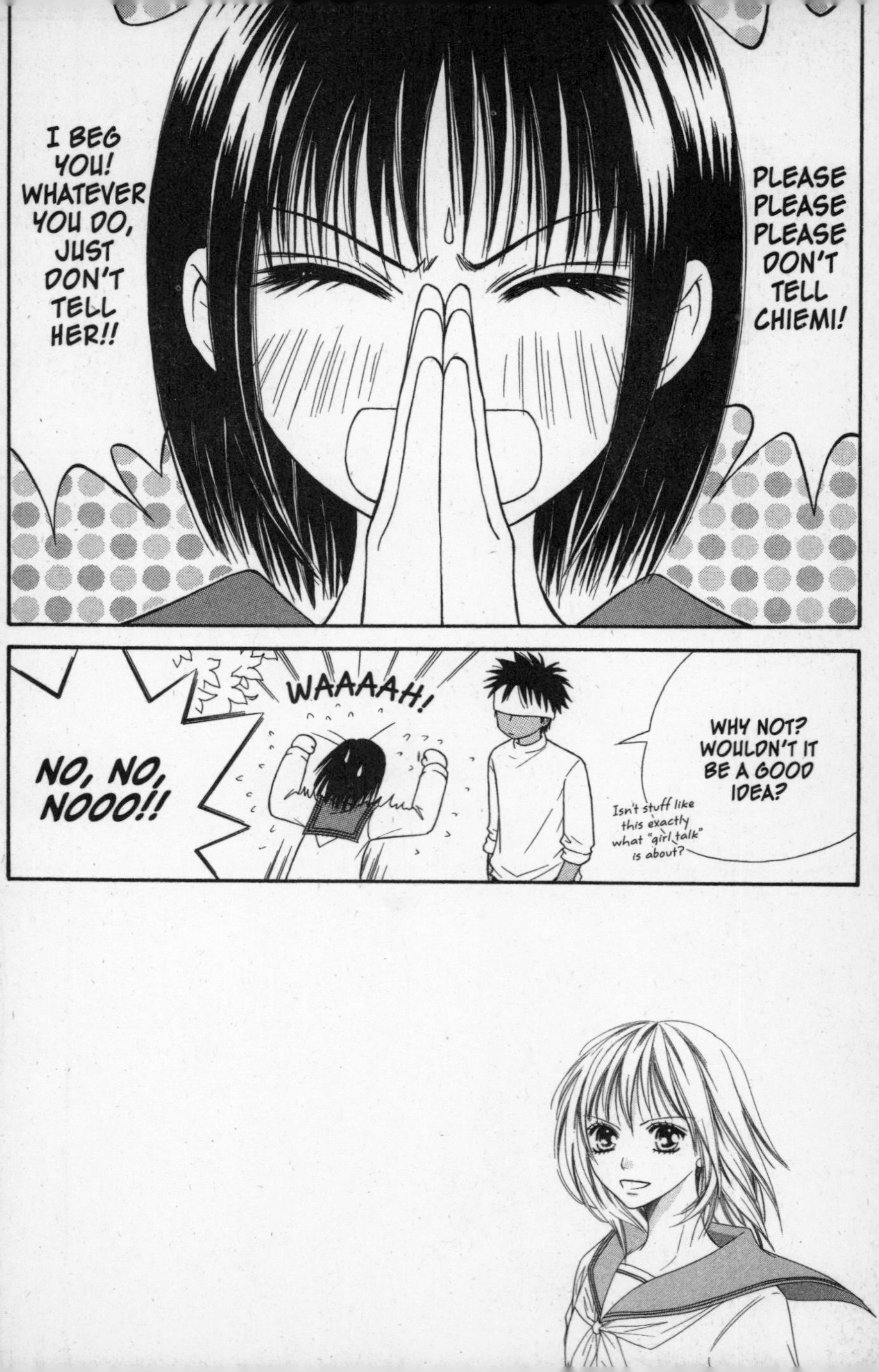
PLEASE PLEASE PLEASE DON'T TELL CHIEMI!
I BEG YOU! WHATEVER YOU DO, JUST DON'T TELL HER!!
WHY NOT? WOULDN'T IT BE A GOOD IDEA?
Isn't stuff like this exactly what "girl talk" is about?
WAAAAH!
NO, NO, NOOO!!

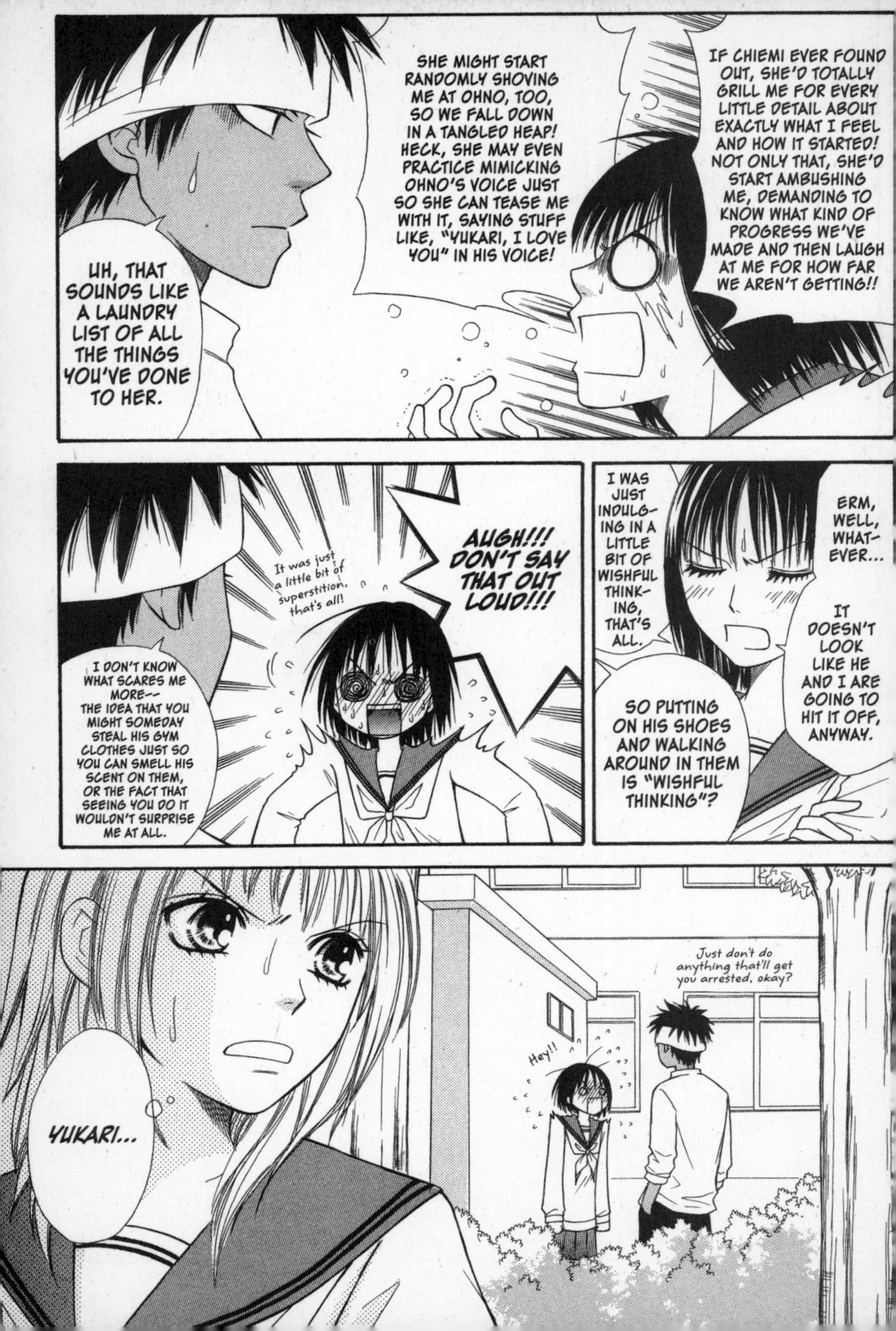
IF CHIEMI EVER FOUND OUT, SHE'D TOTALLY GRILL ME FOR EVERY LITTLE DETAIL ABOUT EXACTLY WHAT I FEEL AND HOW IT STARTED! NOT ONLY THAT, SHE'D START AMBUSHING ME, DEMANDING TO KNOW WHAT KIND OF PROGRESS WE'VE MADE AND THEN LAUGH AT ME FOR HOW FAR WE AREN'T GETTING!!
SHE MIGHT START RANDOMLY SHOVING ME AT OHNO, TOO, SO WE FALL DOWN IN A TANGLED HEAP! HECK, SHE MAY EVEN PRACTICE MIMICKING OHNO'S VOICE JUST SO SHE CAN TEASE ME WITH IT, SAYING STUFF LIKE, "YUKARI, I LOVE YOU" IN HIS VOICE!
UH, THAT SOUNDS LIKE A LAUNDRY LIST OF ALL THE THINGS YOU'VE DONE TO HER.
ERM, WELL, WHATEVER...
IT DOESN'T LOOK LIKE HE AND I ARE GOING TO HIT IT OFF, ANYWAY.
I WAS JUST INDULGING IN A LITTLE BIT OF WISHFUL THINKING, THAT'S ALL.
SO PUTTING ON HIS SHOES AND WALKING AROUND IN THEM IS "WISHFUL THINKING"?
AUGH!!! DON'T SAY THAT OUT LOUD!!!
It was just a little bit of superstition, that's all!
I DON'T KNOW WHAT SCARES ME MORE-- THE IDEA THAT YOU MIGHT SOMEDAY STEAL HIS GYM CLOTHES JUST SO YOU CAN SMELL HIS SCENT ON THEM, OR THE FACT THAT SEEING YOU DO IT WOULDN'T SURPRISE ME AT ALL.
Just don't do anything that'll get you arrested, okay?
Hey!!
YUKARI...

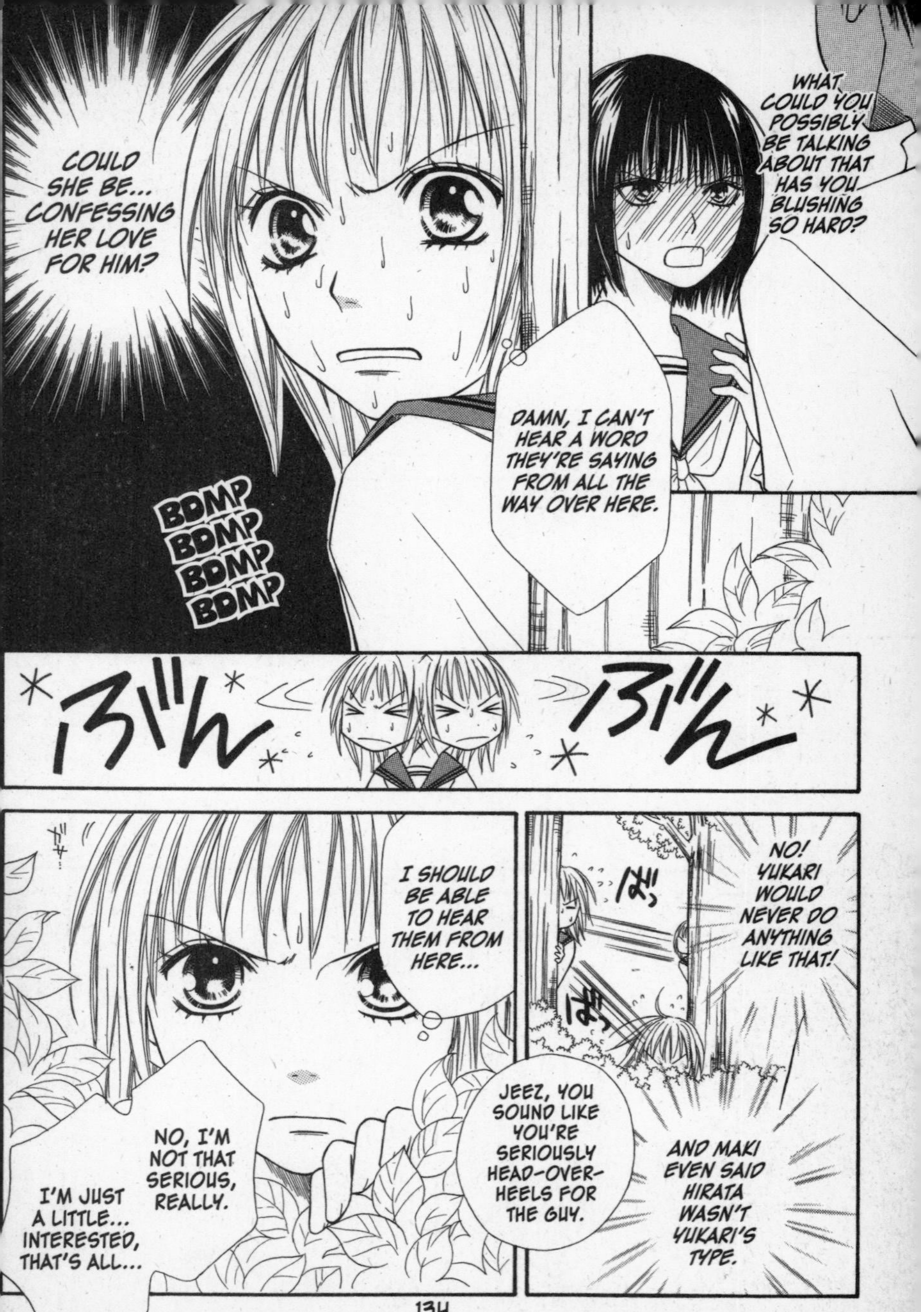
WHAT COULD YOU POSSIBLY BE TALKING ABOUT THAT HAS YOU BLUSHING SO HARD?
COULD SHE BE... CONFESSING HER LOVE FOR HIM?
DAMN, I CAN'T HEAR A WORD THEY'RE SAYING FROM ALL THE WAY OVER HERE.
BDMP BDMP BDMP BDMP
ぶん
ぶん
NO! YUKARI WOULD NEVER DO ANYTHING LIKE THAT!
ぱっ
ぱっ
AND MAKI EVEN SAID HIRATA WASN'T YUKARI'S TYPE.
ガサ…
I SHOULD BE ABLE TO HEAR THEM FROM HERE...
JEEZ, YOU SOUND LIKE YOU'RE SERIOUSLY HEAD-OVER-HEELS FOR THE GUY.
NO, I'M NOT THAT SERIOUS, REALLY.
I'M JUST A LITTLE... INTERESTED, THAT'S ALL...

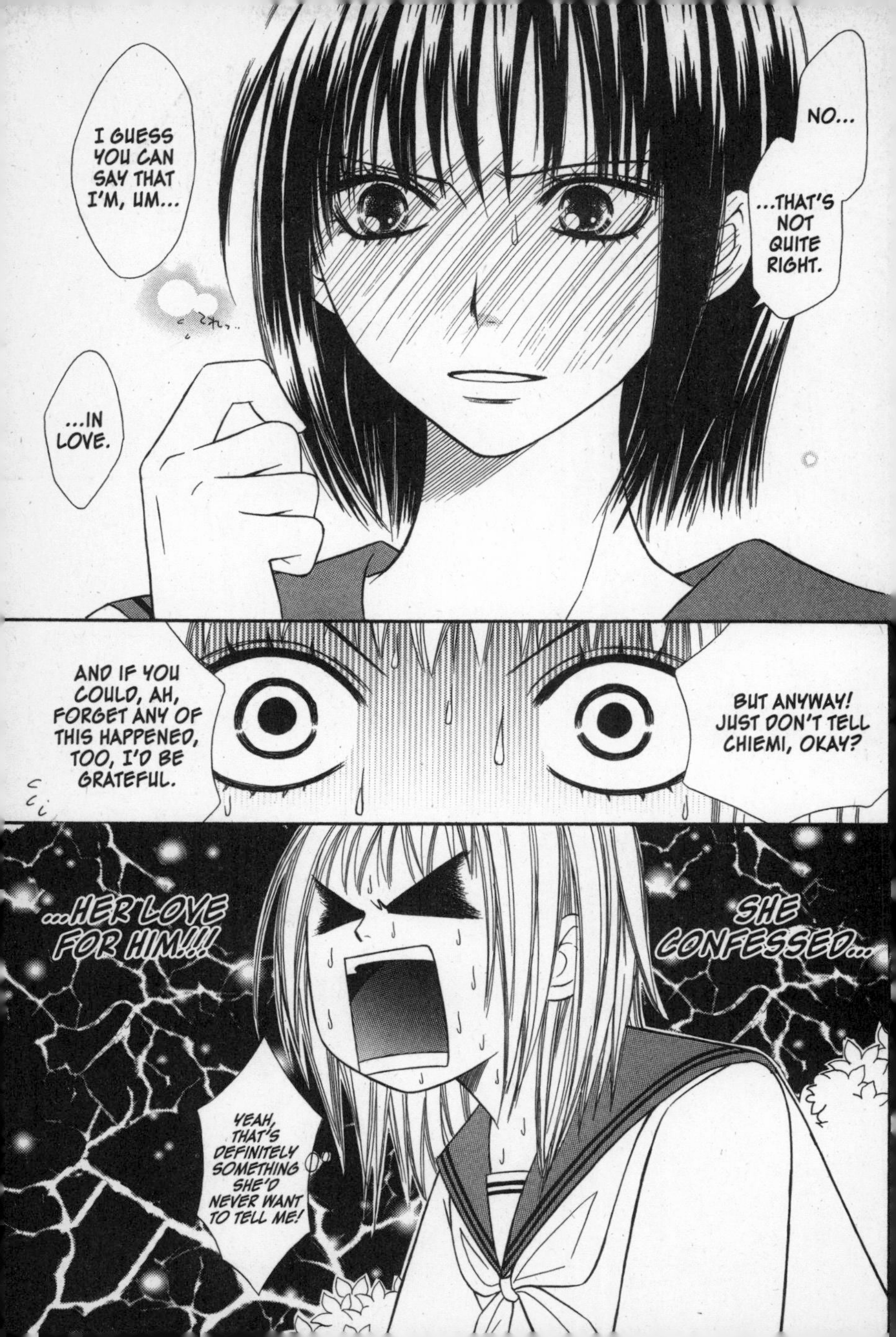
NO...
...THAT'S NOT QUITE RIGHT.
I GUESS YOU CAN SAY THAT I'M, UM...
...IN LOVE.
BUT ANYWAY! JUST DON'T TELL CHIEMI, OKAY?
AND IF YOU COULD, AH, FORGET ANY OF THIS HAPPENED, TOO, I'D BE GRATEFUL.
SHE CONFESSED...
...HER LOVE FOR HIM!!!
YEAH, THAT'S DEFINITELY SOMETHING SHE'D NEVER WANT TO TELL ME!

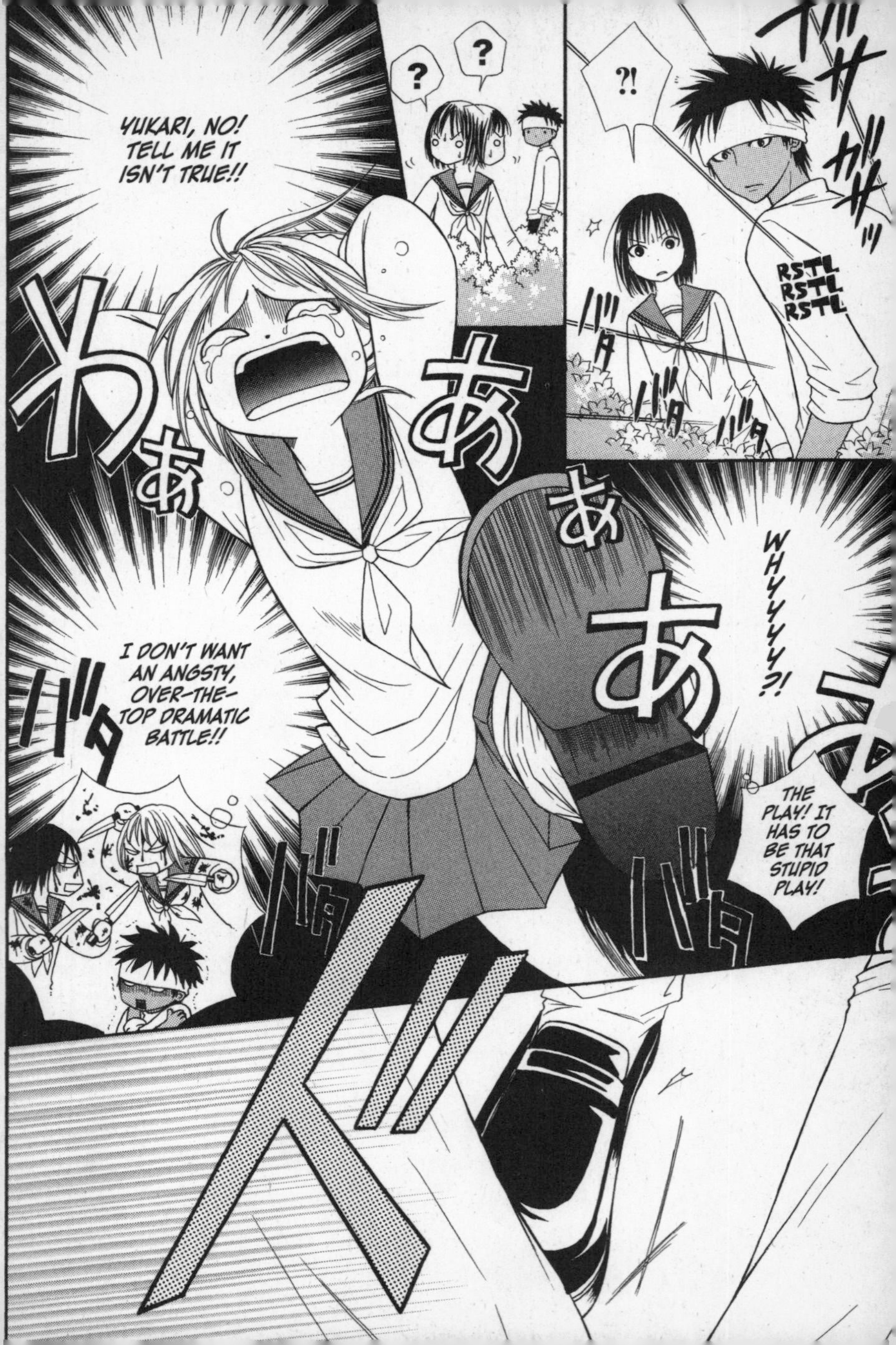

?!
RSTL RSTL RSTL
?
?
WHYYYYYY?!
THE PLAY! IT HAS TO BE THAT STUPID PLAY!
YUKARI, NO! TELL ME IT ISN'T TRUE!!
I DON'T WANT AN ANGSTY, OVER-THE-TOP DRAMATIC BATTLE!!

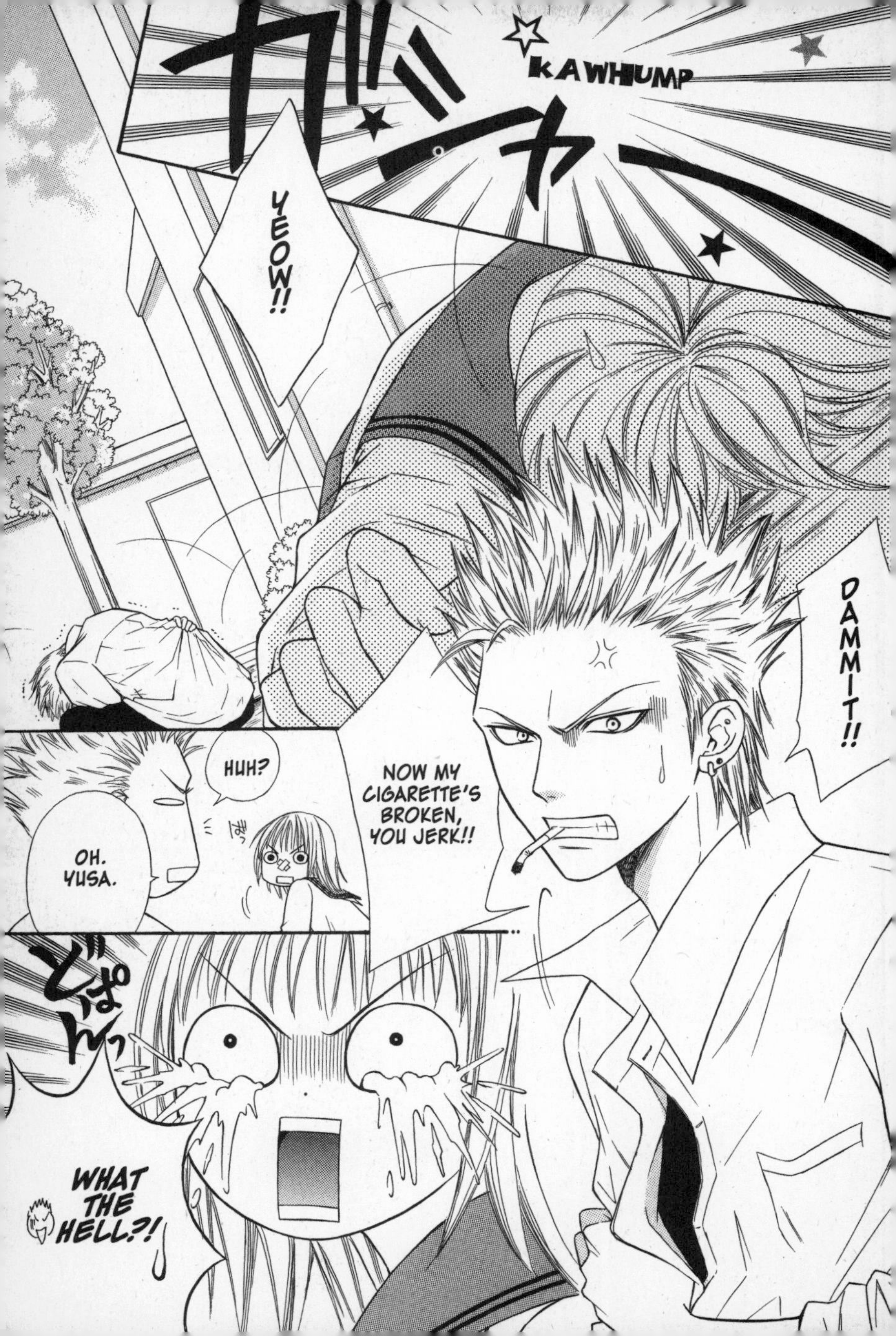
KAWHUMP
YEOW!!
DAMMIT!!
NOW MY CIGARETTE'S BROKEN, YOU JERK!!
HUH?
OH. YUSA.
WHAT THE HELL.?!

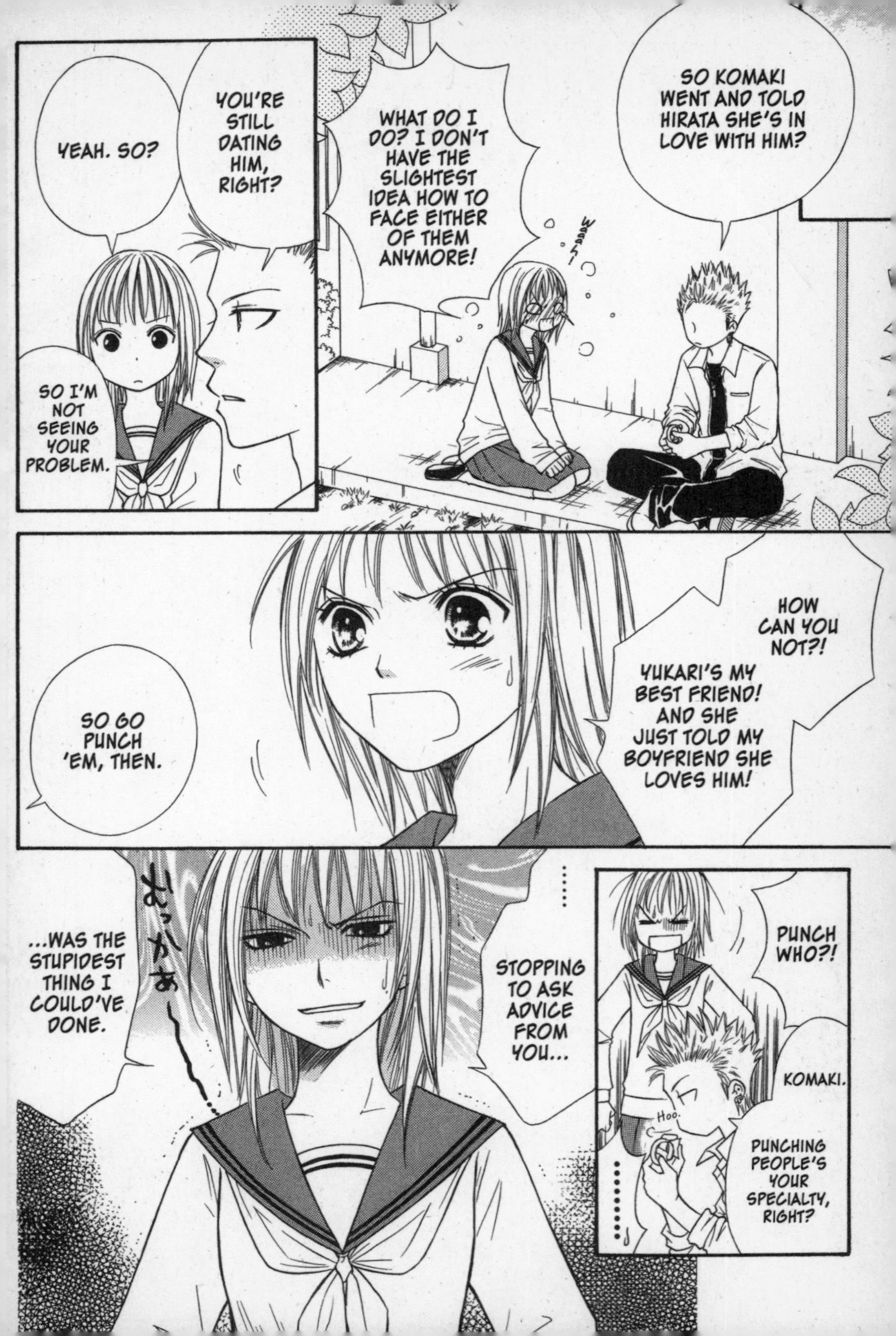
SO KOMAKI WENT AND TOLD HIRATA SHE'S IN LOVE WITH HIM?
WHAT DO I DO? I DON'T HAVE THE SLIGHTEST IDEA HOW TO FACE EITHER OF THEM ANYMORE!
YOU'RE STILL DATING HIM, RIGHT?
YEAH. SO?
SO I'M NOT SEEING YOUR PROBLEM.
HOW CAN YOU NOT?!
YUKARI'S MY BEST FRIEND! AND SHE JUST TOLD MY BOYFRIEND SHE LOVES HIM!
SO GO PUNCH 'EM, THEN.
PUNCH WHO?!
KOMAKI.
PUNCHING PEOPLE'S YOUR SPECIALTY, RIGHT?
……
……
STOPPING TO ASK ADVICE FROM YOU...
...WAS THE STUPIDEST THING I COULD'VE DONE.

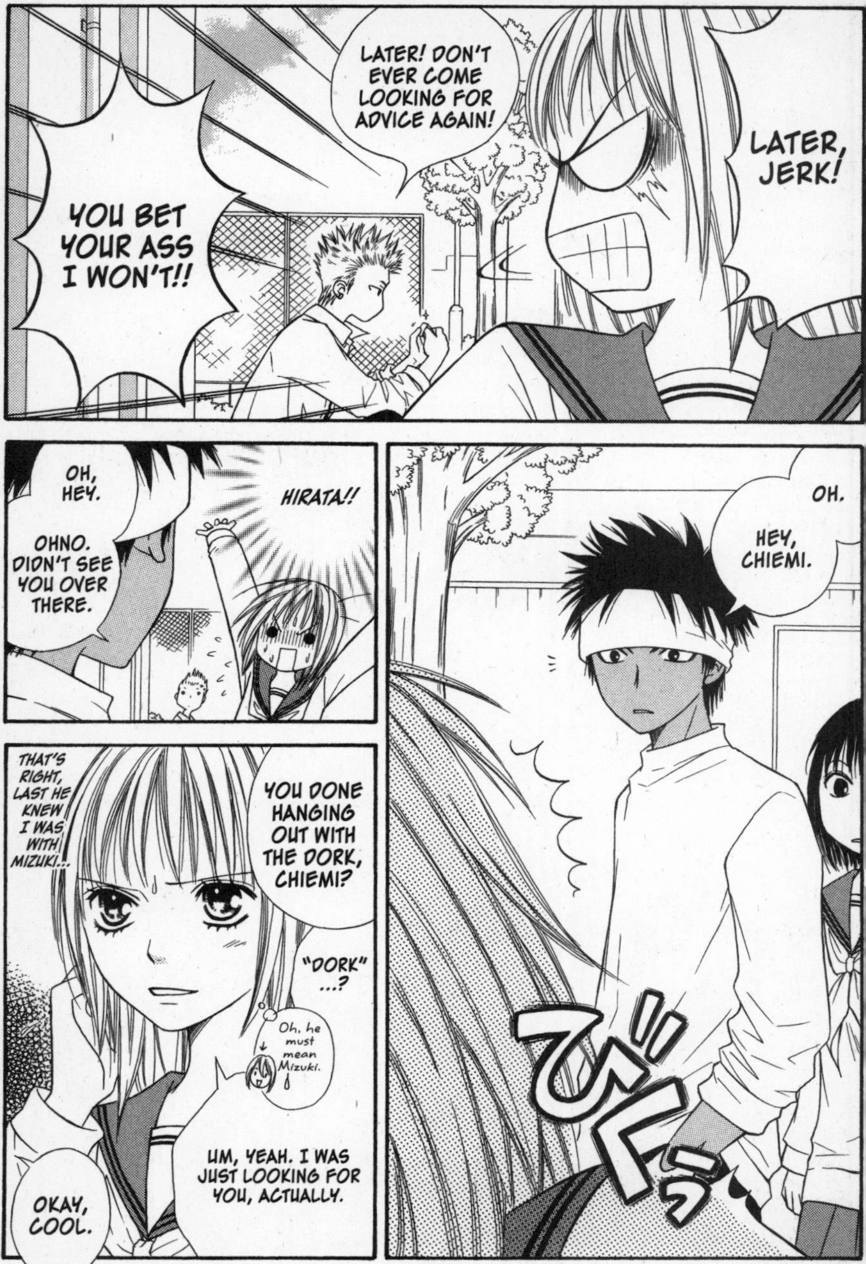
LATER, JERK!
LATER! DON'T EVER COME LOOKING FOR ADVICE AGAIN!
YOU BET YOUR ASS I WON'T!!
OH.
HEY, CHIEMI.
びくっ
HIRATA!!
OH, HEY.
OHNO. DIDN'T SEE YOU OVER THERE.
YOU DONE HANGING OUT WITH THE DORK, CHIEMI?
THAT'S RIGHT, LAST HE KNEW I WAS WITH MIZUKI...
"DORK" ...?
Oh, he must mean Mizuki.
UM, YEAH. I WAS JUST LOOKING FOR YOU, ACTUALLY.
OKAY, COOL.

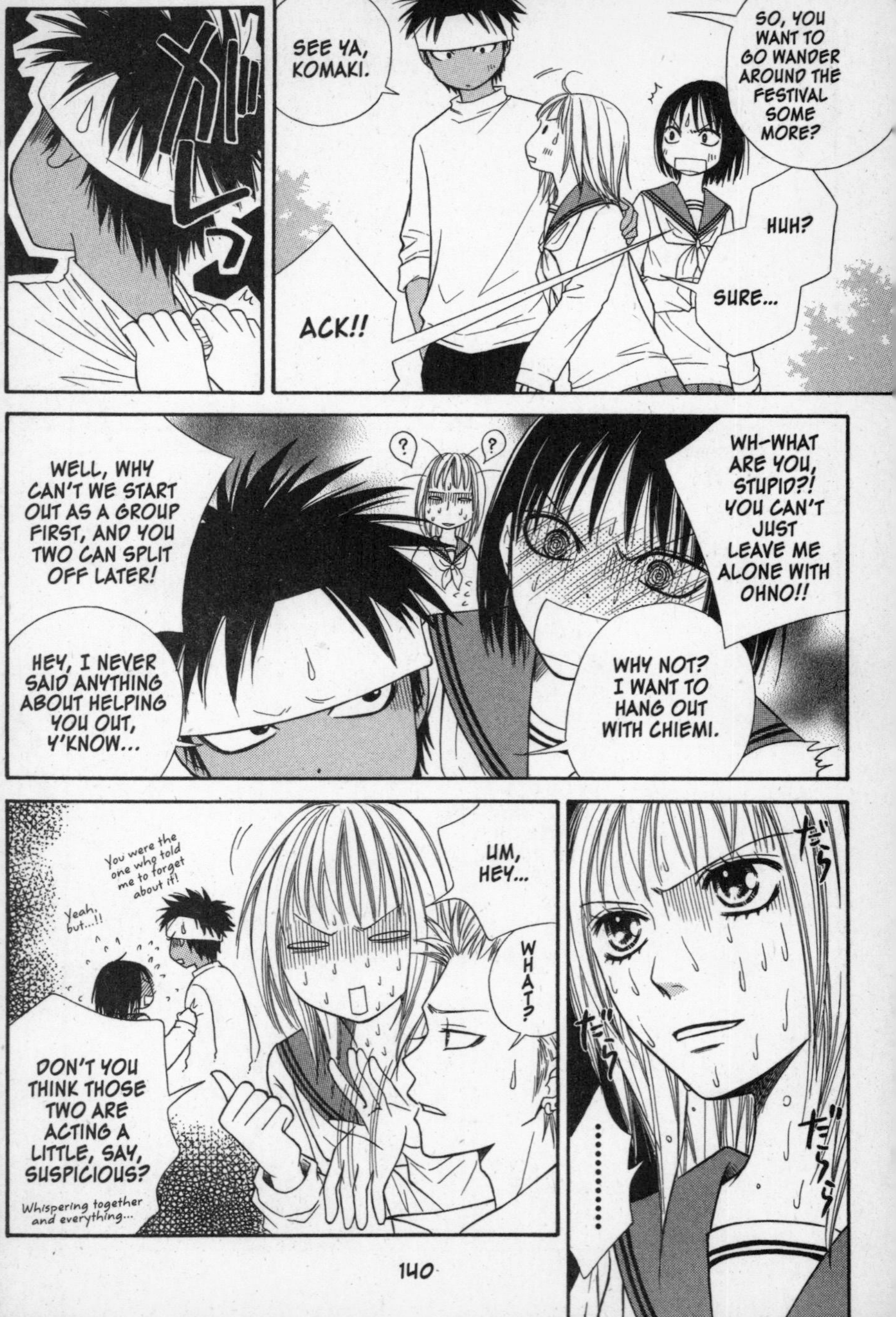
SO, YOU WANT TO GO WANDER AROUND THE FESTIVAL SOME MORE?
HUH?
SURE...
SEE YA, KOMAKI.
ACK!!
WH-WHAT ARE YOU, STUPID?! YOU CAN'T JUST LEAVE ME ALONE WITH OHNO!!
WELL, WHY CAN'T WE START OUT AS A GROUP FIRST, AND YOU TWO CAN SPLIT OFF LATER!
WHY NOT? I WANT TO HANG OUT WITH CHIEMI.
HEY, I NEVER SAID ANYTHING ABOUT HELPING YOU OUT, Y'KNOW...
....
UM, HEY...
WHAT?
You were the one who told me to forget about it!
Yeah, but...!!
DON'T YOU THINK THOSE TWO ARE ACTING A LITTLE, SAY, SUSPICIOUS?
Whispering together and everything...

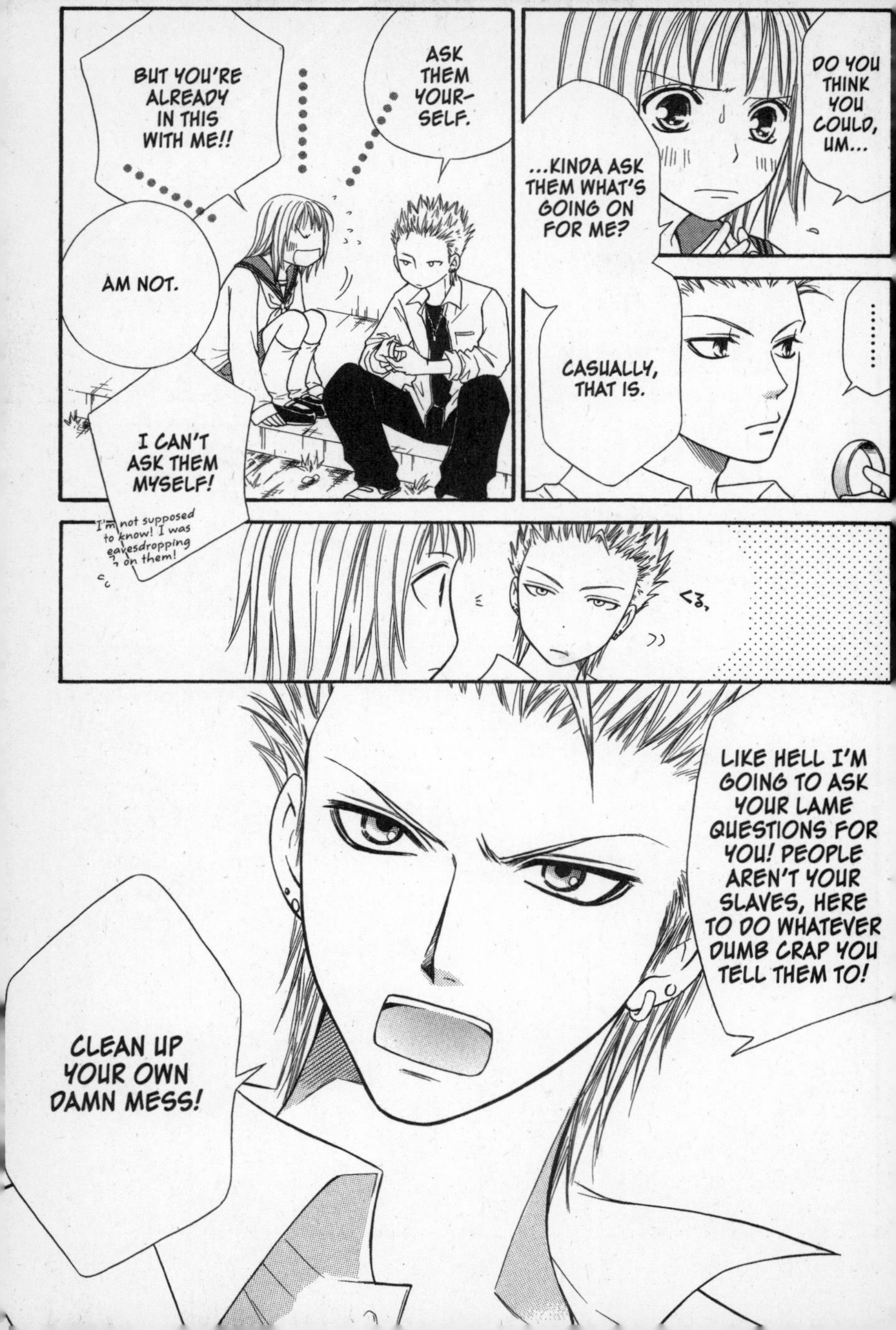
DO YOU THINK YOU COULD, UM...
...KINDA ASK THEM WHAT'S GOING ON FOR ME?
......
CASUALLY, THAT IS.
ASK THEM YOUR-SELF.
BUT YOU'RE ALREADY IN THIS WITH ME!!
AM NOT.
I CAN'T ASK THEM MYSELF!
I'm not supposed to know! I was eavesdropping on them!
くる
LIKE HELL I'M GOING TO ASK YOUR LAME QUESTIONS FOR YOU! PEOPLE AREN'T YOUR SLAVES, HERE TO DO WHATEVER DUMB CRAP YOU TELL THEM TO!
CLEAN UP YOUR OWN DAMN MESS!

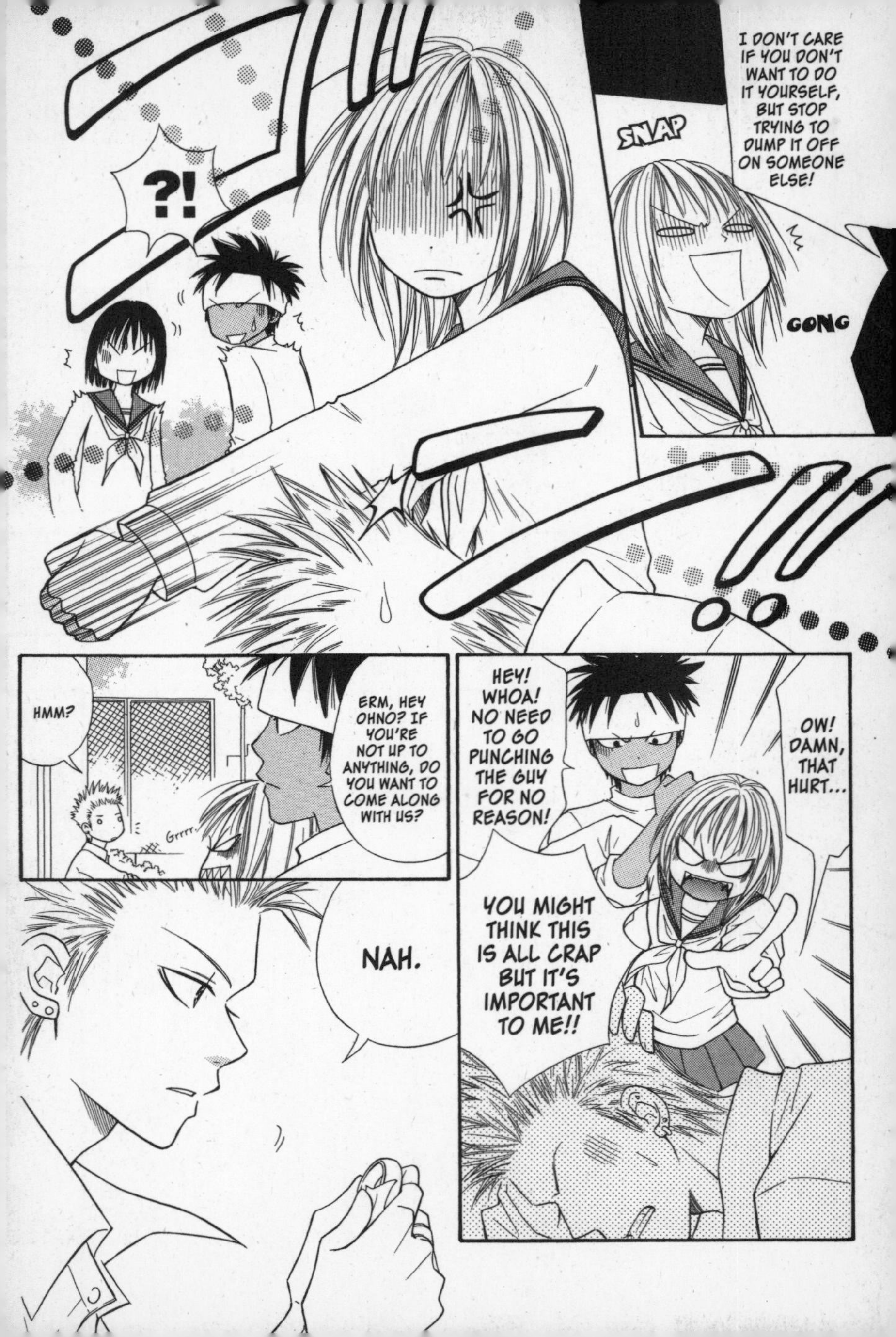
I DON'T CARE IF YOU DON'T WANT TO DO IT YOURSELF, BUT STOP TRYING TO DUMP IT OFF ON SOMEONE ELSE!
SNAP
GONG
?!
OW! DAMN, THAT HURT...
HEY! WHOA! NO NEED TO GO PUNCHING THE GUY FOR NO REASON!
YOU MIGHT THINK THIS IS ALL CRAP BUT IT'S IMPORTANT TO ME!!
ERM, HEY OHNO? IF YOU'RE NOT UP TO ANYTHING, DO YOU WANT TO COME ALONG WITH US?
HMM?
Grrrr.
NAH.

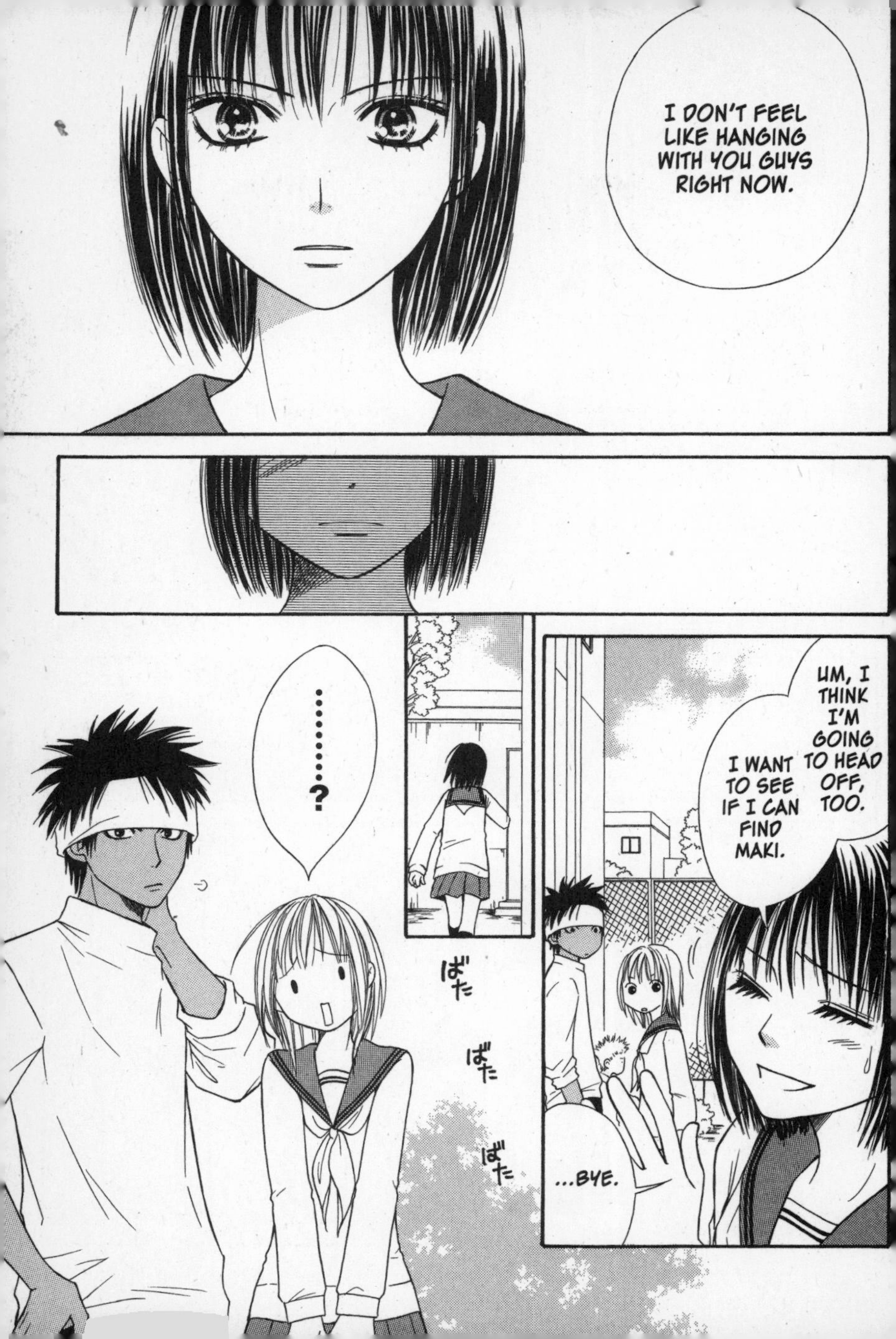
I DON'T FEEL LIKE HANGING WITH YOU GUYS RIGHT NOW.
UM, I THINK I'M GOING TO HEAD OFF, TOO.
I WANT TO SEE IF I CAN FIND MAKI.
...BYE.
ばた
ばた
ばた
......?

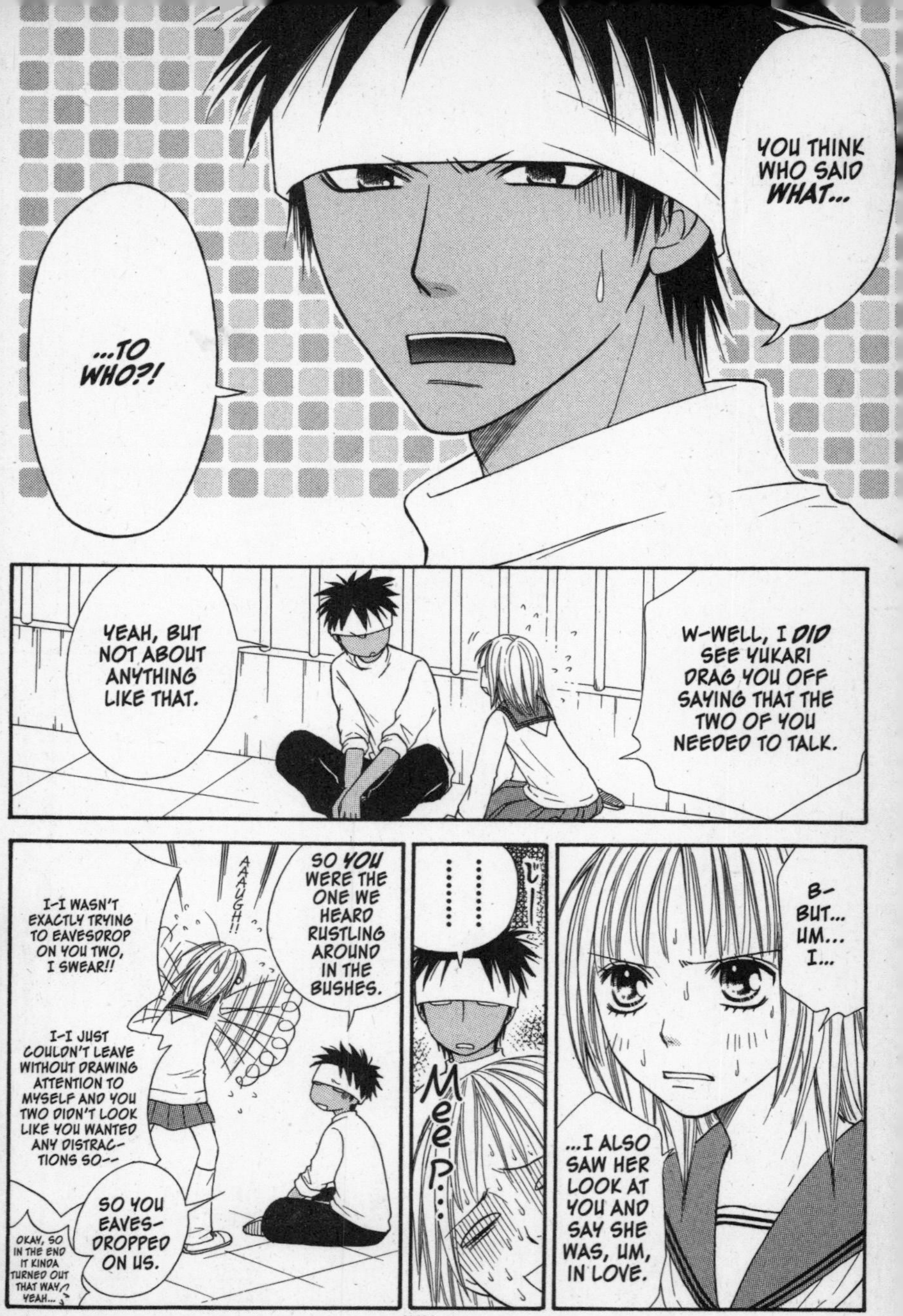
YOU THINK WHO SAID WHAT...
...TO WHO?!
W-WELL, I DID SEE YUKARI DRAG YOU OFF SAYING THAT THE TWO OF YOU NEEDED TO TALK.
YEAH, BUT NOT ABOUT ANYTHING LIKE THAT.
B-BUT... UM... I...
...I ALSO SAW HER LOOK AT YOU AND SAY SHE WAS, UM, IN LOVE.
......
MEEP...
SO YOU WERE THE ONE WE HEARD RUSTLING AROUND IN THE BUSHES.
AAAUGH!!
I-I WASN'T EXACTLY TRYING TO EAVESDROP ON YOU TWO, I SWEAR!!
I-I JUST COULDN'T LEAVE WITHOUT DRAWING ATTENTION TO MYSELF AND YOU TWO DIDN'T LOOK LIKE YOU WANTED ANY DISTRACTIONS SO--
SO YOU EAVES-DROPPED ON US.
OKAY, SO IN THE END IT KINDA TURNED OUT THAT WAY, YEAH...

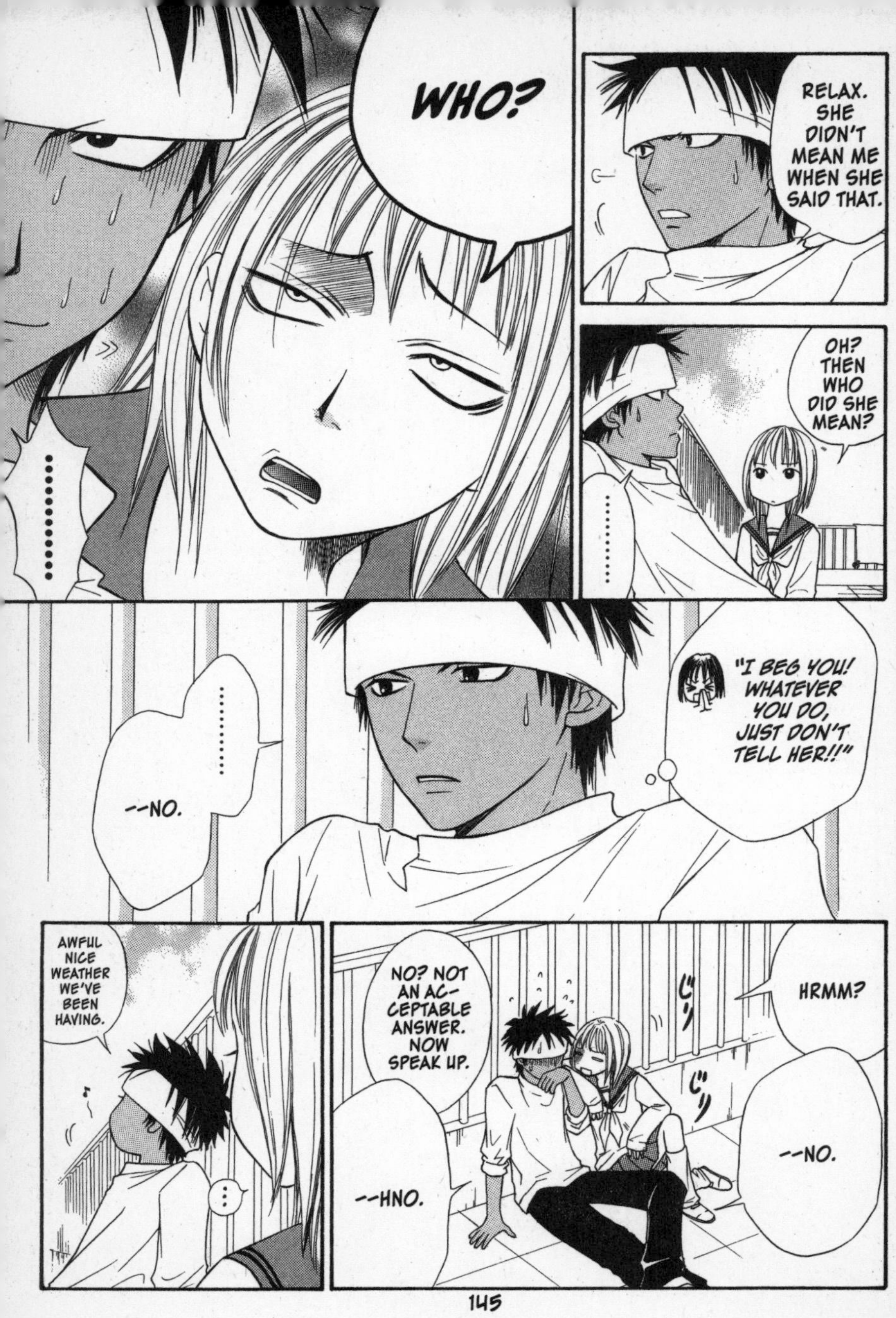
RELAX. SHE DIDN'T MEAN ME WHEN SHE SAID THAT.
OH? THEN WHO DID SHE MEAN?
......
WHO?
....
"I BEG YOU! WHATEVER YOU DO, JUST DON'T TELL HER!!"
......
--NO.
HRMM?
--NO.
NO? NOT AN ACCEPTABLE ANSWER. NOW SPEAK UP.
--HNO.
AWFUL NICE WEATHER WE'VE BEEN HAVING.
...

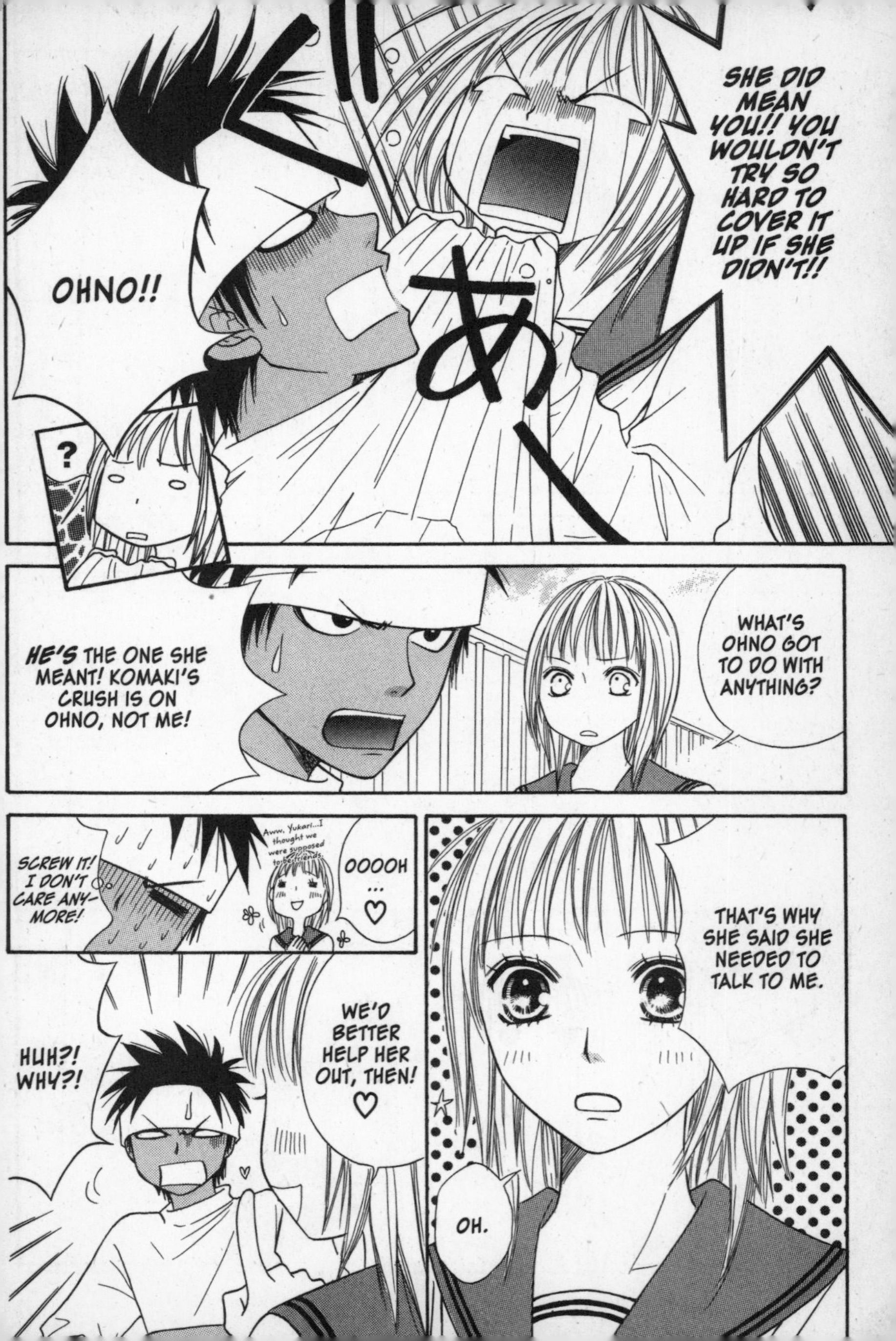
SHE DID MEAN YOU!! YOU WOULDN'T TRY SO HARD TO COVER IT UP IF SHE DIDN'T!!
あ
OHNO!!
?
WHAT'S OHNO GOT TO DO WITH ANYTHING?
HE'S THE ONE SHE MEANT! KOMAKI'S CRUSH IS ON OHNO, NOT ME!
OH.
THAT'S WHY SHE SAID SHE NEEDED TO TALK TO ME.
OOOOH ... ♡
Aww, Yukari...I thought we were supposed to be friends.
SCREW IT! I DON'T CARE ANY-MORE!
WE'D BETTER HELP HER OUT, THEN! ♡
HUH?! WHY?!

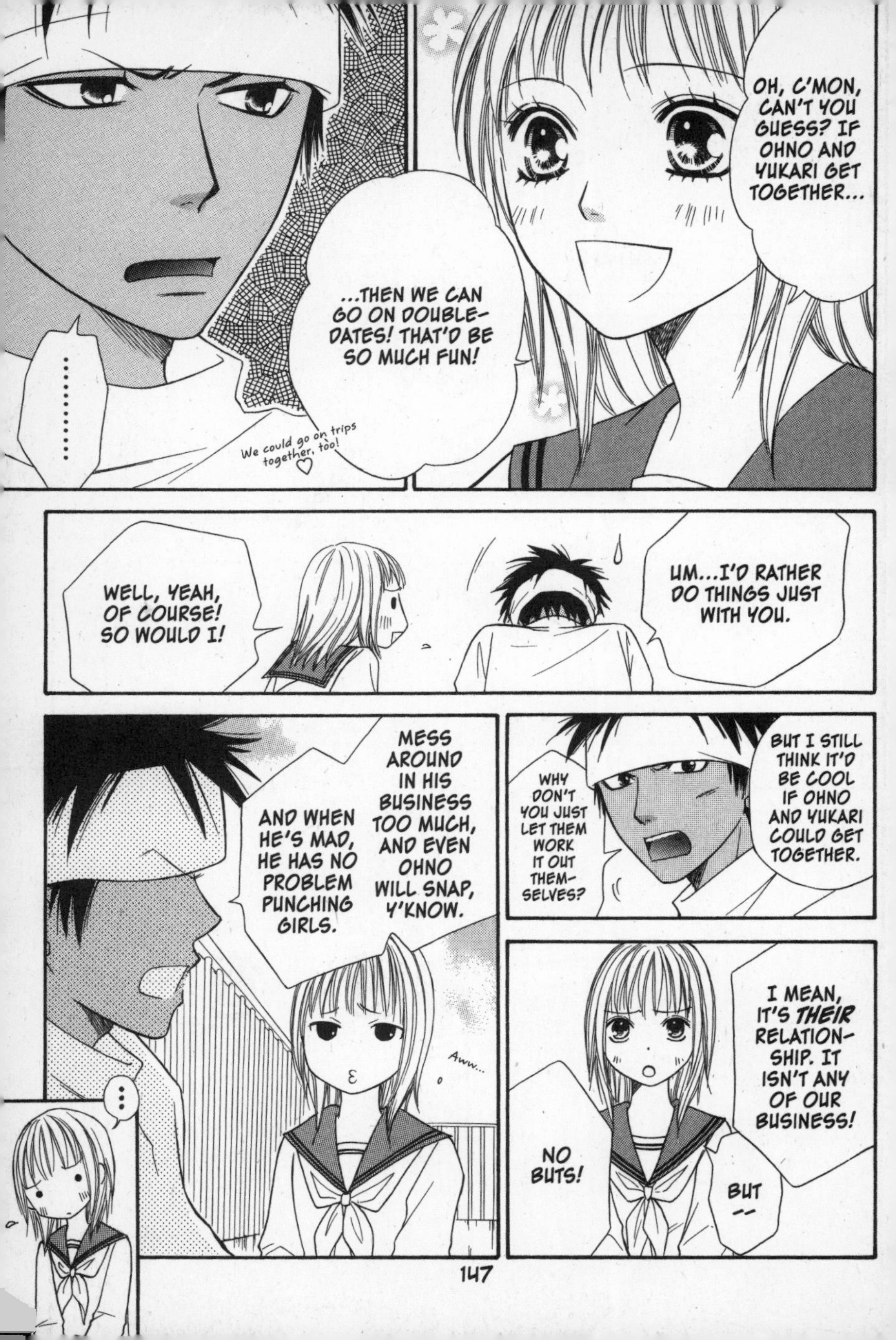
OH, C'MON, CAN'T YOU GUESS? IF OHNO AND YUKARI GET TOGETHER...
...THEN WE CAN GO ON DOUBLE-DATES! THAT'D BE SO MUCH FUN!
We could go on trips together, too! ♡
....
UM...I'D RATHER DO THINGS JUST WITH YOU.
WELL, YEAH, OF COURSE! SO WOULD I!
BUT I STILL THINK IT'D BE COOL IF OHNO AND YUKARI COULD GET TOGETHER.
WHY DON'T YOU JUST LET THEM WORK IT OUT THEMSELVES?
I MEAN, IT'S *THEIR* RELATIONSHIP. IT ISN'T ANY OF OUR BUSINESS!
BUT --
NO BUTS!
MESS AROUND IN HIS BUSINESS TOO MUCH, AND EVEN OHNO WILL SNAP, Y'KNOW.
AND WHEN HE'S MAD, HE HAS NO PROBLEM PUNCHING GIRLS.
Aww...
...

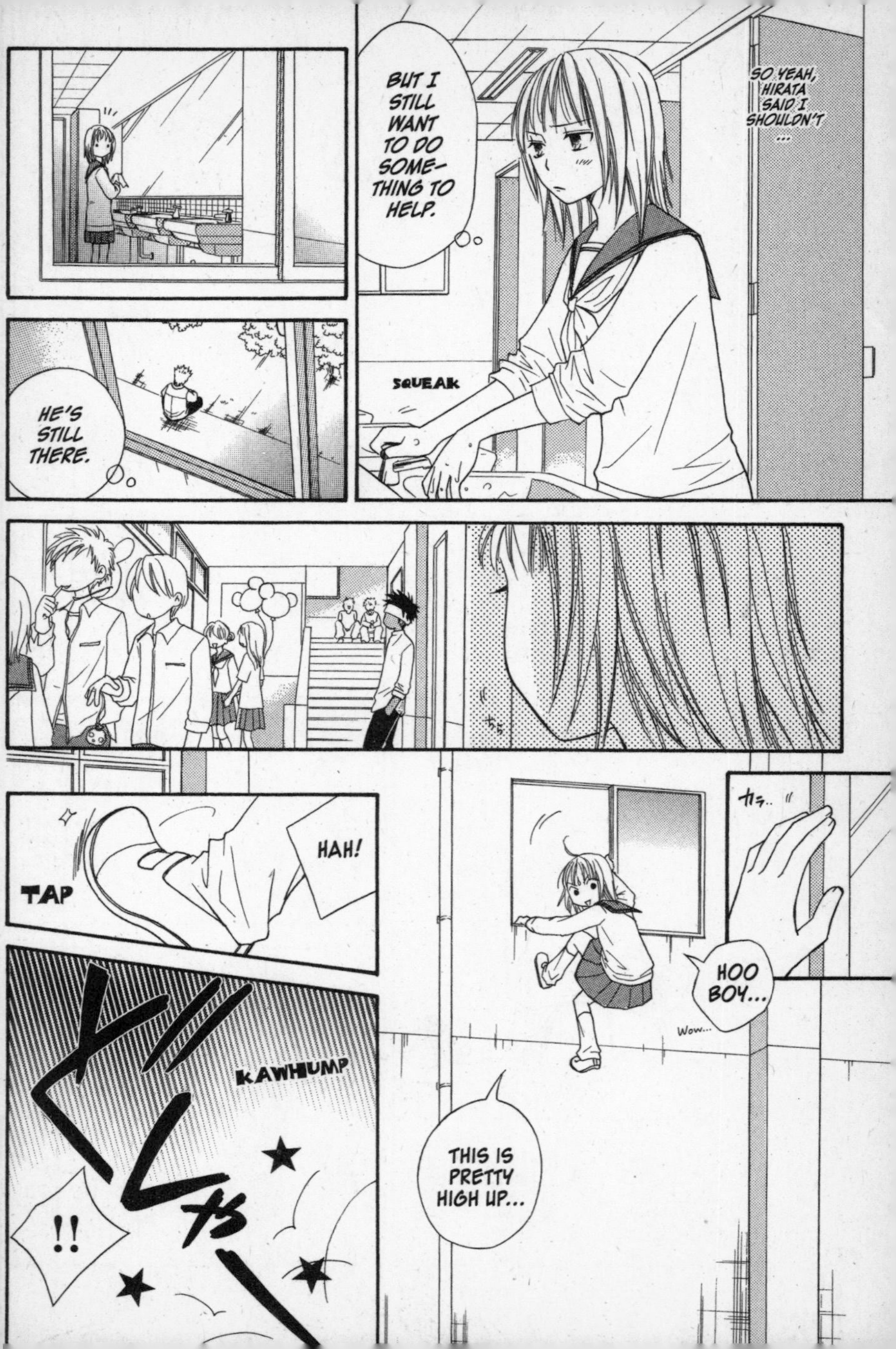
SO YEAH, HIRATA SAID I SHOULDN'T ...
BUT I STILL WANT TO DO SOME-THING TO HELP.
SQUEAK
HE'S STILL THERE.
カラ..
HOO BOY...
Wow...
THIS IS PRETTY HIGH UP...
HAH!
TAP
KAWHUMP
!!

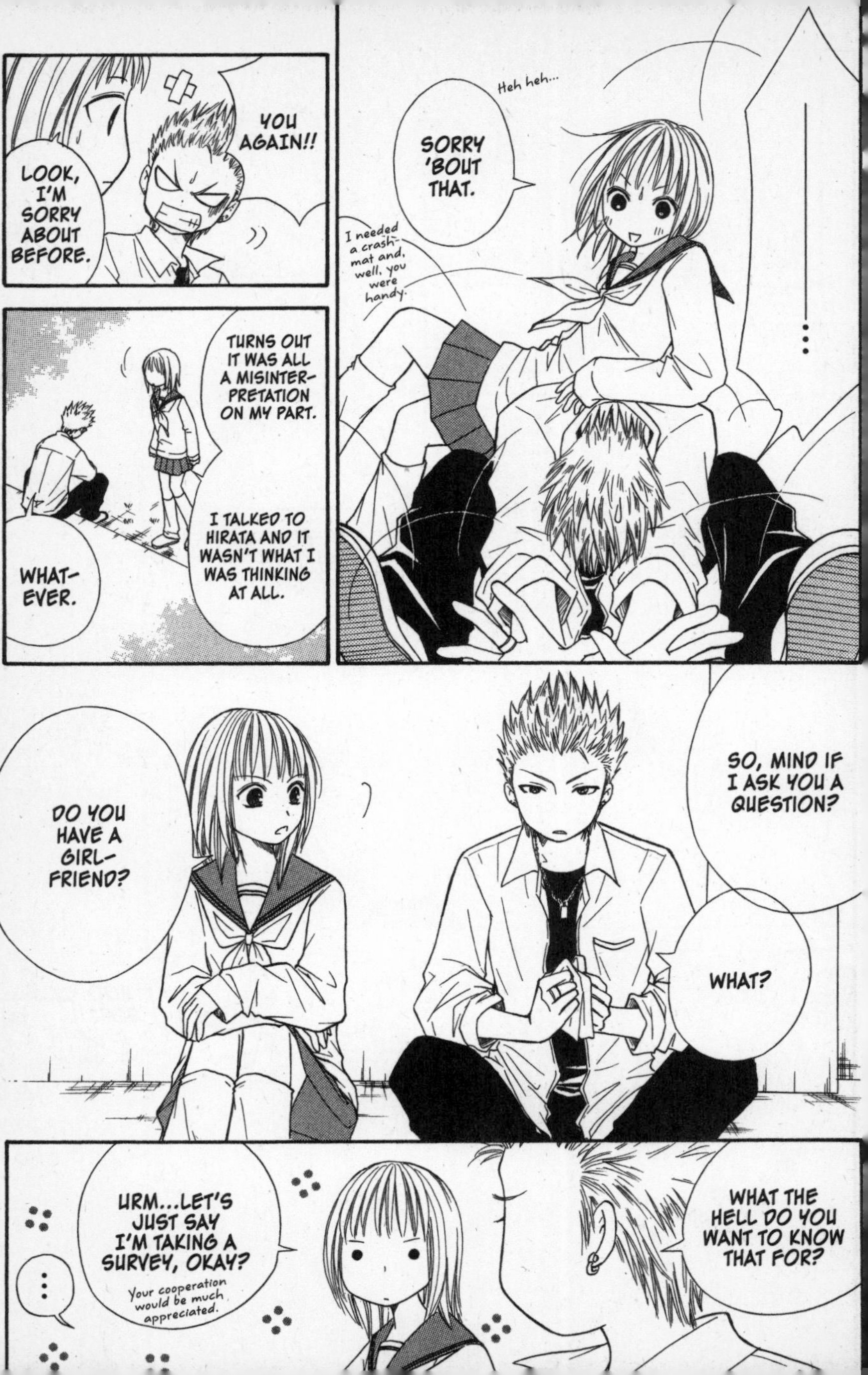
Heh heh...
SORRY 'BOUT THAT.
I needed a crash-mat and, well, you were handy.
...
YOU AGAIN!!
LOOK, I'M SORRY ABOUT BEFORE.
TURNS OUT IT WAS ALL A MISINTERPRETATION ON MY PART.
I TALKED TO HIRATA AND IT WASN'T WHAT I WAS THINKING AT ALL.
WHAT-EVER.
SO, MIND IF I ASK YOU A QUESTION?
WHAT?
DO YOU HAVE A GIRLFRIEND?
WHAT THE HELL DO YOU WANT TO KNOW THAT FOR?
URM...LET'S JUST SAY I'M TAKING A SURVEY, OKAY?
Your cooperation would be much appreciated.
...

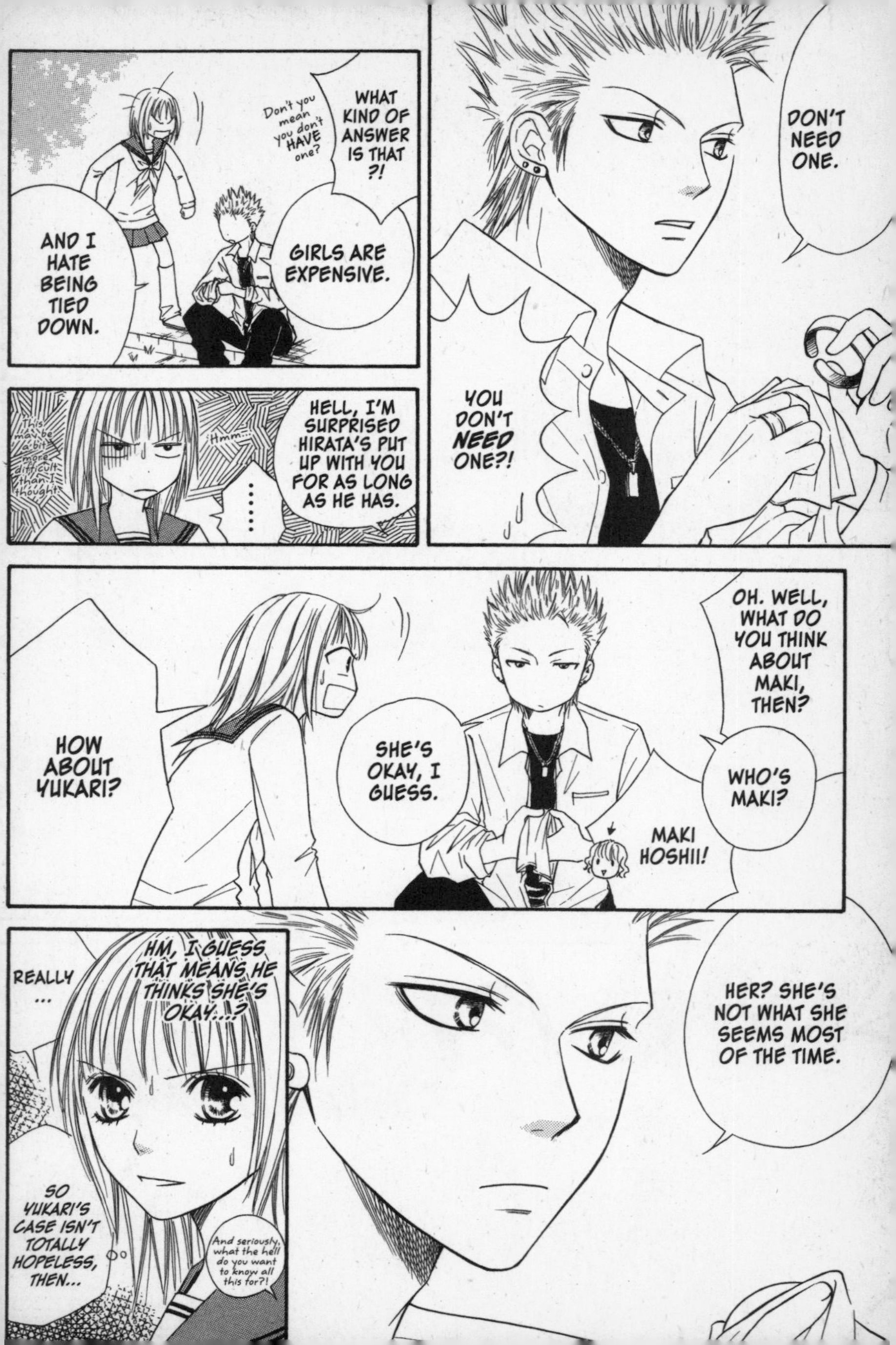
DON'T NEED ONE.
YOU DON'T NEED ONE?!
WHAT KIND OF ANSWER IS THAT ?!
Don't you mean you don't HAVE one?
GIRLS ARE EXPENSIVE.
AND I HATE BEING TIED DOWN.
HELL, I'M SURPRISED HIRATA'S PUT UP WITH YOU FOR AS LONG AS HE HAS.
Hmm...
......
This may be a bit more difficult than I thought.
OH. WELL, WHAT DO YOU THINK ABOUT MAKI, THEN?
WHO'S MAKI?
MAKI HOSHII!
SHE'S OKAY, I GUESS.
HOW ABOUT YUKARI?
HER? SHE'S NOT WHAT SHE SEEMS MOST OF THE TIME.
HM, I GUESS THAT MEANS HE THINKS SHE'S OKAY...?
REALLY ...
SO YUKARI'S CASE ISN'T TOTALLY HOPELESS, THEN...
And seriously, what the hell do you want to know all this for?!

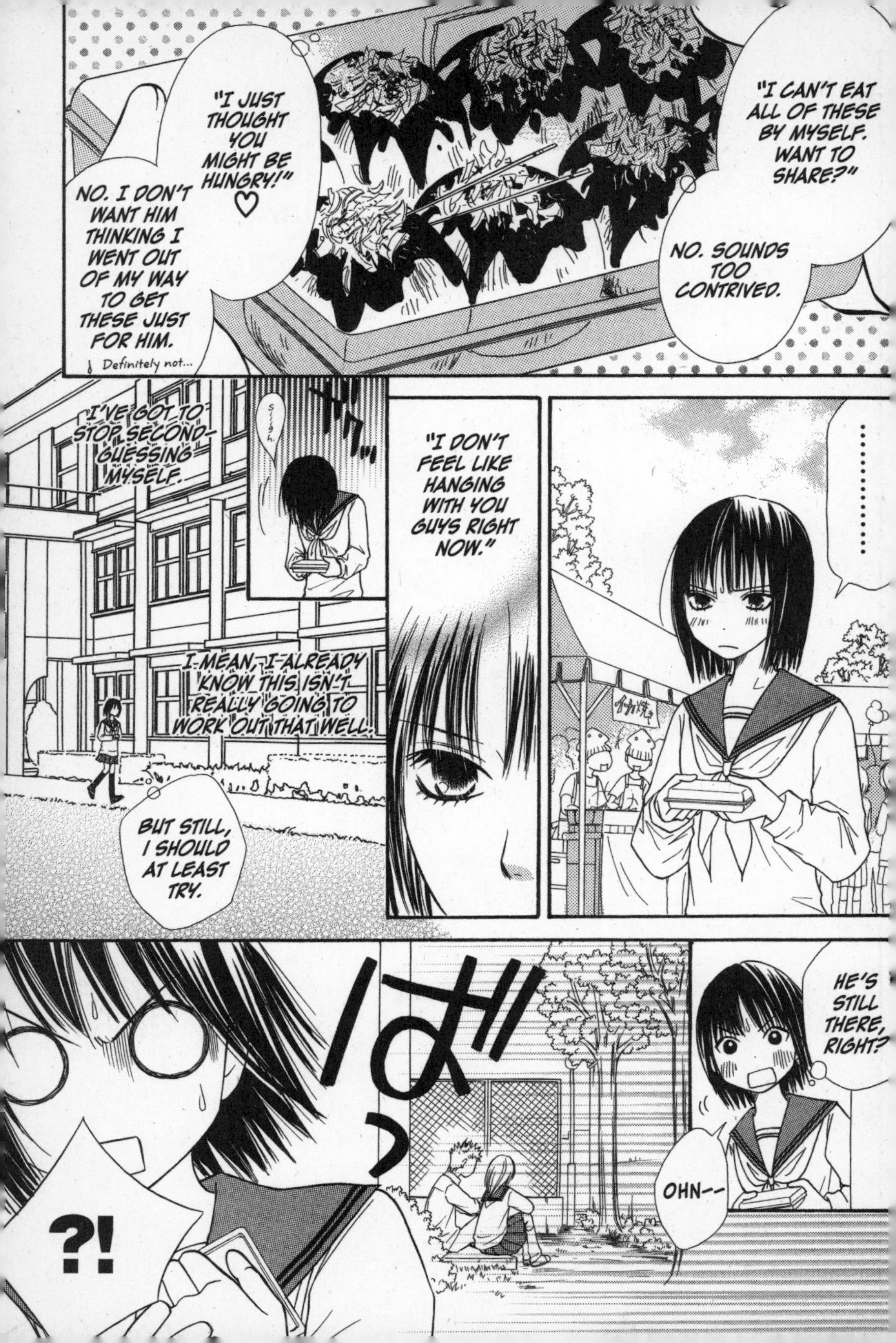
"I CAN'T EAT ALL OF THESE BY MYSELF. WANT TO SHARE?"
NO. SOUNDS TOO CONTRIVED.
"I JUST THOUGHT YOU MIGHT BE HUNGRY!" ♡
NO. I DON'T WANT HIM THINKING I WENT OUT OF MY WAY TO GET THESE JUST FOR HIM.
Definitely not...
......
"I DON'T FEEL LIKE HANGING WITH YOU GUYS RIGHT NOW."
sigh
I'VE GOT TO STOP SECOND-GUESSING MYSELF.
I MEAN, I ALREADY KNOW THIS ISN'T REALLY GOING TO WORK OUT THAT WELL.
BUT STILL, I SHOULD AT LEAST TRY.
HE'S STILL THERE, RIGHT?
OHN--
ばっ
?!

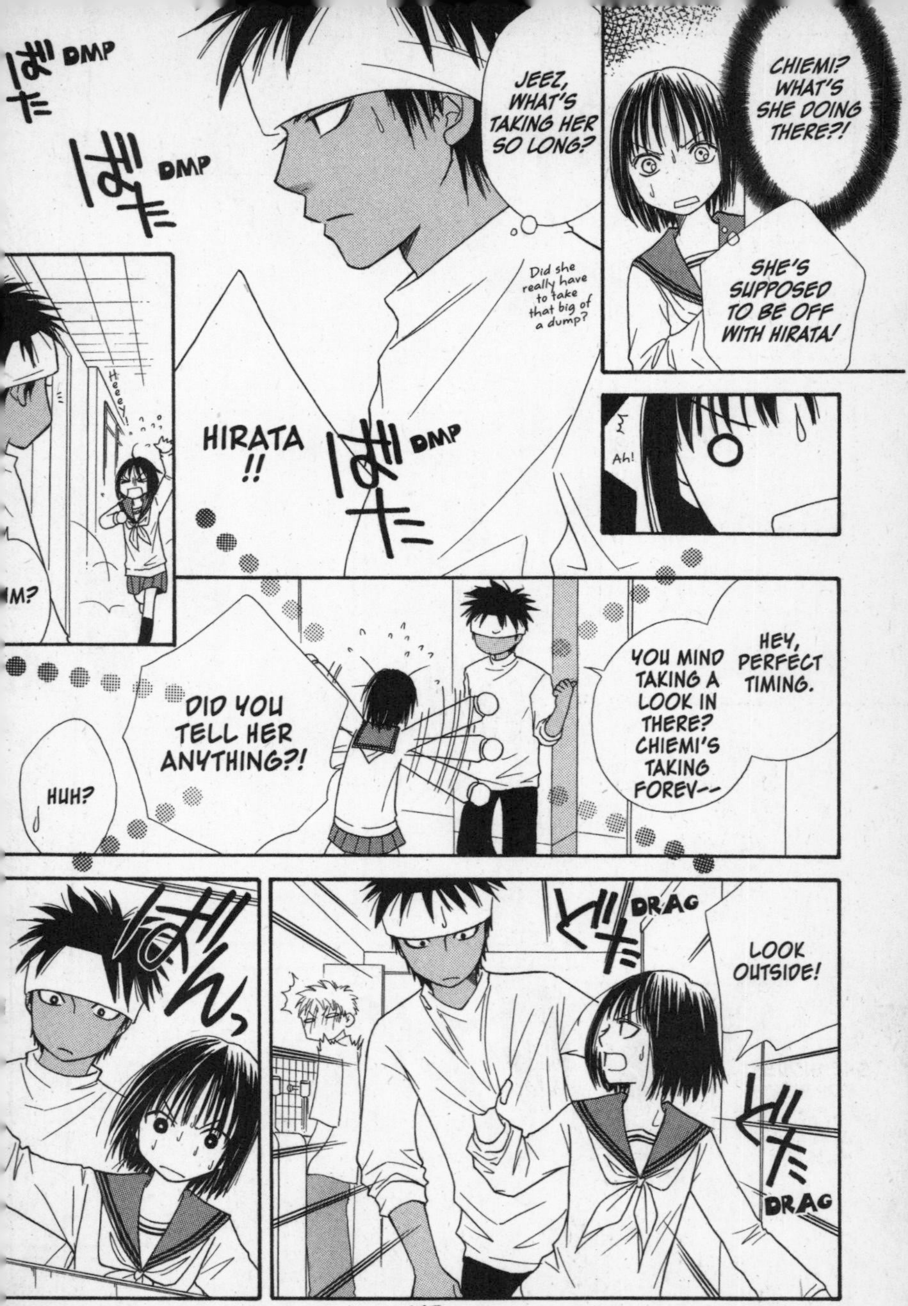

CHIEMI? WHAT'S SHE DOING THERE?!
SHE'S SUPPOSED TO BE OFF WITH HIRATA!
JEEZ, WHAT'S TAKING HER SO LONG?
Did she really have to take that big of a dump?
DMP
DMP
Ah!
HIRATA !!
DMP
Heeey!
M?
HEY, PERFECT TIMING.
YOU MIND TAKING A LOOK IN THERE? CHIEMI'S TAKING FOREV--
DID YOU TELL HER ANYTHING?!
HUH?
DRAG
LOOK OUTSIDE!
DRAG

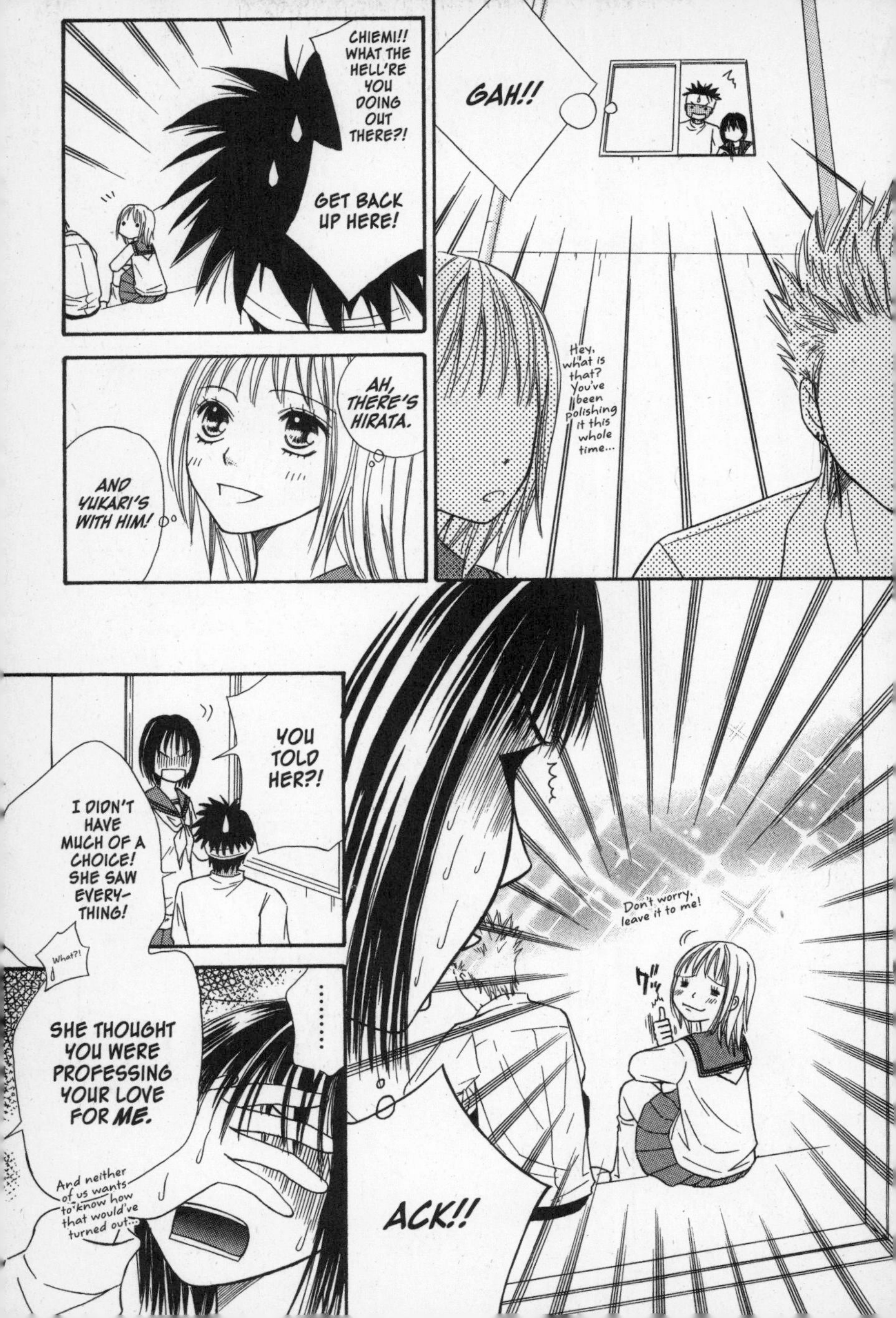
GAH!!
Hey, what is that? You've been polishing it this whole time...
CHIEMI!! WHAT THE HELL'RE YOU DOING OUT THERE?!
GET BACK UP HERE!
AH, THERE'S HIRATA.
AND YUKARI'S WITH HIM!
Don't worry, leave it to me!
ACK!!
YOU TOLD HER?!
I DIDN'T HAVE MUCH OF A CHOICE! SHE SAW EVERY-THING!
What?!
......
SHE THOUGHT YOU WERE PROFESSING YOUR LOVE FOR *ME.*
And neither of us wants to know how that would've turned out...

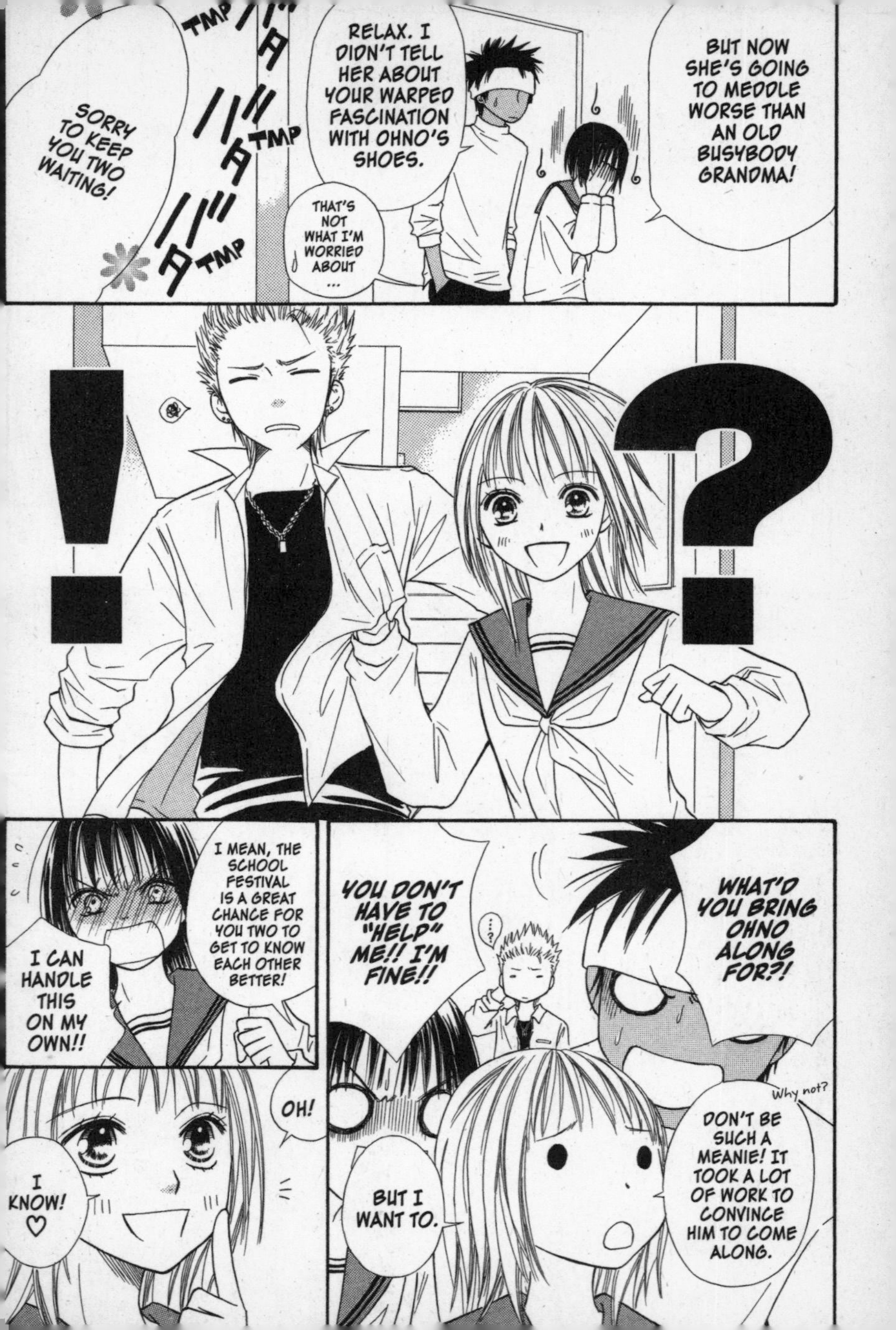
RELAX. I DIDN'T TELL HER ABOUT YOUR WARPED FASCINATION WITH OHNO'S SHOES.
THAT'S NOT WHAT I'M WORRIED ABOUT ...
BUT NOW SHE'S GOING TO MEDDLE WORSE THAN AN OLD BUSYBODY GRANDMA!
TMP
TMP
TMP
SORRY TO KEEP YOU TWO WAITING!
WHAT'D YOU BRING OHNO ALONG FOR?!
...?
Why not?
DON'T BE SUCH A MEANIE! IT TOOK A LOT OF WORK TO CONVINCE HIM TO COME ALONG.
I MEAN, THE SCHOOL FESTIVAL IS A GREAT CHANCE FOR YOU TWO TO GET TO KNOW EACH OTHER BETTER!
I CAN HANDLE THIS ON MY OWN!!
YOU DON'T HAVE TO "HELP" ME!! I'M FINE!!
BUT I WANT TO.
OH!
I KNOW! ♡

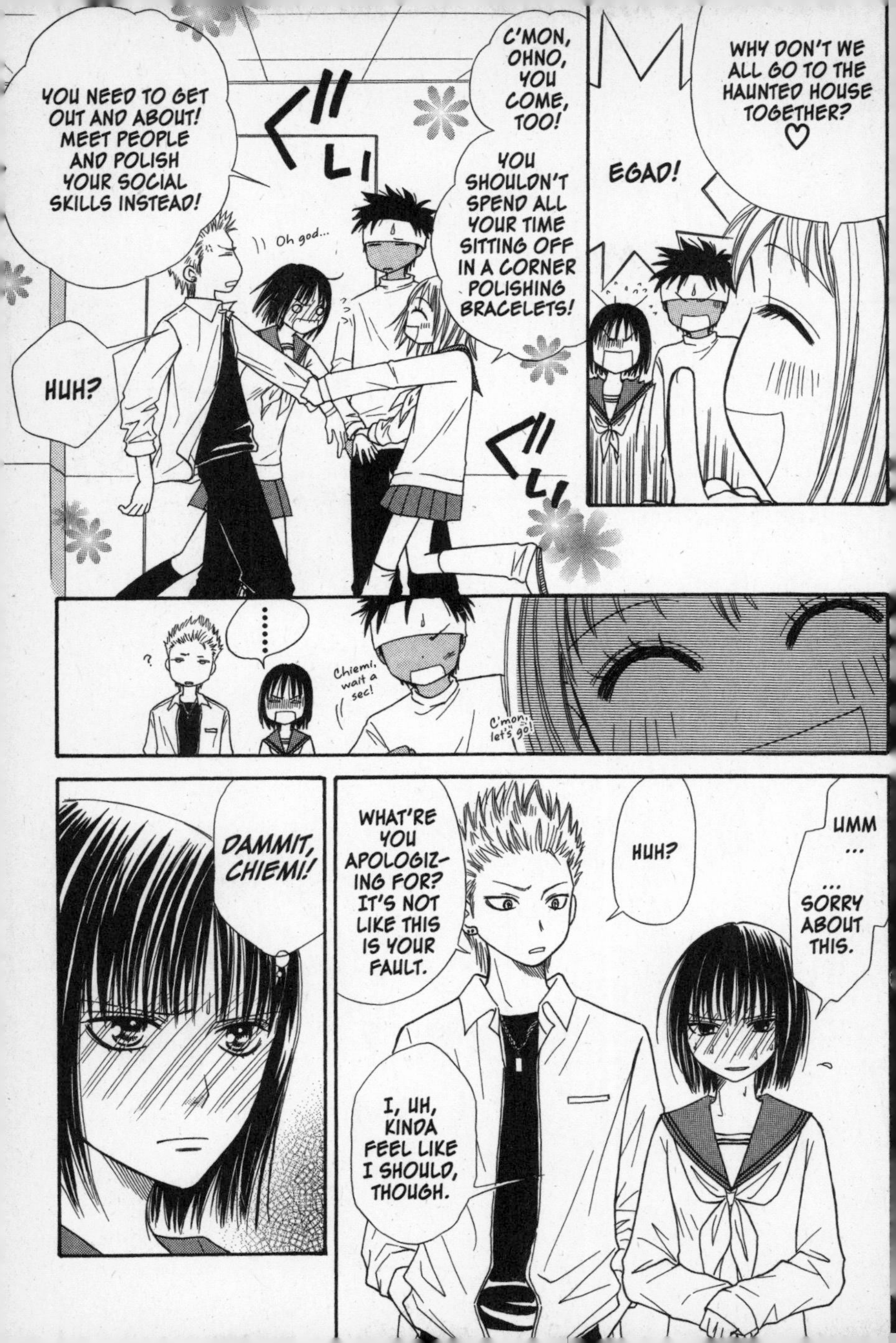
WHY DON'T WE ALL GO TO THE HAUNTED HOUSE TOGETHER? ♡
EGAD!
C'MON, OHNO, YOU COME, TOO!
YOU SHOULDN'T SPEND ALL YOUR TIME SITTING OFF IN A CORNER POLISHING BRACELETS!
Oh god...
YOU NEED TO GET OUT AND ABOUT! MEET PEOPLE AND POLISH YOUR SOCIAL SKILLS INSTEAD!
HUH?
C'mon, let's go!
Chiemi, wait a sec!
......
UMM ... ... SORRY ABOUT THIS.
HUH?
WHAT'RE YOU APOLOGIZING FOR? IT'S NOT LIKE THIS IS YOUR FAULT.
I, UH, KINDA FEEL LIKE I SHOULD, THOUGH.
DAMMIT, CHIEMI!

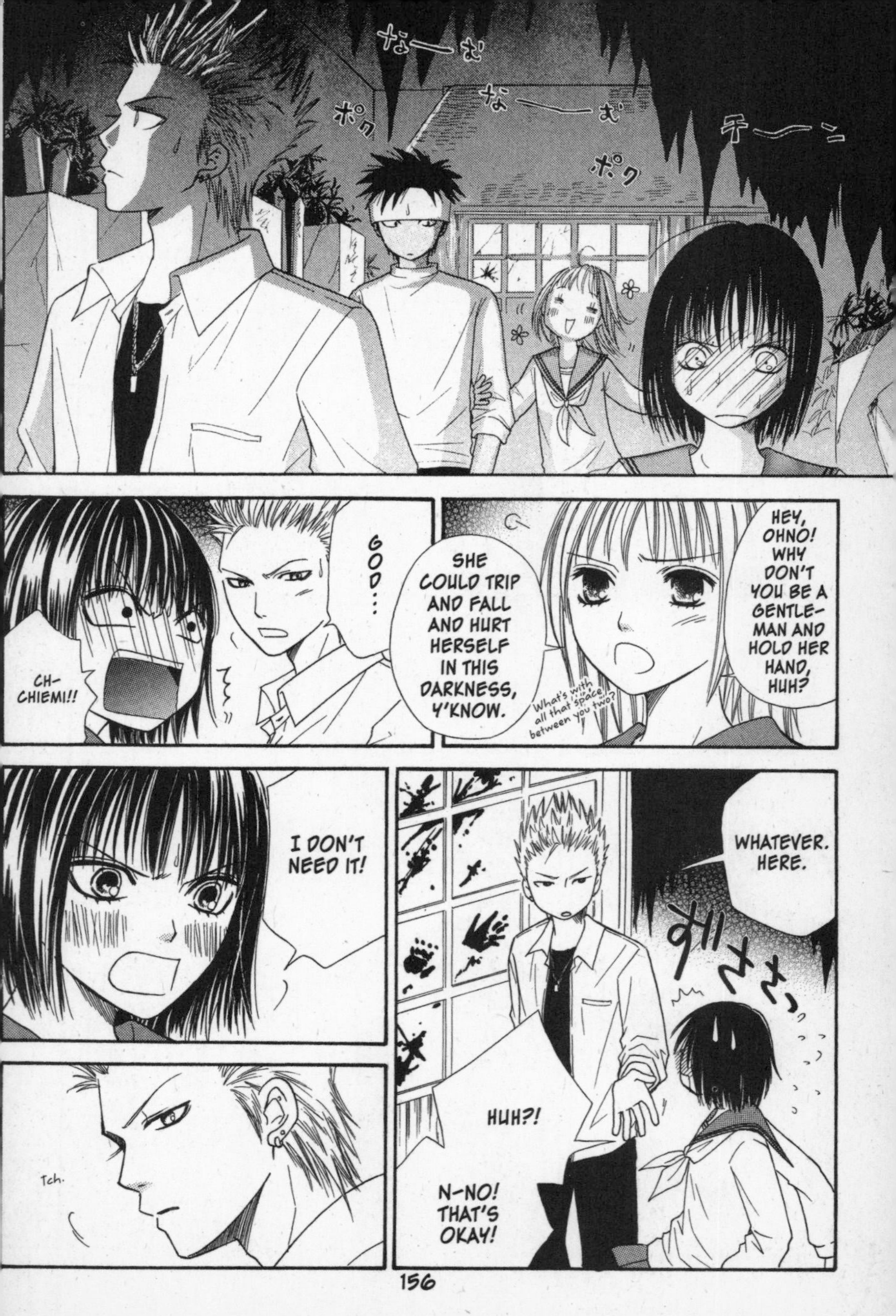
なーむ
なーーむ
ポク
ポク
チーーン
HEY, OHNO! WHY DON'T YOU BE A GENTLEMAN AND HOLD HER HAND, HUH?
SHE COULD TRIP AND FALL AND HURT HERSELF IN THIS DARKNESS, Y'KNOW.
What's with all that space between you two?
GOD...
CH-CHIEMI!!
WHATEVER. HERE.
すささっ
HUH?!
N-NO! THAT'S OKAY!
I DON'T NEED IT!
Tch.

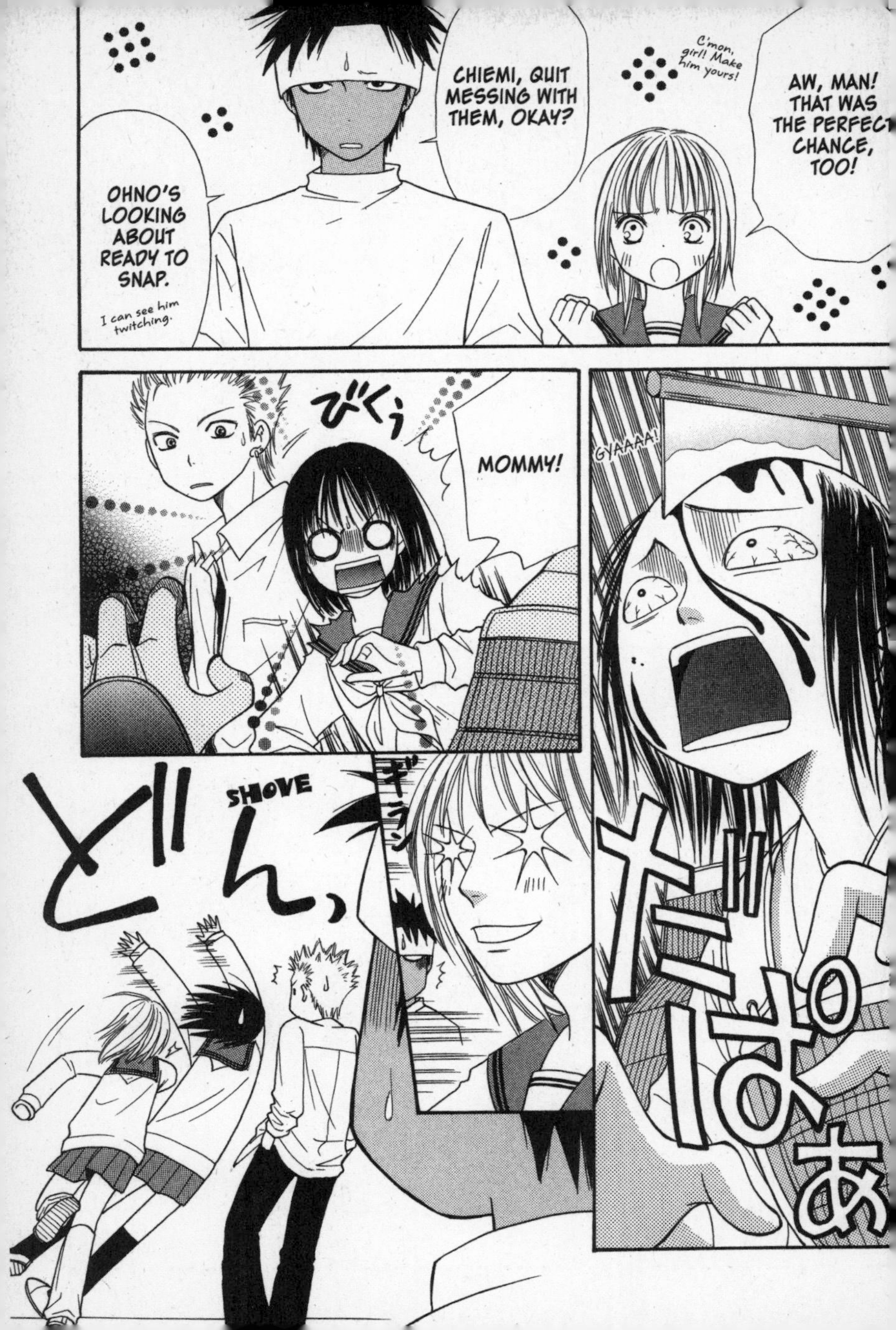
AW, MAN! THAT WAS THE PERFECT CHANCE, TOO!
C'mon, girl! Make him yours!
CHIEMI, QUIT MESSING WITH THEM, OKAY?
OHNO'S LOOKING ABOUT READY TO SNAP.
I can see him twitching.
GYAAAA!
だぱぁ
MOMMY!
びくっ
ギラン
SHOVE
どんっ

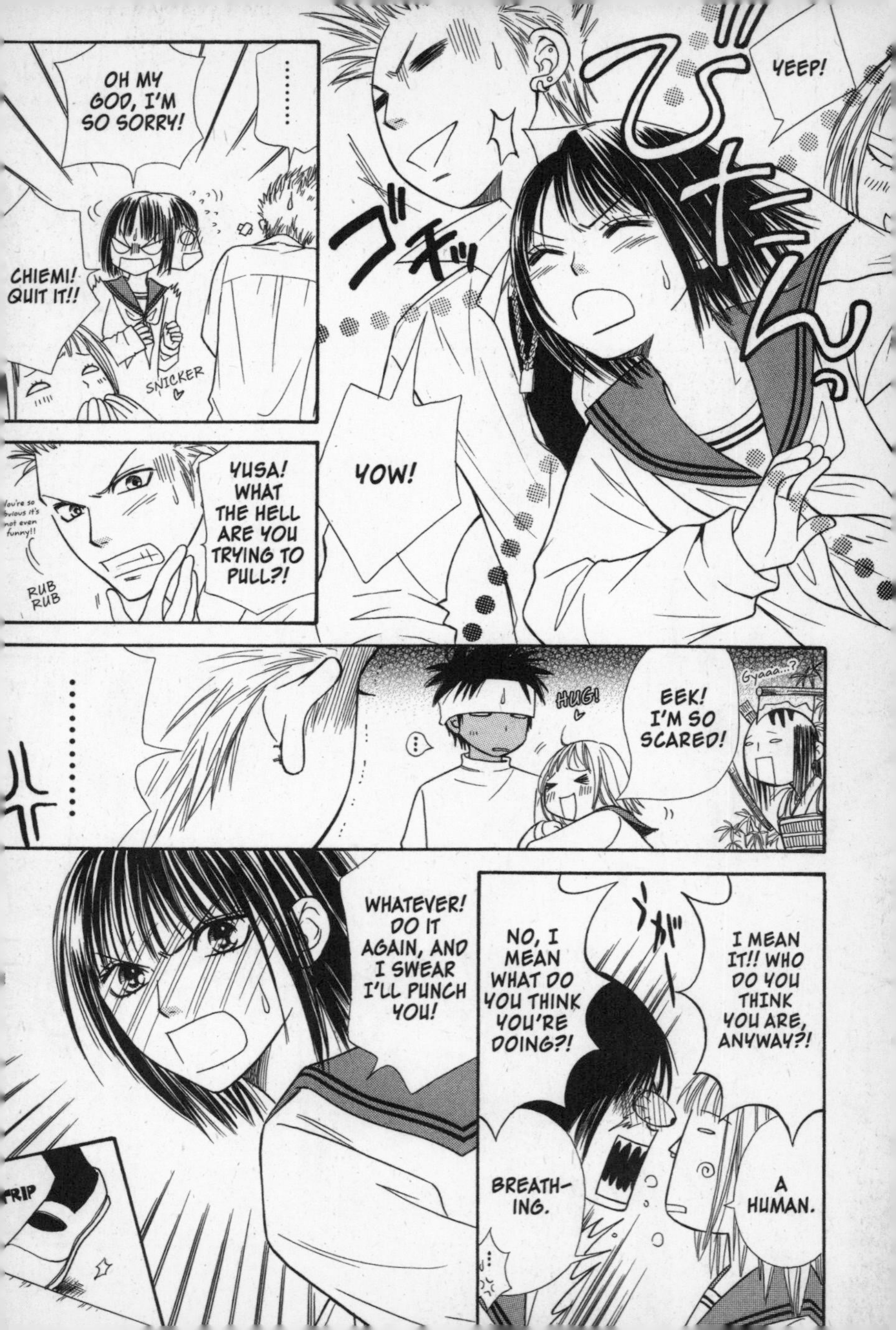
OH MY GOD, I'M SO SORRY!
......
CHIEMI! QUIT IT!!
SNICKER
ou're so bvious it's not even funny!!
RUB RUB
YUSA! WHAT THE HELL ARE YOU TRYING TO PULL?!
ゴキッ
YOW!
YEEP!
....
...
HUG!
EEK! I'M SO SCARED!
Gyaaa...?
RIP
WHATEVER! DO IT AGAIN, AND I SWEAR I'LL PUNCH YOU!
NO, I MEAN WHAT DO YOU THINK YOU'RE DOING?!
BREATHING.
うがー
I MEAN IT!! WHO DO YOU THINK YOU ARE, ANYWAY?!
A HUMAN.

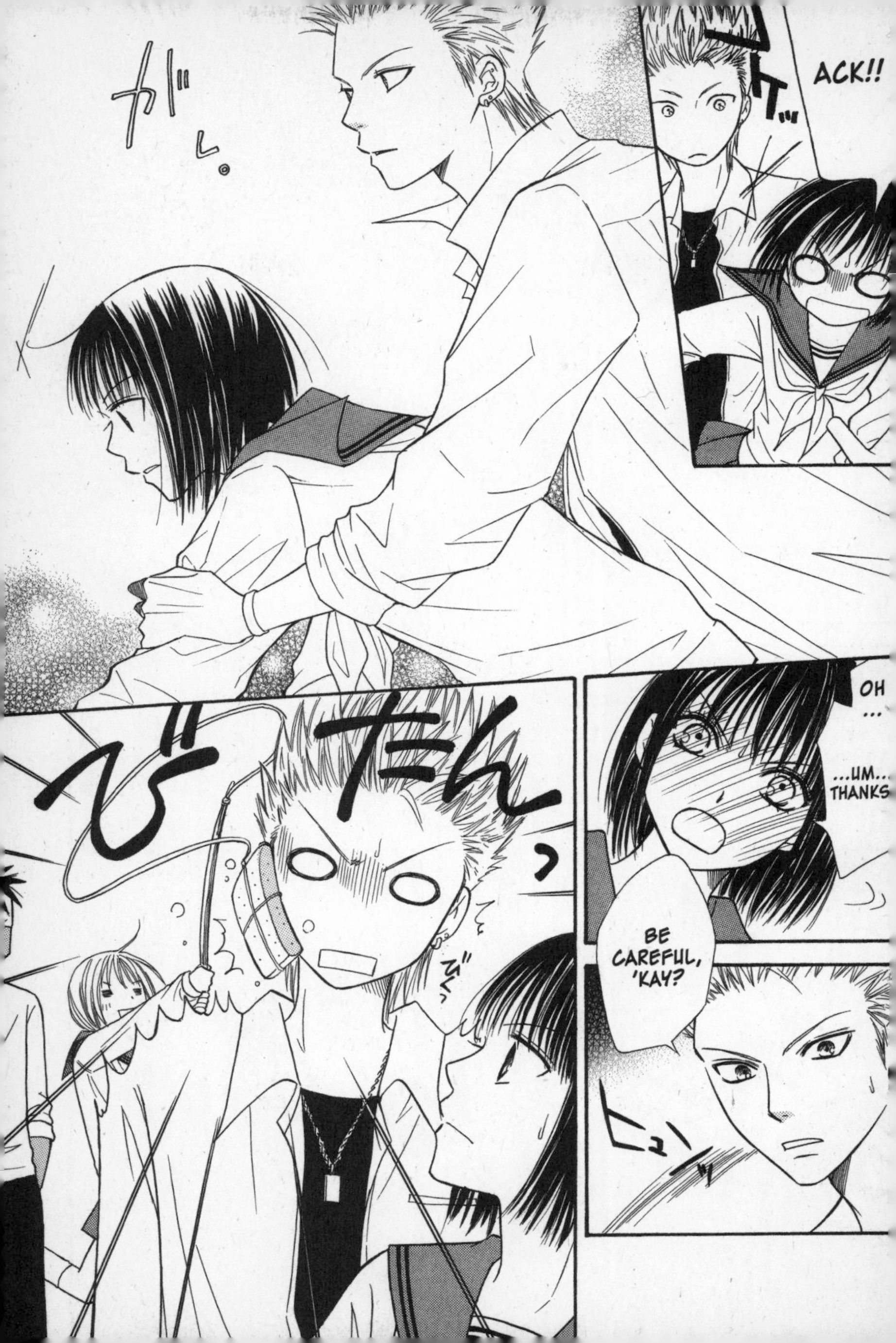

ACK!!
OH ...
...UM... THANKS
BE CAREFUL, 'KAY?

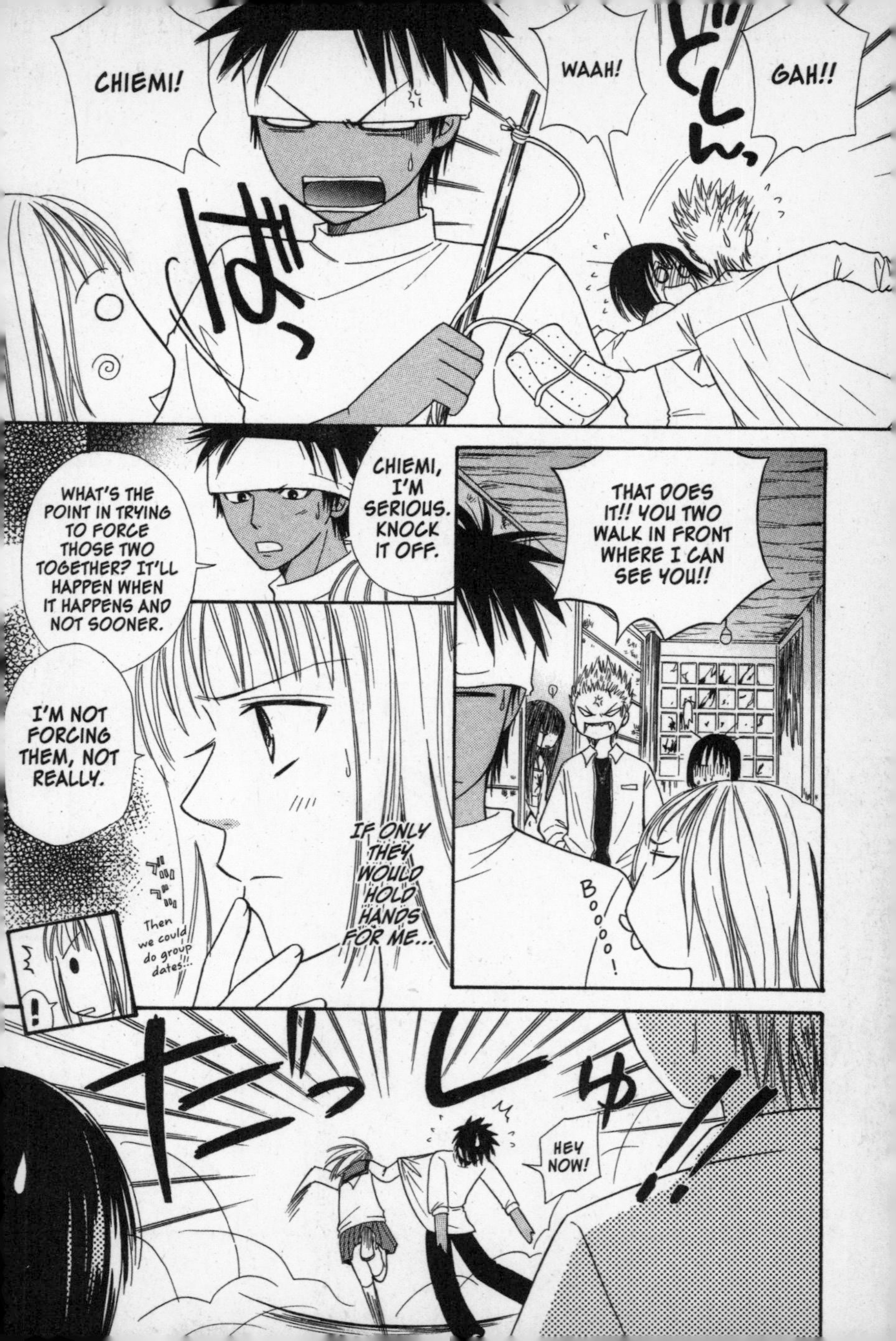
GAH!!
どしんっ
WAAH!
CHIEMI!
ばっ
THAT DOES IT!! YOU TWO WALK IN FRONT WHERE I CAN SEE YOU!!
Boooo!
CHIEMI, I'M SERIOUS. KNOCK IT OFF.
WHAT'S THE POINT IN TRYING TO FORCE THOSE TWO TOGETHER? IT'LL HAPPEN WHEN IT HAPPENS AND NOT SOONER.
IF ONLY THEY WOULD HOLD HANDS FOR ME...
I'M NOT FORCING THEM, NOT REALLY.
Then we could do group dates...
!
だーっしゅ!!
HEY NOW!

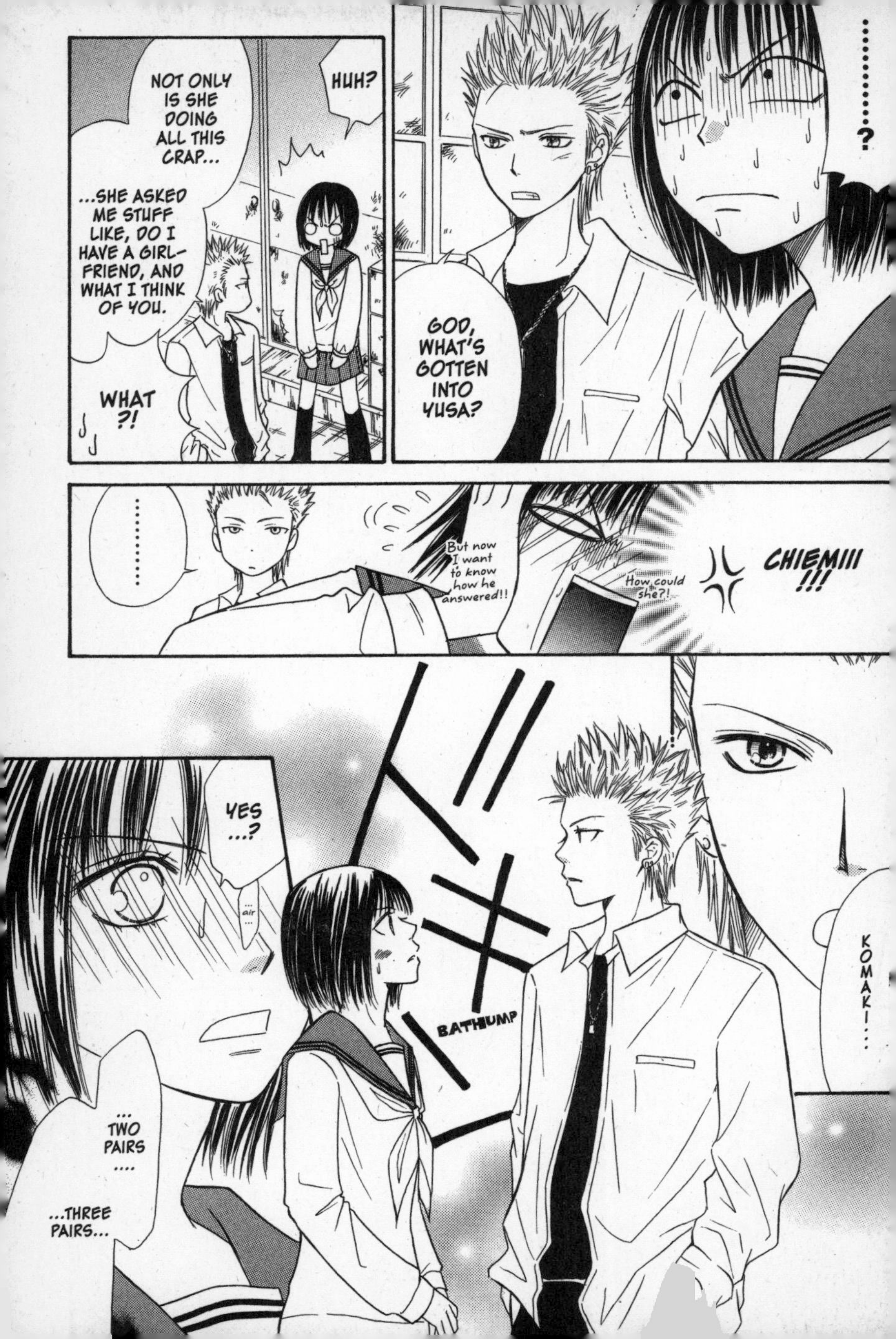
......?
GOD, WHAT'S GOTTEN INTO YUSA?
HUH?
NOT ONLY IS SHE DOING ALL THIS CRAP...
...SHE ASKED ME STUFF LIKE, DO I HAVE A GIRL-FRIEND, AND WHAT I THINK OF YOU.
WHAT ?!
CHIEMIII !!!
How could she?!
But now I want to know how he answered!!
......
KOMAKI...
BATHUMP
YES ...?
...air...
...TWO PAIRS ....
...THREE PAIRS...

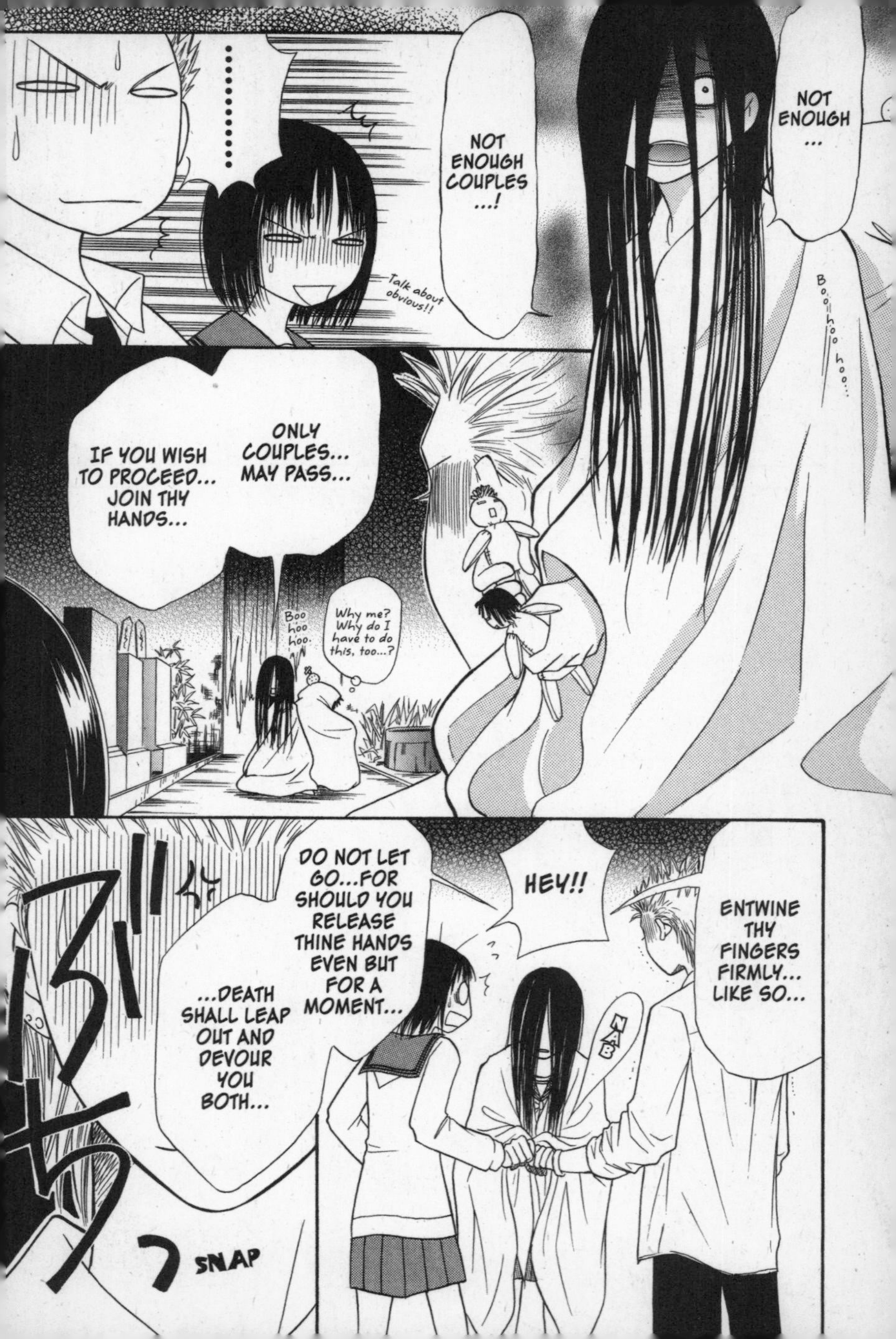
NOT ENOUGH ...
NOT ENOUGH COUPLES ...!
Boo hoo hoo...
......
Talk about obvious!!
ONLY COUPLES... MAY PASS...
IF YOU WISH TO PROCEED... JOIN THY HANDS...
Boo hoo hoo.
Why me? Why do I have to do this, too...?
ENTWINE THY FINGERS FIRMLY... LIKE SO...
HEY!!
NAB
DO NOT LET GO...FOR SHOULD YOU RELEASE THINE HANDS EVEN BUT FOR A MOMENT...
...DEATH SHALL LEAP OUT AND DEVOUR YOU BOTH...
SNAP

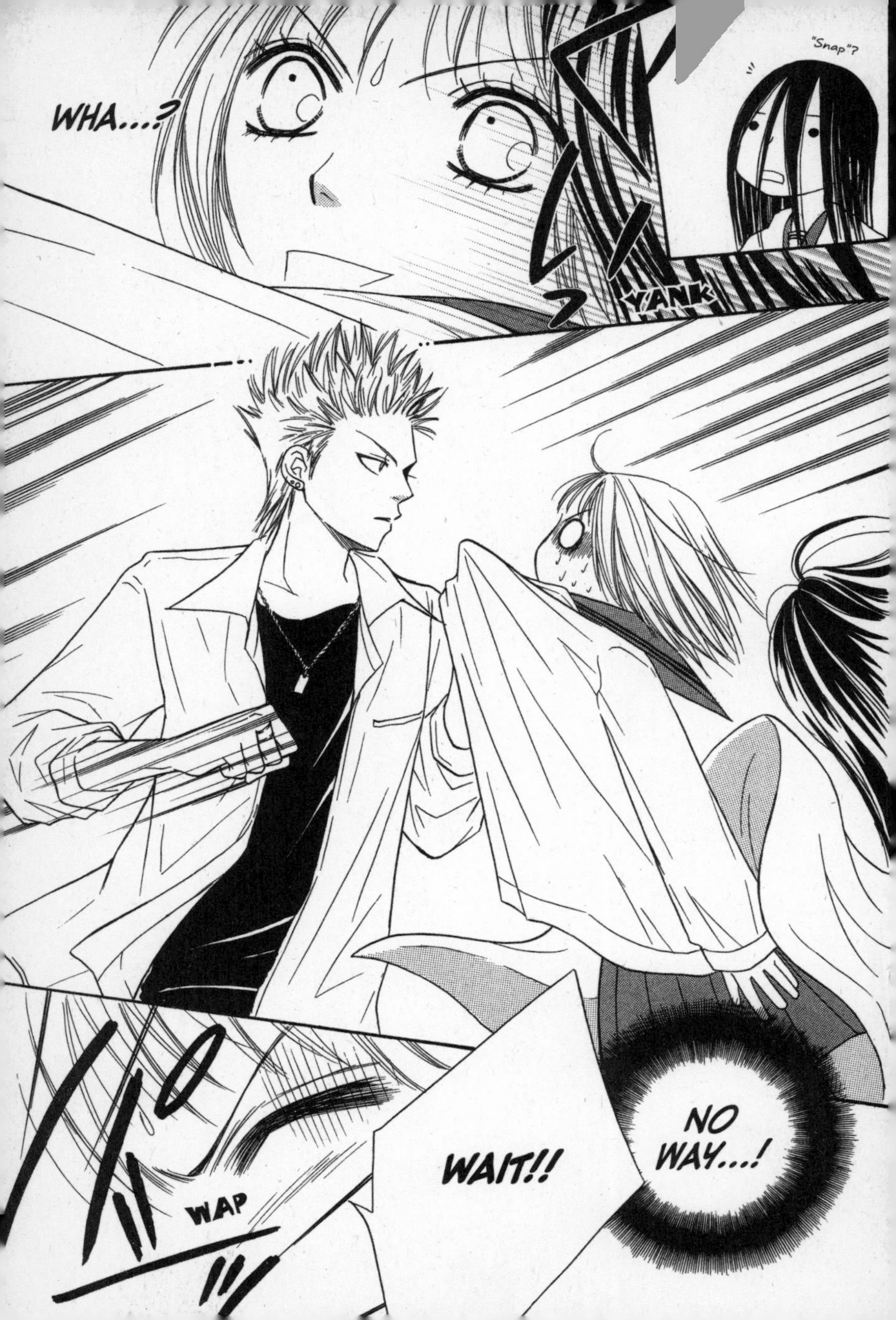
"Snap"?
YANK
WHA...?
NO WAY...!
WAIT!!
WAP

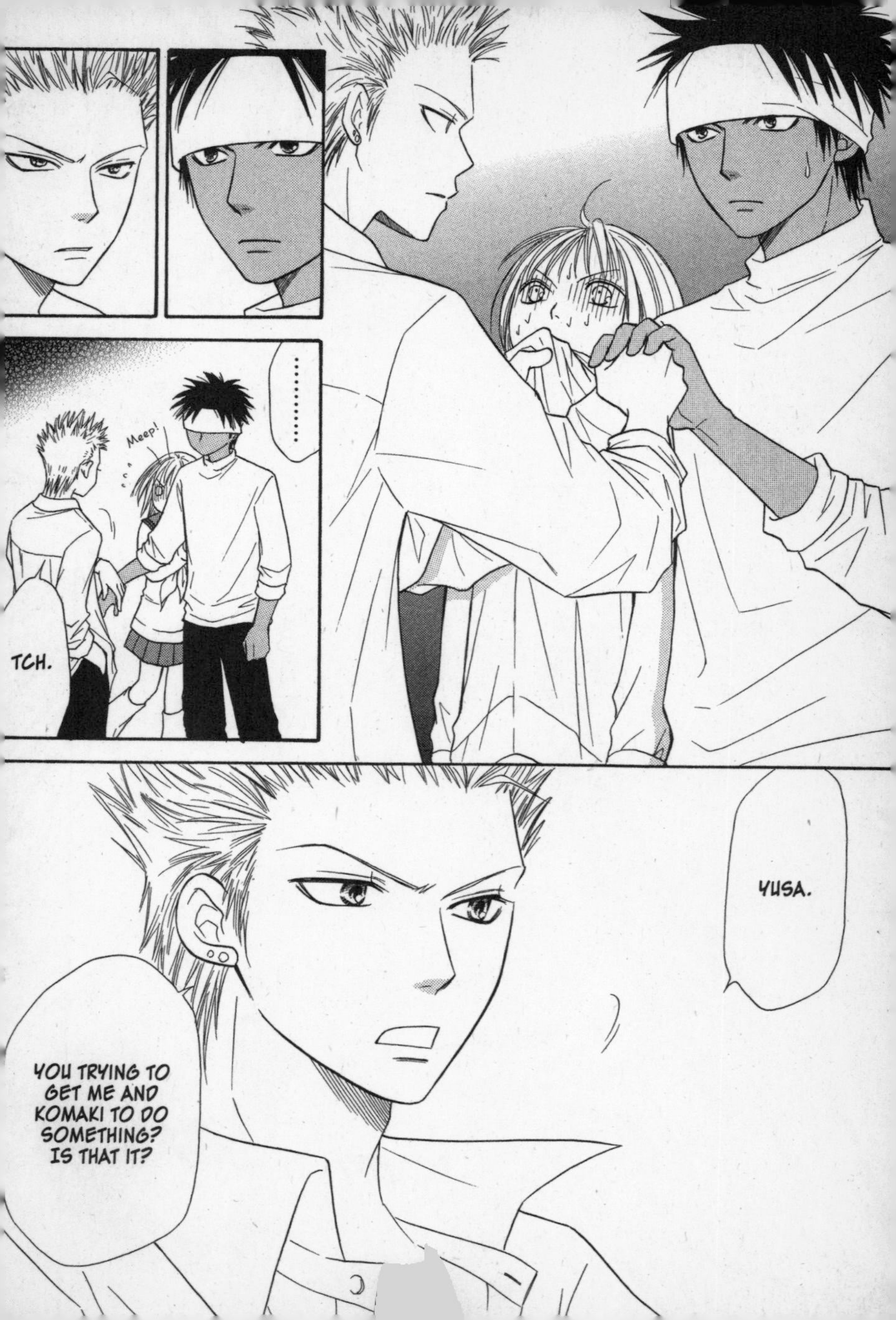
......
Meep!
TCH.
YUSA.
YOU TRYING TO GET ME AND KOMAKI TO DO SOMETHING? IS THAT IT?

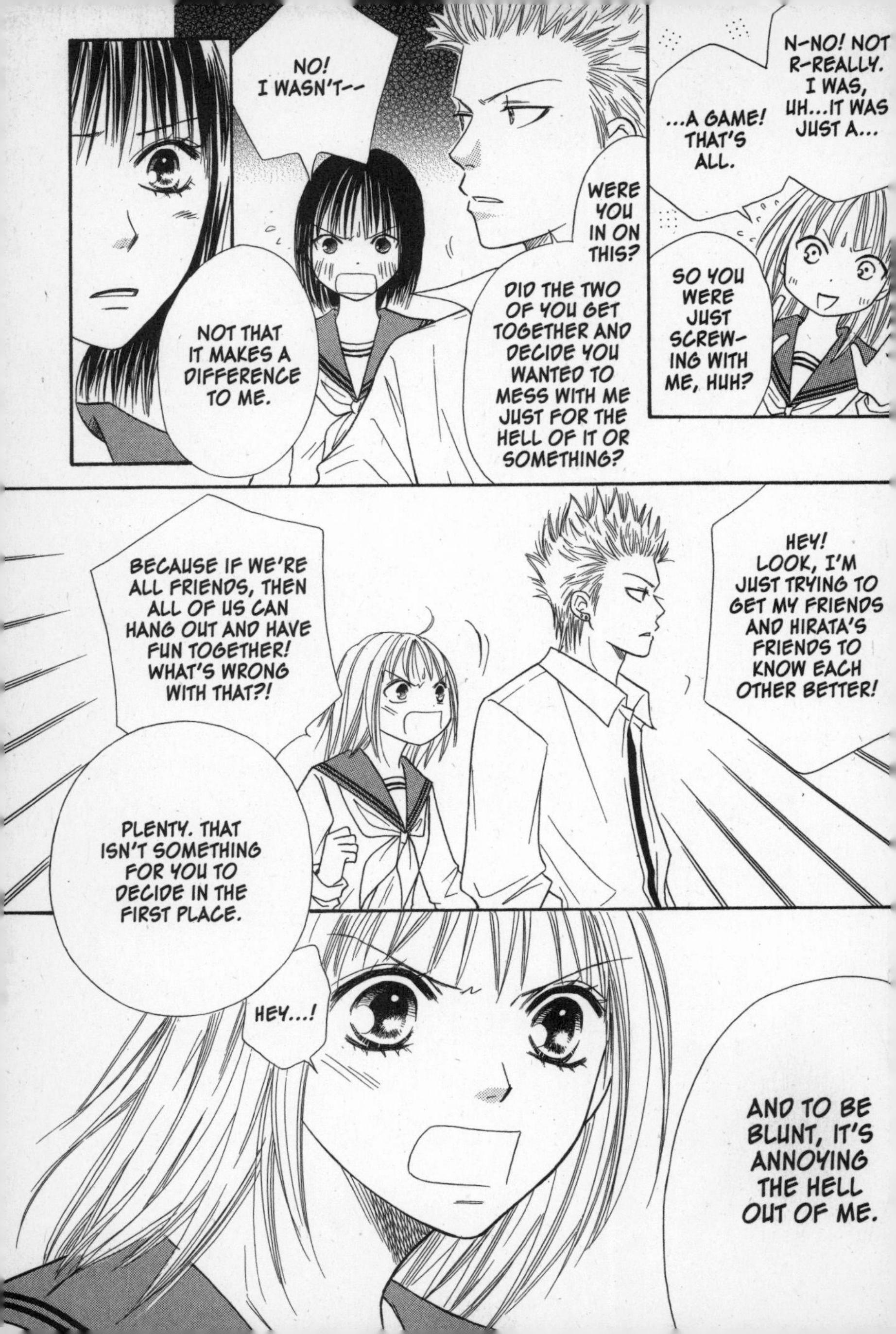
N-NO! NOT R-REALLY. I WAS, UH...IT WAS JUST A...
...A GAME! THAT'S ALL.
SO YOU WERE JUST SCREWING WITH ME, HUH?
WERE YOU IN ON THIS?
DID THE TWO OF YOU GET TOGETHER AND DECIDE YOU WANTED TO MESS WITH ME JUST FOR THE HELL OF IT OR SOMETHING?
NO! I WASN'T--
NOT THAT IT MAKES A DIFFERENCE TO ME.
HEY! LOOK, I'M JUST TRYING TO GET MY FRIENDS AND HIRATA'S FRIENDS TO KNOW EACH OTHER BETTER!
BECAUSE IF WE'RE ALL FRIENDS, THEN ALL OF US CAN HANG OUT AND HAVE FUN TOGETHER! WHAT'S WRONG WITH THAT?!
PLENTY. THAT ISN'T SOMETHING FOR YOU TO DECIDE IN THE FIRST PLACE.
AND TO BE BLUNT, IT'S ANNOYING THE HELL OUT OF ME.
HEY...!

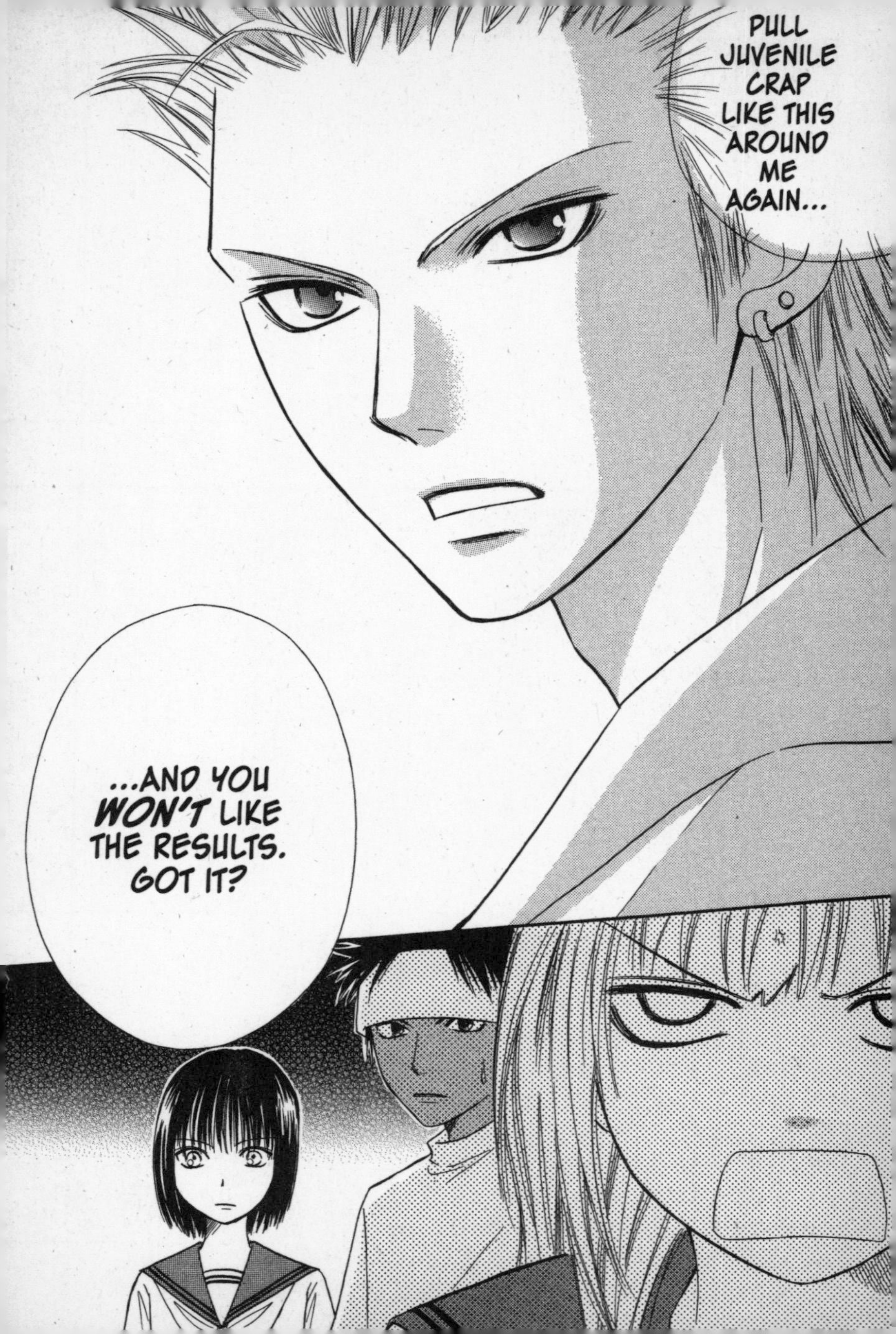
PULL JUVENILE CRAP LIKE THIS AROUND ME AGAIN...
...AND YOU *WON'T* LIKE THE RESULTS. GOT IT?

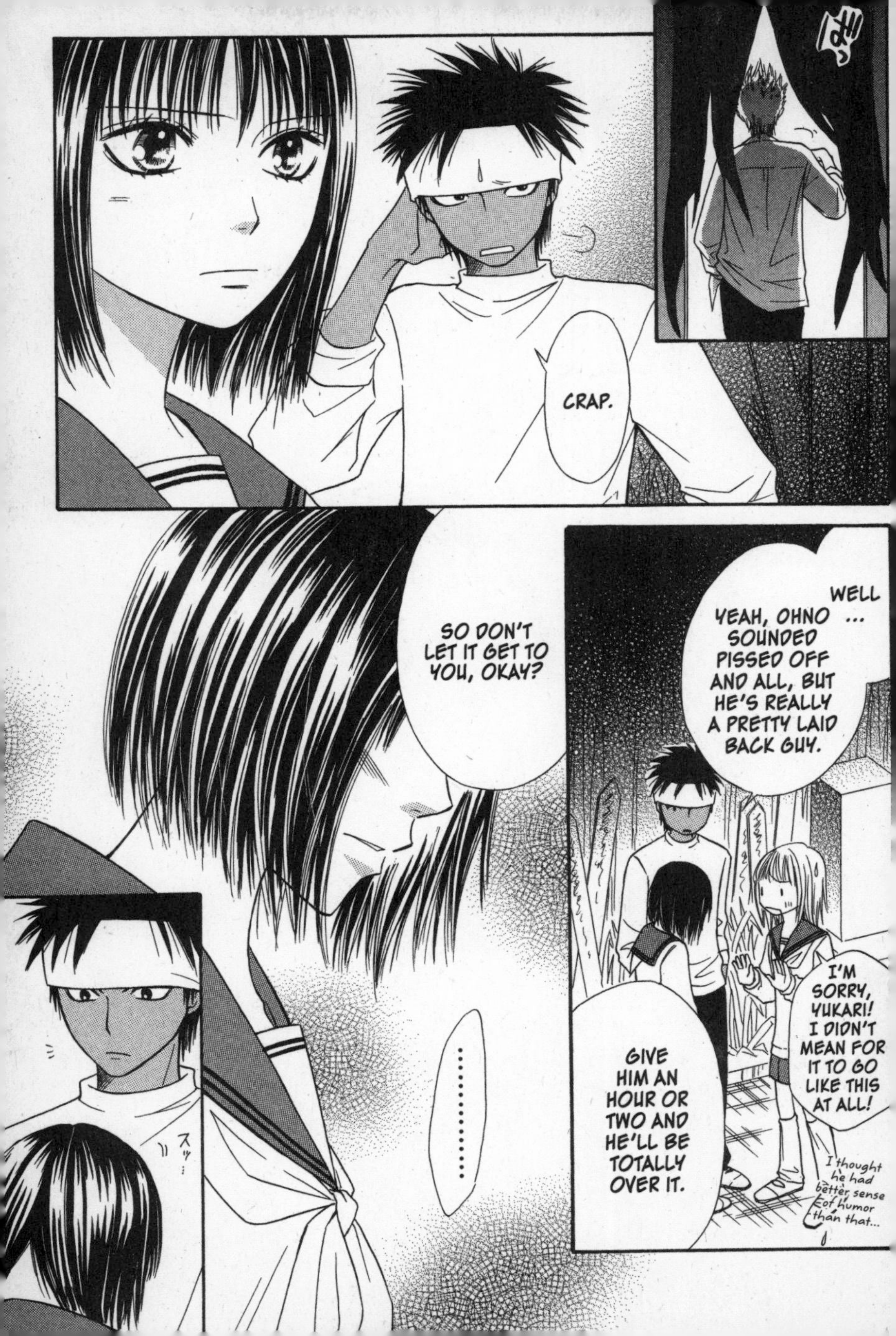
CRAP.
WELL YEAH, OHNO ... SOUNDED PISSED OFF AND ALL, BUT HE'S REALLY A PRETTY LAID BACK GUY.
I'M SORRY, YUKARI! I DIDN'T MEAN FOR IT TO GO LIKE THIS AT ALL!
GIVE HIM AN HOUR OR TWO AND HE'LL BE TOTALLY OVER IT.
I thought he had better sense of humor than that...
SO DON'T LET IT GET TO YOU, OKAY?
......
スッ…

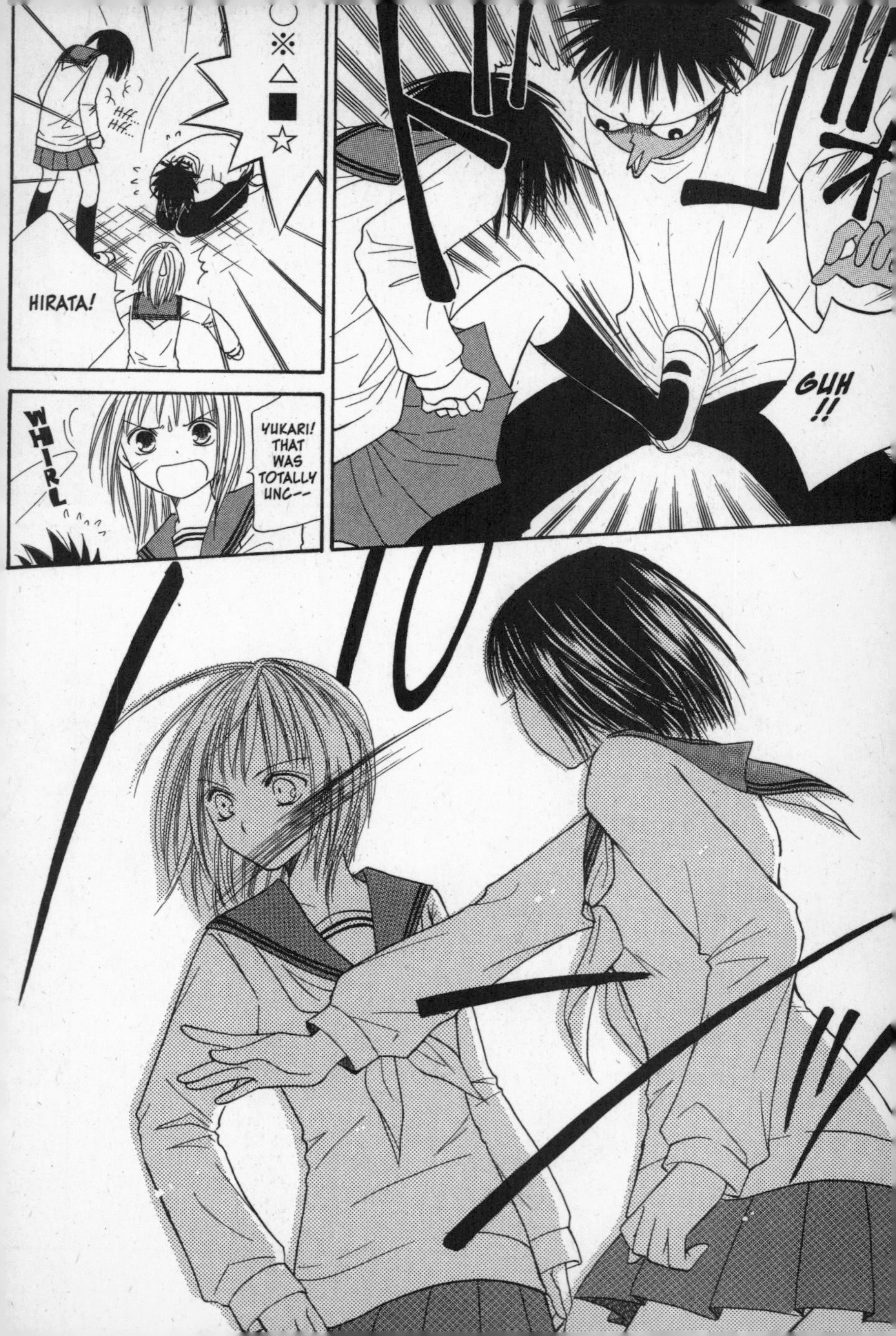
GUH !!
○※△■☆
Hff... Hff...
HIRATA!
YUKARI! THAT WAS TOTALLY UNC--
WHIRL

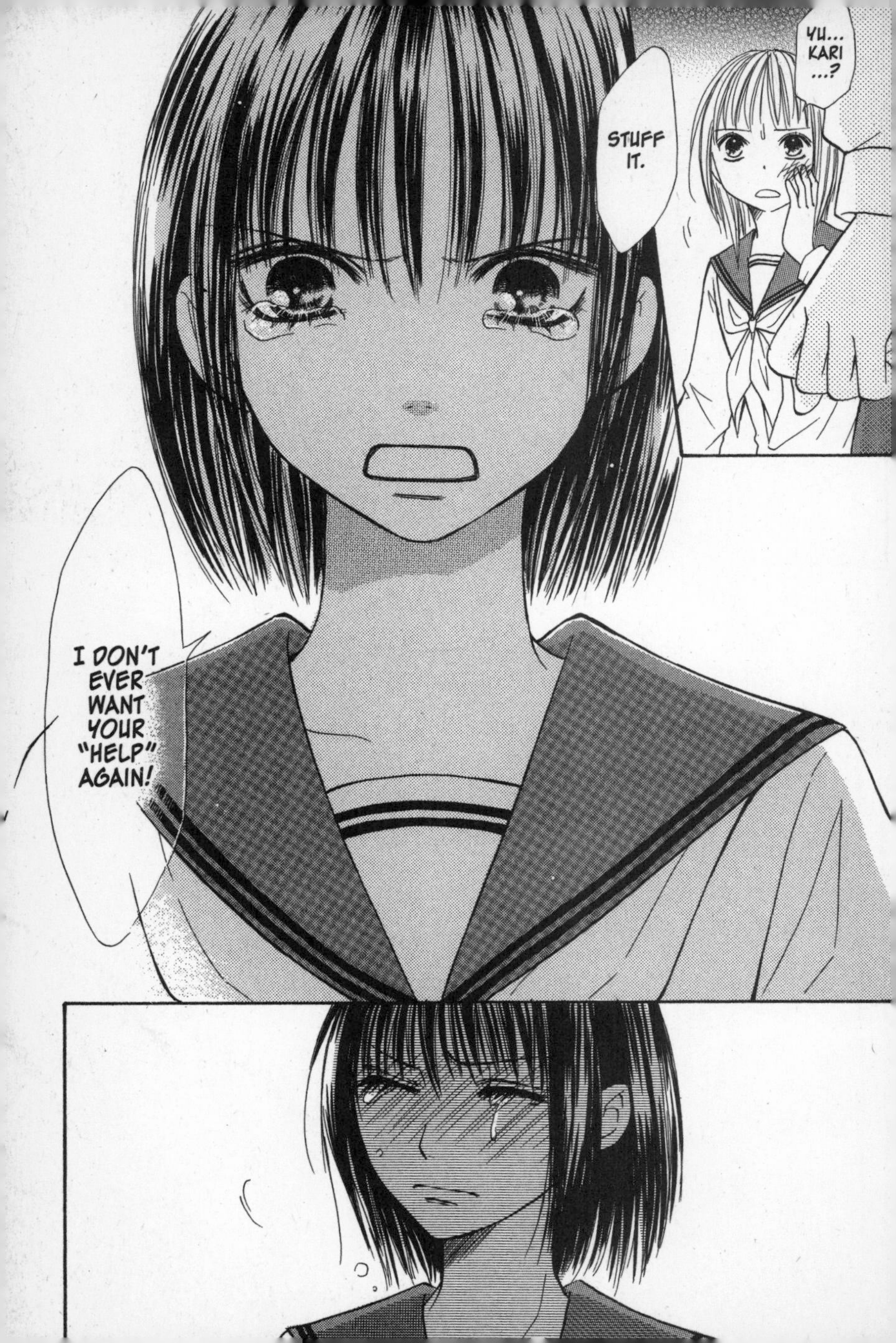
YU... KARI ...?
STUFF IT.
I DON'T EVER WANT YOUR "HELP" AGAIN!

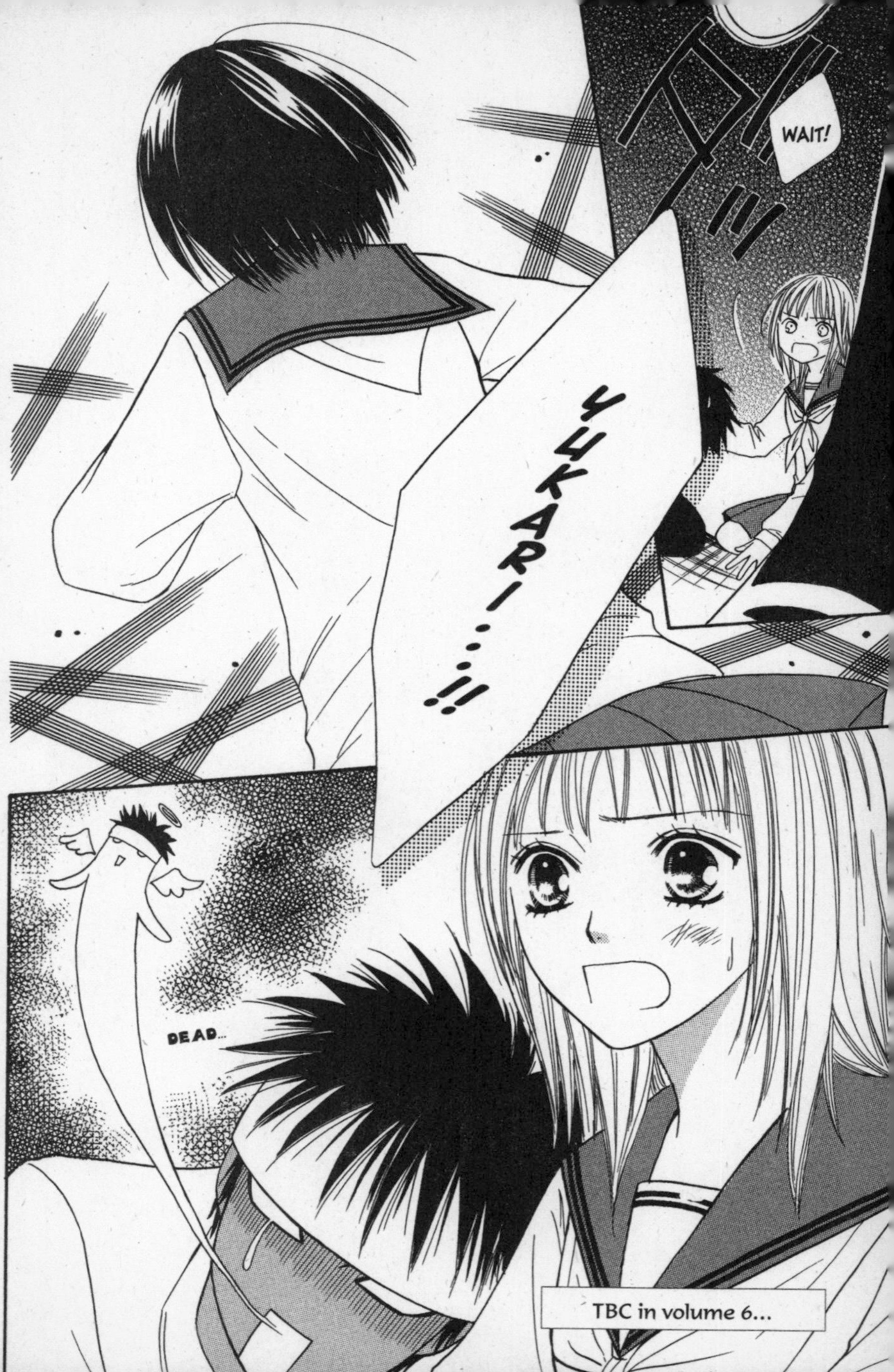
WAIT!
YUKARI......!!!
DEAD...
TBC in volume 6...

LOVE ATTACK™
JUNAI TOKKO TAICHO!

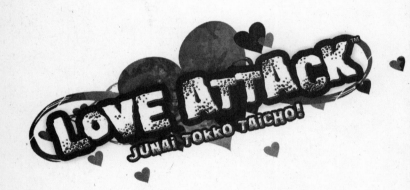

LOVE ATTACK

HERE IT IS, FOLKS!
"LOVE ATTACK: PSYCHOLOGY QUIZ"!
ANSWER THE QUESTIONS BELOW
TO FIND OUT JUST HOW MUCH OF
A ***LOVE ATTACKER*** YOU ARE!

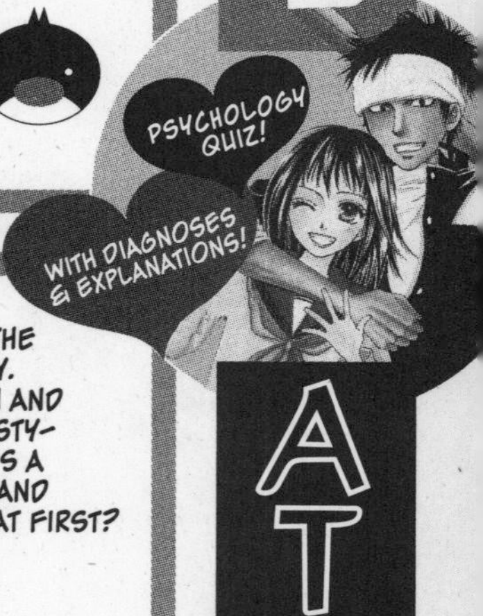

PSYCHOLOGY QUIZ!
WITH DIAGNOSES & EXPLANATIONS!

Q1 TODAY, YOU AND YOUR SIGNIFICANT OTHER ARE OFF ON A DATE TO THE ZOO! THE WEATHER IS PERFECT, AND YOUR MOOD COULDN'T BE BETTER. THERE ARE LOTS OF ANIMALS AT THIS ZOO, AND YOU WANT TO TRY AND FEED SOME OF THEM. WHICH OF THE FOUR BELOW WILL YOU FEED FIRST?

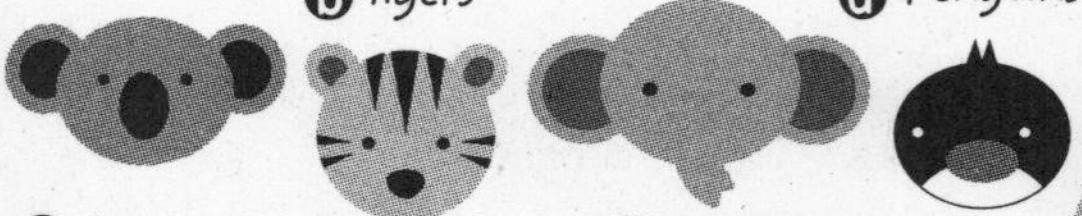

a Koalas
b Tigers
c Elephants
d Penguins

Q2 AFTER SEVERAL FUN HOURS SEEING THE ANIMALS, YOU DECIDE YOU'RE HUNGRY. STOPPING BY THE BURGER STAND, YOU AND YOUR SIGNIFICANT OTHER ORDER A TASTY-LOOKING COMBO MEAL THAT INCLUDES A HAMBURGER, FRENCH FRIES, A COLA AND SOME ICE CREAM. WHICH WILL YOU EAT FIRST?

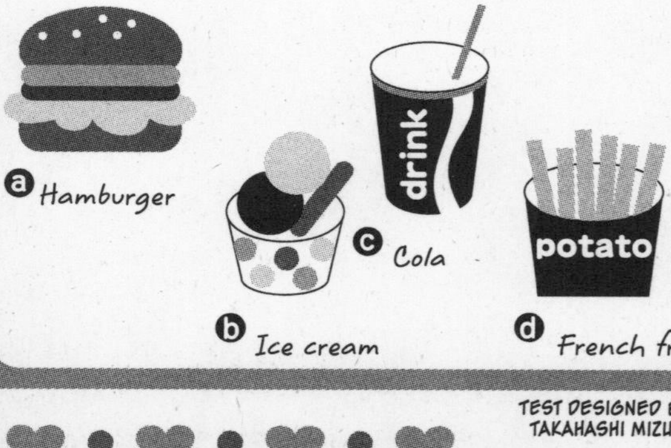

drink
potato

a Hamburger
b Ice cream
c Cola
d French fries

TEST DESIGNED BY /
TAKAHASHI MIZUNA

Q3

IT'S STILL EARLY, SO YOU AND YOUR SIGNIFICANT OTHER HEAD DOWNTOWN. BUT THERE YOU'RE SPOTTED BY THE LAST PERSON YOU'D EXPECT! SINCE IT LOOKS LIKE YOUR DATE IS ABOUT TO GET CRASHED BY UNWANTED COMPANY, YOU BOTH RUN AWAY. WHAT ARE YOU RUNNING FROM?

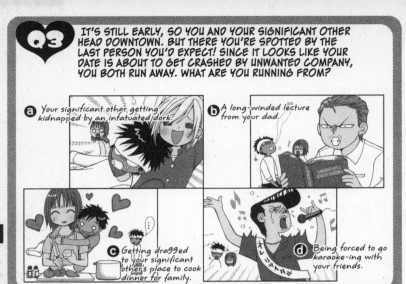

a Your significant other getting kidnapped by an infatuated dork.
b A long-winded lecture from your dad.
c Getting dragged to your significant other's place to cook dinner for family.
d Being forced to go karaoke-ing with your friends.

Q4

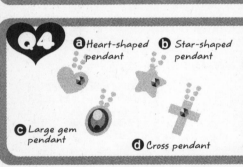

FINALLY LOSING YOUR PURSUER, YOU AND YOUR SIGNIFICANT OTHER FIND YOURSELF IN FRONT OF A LITTLE JEWELRY SHOP. FEELING GENEROUS, YOUR SIGNIFICANT OTHER DECIDES TO BUY A NECKLACE FOR YOU. WHICH ONE WOULD YOU CHOOSE?

a Heart-shaped pendant

b Star-shaped pendant

c Large gem pendant

d Cross pendant

Q5

THE LONG, FUN DAY IS ENDING, AND YOUR DATE IS COMING TO A CLOSE. BEFORE YOU'RE SPOTTED BY YOUR FATHER, YOU GET IN A QUICK GOOD-BYE KISS. WHAT KIND OF KISS IS IT?

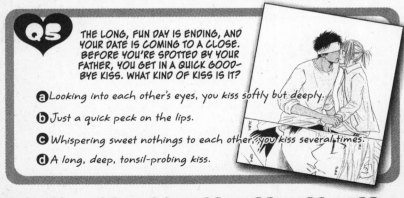

a Looking into each other's eyes, you kiss softly but deeply.

b Just a quick peck on the lips.

c Whispering sweet nothings to each other, you kiss several times.

d A long, deep, tonsil-probing kiss.

GO TO THE NEXT PAGE!

Quiz Explanation & Diagnosis!

READ BELOW TO DISCOVER THE REASONING BEHIND

EACH OF THE FIVE QUESTIONS ASKED ON THE

PREVIOUS PAGES. THEN ADD UP YOUR SCORE FROM

THE GRAPH ON THE BOTTOM OF THE NEXT PAGE.

 Q1

THE ANIMAL YOU CHOSE REFLECTS WHAT KIND OF COUPLE YOU WOULD LIKE OTHERS TO SEE YOU AND YOUR SIGNIFICANT OTHER AS. CHOOSING THE KOALA MEANS YOU WANT TO BE SEEN AS A CUTE COUPLE. THE TIGER MEANS A COOL COUPLE. THE ELEPHANT MEANS A ROMANTIC COUPLE, AND THE PENGUIN MEANS A FASHIONABLE COUPLE.

 Q2

WHAT PART OF THE MEAL YOU EAT FIRST REVEALS WHAT KIND OF LOVE YOU WANT FROM YOUR SIGNIFICANT OTHER. STARTING WITH THE COLA MEANS YOU'D LIKE AN EASY-GOING RELATIONSHIP. PICKING THE SALTY FRIES FIRST MEANS YOU'RE LOOKING FOR AN ELABORATE AFFAIR. GOING WITH THE ICE CREAM FIRST MEANS YOU WANT LOTS OF SWEET ROMANCE. CHOOSE THE MAIN DISH HAMBURGER TO START WITH, AND THAT MEANS YOU'RE LOOKING FOR ONE ACTIVE, MEATY RELATIONSHIP!

 Q3

WHAT KIND OF SUDDEN INTERRUPTION YOU SAW IS A REPRESENTATION OF WHAT KIND OF DANGER YOU EXPECT YOUR RELATIONSHIP TO FACE. THE NASTIER THE INTERRUPTION YOU'RE WILLING TO TAKE ON, THE GREATER THE STRENGTH OF YOUR LOVE. THE WORST INTERRUPTION OF THE FOUR, OF COURSE, IS GETTING A LONG-WINDED LECTURE FROM DAD!

Q4 THE TYPE OF PENDANT YOU CHOOSE REFLECTS WHAT IT IS YOU MOST WANT FROM YOUR SIGNIFICANT OTHER. PICKING THE HEART-SHAPED PENDANT MEANS YOU'RE LOOKING FOR LOVE. CHOOSE THE STAR-SHAPED PENDANT AND YOU'RE EXPECTING A VERY PHYSICAL RELATIONSHIP. THE GEM PENDANT MEANS YOU'RE SEARCHING FOR WEALTH, AND THE CROSS PENDANT SHOWS THAT YOU WANT A DEEP, SPIRITUAL CONNECTION.

Q5 WHAT KIND OF GOODBYE KISS YOU WANT IS A SIGN OF HOW CLOSE YOU'RE GETTING TO CHEATING ON YOUR LOVED ONE! CHOOSE ANSWER A AND IT MEANS YOU'VE THOUGHT ABOUT CHEATING, BUT YOU WON'T GO THROUGH WITH IT. ANSWER B MEANS YOUR MIND HAS ALREADY MOVED ON TO WHAT HAPPENS AFTER KISSING—MEANING YOU HAVE THE HIGHEST CHANCE OF CHEATING! ANSWER C SHOWS THAT YOU'RE QUITE THE INQUISITIVE ONE, AND WHILE YOU'RE SATISFIED FOR NOW, YOU MAY NOT BE FOREVER. ANSWER D SHOWS THAT YOUR CURRENT LOVED ONE IS ALL YOU HAVE ON YOUR MIND—NO CHANCE OF CHEATING HERE!

YOUR SCORE IS:

.... POINTS

TURN THE PAGE FOR WHAT YOU'RE ALL WAITING FOR: THE DIAGNOSIS!

	a	b	c	d
Q1	3	1	4	2
Q2	4	3	1	2
Q3	3	4	1	2
Q4	4	2	1	3
Q5	3	1	2	4

How high is your Love Attacker rank?!

18-20 PTS.

A

LOVE ATTACKER!!

THE PURITY OF YOUR LOVE IS BEYOND QUESTION, AND YOU'RE READY TO TACKLE WHATEVER OBSTACLES MAY COME YOUR WAY. CONGRATS! YOU ARE THE DEFINITION OF A "LOVE ATTACKER"! USE YOUR GUTS AND YOUR PURE HEART TO GO OUT THERE AND GRAB LOVE BY THE HORNS!

14-17 PTS.

B

WHOA! NOT BAD!!

YOUR TALENT FOR PURE LOVE IS JUST BEGINNING TO BLOOM, AND IT LOOKS LIKE THERE ARE MANY WONDERFUL DAYS OF LOVE WAITING FOR YOU. BE SURE TO FOLLOW YOUR GUT FEELINGS, BECAUSE THEY'LL LEAD YOU TO AN EVEN MORE WONDERFUL, HAPPY FUTURE. NO NEED TO STRETCH YOURSELF. YOU ALREADY HAVE EVERYTHING YOU NEED.

HMM...COULD BE BETTER

10-13 PTS.

C

A PURE LOVE FIGHTER, YOU MAY BE FACING OFF WITH SOME OF YOUR LESS PURE IMPULSES, BUT YOU ARE STILL STRUGGLING TO WALK THE PATH TO TRUE LOVE. DON'T GET TOO CAUGHT UP IN YOUR BATTLES, THOUGH. TAKING A STEP BACK AND ASSESSING YOUR RELATIONSHIP EVERY NOW AND AGAIN IS IMPORTANT.

UH-OH! BE CAREFUL!

6-9 PTS.

D

CAREFUL NOW! WITH THE NUMBER OF WORLDLY PASSIONS YOU HAVE TO REIN IN, PURE LOVE IS A LONG WAY OFF! BUT IF YOU LET THINGS STAY AS THEY ARE, ALL THAT WAITS FOR YOU IN THE FUTURE IS A BROKEN HEART. CURB YOUR SELFISHNESS, PUT A LEASH ON YOUR CHEATING TENDENCIES AND TRY BEING TRUE TO YOUR LOVE.

YiKES! SERiOUS LACK OF PURE LOVE!

5 PTS.

E

YEOW! IT LOOKS LIKE YOU HAVEN'T EVEN GRASPED THE BASICS NEEDED TO BE A LOVE ATTACKER! BUT DON'T GIVE UP HOPE! GO OUT AND GRAB COPIES OF *LOVE ATTACK* VOLUMES 1-5 AND STUDY, STUDY, STUDY! DON'T FORGET, READING IT ALOUD WILL INCREASE ITS EFFECTIVENESS! ♥

USE THE RESULTS OF THIS QUIZ TO MAKE YOURSELF INTO A BETTER LOVE ATTACKER! ♥

IN THE NEXT...

LOVE ATTACK™

JUNAI TOKKO TAICHO!

CHIEMI IS GOOD AT MANY THINGS, BUT A MATCHMAKER SHE MOST DEFINITELY IS NOT. BUT NEVER ONE TO ADMIT DEFEAT, SHE SETS OFF ONE LAST DOOZY OF A PLAN TO CREATE A LOVEY-DOVEY ALLIANCE BETWEEN YUKARI AND OHNO. WILL SHE SUCCEED IN CREATING THE SECOND-MOST VIOLENT COUPLE AT SCHOOL, DESPITE HER BEST FRIEND'S RELUCTANCE?

YUKARI'S BFF VS.
CHIEMI'S IFFY-BFF

COMING IN APRIL 2009!

LOVE IS...

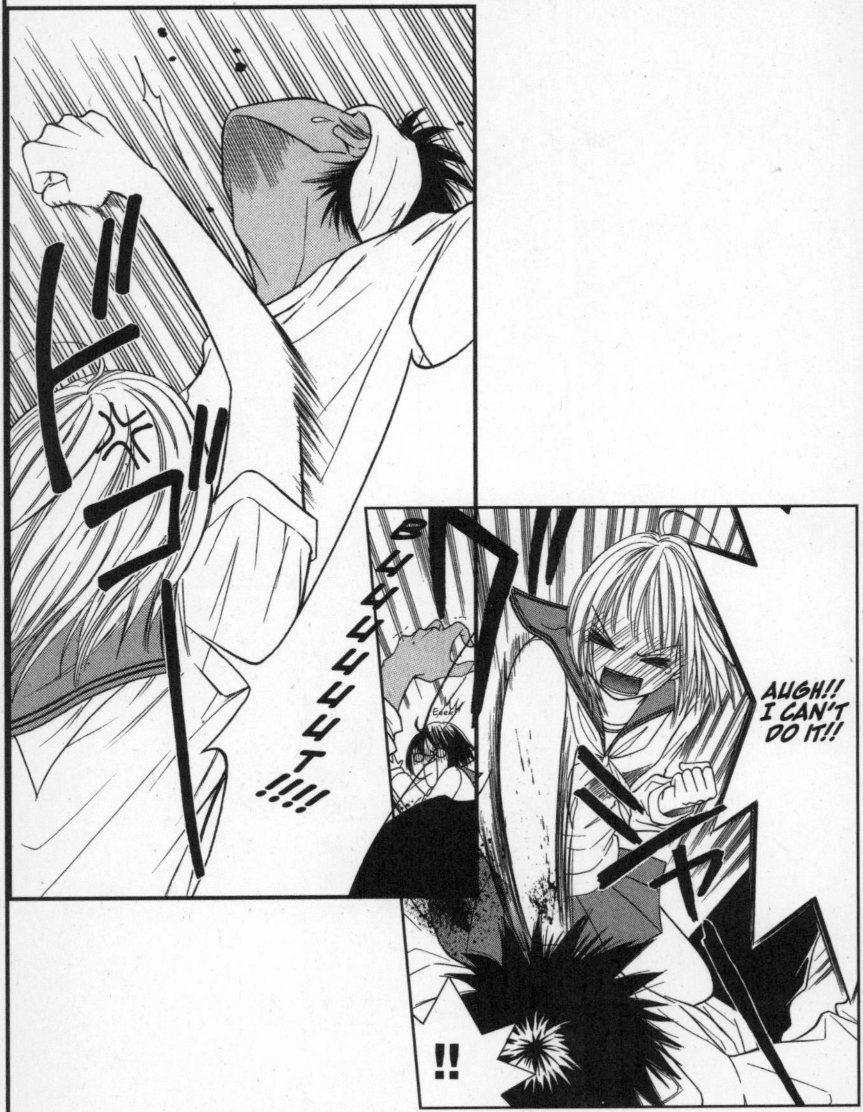
BUUUUUUUT!!!!!
Eeek!!
AUGH!! I CAN'T DO IT!!
!!

...getting your molars knocked out.

LOVE IS...

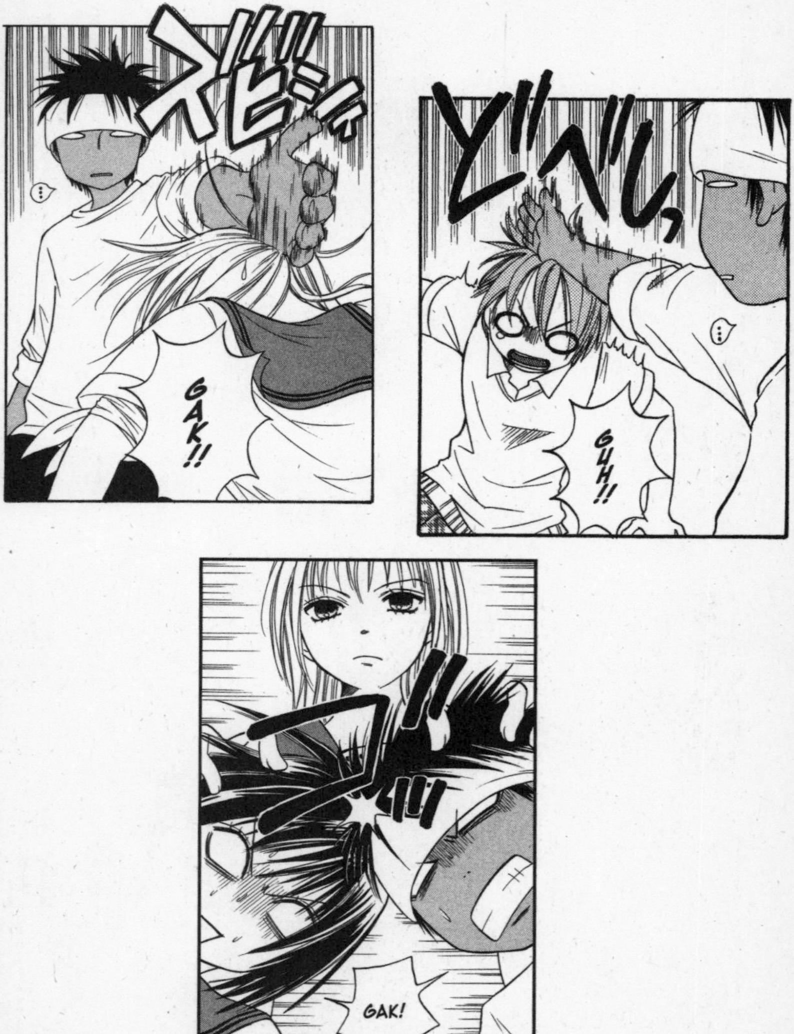
GUH!!
GAK!!
GAK!

...needing a good conk on the noggin.

LOVE IS...

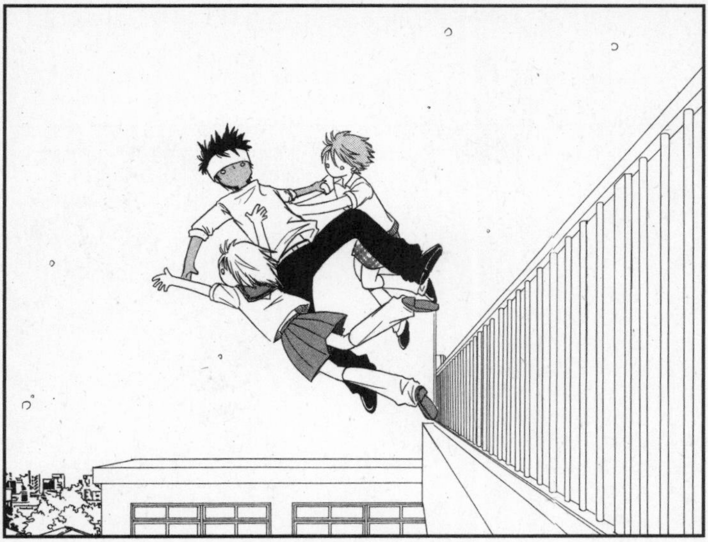

...risking your life...

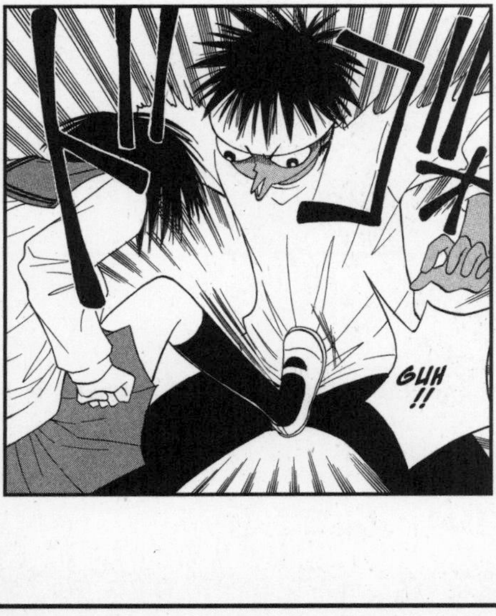
GUH !!

...and your future children's lives.

LOVE IS...

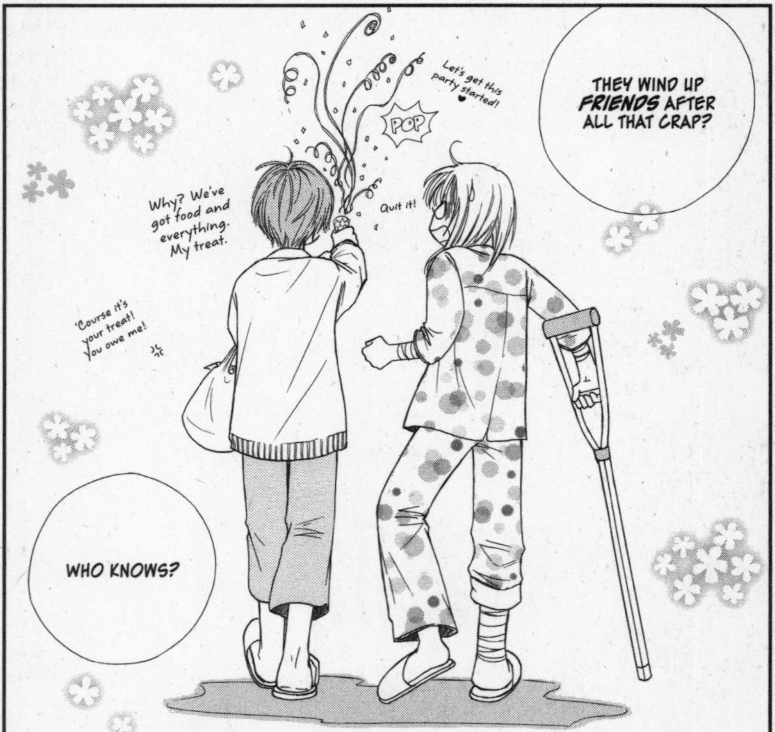
THEY WIND UP FRIENDS AFTER ALL THAT CRAP?
Let's get this party started! ♥
POP
Quit it!
Why? We've got food and everything. My treat.
'Course it's your treat! You owe me!
WHO KNOWS?

...knowing your way to the nearest hospital.

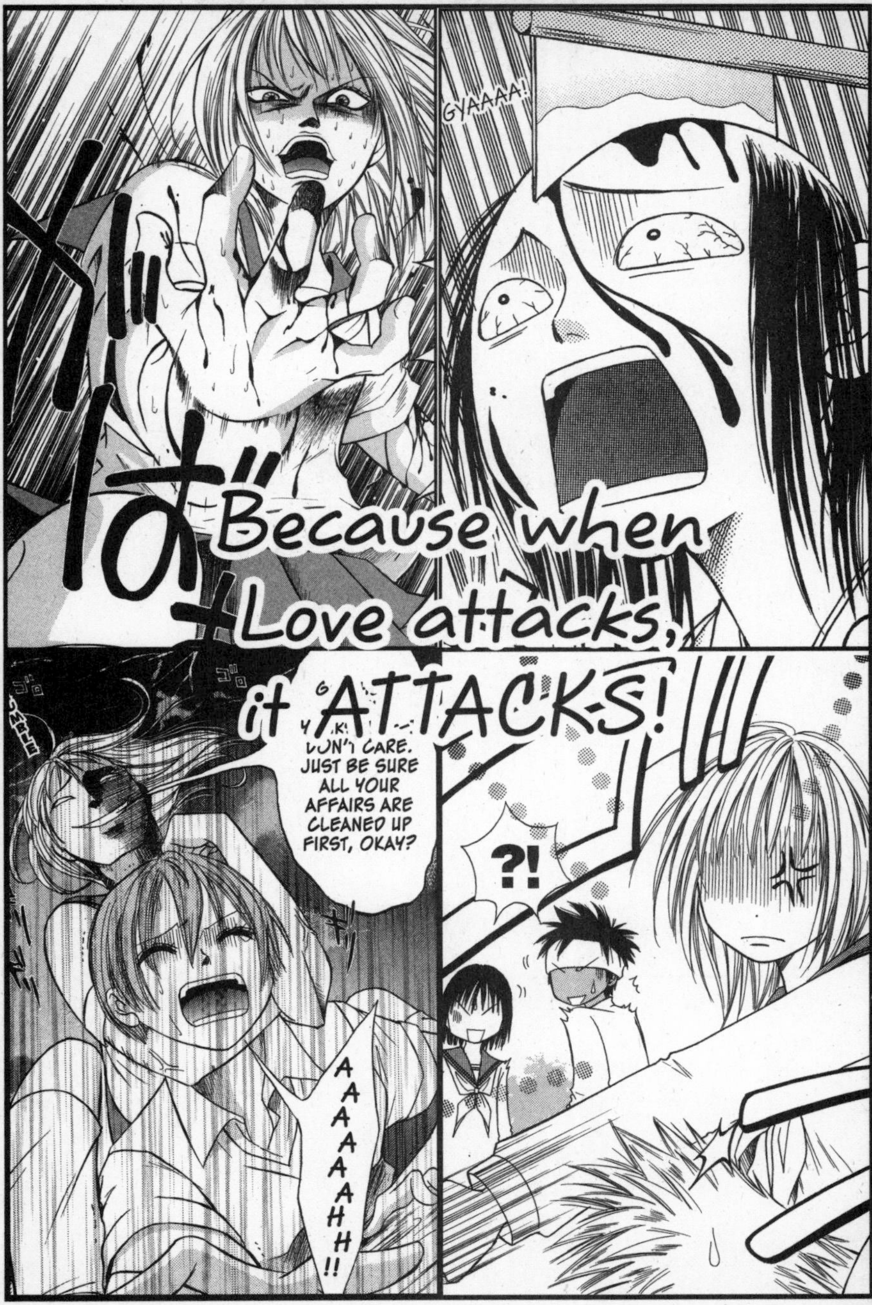
GYAAAA!
Because when Love attacks, it ATTACKS!
?!
DON'T CARE. JUST BE SURE ALL YOUR AFFAIRS ARE CLEANED UP FIRST, OKAY?
RUMBLE
AAAAAAAAHH!!

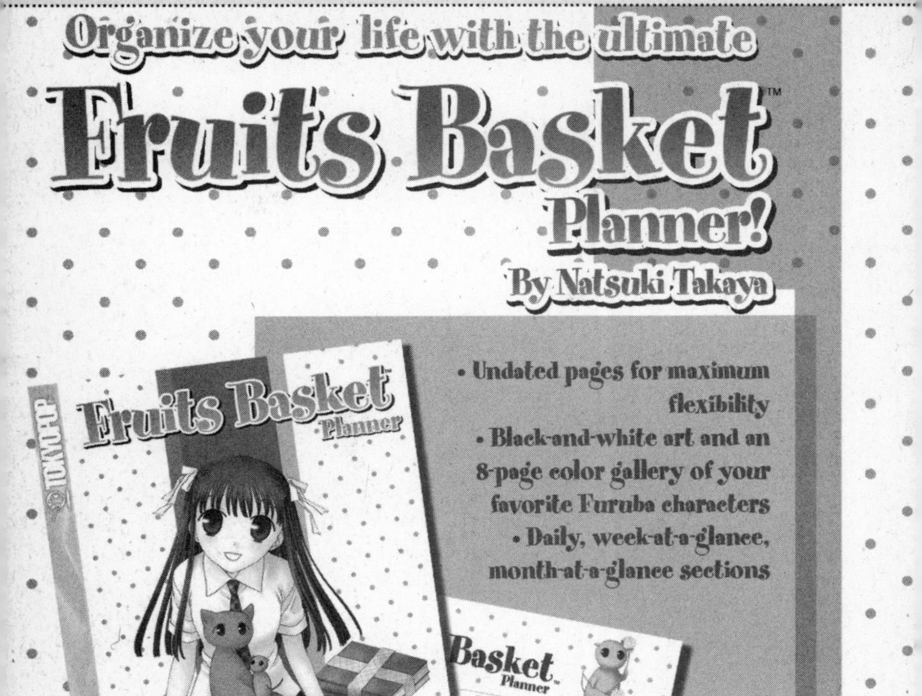
Organize your life with the ultimate
Fruits Basket™ Planner!
By Natsuki Takaya
• Undated pages for maximum flexibility
• Black-and-white art and an 8-page color gallery of your favorite Furuba characters
• Daily, week-at-a-glance, month-at-a-glance sections
Fruits Basket™ Planner
TOKYOPOP
Basket Planner
Tuesday
Wednesday
Fruits Basket Planner
Monday
Tuesday
Wednesday
Read Fruits Basket at www.TOKYOPOP.com/Fruits_Basket
© 1998 Natsuki Takaya / HAKUSENSHA, Inc.

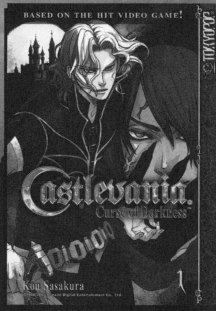

STOP!

This is the back of the book.
You wouldn't want to spoil a great ending!

This book is printed "manga-style," in the authentic Japanese right-to-left format. Since none of the artwork has been flipped or altered, readers get to experience the story just as the creator intended. You've been asking for it, so TOKYOPOP® delivered: authentic, hot-off-the-press, and far more fun!

DIRECTIONS

If this is your first time reading manga-style, here's a quick guide to help you understand how it works.

It's easy... just start in the top right panel and follow the numbers. Have fun, and look for more 100% authentic manga from TOKYOPOP®!